The New Elegance

THE NEW ELEGANCE

Stylish, Comfortable Rooms for Today

TIMOTHY CORRIGAN
WITH MICHAEL BOODRO

TO

ELAINE MALTZMAN, MY MUSE, WHO CONTINUALLY INSPIRES ME

AND BRINGS A SENSE OF THE POSSIBLE TO ALL THAT I DO,

AND

KATHLEEN SCHEINFELD, WHO HAS BEEN THE CONSTANT SOURCE

OF BALANCE, ENTHUSIASM, AND SUPPORT IN MY LIFE.

Table of Contents

Introduction 9

Classic Mayfair 12
SCALE AND PROPORTION 32

Parisian Pied-à-Terre 36
SYMMETRY 54

Gracious Glamour 59
ARCHITECTURAL DETAILS 76

Royal Palms 80
IMPACTFUL SURFACES 104

California Colonial 108
THE LAYERED LOOK 128

Shoreline Sophistication 130
ART AND MIRRORS 150

Family Hangout 153
THE POWER OF COLOR 168

Packing a Punch 172
DRAMA AND SURPRISE 186

Country Cosmopolitan 189
COMFORT 206

Western White House 208
MIXING ELEMENTS 230

Royal Residence 232
DETAILS ARE THE DESIGN 252

Acknowledgments 254

Credits 256

Introduction

Elegance is misunderstood. Too often, people think of elegance as being stiff or formal, as something that is applied or put on, a pose one strikes and then struggles to maintain. In our modern world of casual Fridays and athletic/leisure wear every day of the week, elegance seems to require too much time and too much thought. It is dismissed as studied, mannered—even affected. The quality once considered the highest compliment for a person, a work of art, or an interior is now often regarded as dated and no longer relevant.

Nothing could be further from the truth. Elegance is not something that adds stress or difficulty to our lives—quite the contrary. True elegance, to me, means confidence in who you are and what you love, grace in how you handle yourself, and openness to the best in others.

Elegance adds immense pleasure to life. To seek elegance—in your behavior, in what you wear and surround yourself with—is a treat you give to yourself and, almost inadvertently, share with those around you. Elegance is not something you save for a special occasion, something you wait to pull out, like your finest china or crystal on the holidays. Elegance, like beauty, should be part of your life every single day.

I like to think that the rooms in this book are elegant, but I also know that they are more relaxed and comfortable than they initially appear. Partly, that is the nature of a design book. When a photographer comes in, the impulse is to make the room look as perfect as possible—not unlike the way you might dress up to look your best when posing for a formal portrait. But all of these rooms, no matter how grand they look or how many valuable objects they contain, are—first and foremost—comfortable. I know because I not only created them, I have also lived in some of them, and I have used many others with my clients. I have seen them in operation, and I have heard from my clients and friends how conducive they are to relaxation and enjoyment, how often they are used, and how much they are loved.

Comfort is not antithetical to elegance, but rather its support and backbone. No one can feel truly elegant (at least not for long) if he or she doesn't feel at ease. A certain level of nonchalance and relaxation is required. Creating a sense of security is one of the underlying roots of all of my designs. Looking through these projects, I realized that the one effect I consistently try to accomplish is an innate feeling of safety. In fact, the notion of feeling cocooned, protected, and pampered underlies my whole design ethos.

And it is no crime to design with comfort in mind. My problem with minimalist rooms and austere spaces is that they look beautiful in photos, but not many people actually want to be in them—at least not for an extended period. The sleek severity that Le Corbusier and Mies van der Rohe extolled and taught for decades to generations of younger architects and designers was hugely influential, but never easy to achieve—and never truly embraced by the American public. The truth is, very few people live that way—or even aspire to. And we shouldn't feel guilty if we don't.

At the same time, people today don't want trade-offs. We want to surround ourselves with objects that are beautiful, but not delicate or fragile. Most of us don't have staff, or the free time to attend to the traditional household duties of ironing, polishing silver, waxing furniture, etc. We may enjoy watching *Downton Abbey* and imagining our lives in similarly grand homes, but even the English aristocracy no longer lives that way, nor do they want to. Of course, the secret to avoiding polishing silver is not to put it away, but to use it every day—then you won't have to polish it.

And that is another lesson about living an elegant life. Use what you have. Use it all. Use it now. Few things are sadder than piles of exquisite porcelain and china hidden away in a cupboard, or a large house in which many of the rooms go unused. That is one reason why in every home I design, each room has a specific purpose, guaranteeing it will be used. And if something you own doesn't work for you, give it away. If a room doesn't function for the way you live, change it to make it work for you. Turn the dining room into a library, or an unused bedroom into a home gym. Fit out an underutilized living room with a desk to make it a place you turn to when paying bills or researching a project.

Too often, we succumb to visions of how we want to live—in a sleek, white space, a country cottage, or a grand manse—then feel bad when we can't live up to those fantasies. We all deal with enough difficulties and failures day to day. Design, and the way we live, shouldn't add to them. Never buy into a trend. Just as one should never adopt a fashion look from head to toe, an elegant home needs to acknowledge its time, but also transcend it.

I won't deny that many of the homes in these pages are grand and expensive. But even in these rooms, there are lessons to be learned that apply to any home. Great design is not about the size of your space or the budget you spend. It is a reflection of knowing who you are and what makes you comfortable, and living confidently and happily with the objects you choose and assemble.

It is easier today than ever, thanks to online sites and auctions, to find beautiful furniture and objects at reasonable—and often bargain—prices. I recently bought a stunning painting online from a Copenhagen auction house for $250. You should always buy the best-quality items you can afford, but not everything in a room needs to be expensive. A mix of items of different prices, different eras, and differing qualities is far more appealing. No one wants to live in a museum of decorative arts.

But I can assure you that spending each day in beautiful rooms, rooms full of personal items and objects you love, will bring meaning and solace to your life, satisfaction, and even joy. And if there is one lesson I hope you take from this book, it is that there is no reason not to live comfortably and with elegance.

Classic Mayfair

London is known for its elegant townhouses, and no neighborhood embodies the ideal of city living more than Mayfair, an area that encompasses Hanover, Berkeley, and Grosvenor Squares. Lined with elegant Georgian houses dating to the mid-eighteenth century, this section of the city has long been a favorite of the aristocracy, and for good reason.

This house, called "Belgravia House," was in fact built even before neighboring Belgrave Square was laid out in the 1820s, so it was rich in history and elegant detailing—so much so that it had been landmarked by the City of London. However, its history has not been without conflict. In the early twentieth century, after World War I and the decline of the aristocracy, Mayfair had deteriorated and become a more commercial area. This house, along with many of its neighbors, had been repurposed as offices. In the 1990s, it became the private home of a Russian family.

By the time it was acquired by my client, a Qatari prince, the interior had been so bastardized and stripped of its period details that, unlike the facade, it was no longer landmarked. The silver lining to this cloud was that we faced no restrictions on how we could proceed, and we were able to strip all seven floors down to the studs.

But although we were starting with a virtual blank slate, the last thing my client or I wanted was to create a modernist or minimal house. In fact, we sought to design a classic British interior—but one adapted to today's needs in terms of technology, heating and air-conditioning, and ease of use. Within the envelope of the existing walls and windows, we reconfigured all the rooms and devised new architectural detailing that would evoke the period when the house was built. In a major feat of engineering, the mechanical services were installed on the roof, and air-conditioning and heating units, vents, and speakers were hidden throughout, behind new pilasters or incorporated into bookcases or furniture.

Because we thought of the house as an ode to the best of British style, with all the comforts and tradition of a country house, we

In the entrance hall, the pilaster on the right was installed to conceal ductwork, and the one on the left was added for symmetry. A custom console hides a radiator grille, and the mirror is George II.

tried whenever possible to use British materials, British craftsmanship, and British antiques. A huge inspiration for the look were the wonderfully layered, comfortable houses that John Fowler devised throughout the twentieth century, often working with his partner, Sibyl Colefax. Since textiles are such a major element of any great British interior, we used as many Colefax and Fowler fabrics as possible, and books on Fowler's work became my touchstone for the design. I was once lucky enough to spend a weekend at Fowler's last commission, Cornbury Park, and it brought home to me how adept he was at combining elegance and comfort into the same space.

We replicated the traditional London multilevel Georgian townhouse layout, with grand rooms at the front and smaller rooms overlooking the garden at the back. This structure gives an intimate appeal to even the grandest houses.

London is known for its gray days, and one of the greatest challenges was to bring light into the rooms. This starts in the entry hall, where we installed pale marble floors to reflect light, gleaming white pilasters (which also hide mechanical systems), and highly polished mahogany doors with fanlights overhead to admit as much light as possible while ensuring privacy. Throughout the house, we installed dozens of mirrors to multiply light and add sparkle and glamour to a room.

Because I very consciously wanted to mark the transition from the outside to the interior, the ground-floor sitting room is lined with a custom, hand-painted Fromental wallpaper that evokes an English park and garden, a conceit reiterated in the oak-leaf chandelier and floral-motif rug.

My client does not entertain on a large scale but prefers small family gatherings. He requested an American-style kitchen with an island and an adjacent family-room area with a sofa for hanging out. So we transformed what had originally been the formal dining room at the front of the house into a warm and cozy kitchen area that incorporates a dining table, television, and seating area, all unified with a palette of blue, white, and silver and accented

ABOVE: A custom three-tiered lantern rises the full height of the staircase. OPPOSITE: On the second-floor stair landing, an early-eighteenth-century Italian mirror hangs above a custom console that encases a radiator.

The ground-floor sitting room was designed to create a connection with the outdoors. The hand-painted wallpaper is by Fromental, the oak-leaf chandelier was found in London, and the mirror above the mantel hides a television and reflects an eighteenth-century French trophy depicting garden tools. The curtain fabric is one of my designs for Schumacher. FOLLOWING PAGES: The main drawing room on the second floor faces north, so we chose a palette of sunny and bright colors. The room is anchored by a double sofa upholstered in a blue velvet, the walls are covered in a velvet embossed with a damask pattern, and the paintings and mirrored girandoles are eighteenth-century Venetian.

with Delft tiles and a witty wallpaper that repeats the blue-and-white motif. We painted the ceiling with softly reflective eggshell paint and upholstered the sofa in an indoor-outdoor fabric for practicality.

English homes are known for their dramatic, showstopping window treatments, and this is one tradition we happily embraced. The drapes and pelmets frame the view, but just as important, on London's many gray, rainy days, they divert attention from the dreary weather outside. Here, again, John Fowler was my inspiration, and I looked to his window treatments for ideas, including the pelmets outlined in navy in the kitchen, the ball gown–worthy swags of the golden curtains in the grand upstairs rooms, and the dressmaker details of hand-embroidered sheers, passementerie trims, embroidery, and fringe throughout the house.

Upstairs on the first floor (considered the second floor in the United States) is the grandest room in the house. But even here, despite its formality and soaring thirteen-foot ceilings, we wanted to create a bright and

OPPOSITE: The drawing room features a wall paneled with mirrors and fitted with gilt brackets that hold an assortment of Delft jars. ABOVE: The custom commodes are hand-painted, and the mirror above the mantel also conceals a television.

THE NEW ELEGANCE 21

The upstairs sitting room was designed to evoke global travels, with wallpaper illustrating antique maps and a pair of eighteenth-century Venetian overdoors above the sofa. The desk is antique, and the cocktail table is from my furniture collection for Moissonnier.

cheerful atmosphere. The palette is a pale yellow, gold, and blue. But the double sofa is upholstered in a blue that is brighter and more vivid than any that would ever have been used in the eighteenth century. And playful elements throughout make it clear that this is a room made for use today. The carpet is an eighteenth-century Savonnerie, the floor is traditional *parquet de Versailles*, and the porphyry urns by the windows stand on George III pedestals. In contrast to this formality, the chairs all swivel to make conversation easy, and a television hides behind the mirror over the fireplace. The walls are sheathed in velvet, but the velvet is embossed with a damask pattern, so the effect varies as you move about the space, bringing liveliness to the room. Gold brackets hold antique blue-and-white vases and jars, but they are set against mirrored panels that multiply and playfully distort their effect. And the cabinets flanking the fireplace are hand-painted with a bold chinoiserie pattern in a vivid turquoise. With the nineteenth-century Venetian touches throughout—sconces and painted panels, as well as the carpet—the whole effect is of a room crafted to display the trophies gathered on the traditional grand tour of the Continent, but one made via jet and motorcycle.

The family sitting room on the same floor replicates the proportions and layout of the garden sitting room below it, but here the effect is cozier and more intimate, with a witty wallpaper by Cole & Son that looks like an accumulation of old maps, a pair of overstuffed Knole sofas in another vivid shade of blue, an arabesque-patterned rug of my own design, and a collection of nineteenth-century photographs of travels in Egypt.

On the landing between the two rooms, the walls are lined in the same practical soft blue vinyl wallpaper used in the entry, and a madly exuberant gilded Italian mirror hangs over a slim custom console that hides the radiator. A custom-designed triple lantern is suspended over the stair, bringing light to the three landings.

The third level is devoted to a large master suite that picks up the blue-and-gold palette, but in a far more minor key. The traditional bed is encased with fabrics, the wallpaper is an archival design by Watts of Westminster, and even the chandelier adds to the color scheme. An almost abstract photograph of the watery Thames by Michael T. Noonan adds a contemporary element, even as it reinforces the aqueous atmosphere.

On the fourth floor are three additional bedrooms and bathrooms. The largest is adorned with an archival floral wallpaper pattern re-created on silk, a crown molding that reiterates the motif, and mirrored cabinetry accented with panels of gilded sheaves of wheat. The others are simpler, but still embody the playful atmosphere that makes the best English homes such a pleasure.

The breakfast area in the family kitchen is fitted with an outdoor rug and indoor-outdoor upholstery fabrics for ultimate practicality; the marble table is a custom design, and the curtain fabric is from my collection for Schumacher.

OPPOSITE AND ABOVE: In the wife's bedroom, the bed and drapery fabrics are from my collection for Schumacher, the commodes that serve as nightstands are eighteenth-century Italian, and the wallpaper was custom made based on an antique fragment.

THE NEW ELEGANCE 27

OPPOSITE AND ABOVE: The client's bedroom is appointed in shades of his favorite color, even in unexpected places, such as the chandelier. Above an antique desk hangs a contemporary photograph of the Thames by Michael T. Noonan that reiterates the watery palette, and the back of the desk chair is embroidered to add richness.

THE NEW ELEGANCE 29

ABOVE AND OPPOSITE: To give it a cozy feel, the walls of a fourth-floor guest room are upholstered in a classic Colefax and Fowler fabric, which is also used for the curtains and bed hangings. The Italian-strung curtains echo the shape of the bed hangings.

INTERLUDE
SCALE AND PROPORTION

You don't have to be a designer, or even visually sophisticated, to realize that some rooms strike you immediately as comfortable and appealing, while others, as interesting as they might initially seem, ultimately feel awkward and off-putting, even if you can't put your finger on why.

More often than not, these subconscious reactions have to do with scale and proportion. Crucial as they are, those two factors are often the most difficult to work with. Few of us get to enjoy the perfect proportions of an Italian villa or a classic *hôtel particulier* in Paris. All too often, designers have to contend with awkward rooms, low ceilings, narrow dimensions, or ungainly layouts.

Fortunately, there are ways to minimize, if not eliminate, problems with scale and proportion and disguise their effects. There are a few standard precepts: In rooms with low ceilings, keep the furniture low as well. Hang artworks and mirrors low, and hang curtains a few inches above the top of the window. Paint the ceiling in an eggshell finish to reflect the light, or even add painted clouds to evoke the sky rising overhead. Conversely, in rooms with tall ceilings, use overscale furnishings, vertical elements such as screens and pedestals, or artworks and mirrors hung on top of one another to lift the eye.

What is important is to analyze the space first, acknowledge and understand its defects, and then work to compensate for any shortcomings. Don't try to pretend they don't exist. Design doesn't have to be perfect to be beautiful, and there are endless ways to make even awkward spaces comfortable and appealing.

1

This house in Los Angeles was designed by architect John Elgin Woolf, a Hollywood favorite in the 1950s and '60s. His glamorous approach was instrumental in establishing the style that became known as Hollywood Regency. For this room, we wanted to honor that stylish pedigree, so rather than playing against the height of the room, we choose to emphasize it with vivid curtains that frame the vertical views of the pool and garden beyond. Tall-backed chairs and busts on high pedestals reinforce the lofty feel.

2

A dining room in Paris that was tiny and narrow became a jewel box for intimate dinners, thanks to a central ceiling medallion painted with clouds, which seems to open the room to the sky. This effect is supplemented by an array of tall items, including a secretary, obelisks, and a portrait hung high against the red wall. The rich blue floral carpet and the dark wood paneling ground the space under the faux sky, turning it into a fantasy garden at night, when the room glows in candlelight.

3

The ceilings in this Beverly Hills house were only nine feet high, and the room is both long and narrow. To disguise the lack of height, we hung the curtains several inches above the arched windows and placed the large furniture pieces around the perimeter of the room, with smaller, lighter pieces in the center, to make the space seem as expansive as possible. We anchored it with a pale rug, then followed through with a monochromatic palette that softens edges and blurs the distinction between walls, floors, and ceilings.

In this living room in Los Angeles, with twenty-two-foot ceilings that seemed to dwarf everything, I hung a wide, overscale chandelier to lift the eye. I continued the effect by placing very tall mirrors above the consoles, which I then topped with plaster medallions, lifting the eye even further. Even the lamps on the consoles are much taller than the norm. The upholstered pieces are the same color as the walls so that the focal point becomes the darker elements in the room—the light fixture, the beamed ceiling, the medallions, and the opening and grille over the arched doorway. Every item was positioned to activate the eye and draw it upward.

5

The problems with this galley kitchen in Los Angeles were its narrow proportions and very high ceilings. The checkerboard floor tiles were laid on the diagonal to visually stretch the space and make it appear wider than it is. The height of the table and stools are exaggerated to fill the vertical space, and two chandeliers, layered and far more elaborate than the usual kitchen light fixtures, lift and dazzle the eye, disguising the unusual height of the space.

In this Paris living room, the challenge was to bring comfort and warmth to a small space that was broken up by way too many doors. To overcome the awkward layout, we treated some of the doors as walls and hung artworks on them. And although the general precept is to use small-scale furniture in small rooms, here we selected overstuffed, full-size pieces to denote comfort and to encourage sitting and relaxing. But to maximize the space as much as we could within the limited confines, we positioned all those pieces around the perimeter of the room.

For this entertaining space in a Los Angeles home, we disguised the long, low proportions by installing a custom tufted banquette that runs the full length of the space, then enclosed it on both ends to make it seem even more welcoming and comfortable—and not incidentally, to make the room itself seem wider. The back of the banquette is higher than usual, and we placed a mirror directly above it, both of which make the room seem taller. The last visual trick was to put disproportionately low tables in front, which furthered the illusion.

4

5

6

7

Parisian Pied-à-Terre

For anyone interested in design—anyone interested in beauty in any form—Paris is essential. Long before I was a designer, I became entranced by the city. With its beautiful Gothic and neoclassical architecture, Paris—wherever you look—is a lesson in scale, proportion, and the beauty of symmetry. And with its museums large and small, the antiques shops that cluster near the Seine on the Left Bank, the high-end fabric and textile shops that entice designers and casual strollers alike with their sumptuous wares, each day in the city becomes an informal seminar on the history of decorative arts. Of course, Paris is the ultimate heaven for any shopper, with its famous flea markets, the Marché aux Puces and Puces de Vanves, and the city's famed auction houses, where treasures of some kind or other come under the gavel virtually every day.

I have been fortunate enough to live in four different apartments in Paris over the past thirty years. More than two decades ago, when I worked in advertising, I rented one near the Parc Monceau. Later, I had an apartment not far from Drouot, the oldest of the city's many auction houses, and its salesrooms not only furnished my apartment, they also became a bit of an obsession. Some have even described me as an auction addict. I wouldn't go that far, but I will admit that the experience of being in those rooms was formative in my subsequent decision to change careers.

After returning to New York, I realized that I was no longer happy in advertising. So I moved to my hometown of Los Angeles, where I began my new career. Seven years later, I had enough projects in Europe that I could finally open an office in Paris and justify indulging the dream that so many designers have of owning a pied-à-terre in the City of Light.

My current apartment is in an ideal location, very near the Place de la Concorde and the Place de la Madeleine. It is close to some of the finest shopping in Paris, but it is located on a tiny two-block-long street, near the Japanese and British embassies, that is so quiet you could almost be in the country. And the view from the windows reveals only nineteenth-century buildings, so it is a bit like being outside of time, as well as removed from the bustle of the city.

My apartment is on the third floor of a traditional Haussmann-style building built in the second half of the nineteenth century.

To add nuance and depth to the living room of my Paris apartment, the paneling is painted with six shades of white and two grays, as well as a red pinstripe. Here, one of the many doors is disguised with a mirror above an antique console. FOLLOWING PAGES: In a play of reflections, the mirror over the mantel reflects an interior window that looks onto a matching mirror in the dining room beyond. The seating and cocktail table are from my furniture collection for Schumacher, and the rug is one I designed for Patterson Flynn Martin.

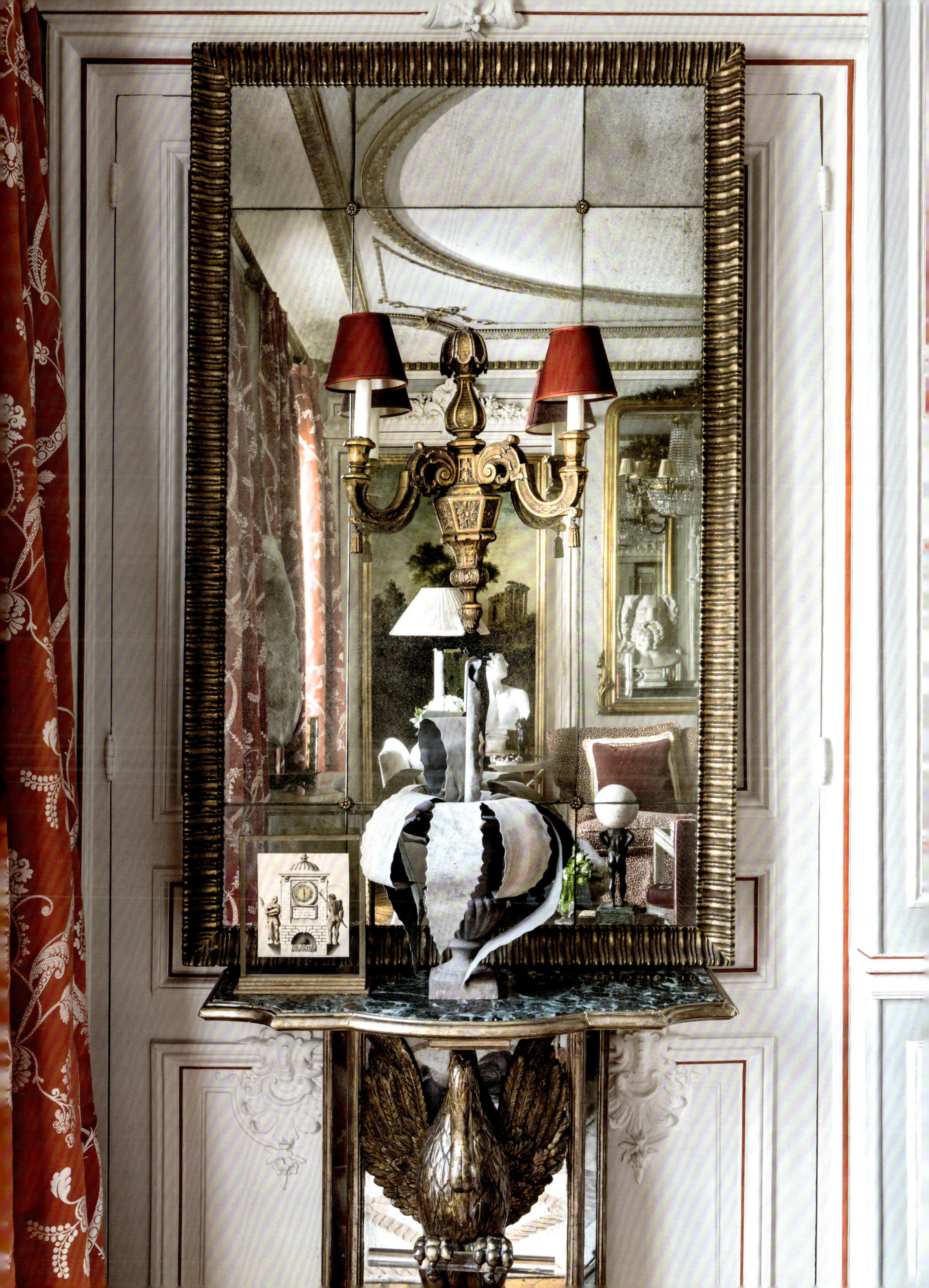

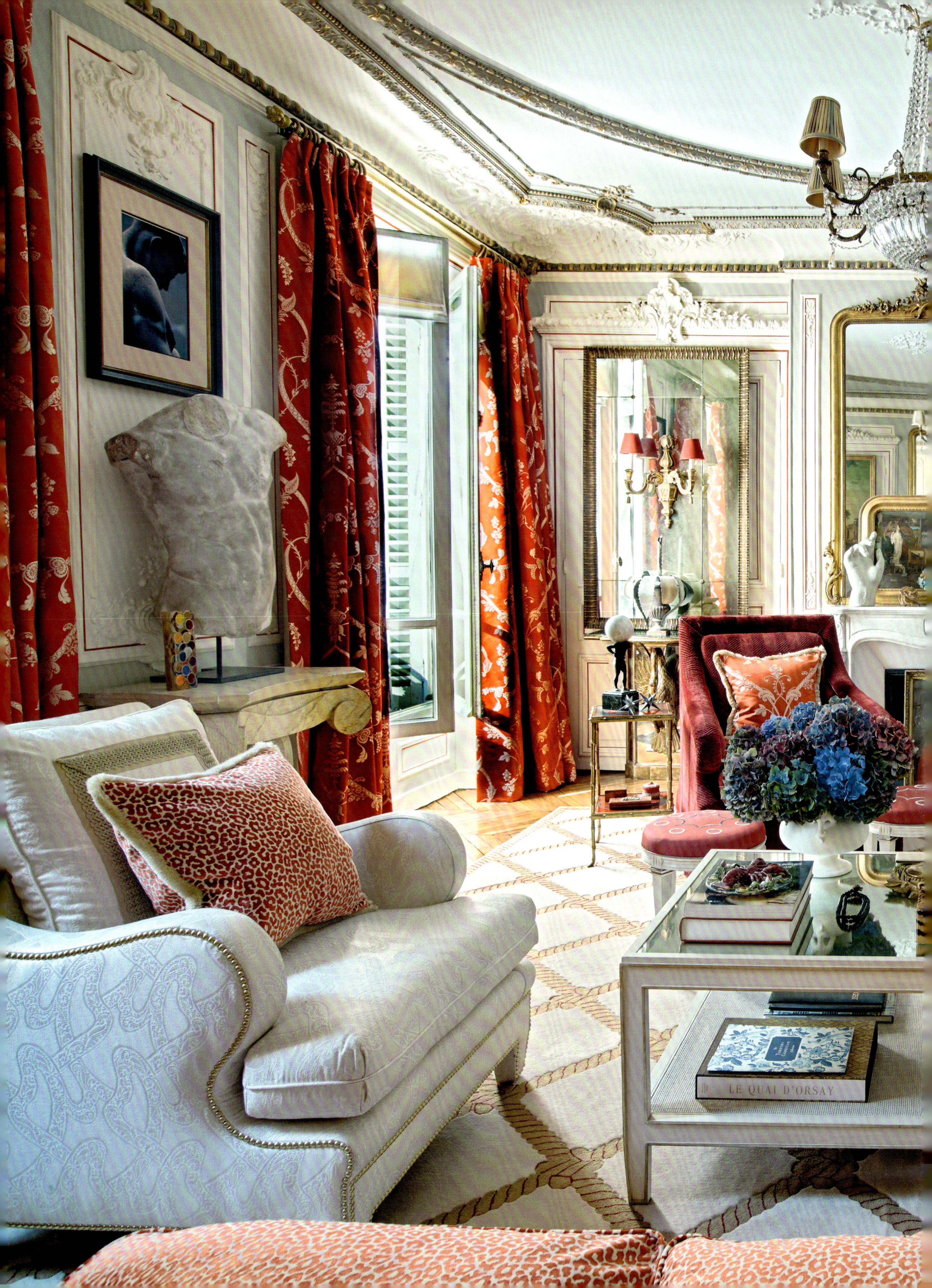
LE QUAI D'ORSAY

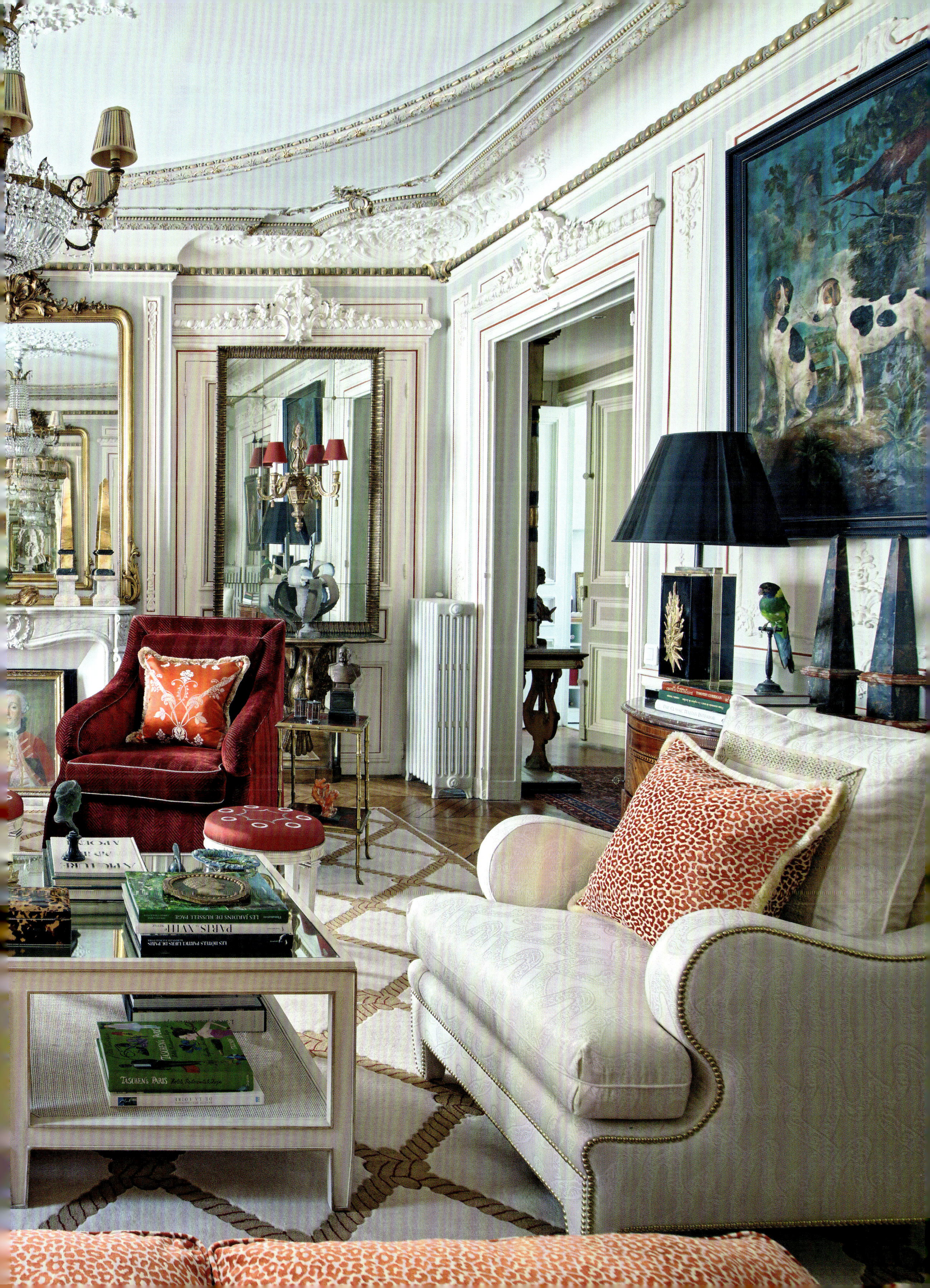
LES JARDINS DE RUSSELL PAGE
TASCHEN'S PARIS

There is only one apartment per floor, so each receives light from both east and west. The layout is severely symmetrical, with a long central corridor with double doors on both sides. Fortunately, the apartment had retained all its original paneling and plasterwork, parquet floors, and fireplaces in every room. As elegant as it was, however, the layout didn't really correspond with the way I wanted to use the space. I wanted it to serve as a showplace for decorative arts from the eighteenth through the twentieth centuries, yes, but also as a place where I could relax, put my feet up, have a drink, invite friends for the weekend, or host intimate dinner parties for six. (I don't cook, but Fauchon is just a block away.)

I made no permanent changes to the historic interior, but I reconfigured the ways the rooms are used to make the apartment more livable. It now consists of an entryway, living and dining rooms, a study, three bedrooms with baths, and an eat-in kitchen.

In the living room, for example, there were six pairs of doors opening onto other rooms, as well as French doors with Juliet balconies. With all those doors, furniture would have had to be placed in the middle of the room, which was neither practical nor convenient. I removed one pair of doors, set an antiqued mirror panel into another, and disguised the other four by placing consoles, mirrors, and paintings in front of them, with the ornate plasterwork serving as frames. This gave the space, which had been more of passageway than a room, greater versatility and a sheltering, comforting atmosphere.

The great conceit of the room is what appears to be a large gilded mirror behind the sofa, but is in actuality an internal window looking onto what is now the dining room beyond. I furthered the illusion by placing an

ABOVE: The open window in the living room looks onto the mirror in the dining room; the identical frame and matching chandelier create an amusing trompe l'oeil effect. OPPOSITE: The sofa is upholstered in a velvet I designed for Schumacher, inspired by Madeleine Castaing; the side table is a custom design, and the painting by Hubert Robert disguises yet another door.

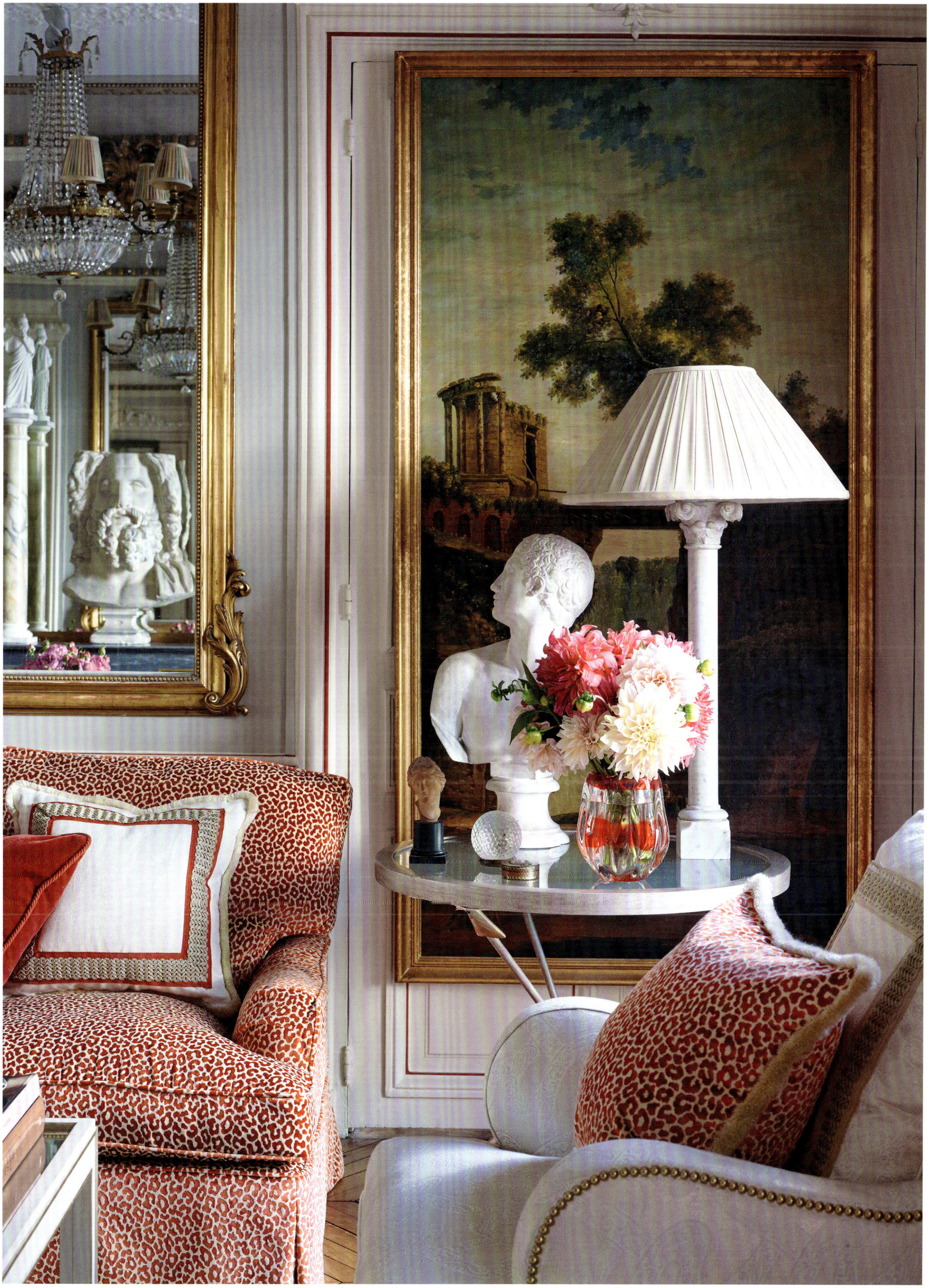

A whimsical painting of Nero hangs on a panel of mirror inset into what had been a door; the dog painting is a nineteenth-century copy of a seventeenth-century original by Alexandre-François Desportes, and the demilune console is from the eighteenth century.

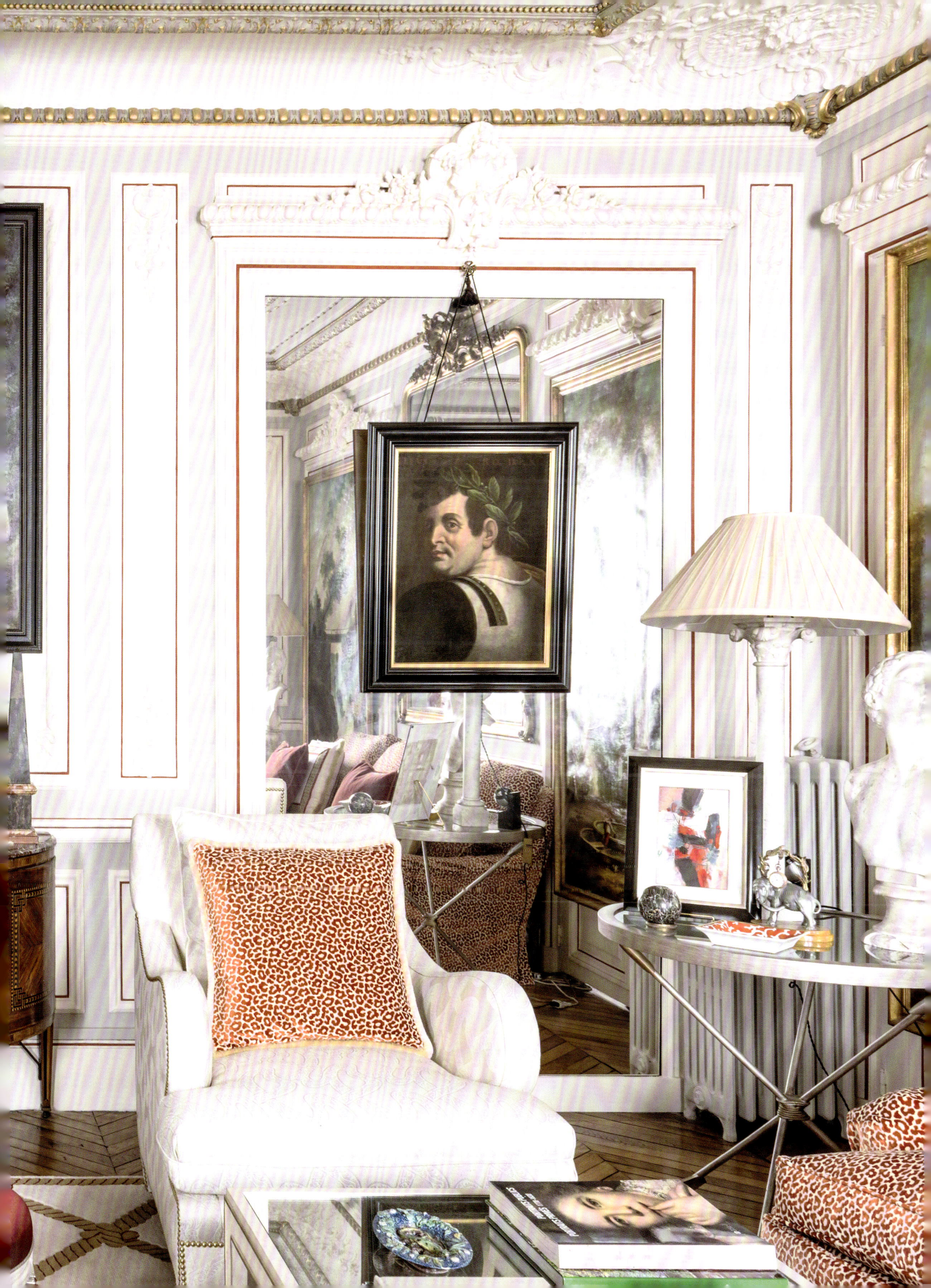

identically framed mirror in line with it in the dining room, and another mirror on the opposite wall of the living room. I then hung matching crystal-bedecked Napoleon III chandeliers in each room. This seems to set up an infinite succession of reflections, and what is real and what is mere reflection is brought playfully into question. Symmetry is both reiterated and undermined, and the trompe l'oeil game always surprises and delights my guests.

I enlivened the ornate paneling and plasterwork by painting them in multiple shades of gray and white and added a thin red line around the paneling for extra oomph. Since the rooms are visually linked through the internal window, I used the same color scheme in the dining room, which features a circa-1970 Italian table surrounded by Louis XVI–style chairs. They come from very different periods but share a similar strong geometric presence.

Because this is my own home, I felt I could freely use my fabric designs for Schumacher and rugs that I designed for Patterson Flynn Martin. Bold curtains add a contemporary element amid all the eighteenth- and nineteenth-century pieces. In the living and dining rooms, the vivid red colorway of my Parc Monceau fabric used for the curtains reiterates the thin red stripe on the paneling and makes it clear that this is no eighteenth-century room. The 1980s mirror over the fireplace in the study fulfills much the same function—a bold reminder of today. The master bedroom is literally cocooned in my blue-and-white Cap Ferrat linen blend, which even covers the walls (and disguises the lack of closet doors), making the room soothing, serene, and restful. I love sleeping there.

For all my love of French decorative arts—and that passion is abundantly evident throughout the apartment (as is my obsession with auction houses)—the apartment works for me and the way I live today. The rooms retain all their historic detail, yet they still reflect my style, my needs, and my desires. To me, that is the definition of any successful decorating effort.

ABOVE: The entrance hall, looking into the living room. OPPOSITE: In the dining room, a 1970s Italian table is surrounded by Louis XVI–style chairs by Moissonnier that echo its clean lines; the rug is a nineteenth-century Tabriz, and the chandelier is identical to the one in the living room. FOLLOWING PAGES: The dining room mirror is flanked by eighteenth-century illustrations by the Comte de Buffon; the urns and pedestals are eighteenth-century Italian.

44   THE NEW ELEGANCE

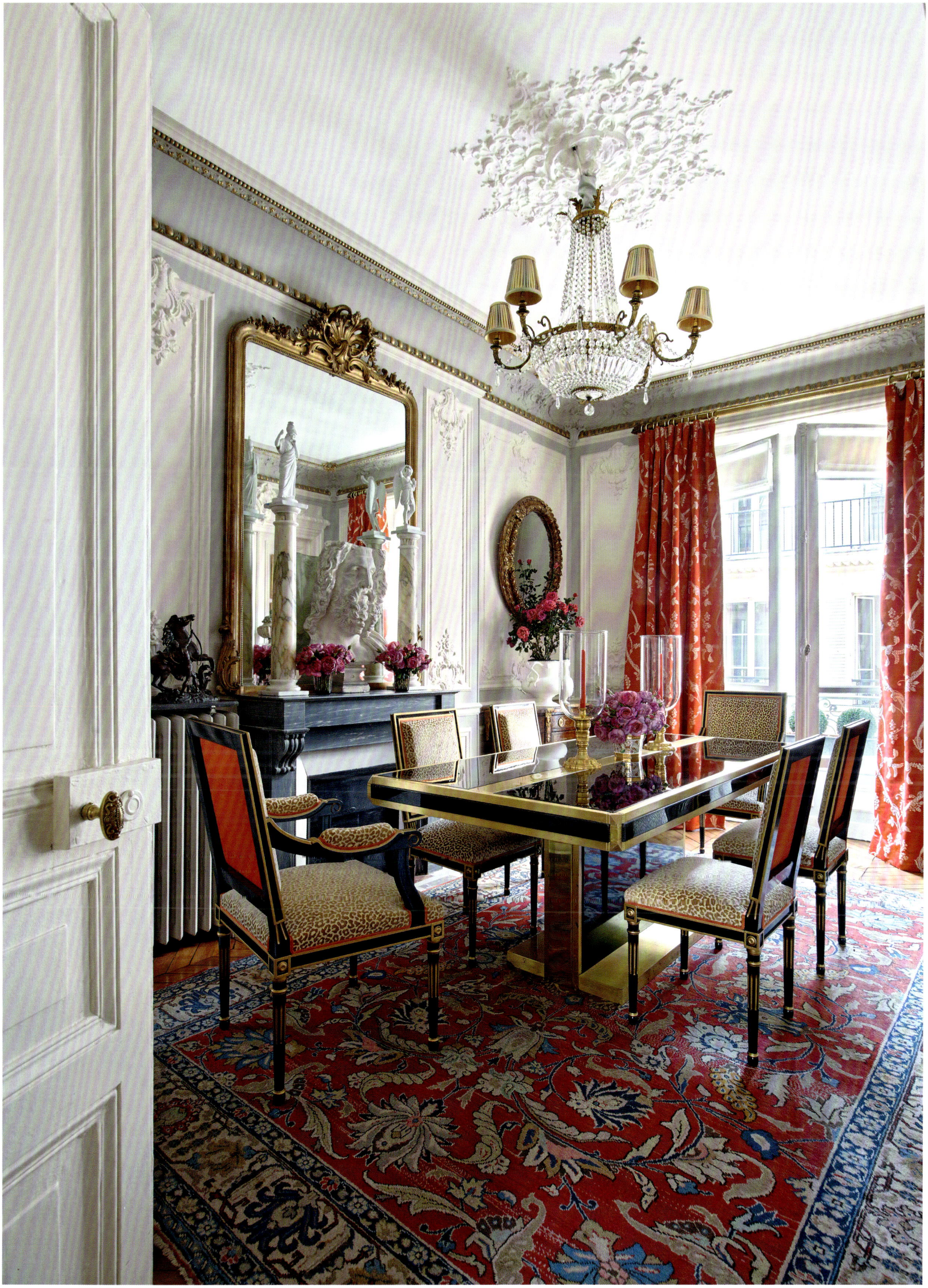

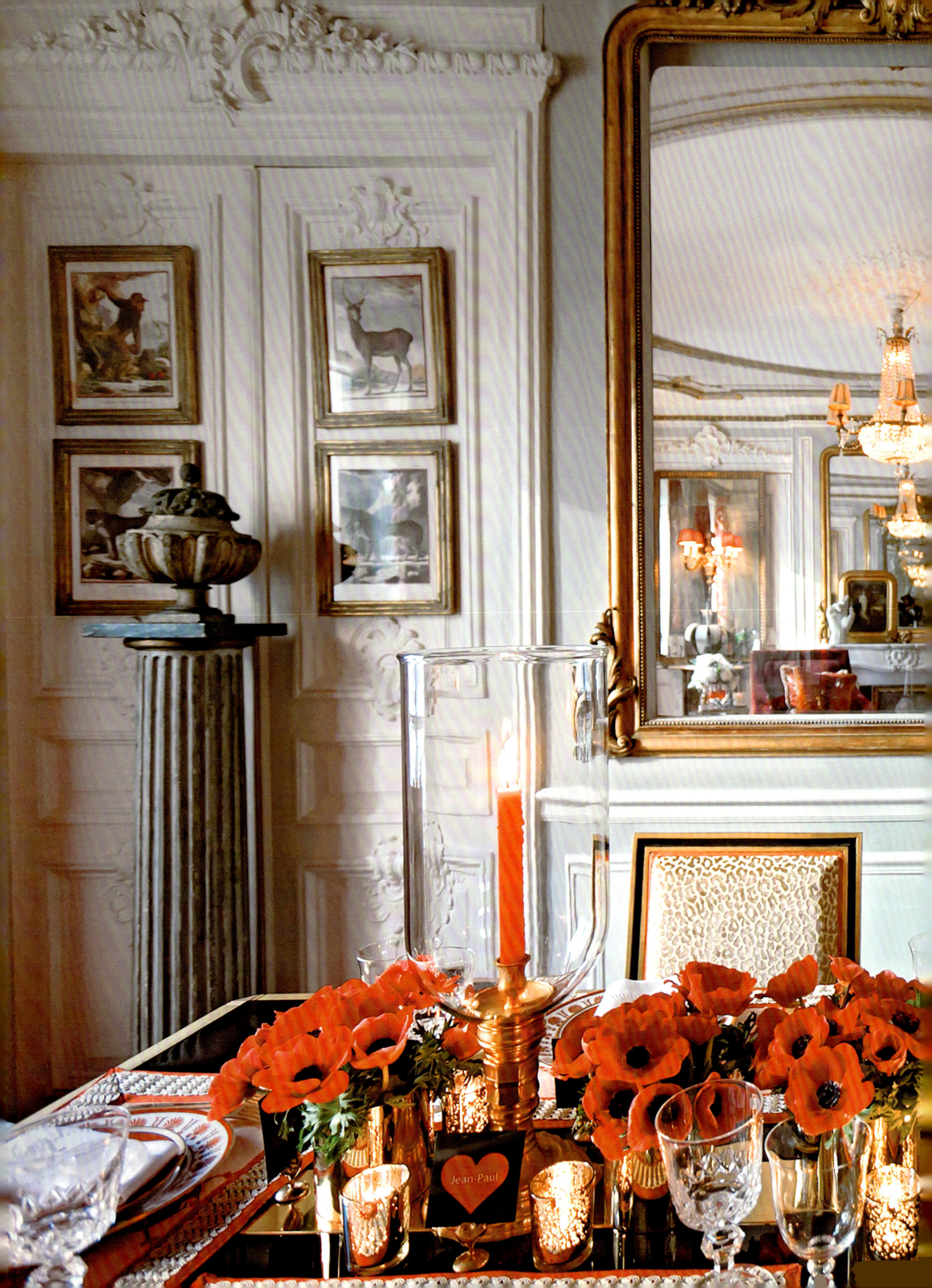
Jean-Paul

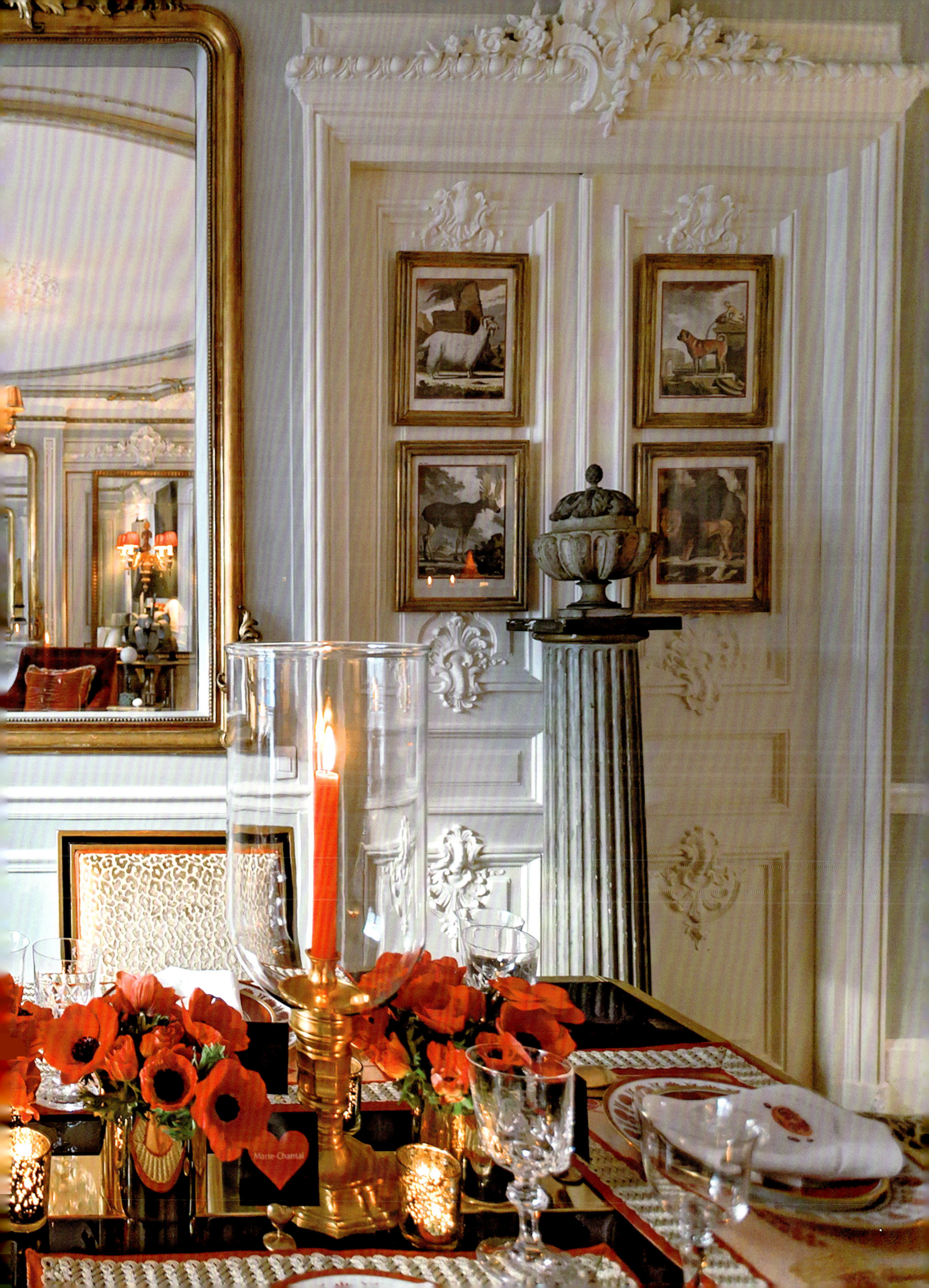
Marie-Chantal

In the study, the wallpaper is a custom design, and the doors are embellished with gilded boiseries representing the four seasons, copies by Iksel of the originals in the Musée Carnavalet. The mirror is contemporary, the desk is Louis XV, and the staircase model is one of hundreds made in the eighteenth and nineteenth centuries by apprentice carpenters as proof of their skills.

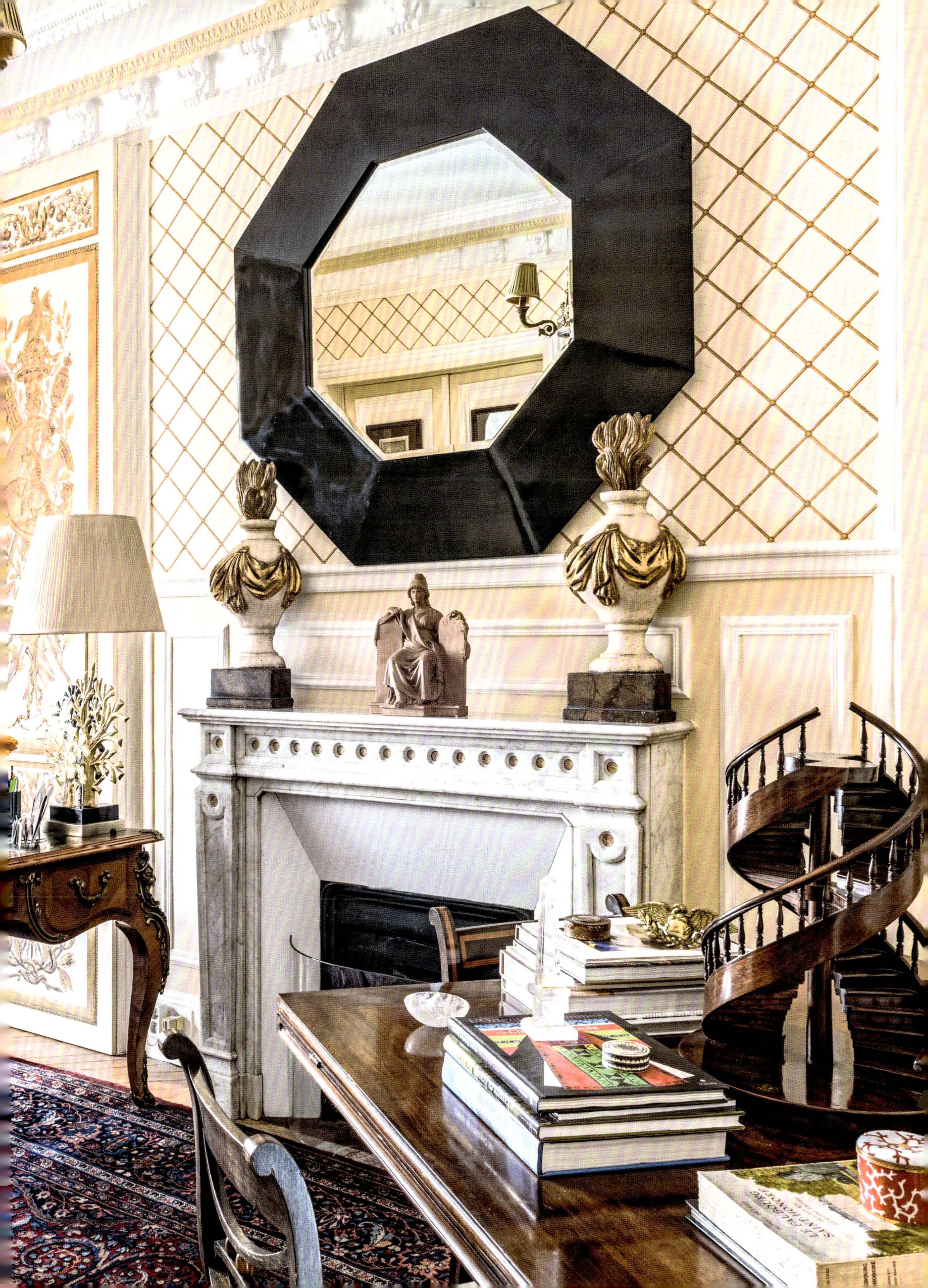
LE FAUBOURG
SAINT-HONORÉ

ABOVE AND OPPOSITE: To create a sheltering feel in my bedroom, I lined the walls with my Cap Ferrat fabric for Schumacher. The mirror over the original mantel evokes a window, the chandelier is 1940s French, and the Empire mahogany chest of drawers is topped with an eighteenth-century Italian gilt mirror.

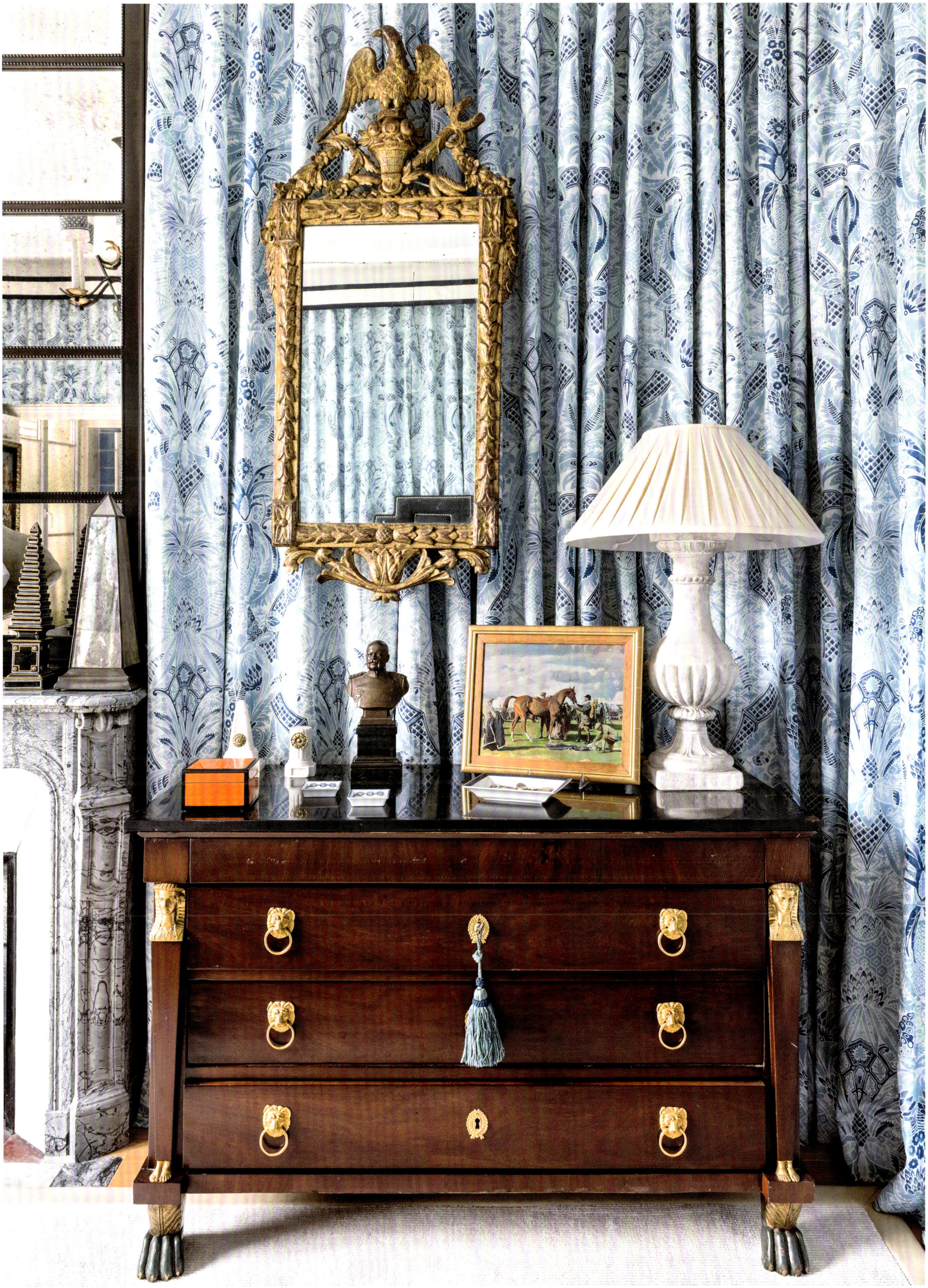

ABOVE: A guest room bed is dressed with fabrics I designed for Schumacher and flanked by eighteenth- and nineteenth-century architectural drawings. OPPOSITE: At the end of the long hallway, a segment of graphic wallpaper stands sentry.

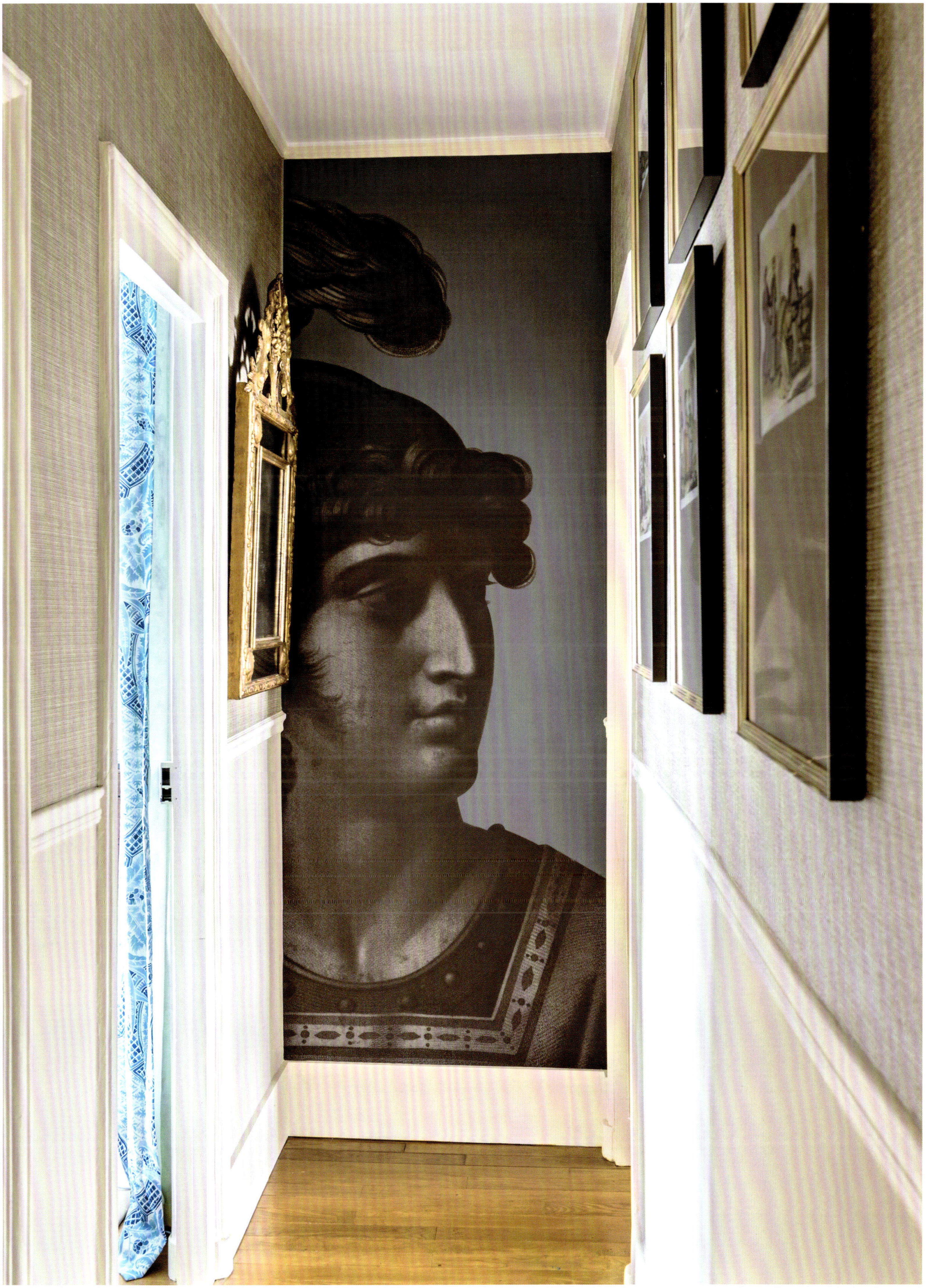

INTERLUDE
SYMMETRY

As even a cursory glance at these pages will make clear, I am a fan of symmetry. Symmetry endows a room with a sense of logic and rationality, serenity and peace. But symmetry is far more complex—and the opportunities far richer—than simply playing with matched pairs. In fact, there are three kinds of symmetry to consider, as well as asymmetry.

Reflectional symmetry is the most pervasive and easily understood. Reflectional symmetry is when both the left and right sides of an image match. Our faces, which are the most recognizable form to the human eye, are reflectionally symmetrical. Psychological research proves that we subconsciously find highly symmetrical faces to be more attractive and more trustworthy. So it is not at all surprising that reflectional is the most common form of symmetry.

Rotational symmetry is another common form, where all elements are distributed equally around a central focal point, much like the petals around the pistil and stamen of a flower. This type of symmetry gives any image, or any room, a central focus such as a dining or cocktail table, which is reassuring to the eye and allows it to absorb elements at its own pace, knowing that the center will hold.

Translational symmetry is the use of a repeated pattern or motif throughout a space so that it creates visual echoes, reinforcing the unity of a room and giving a sense of coherence, cohesion, and care. This kind of considered effort can be bold or subtle, but the result is often the same—a sense that all details have undergone careful consideration, which lends a feeling of security and calm.

Asymmetry is not the opposite of symmetry, which could lead to confusion and cacophony. But deliberately breaking the evenness and regularity of a symmetrical space helps to avoid predictability and a soporific effect. Too much symmetry lulls the eye, and no room should be able to be understood with a single glance. The trick with asymmetry is to use it wisely—you don't want to create a space that is off-putting or subliminally disturbing. The eye and mind have to work harder when an object or a space is asymmetrical. Psychological comfort is as important as the physical kind. So asymmetry is best used in a small area or as small touches, as in a balanced but irregular display of artworks, or a still life of objects on a mantel or cocktail table.

1
This entrance hall in Bel Air is a prototypical example of reflectional symmetry, with matching mirrors, consoles, even vases and floral arrangements flanking the French doors. The balance of elements signals that this is a welcoming space and that the rooms beyond it will be equally as comfortable and soothing.

2
In this gentleman's bedroom in Paris, the traditional Greek key border becomes the motif that unifies the room, in an example of translational symmetry. The Greek key appears on the headboard, on the bed-curtains, and even on the nightstands flanking the bed. The motif never draws attention to itself, but rather acts as a subtle graphic background element, like the backbeat to a favorite song.

3
In the dining room of my former home in Hancock Park, rotational and reflectional symmetry work together. The dining table is centered under a traditional chandelier and dramatic ceiling rosette, and the table is lined up with the window, which is flanked by identical bookcases.

4
A perfect example of rotational symmetry is this red dining room in the Hollywood Hills. The chairs are placed evenly around a circular table, under a circular light fixture. Adding further to the regularity of the room is a set of six framed rolled-glass mirrors placed opposite the windows to expand the light and to echo their geometry.

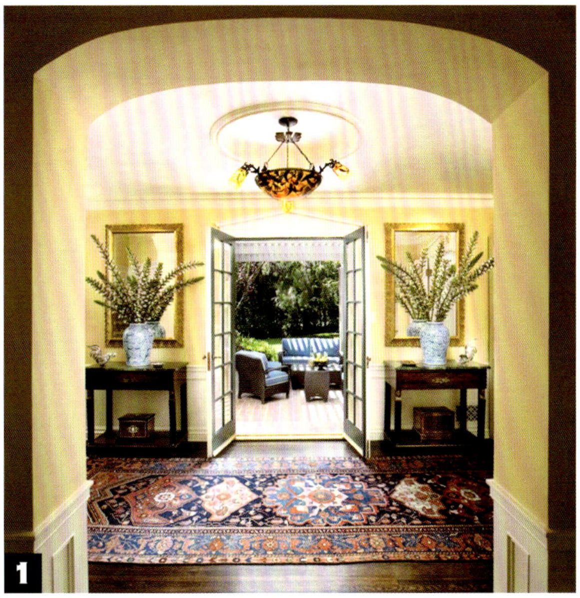

1

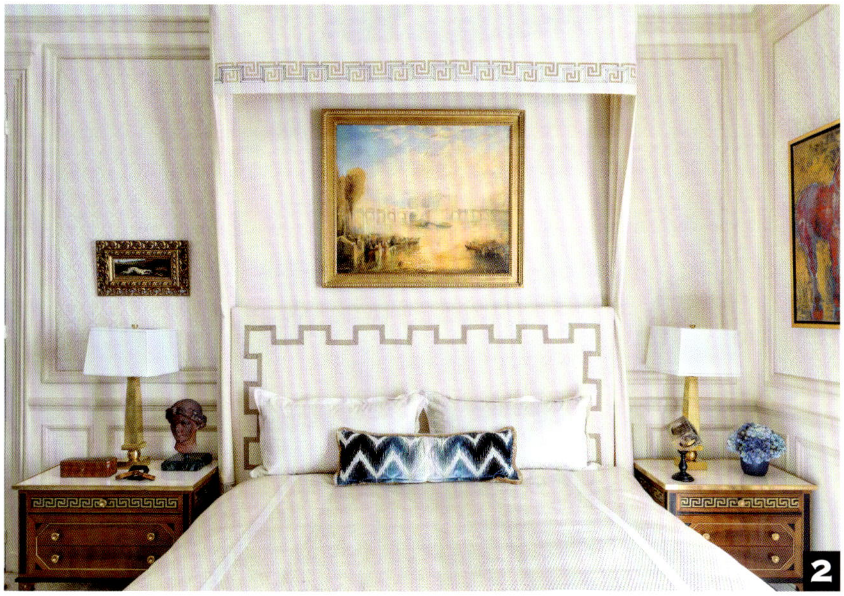

2

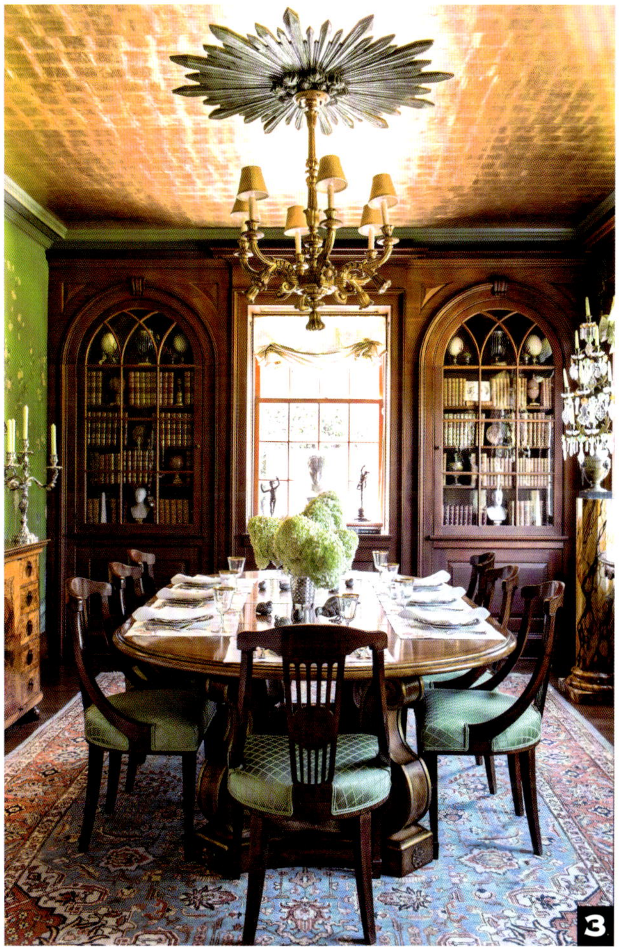

3

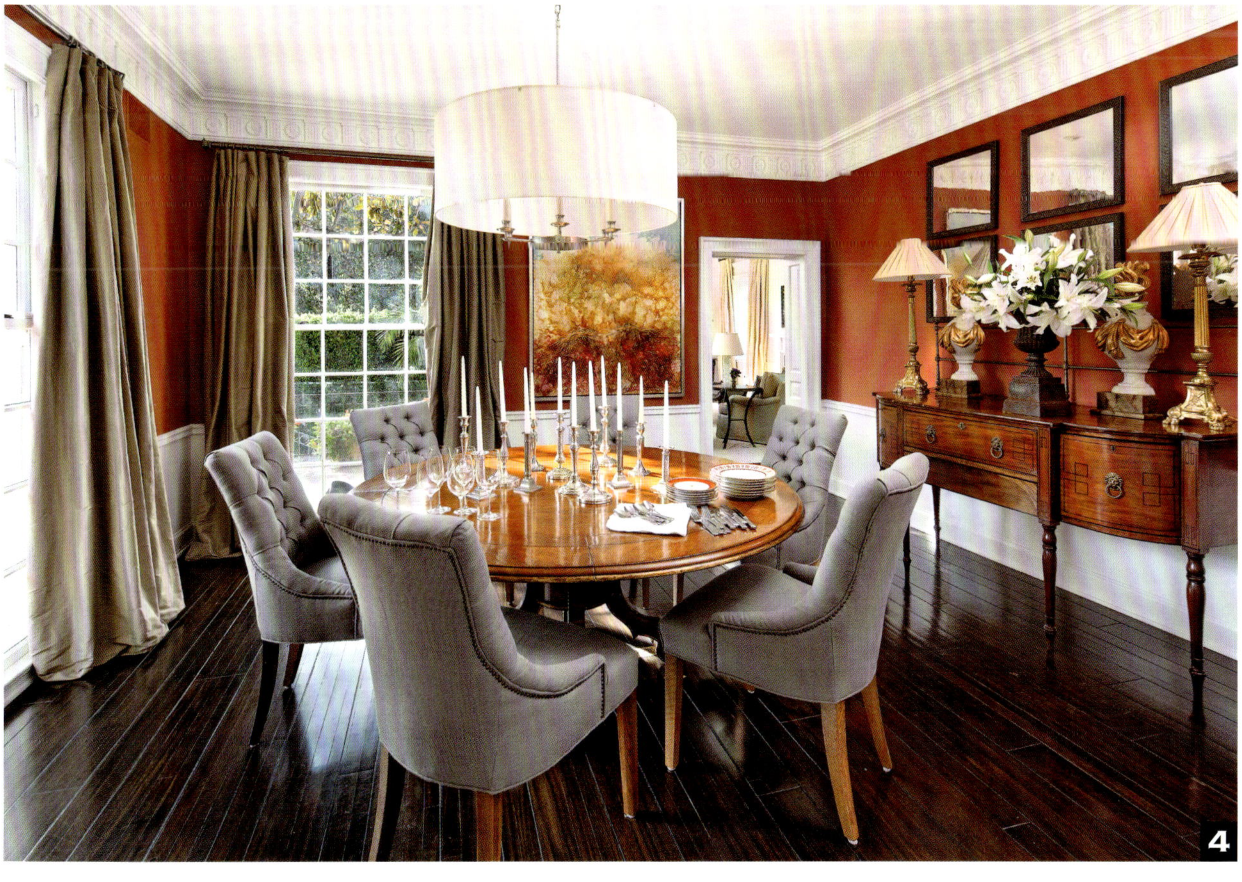

4

5

At first glance, this entry hall in Doha, Qatar, looks completely symmetrical, with the console flanked by matching chairs and the mirror centered and lined up with the pendant light. But something more interesting is going on: the base of the console itself is slightly asymmetrical—organic and rooted, balanced but not perfectly even. The effect is subtle, which makes the entire space more intriguing.

6

Roses are the theme in this lady's bedroom in London, blooming not only on the wallcovering, but also on the painted-plaster ceiling border and even in fabric at each corner of the curtains. This repeated feminine detail, an example of translational symmetry, is unlikely to be noticed immediately; it emerges over time as a kind of low-key delight that furthers the sense of warmth and cosseting within the room.

7

For the entry of this Venice Beach home, I chose a console that is balanced but not even. The sconces are the only symmetrical element—even the accessories are asymmetrically displayed. Yet the overall feel is one of balance and serenity.

8

A bathroom in a house in Hancock Park features a freestanding tub centered between two identical mirrored doors. This kind of reflectional symmetry is a platonic ideal and is possible only when the architecture (window and door placement, for example) allows it. But even when employed on a smaller scale—the layout of furniture, the placement of accessories—reflectional symmetry can be a powerful tool.

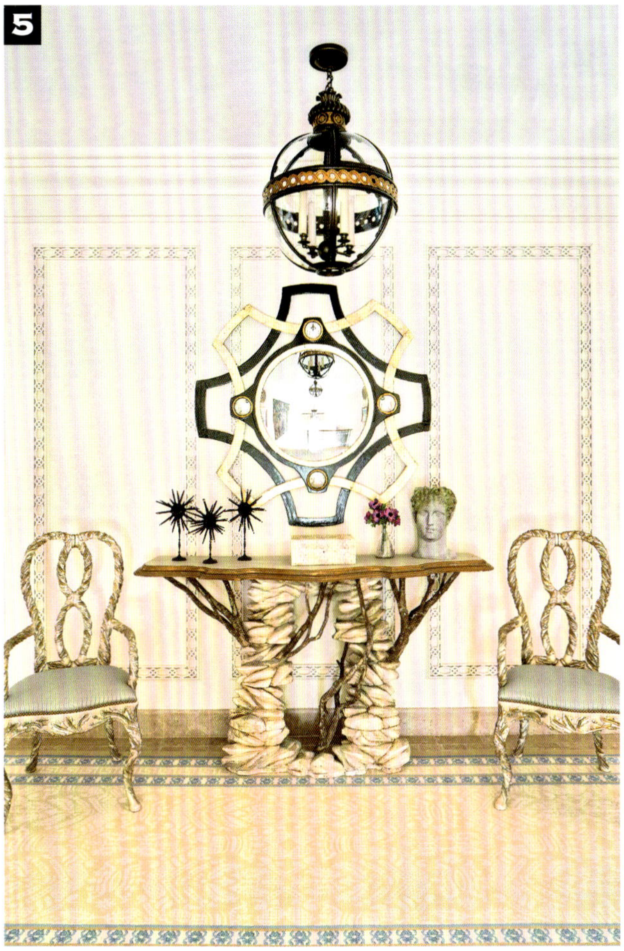
5

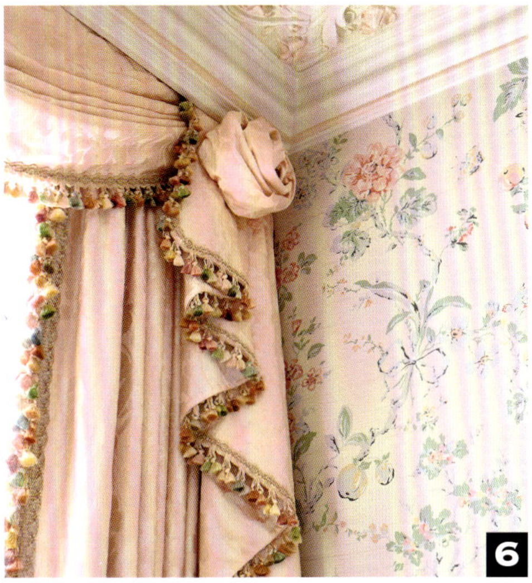
6

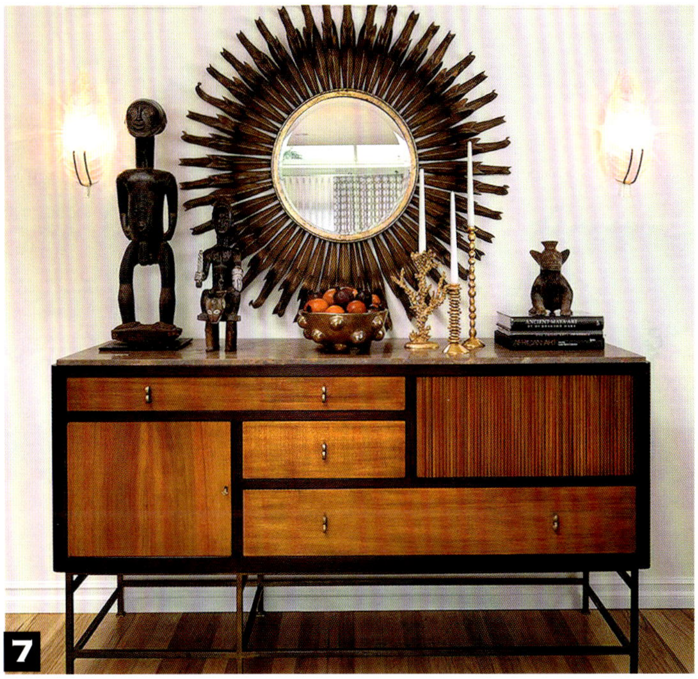
7

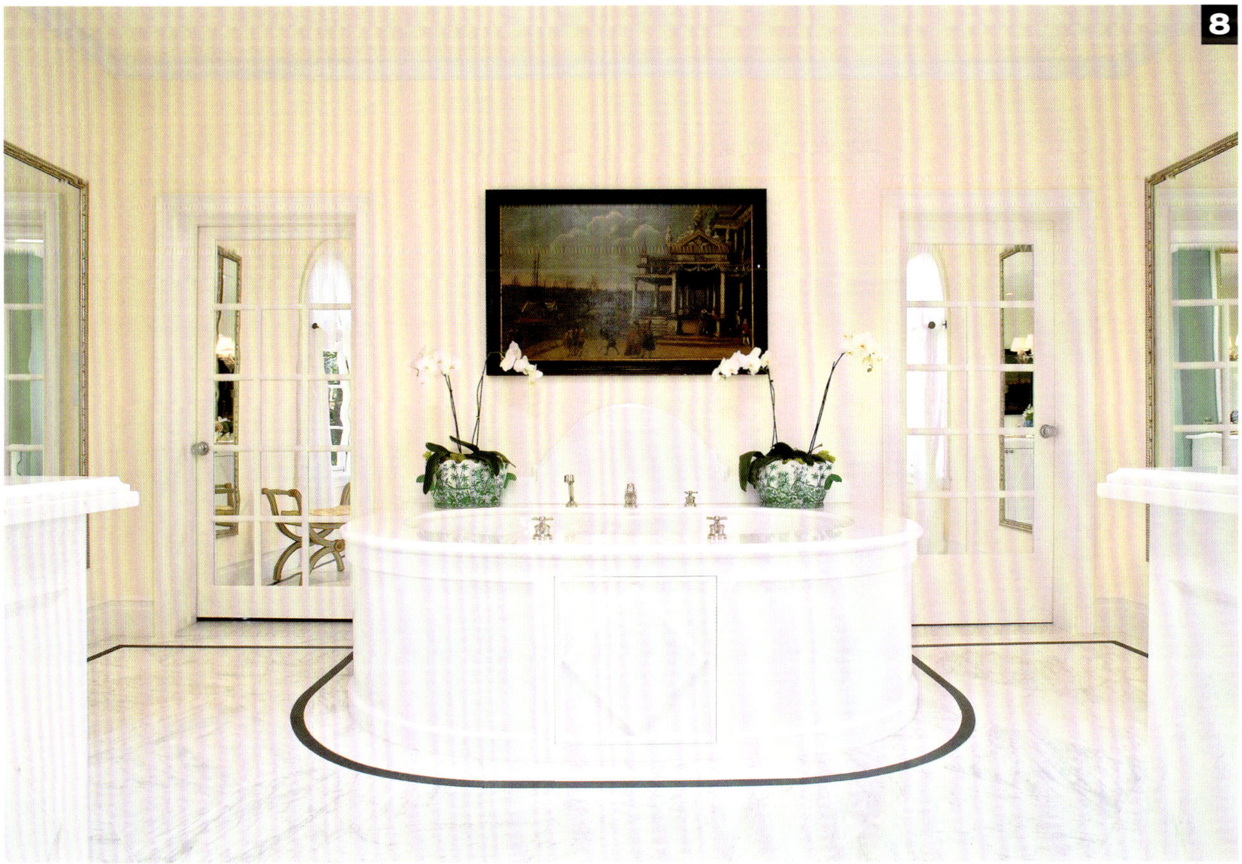
8

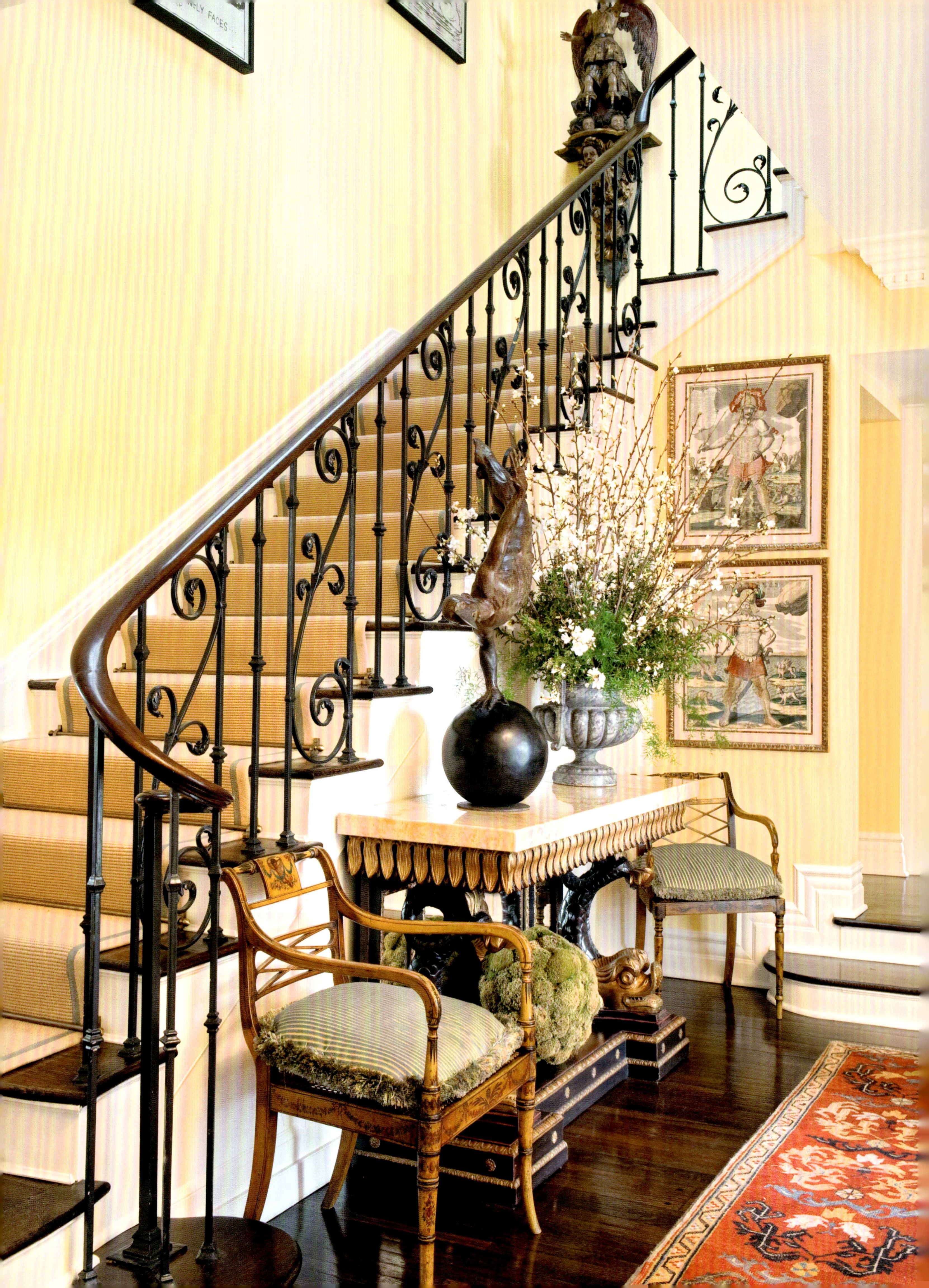

Gracious Glamour

Los Angeles is not only my home, it is also my hometown. I grew up there, and I have always loved its mild climate and the year-round indoor-outdoor lifestyle it inspires. There is nothing more wonderful than throwing open the doors and windows of your house and being able to wander into the garden at a moment's notice—especially in December or February. There is a reason that California has come to symbolize the good life for so many people—here and abroad—and why the California lifestyle has become a touchstone of popular culture.

And who among us isn't fascinated by the myth of Hollywood? For decades, movies and television shows have made Hollywood a site of dreams—and a few nightmares. It is a city of glamour and decadence as well as sunshine and vitality. I am especially enamored with the idea of Hollywood from the 1920s through the 1950s, when it was still a small town and the entertainment community was cohesive, friendly, and accessible—before paparazzi staked out the streets and restaurants, before buses filled with tourists followed the map of stars' homes, and before huge estates began changing the scale of Hollywood and Beverly Hills. I love the black-and-white photos of stars of the '40s and '50s dancing in nightclubs, lazing around each other's pools, mixing cocktails and barbecuing steaks in their backyards. Undoubtedly, the reality was never quite that rosy and relaxed, but the myth still retains its power to enchant.

Part of the appeal of this house is it seems to embody that era, with all its charms—at least from the outside. Located in the Hollywood Hills, above the Sunset Strip, it has dazzling views over the city. And with its straightforward lines, elegant proportions, and charming bay windows, it is a fine example of Hollywood Regency style. The house was built in 1926, and its understated glamour seems to reflect the intimate scale and openness of that simpler era.

Yet inside it was totally undistinguished. Either the house had been stripped of its architectural detailing, or it had never had any (neither the owners nor I were ever able to ascertain which). Perhaps the original owner had wanted the elegance and whimsy of a Paul R. Williams house but wasn't willing to lavish the care and money required. By the time I was hired, the house had been renovated several times over, without noticeable improvement.

The warm and welcoming yellow-and-white scheme in the entry to this Hollywood Hills house contrasts with the gleaming dark floors and vivid rug. The staircase, which is original to the house, is fitted with a practical wool sisal runner.

The appeal of the house still resided completely in its facade—as if it were part of a movie set, not a real home.

Fortunately my clients, a studio executive and his husband, a real estate developer, understood the problem. They are involved in many philanthropic organizations and entertain often on their behalf, so they wanted a place that celebrated Hollywood's past and could dazzle a crowd, but one that would also work efficiently and comfortably for them day to day.

We retained much of the downstairs floor plan, with its gracious entry, living room on the left, dining room to the right, and a view straight through a pair of French doors to the garden. Yet the only original detail worth retaining was the wrought-iron stair rail that rises to the second floor. There, we converted what had been three bedrooms and baths into two of each, allowing for larger and more graceful spaces.

Then came the opportunity to add drama and a sense of scale. We wanted to enhance the house with the kind of architectural detailing that was so popular when Hollywood Regency was at the height of its popularity. I replaced the simple door surround that led from the entry to the living room with an imposing, richly detailed archway. I also added another door leading from the living room into the library, which we enlarged by bumping out the back wall several feet and installing a bay window that echoes the pair on the front facade. Adding the window also made it possible to see straight through these rooms to the garden beyond, emphasizing the indoor-outdoor connection so important to California living.

The coup de théâtre in the living room comes from a place too often overlooked in design: the ceiling. Here we installed a plaster fretwork pattern that adds a gentle rhythm to the space, even as it lifts one's eyes up. We followed this by installing raised wood paneling on the walls, painted in various shades of cream, to give the room heft and a sense of solidity. The fireplace surround and mantel are rather grand, inspired by ones at the Château de Groussay, near Paris, but we undercut any sense of pomposity with a convex mirror and an array of charming Delft pottery. The furniture in the room is quite simple and understated, with a pair of graceful, sweeping Avery Boardman sofas flanking the fireplace and a custom shagreen-and-bronze coffee table between them.

The ceiling in the dining room marks another dramatic gesture: It is covered in gold leaf with an eighteenth-century crystal chandelier hanging from an overscale plaster starburst medallion. To achieve the effect of antique Chinese celadon porcelain on the walls, we glazed linen and then crackled it before applying. The dining table is Biedermeier and we surrounded it with coral velvet–upholstered chairs by Billy Haines, the glamorous Hollywood designer of the 1930s and '40s. The final flourish is the curtains, made

To bring architectural interest to the house, we added the archway, moldings, and ceiling medallion. FOLLOWING PAGES: The living room ceiling was enriched with plaster detailing, the walls with paneling. The marble mantel and the carved wood overmantel decorations were inspired by ones at the Château de Groussay; the rug is nineteenth-century Persian.

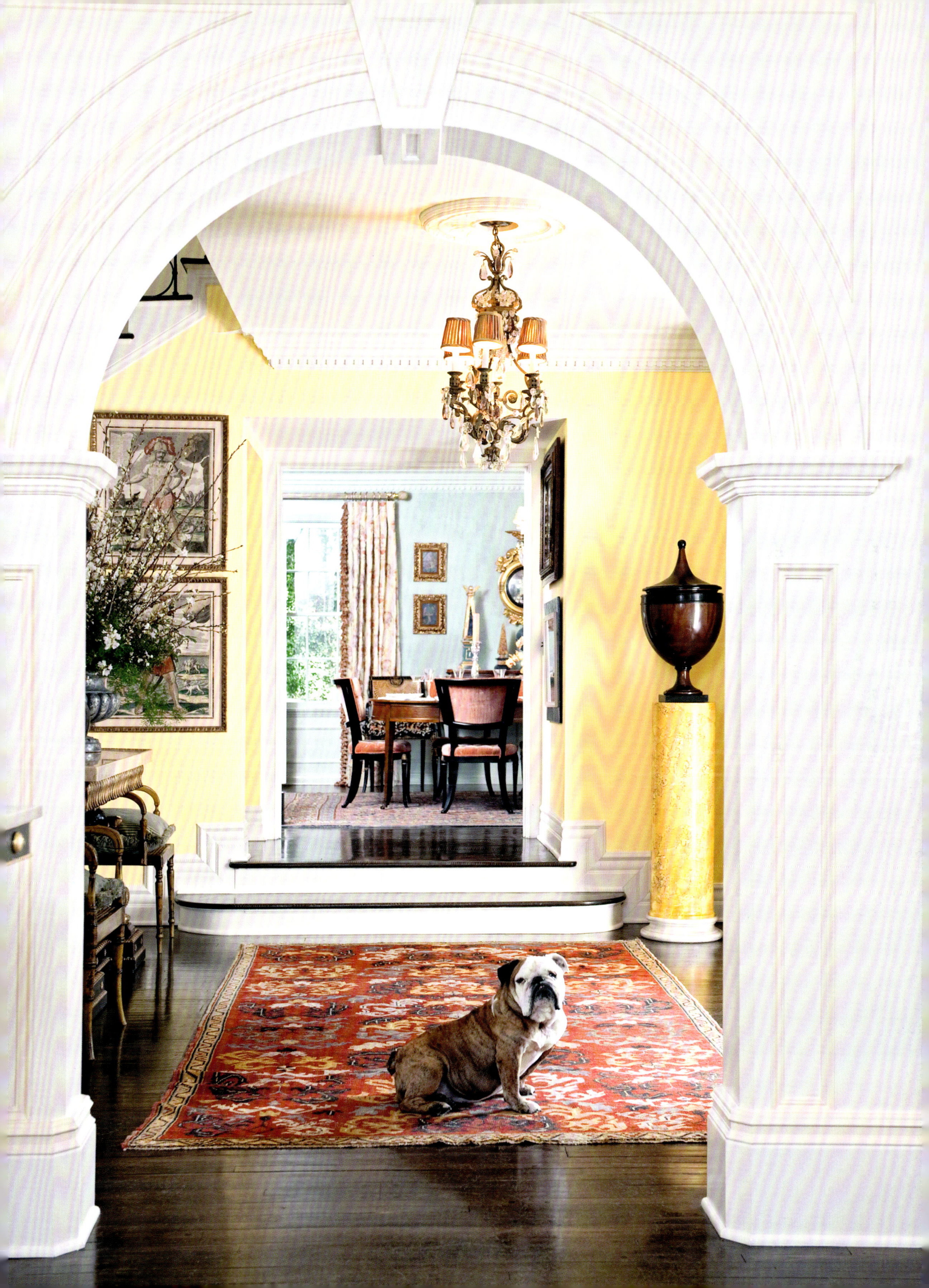

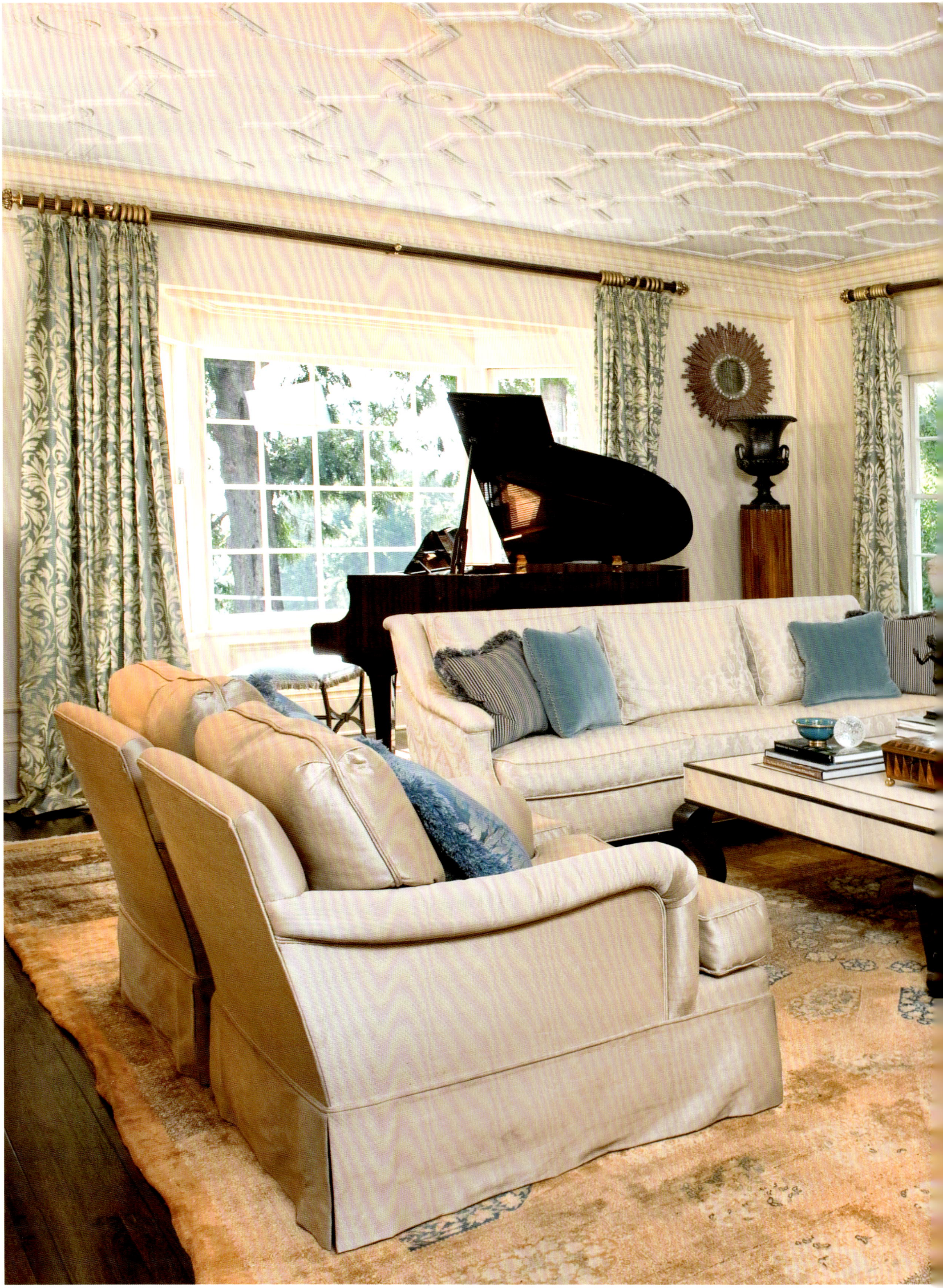

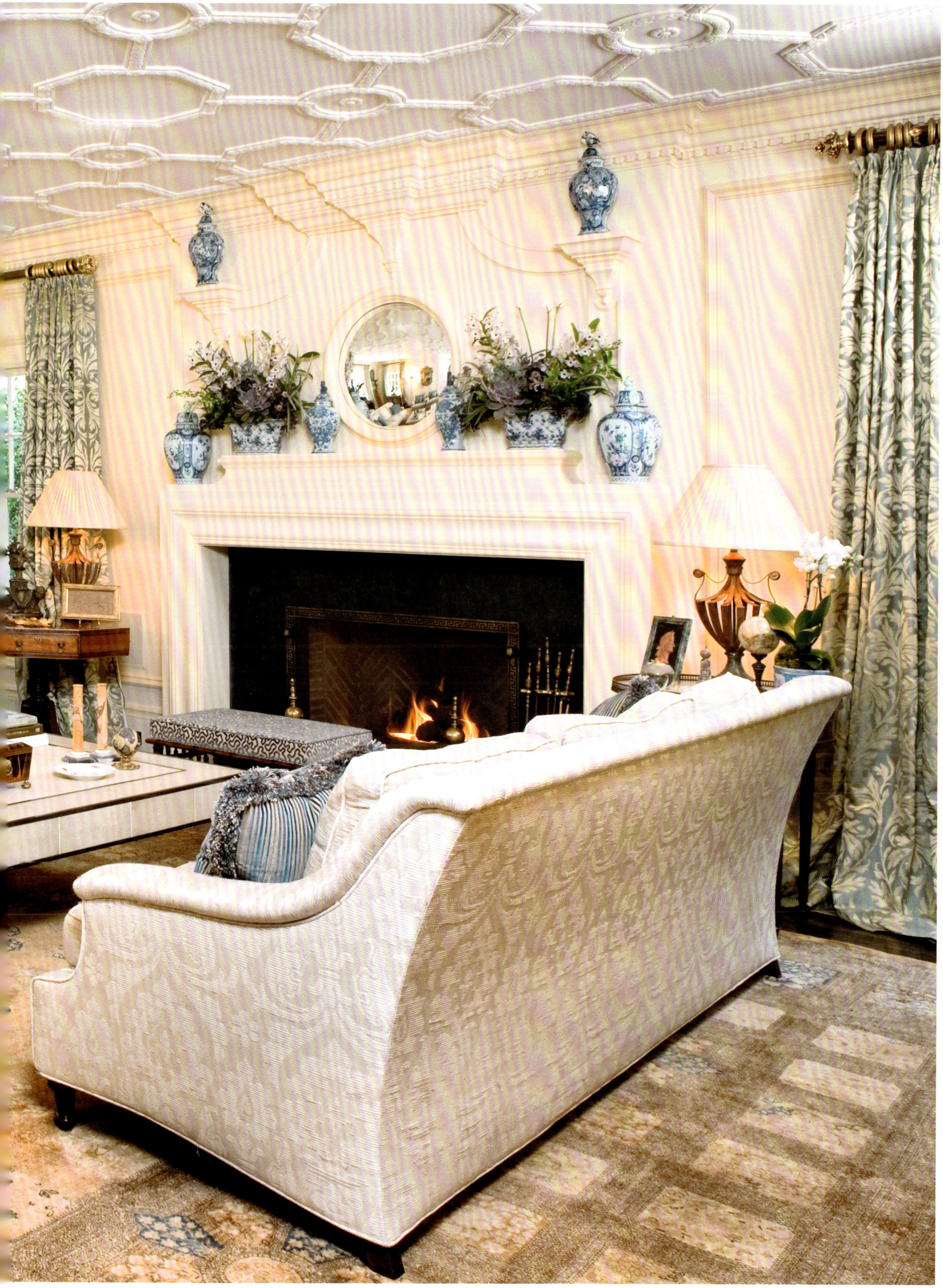

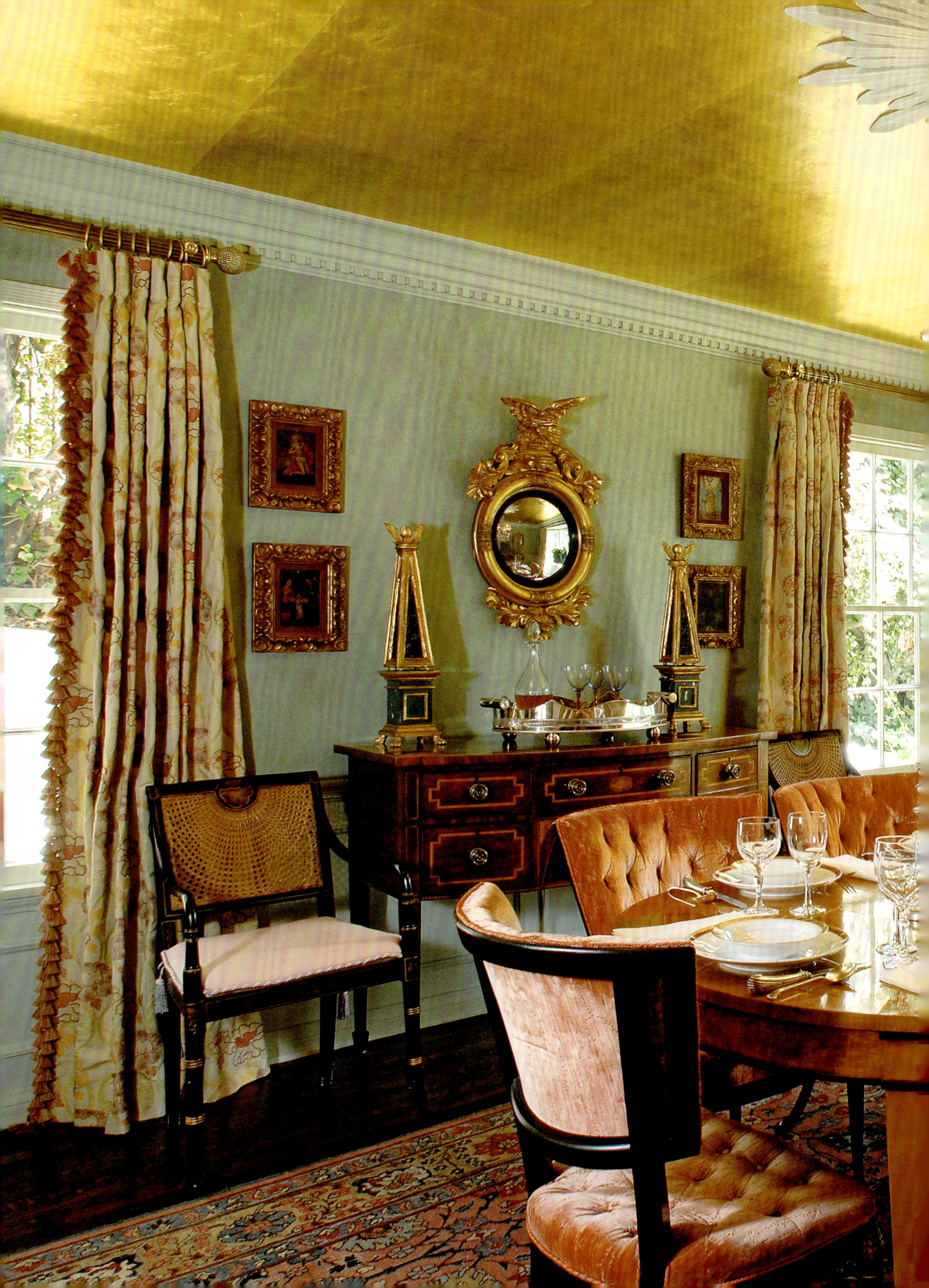

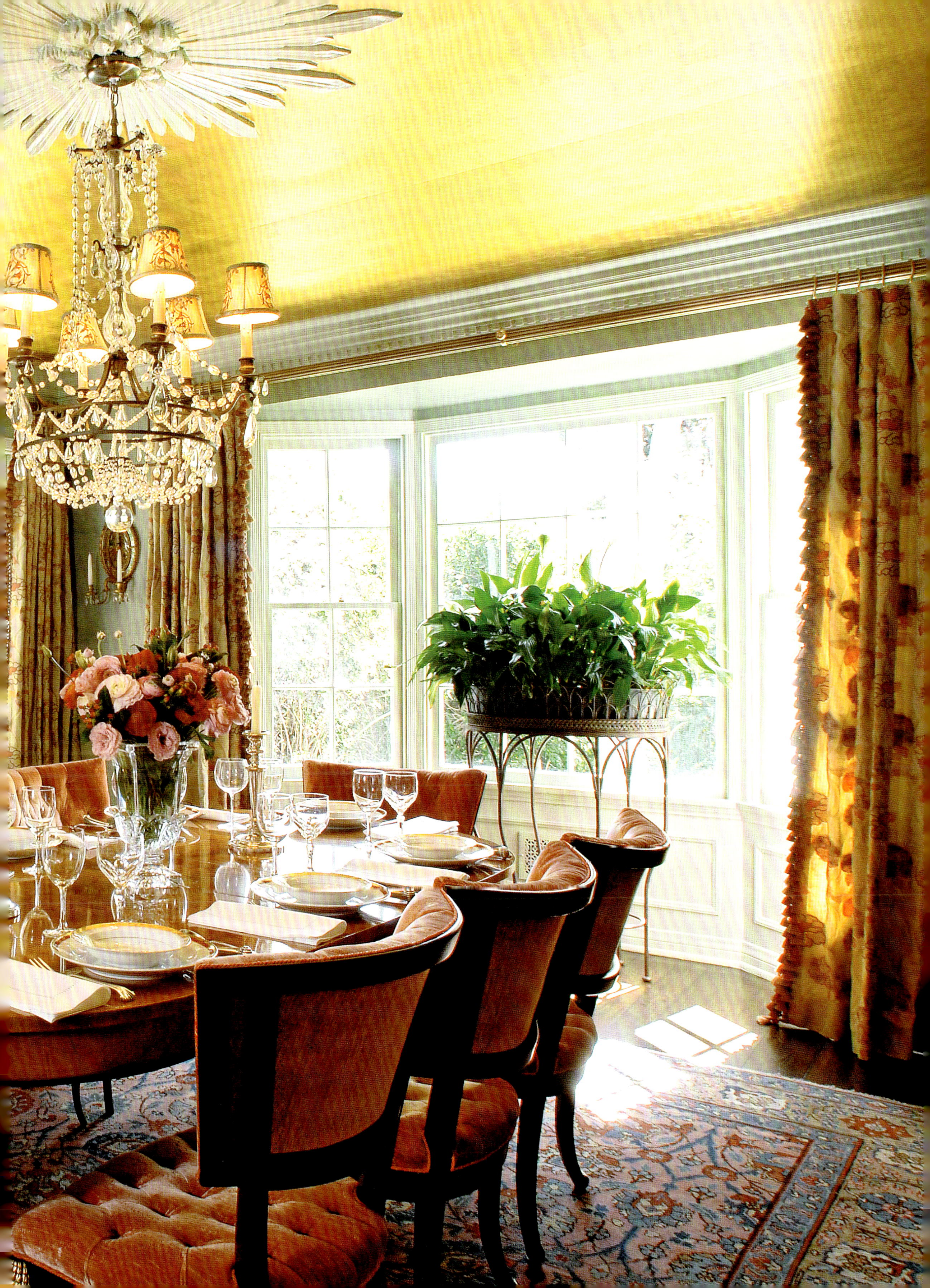

PREVIOUS PAGES: In the dining room, the crown moldings and ceiling medallion were added, gold leaf was applied to the ceiling, and the canvas on the walls was glazed and then crumpled before being applied; the dining chairs are by Billy Haines.
ABOVE AND OPPOSITE: The family room/library was a new addition and is paneled in English knotty pine. The chairs and sofas are covered in outdoor fabrics, the cocktail table is a custom design, and the artwork is by David Hockney.

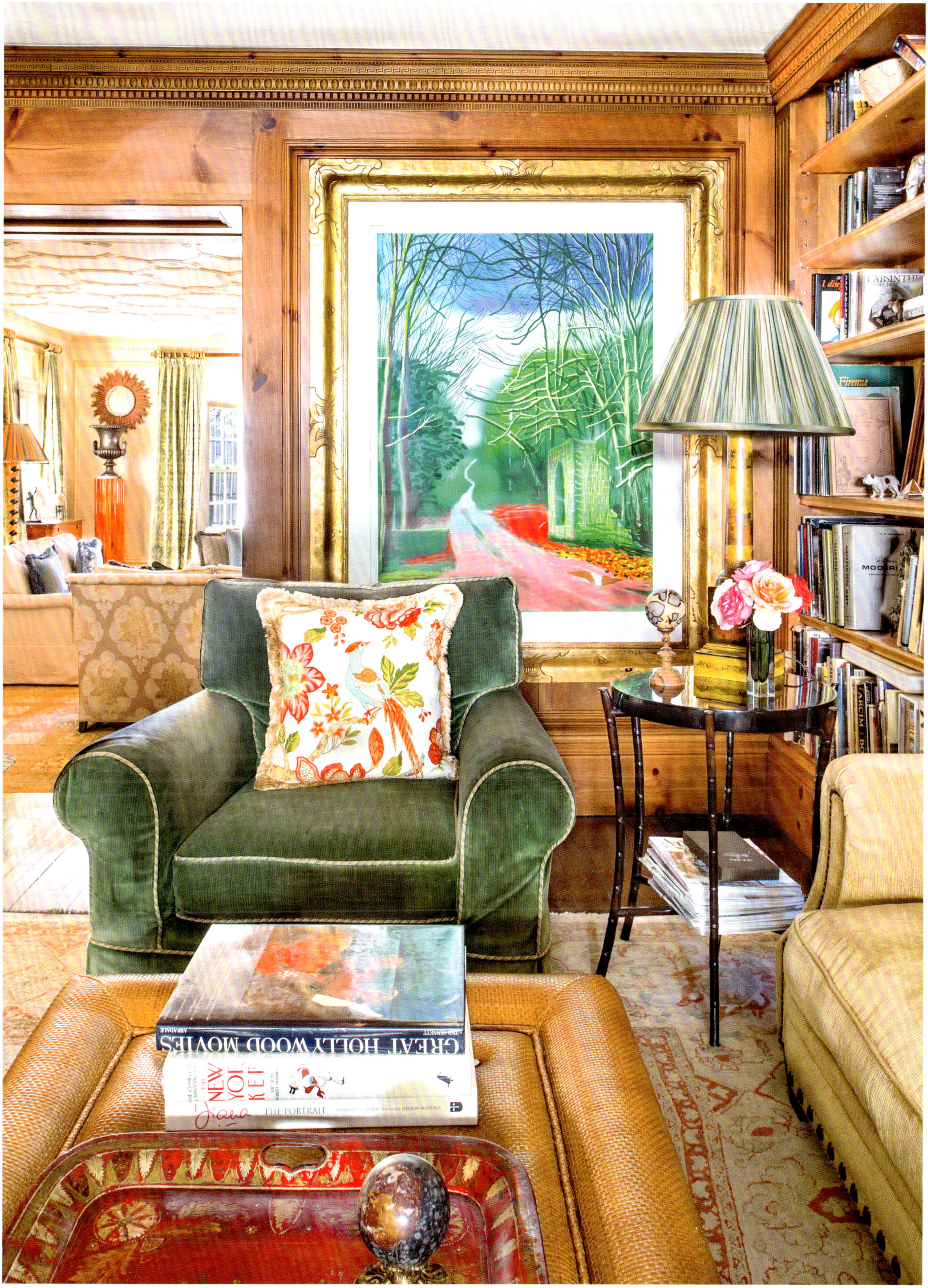

ABOVE: The powder room channels the glamour of old Hollywood with an exuberant wallpaper by Mauny and a 1940s French mirrored chest of drawers. OPPOSITE: In the octagonal breakfast room, we stripped out the cabinetry and installed a scenic wallpaper by Zuber to bring the outdoors in. The rug and table reiterate the room's octagonal shape.

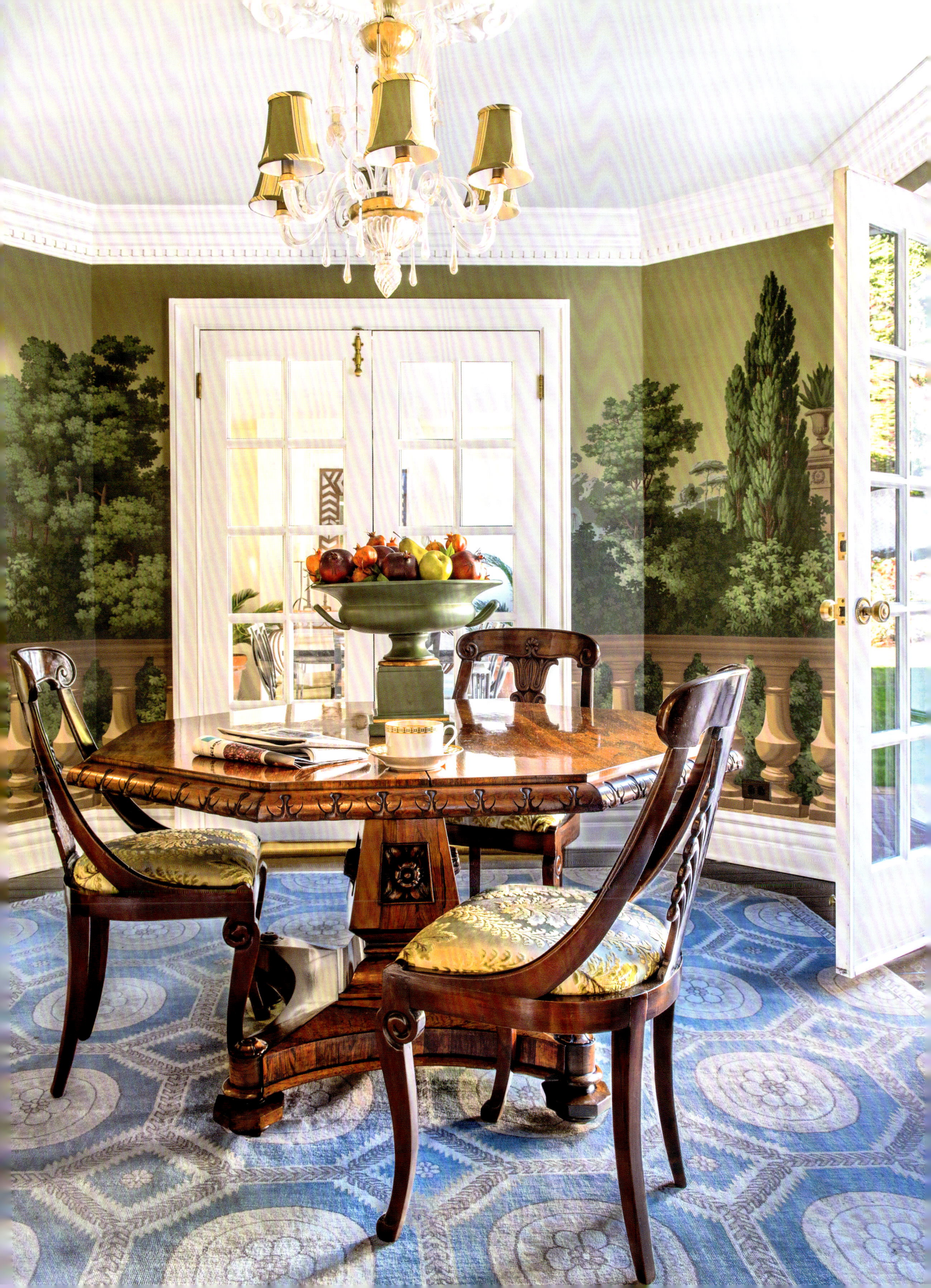

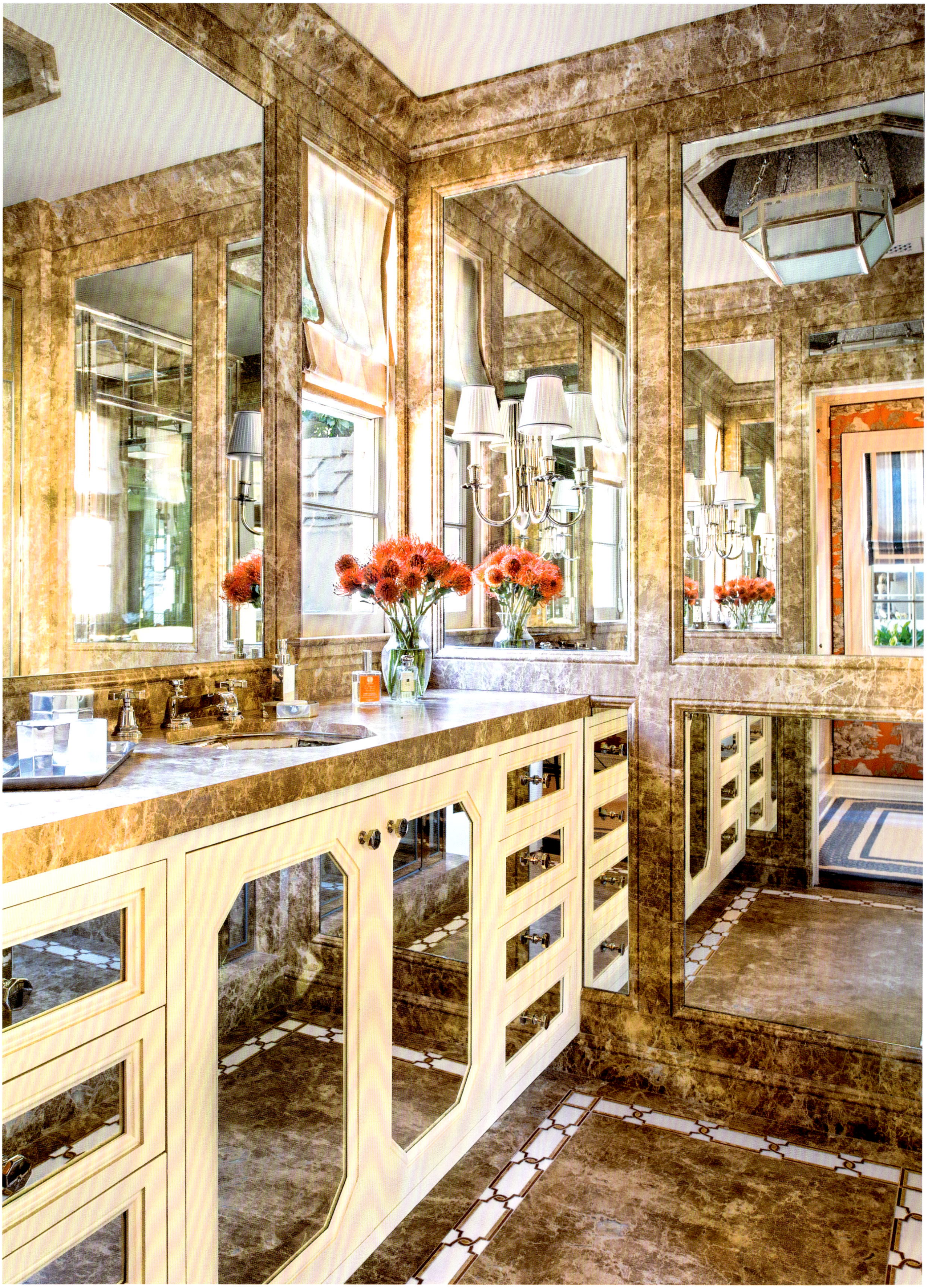

OPPOSITE: In a guest bath, we replaced tile with paneling of richly veined marble inset with panels of mirror.
ABOVE: Because the master bedroom receives light from three sides, we upholstered its walls in a durable, fade-resistant outdoor fabric. The monochromatic color scheme gives the room a soothing, masculine appeal. The armchair and ottoman are upholstered in a fabric by Fortuny.

A guest room takes the opposite approach to color with a vivid and whimsical orange-and-cobalt scheme. The walls are upholstered in a toile, which is contrasted with striped bed hangings and curtains.

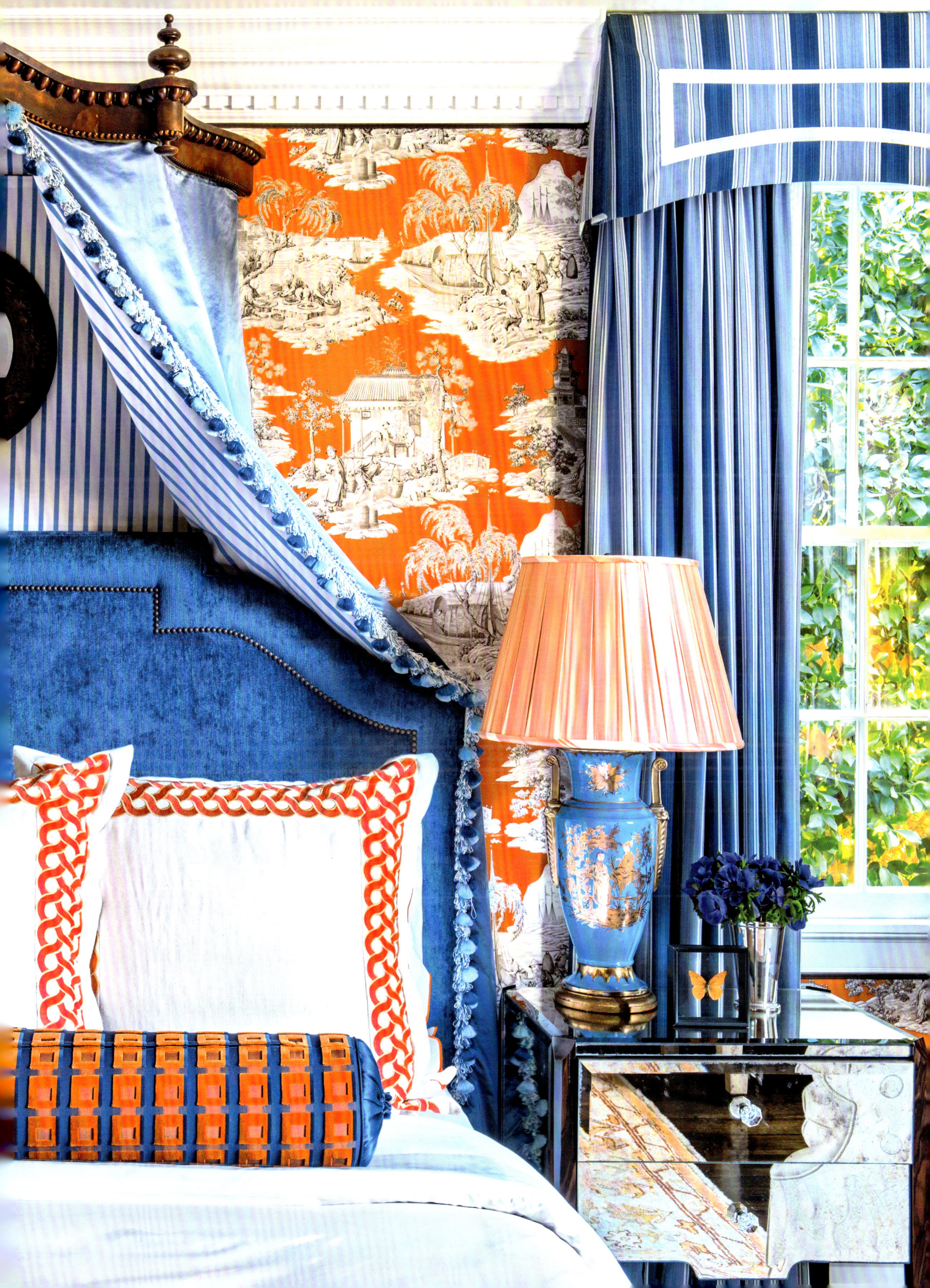

of an updated damask pattern of celadon and coral silk and embellished with an extravagant tassel fringe. The tiny powder room off the foyer is given a dose of drama with mirrored furniture and a bold Art Deco wallpaper that I found in the Mauny archives in Paris.

The library had been paneled in a dark and dreary wood, more evocative of London than a sunny Los Angeles home, so we replaced it with warm, hand-waxed English knotty pine. To up the comfort factor, we covered the upholstered pieces in plush outdoor fabrics that resist stains and the inevitable wear that comes with two beloved English bulldogs. We installed a large-screen television and centered the room on an oversize ottoman with a plush outer perimeter for sitting or resting feet and a firm table at its center to hold drinks, snacks, books, and remote controls. We finished off the room with an ornate, graphic eighteenth century French inlaid-wood desk.

The octagonal breakfast room, which is accessible from both the kitchen and the dining room, provided a chance to be whimsical and a bit theatrical. So we chose a hand-blocked Zuber wallcovering depicting a balustrade with a French landscape beyond, creating the illusion that you are having coffee within a shady bower. The octagonal antique table and rug both reiterate the unusual shape of the room.

And because the breakfast room, library, and kitchen all have glass doors that open to the terrace, with the gardens and swimming pool beyond, the link to nature is ever present. We brought a bit of French fancy to the garden by covering the terrace with a striped awning, installed a columned pergola with climbing roses and wisteria, and enclosed the pool in white-painted treillage, a favorite of the French court—and of mine.

Upstairs, the master bedroom is a quiet refuge done in tones of tan and cream. We upholstered the walls and covered the windows in a practical yet tactile outdoor fabric, laid down a graphic rug, and finished the room with a mix of furnishings, including an Italian inlaid secretary, a 1960s stainless-steel klismos chair, and a Biedermeier side table. Contemporary works of art, including a large-scale photograph by Michael Richard Lambert, add a sense of immediacy.

But if the master bedroom is understated, the guest bedroom is dramatic and decidedly playful. We upholstered the walls in a vivid orange toile and used a variety of deep blues for the upholstered headboard, the drapery framing the bed, and the striped curtains. The bathroom is equally dramatic, with walls sheathed in richly veined marble, expansive mirrors, and even mirrored panels inset in the cabinetry, all reflecting light and creating a dazzling effect. The intent here, as in all the rooms, was to indulge in a bit of Hollywood fantasy without ever losing sight of practicality or comfort.

The attention to architectural detailing extends to the garden, where we installed a gate and archway of trellis. The false-perspective arch is backed with mirror to make the garden appear larger than it actually is.

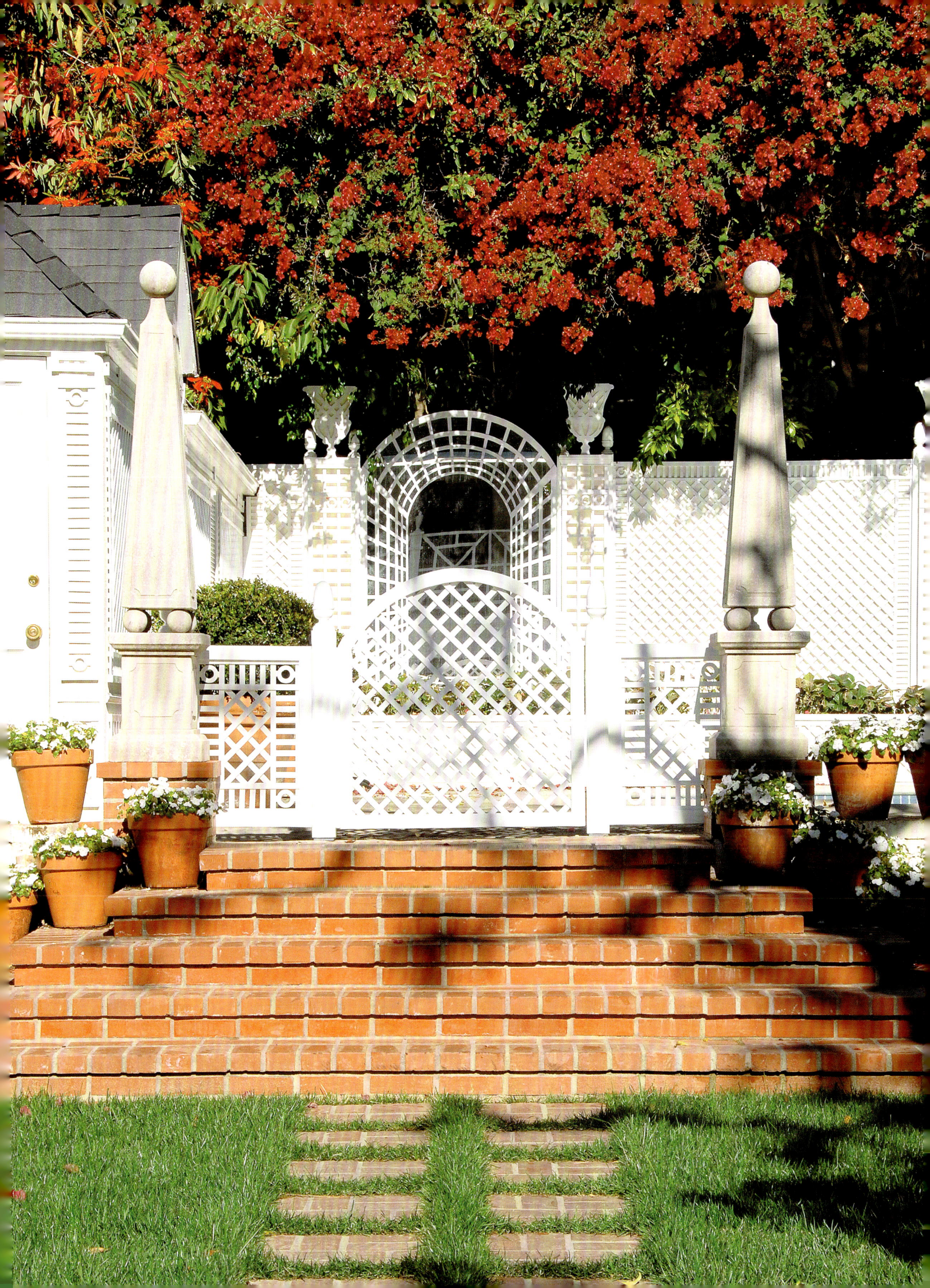

INTERLUDE
ARCHITECTURAL DETAILS

Once a home's basic structure, scale, flow, and principal materials are established, you can turn your attention to the architectural details that add richness, texture, and visual interest. And where it is impossible to get the scale and structure precisely right, architectural details become even more important, as they can compensate for weaknesses and awkwardness.

Architectural details are like sartorial embellishments—a gentleman's tie and pocket square, a woman's earrings or necklace. They don't change the basic structure or meaning, but rather enhance and enliven them. Moldings, cabinetry, millwork, flooring, window frames and treatments, plasterwork, ceilings, stair railings, and other choices all add to the success of a home. They are subtle yet potent, bringing visual interest, texture, and cohesiveness to a room and making it feel complete, composed, and comfortable. You will want to think about them early on in the design process.

Floors, for example, constitute an expansive area in any home and can have an enormous impact on the look, feel, and function of a room. If your floor is marble, it will convey a totally different vibe than if it is *parquet de Versailles*. Whether floors are light or dark; carpeted or bare; wood, marble, or tile; or plain or patterned, what's under our feet is crucial in setting and sustaining the style and comfort of a room. Ceilings provide another opportunity, often overlooked, to enhance a room in a number of ways, with beams, moldings, paint, and plaster details, even wallpaper.

All of these details create a mood, and it is one that should be appropriate to the style, period, and site of the house. If your millwork is gilded, it will have a far different effect than if it is painted or stained, and while gilding might be marvelous in a Paris apartment, it is not going to work at a casual beach house. If materials, shapes, and textures are in harmony with one another and with the intent and character of the room, you are well on your way to success.

1

For a house in Los Angeles that was short on distinguishing features, simply hanging an impressive chandelier in the dining room was not enough. To add a dramatic flourish, we installed an over-the-top sculptural plaster starburst rosette, from which the chandelier now hangs. Like floors, ceilings are too often afterthoughts in devising the decor of a room, yet whether painted with soft colors, sporting a mural of clouds (or even putti!), fitted out with beams, or covered with gold- or silver-leaf squares to add a subtle shimmer and glow, ceilings provide a huge opportunity to affect the look and feel of a room.

2

The carved and painted ceiling in this Beverly Hills house was also a standout element. We had it carefully cleaned, but then we created a custom light fixture to make it even more prominent. We choose a traditional shape, but the fixture's unusual size (it has eighteen arms) and its unexpected material (gleaming chrome) make it clear that this is a contemporary piece in a contemporary room.

3

This hall in a Beverly Hills home is a case where the architectural details are not background elements, but virtually the stars of the room. There was no way to minimize or compete with the richly carved wood archways, columns, and balustrades, or the ornate plaster ornament on the ceiling, so we decided to highlight them with the unexpected deep rose color of the walls. The rich color showcases the classical elements while also bringing a modern edge.

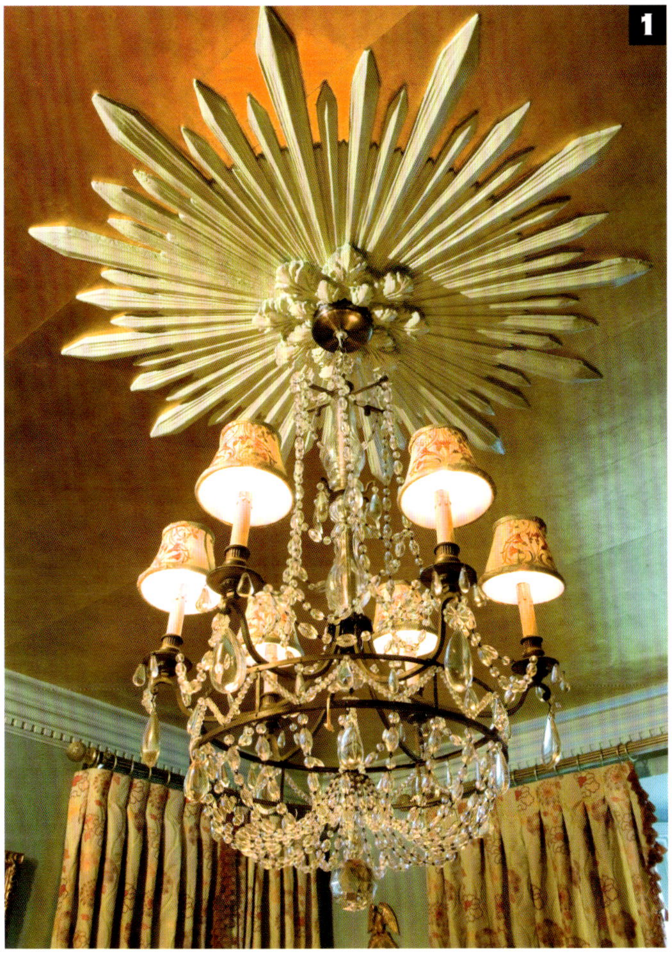
1

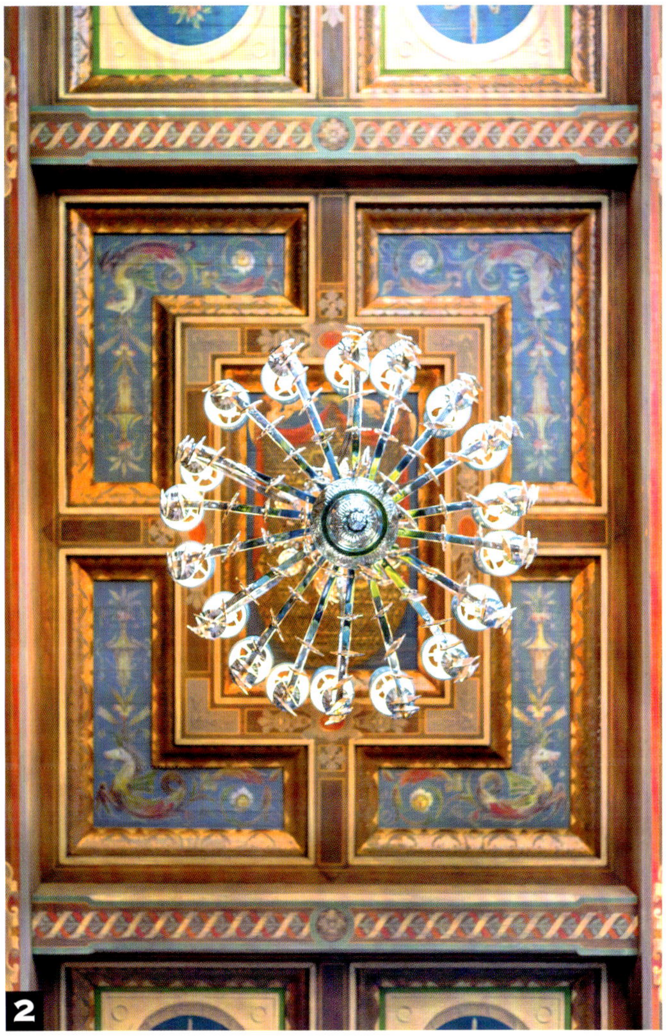
2

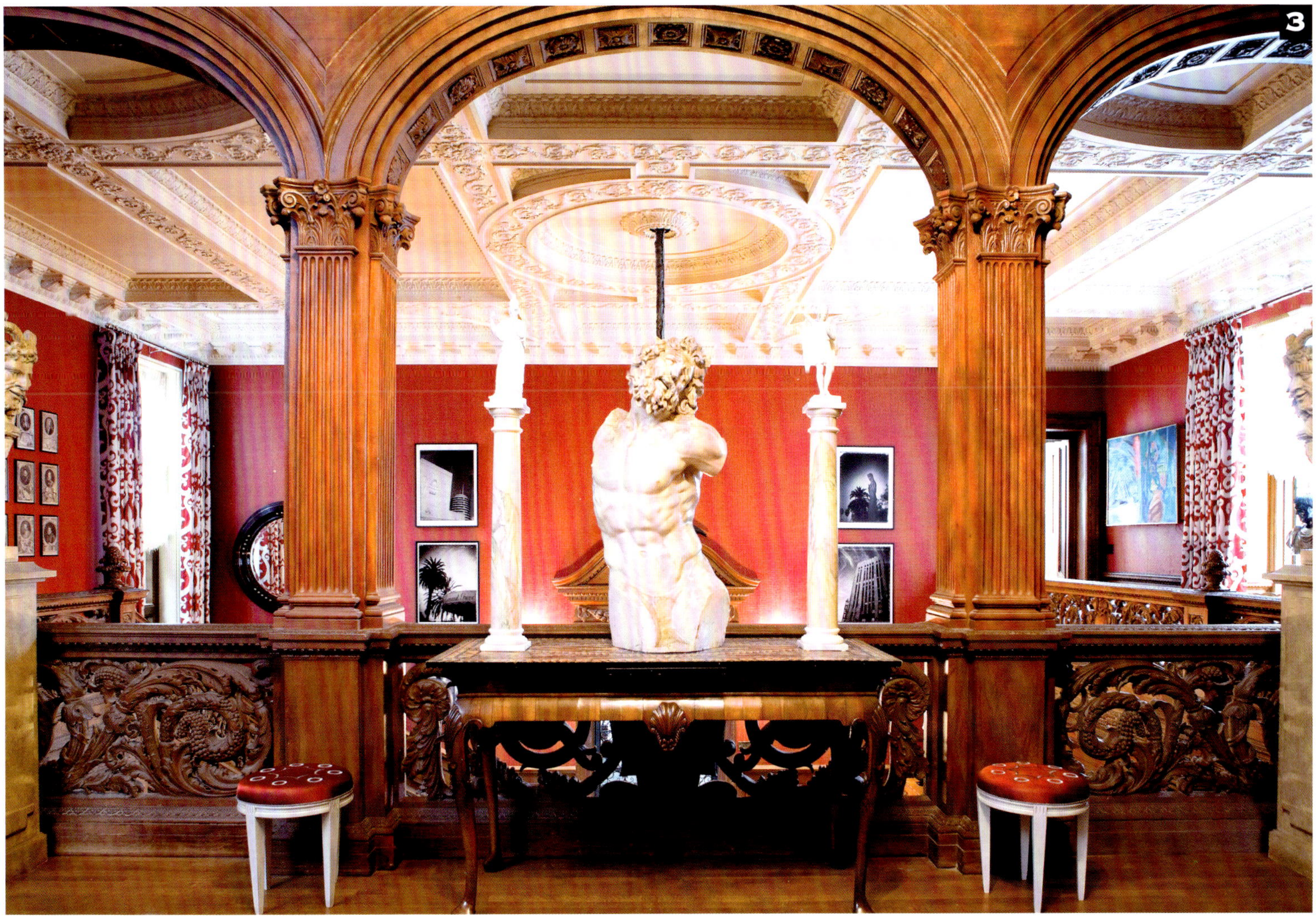
3

4

To add femininity and grace to a lady's bedroom in a home in London, I created custom paneling that would frame the mirrored cabinetry. Inspired by a piece of cabinetry at the Wallace Collection in London, I opted for subtly gilded decorative patterning that contrasts with the cream-painted background for a discreet yet lush effect, turning what would otherwise be a bland background piece into an integral element of the room's feminine and fanciful atmosphere.

5

I am not a fan of open skylights in traditional homes. The light they supply is usually welcome, but I find it unappealing to look directly up into them and see the fittings, and the shafts of light they admit can be harsh at certain times of the day. To mitigate that effect, in this Los Angeles home, I fitted the skylight with white Plexiglas and then softened the light further with a white fabric scrim. The crisp, black iron star frame turns the skylight into a decorative element in keeping with the architecture of the house.

6

For this playful house in Beverly Hills, we wanted to use traditional materials—in this case, marble—for the floors, but in unusual shapes. I looked to a sixteenth-century Venetian floor for the many vivid colors, but used polka dots instead of stripes, inset with circles of glass that, at the flip of a switch, go from opaque to transparent. This is a somewhat extreme version of the kind of energy that flooring can bring to a room, but even simple wood planks, depending on how they are installed and treated, can have a strong impact.

7

Mirrors are not just decorative, they can also be used to delineate and multiply architectural details. In this house by the sea in La Jolla, I used arches of mirror to flank—and reiterate—the impressive arched opening to the room. The mirrors amplify not only the light, but also the elegance of the boiserie that panels the room. The fanciful eighteenth-century carved mermaids over the mantel hold court above a mirror that rises to reveal a television. And to further the playful oceanic motifs, the coffered ceiling is inset with canvas panels of grotesque sea monsters, hand-painted in France.

4

5

6

7

Royal Palms

There's nothing more charming than watching children at the beach building castles in the sand. In a way, that's what I had to do here—create a residence that was both grand in scale and luxury, but also embodied a sunny, relaxed, and beachy vibe.

When my firm took on the assignment, nothing of the structure existed except for its steel frame. But it was quite a frame, for a house of more than 43,000 square feet right on the beach yet also in the midst of Doha, Qatar, called the world's richest city. This clearly wasn't a simple beach shack; rather, it was a place worthy of three generations of an important Qatari royal family, somewhere they could gather, relax, entertain, and enjoy the clear waters of the Persian Gulf.

I struggled with the concept until I remembered how much I enjoyed looking at historic photographs of Palm Beach, Florida, in the 1920s and '30s. "Palm Beach casual"—luxury and glamour tempered by a sunny palette, crisp, clean lines, and a certain relaxed sophistication—became a touchstone for this project. The image we wanted to evoke was not so much a pool house and swimsuits at noon, but a terrace at twilight, the kind of place that brings to mind caftans, palazzo pants, and silver cocktail shakers.

One way to achieve this effect was to define a palette of golden beiges contrasted with a range of rich blues and bright colors throughout the house, to echo the sea visible from the many windows. I also sought to break up the scale of the rooms by establishing numerous sitting areas and embellishing nearly every surface—from walls to floors to ceilings—with a variety of decorative treatments. These range from barely noticeable painted murals to trellising to gold leaf, as well as plasterwork and hand-painted wallpapers. This array of surfaces, treatments, textures, and colors assures that the eye never tires or grows bored.

The mix of grand spaces with subtle details is immediately evident in the entry foyer, with its graphic, circular-patterned marble floor. In contrast, a ceiling mural of soft clouds shimmers above, an effect we created by mixing crushed pearls in with the white pigments. Long before the discovery of the country's immense oil and natural gas reserves, Qatar was a major source of pearls, so it seemed appropriate to use pearls as a symbol of the country's past.

The abundance of arched windows ensures that light is a constant and changing presence in the space. The shallow groin-vaulted ceiling

The seaside rotunda entrance hall of a palatial villa in Qatar features a ceiling mural of clouds enriched with crushed pearls, a Murano glass chandelier, and a floor of semiprecious stones. The eighteenth-century table base is fitted with a top of mother-of-pearl and malachite, and the walls are embellished with a trompe l'oeil mural of gauzy curtains.

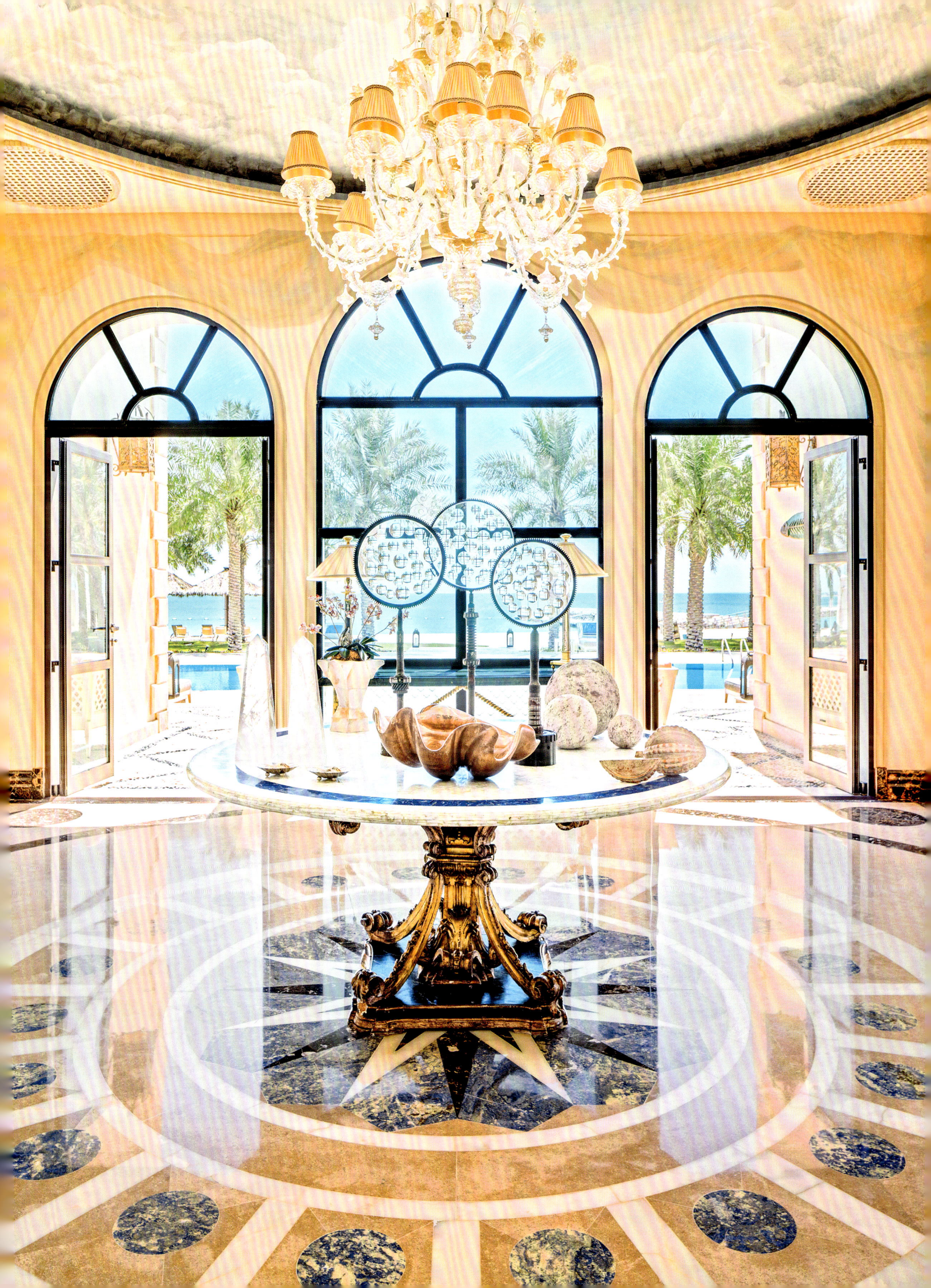

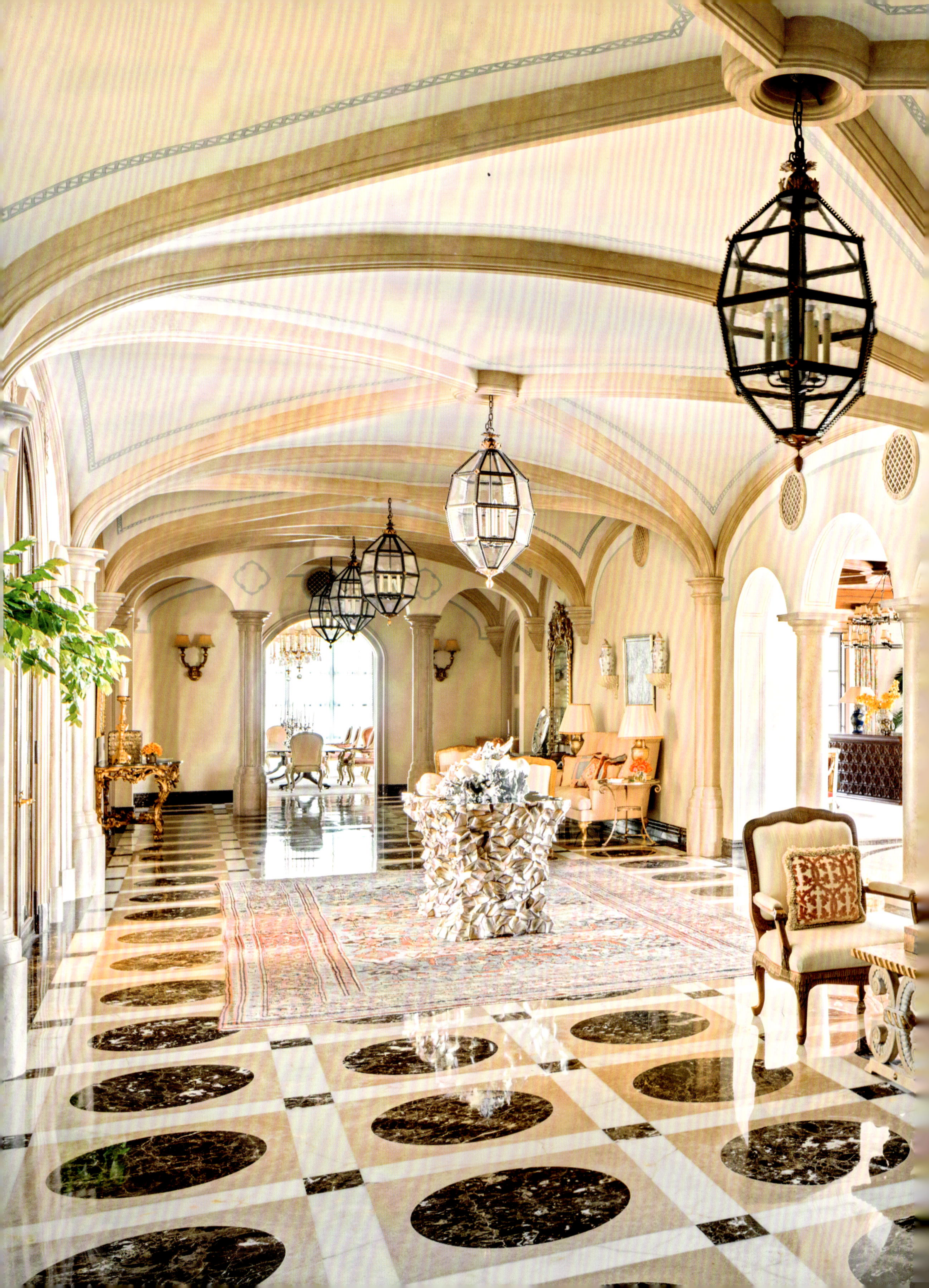

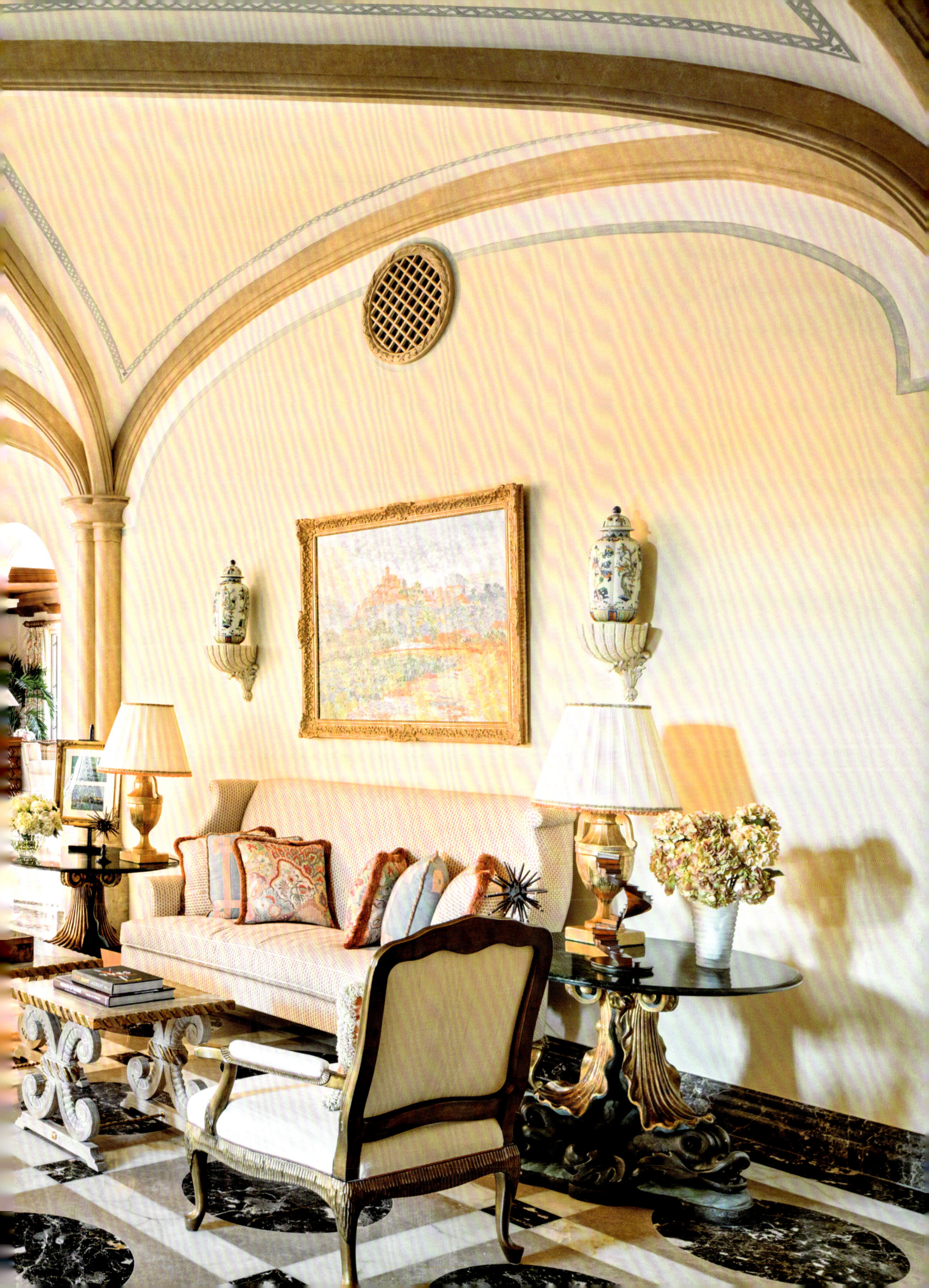

of the adjacent arcade, its ribs contrasted with darker plaster and a decorative painted chain, provides a gentle, almost dancing rhythm that plays off the bold marble floor, inspired by the one in the dining room at the Château de Groussay.

The formal reception room is a confection of blue and gold, with trelliswork in a lighter shade of blue layered over those colors—all the way to the ceiling. The color scheme is reiterated in the upholstery fabrics, in the massive antique rug adorned with a gentle pattern of flowers, sprigs, and leaves, and even in the small shades of the crystal chandeliers.

The formal dining room picks up the trelliswork in its wainscoting, layered over mirror, but here the star is the hand-painted de Gournay wallpaper of flowers and birds in flight against a rich blue sky. The dining chairs are upholstered in a coral velvet, and the room is presided over by an impressive eighteenth-century gilt-wood mirror.

In the more casual living rooms that flank the entry, I employed a favorite device of one of my heroes, the Spanish painter Josep Maria Sert. I had the walls painted with very pale shadows of the palm trees outside—the actual shadows that occur during one moment of the day, but in this case the shadows linger softly, an unobtrusive yet haunting presence that allows the surrounding landscape to infuse the house. The wood-paneled ceilings add warmth and intimacy.

As in most houses, no matter their size, the kitchen and adjacent family room are the most frequent gathering spots. I accented the traditional white cabinetry of the kitchen with a silver-leafed rope detail and topped the oversize island with an engineered-stone countertop in a striking shade of blue, a color that, in a deeper shade, also carpets the family room. There are multiple areas to dine and a large seating area with upholstered furniture to complete the feeling of comfort and warmth.

At the opposite end of the ground floor, his-and-hers master bedrooms are separated by a dramatic barrel-vaulted sitting area that is paneled from floor to ceiling. The recessed area around each of the square panels is painted in shades of blue that fade to white as they rise to the top, a subtle ombré effect that gives richness to the space and serves as a wonderful surprise that you don't immediately notice when you enter the room. His bedroom and bath are restrained and spare, in shades of turquoise and white; hers is more fanciful, with walls covered in a lavender-pink silk, a gilt four-poster bed, and a crystal chandelier. The upstairs also includes four guest suites, each with its own sitting room and terrace. I intentionally designed them to be unique, to appeal to different guests.

On this floor is another large living room. The walls are covered in faux-bois wallpaper squares that give the effect of driftwood. Over the sofa hangs a metal wall sculpture of a

PREVIOUS PAGES: The eighty-two-foot-long beachside entry hall is supported by a series of stone groin vaults with painted detailing that we added. The floor was inspired by the dining room at the Château de Groussay, and many of the decorative details play off the home's seaside location, including the shell-shaped brackets, the rope detailing on the small cocktail tables, and the center table made with abalone shells. OPPOSITE: The hallway to the kitchen features a seventeenth-century Aubusson tapestry.

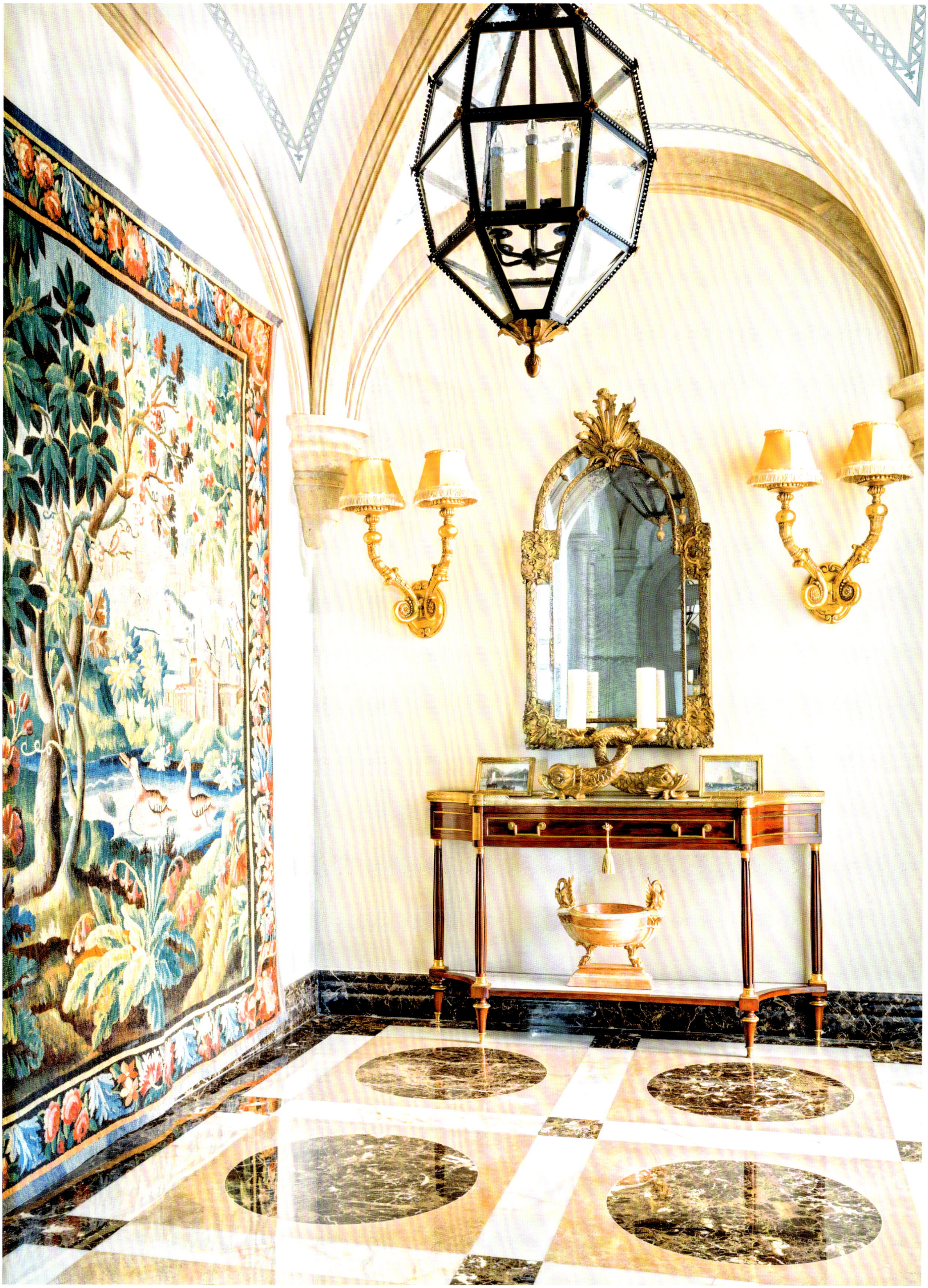

ABOVE: The formal entry has a floor of semiprecious stones that I designed. OPPOSITE: The wave motif at the top of the treillage in the formal living room is another subtle reference to the sea.

Mercedes
Seuil
OCEANS
Jacques Perrin
François Sarano
Stéphane Durand
BVLGARI SERPENTI COLLECTION

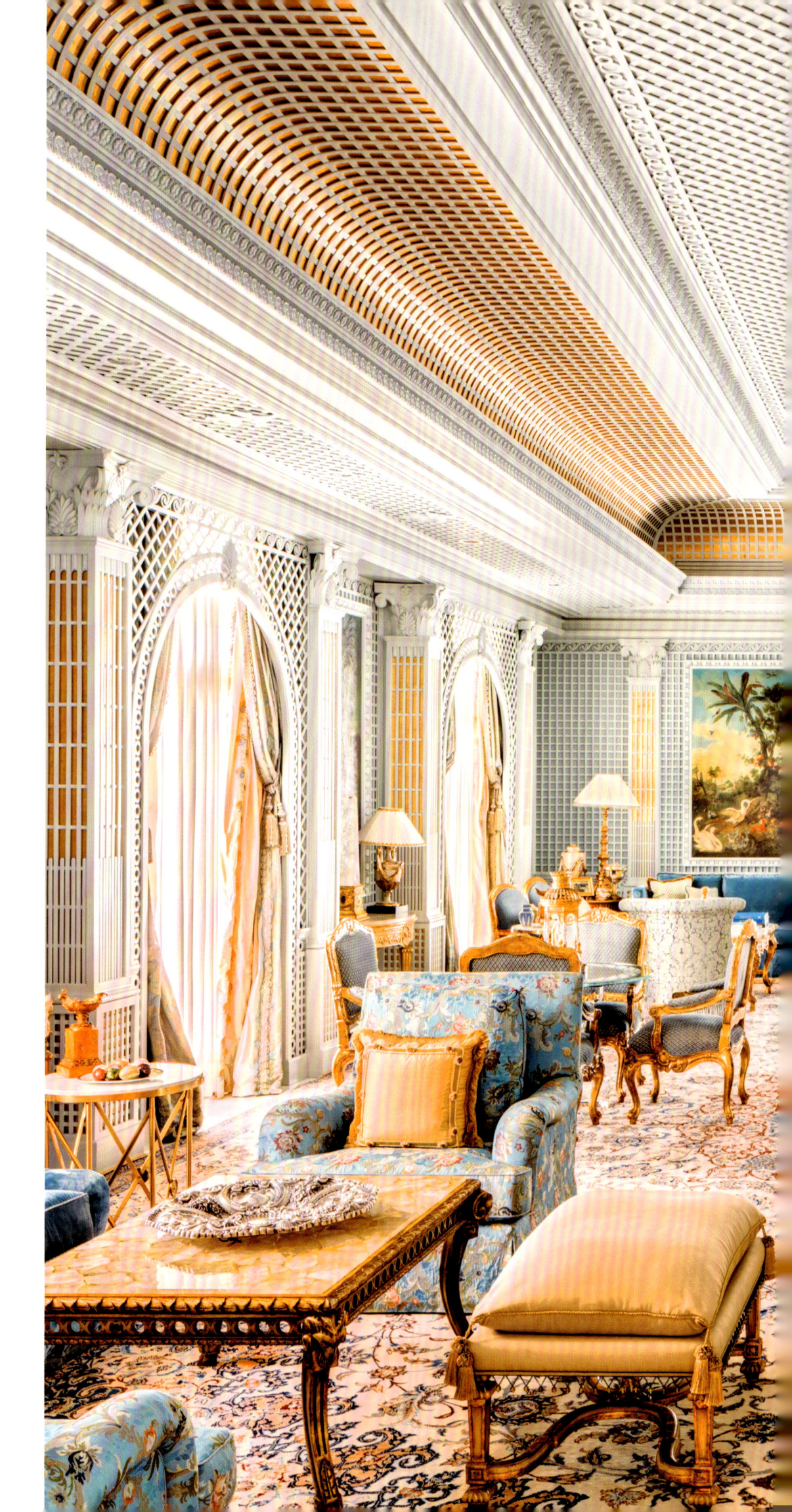

The formal living room is so expansive that it allows for six seating areas. The treillage on the walls and ceiling, by Accents of France, unifies the room and adds architectural elements that prevent the scale from being overwhelming; the pilasters and the ceiling recess are gold leafed, and the oversize rug is antique.

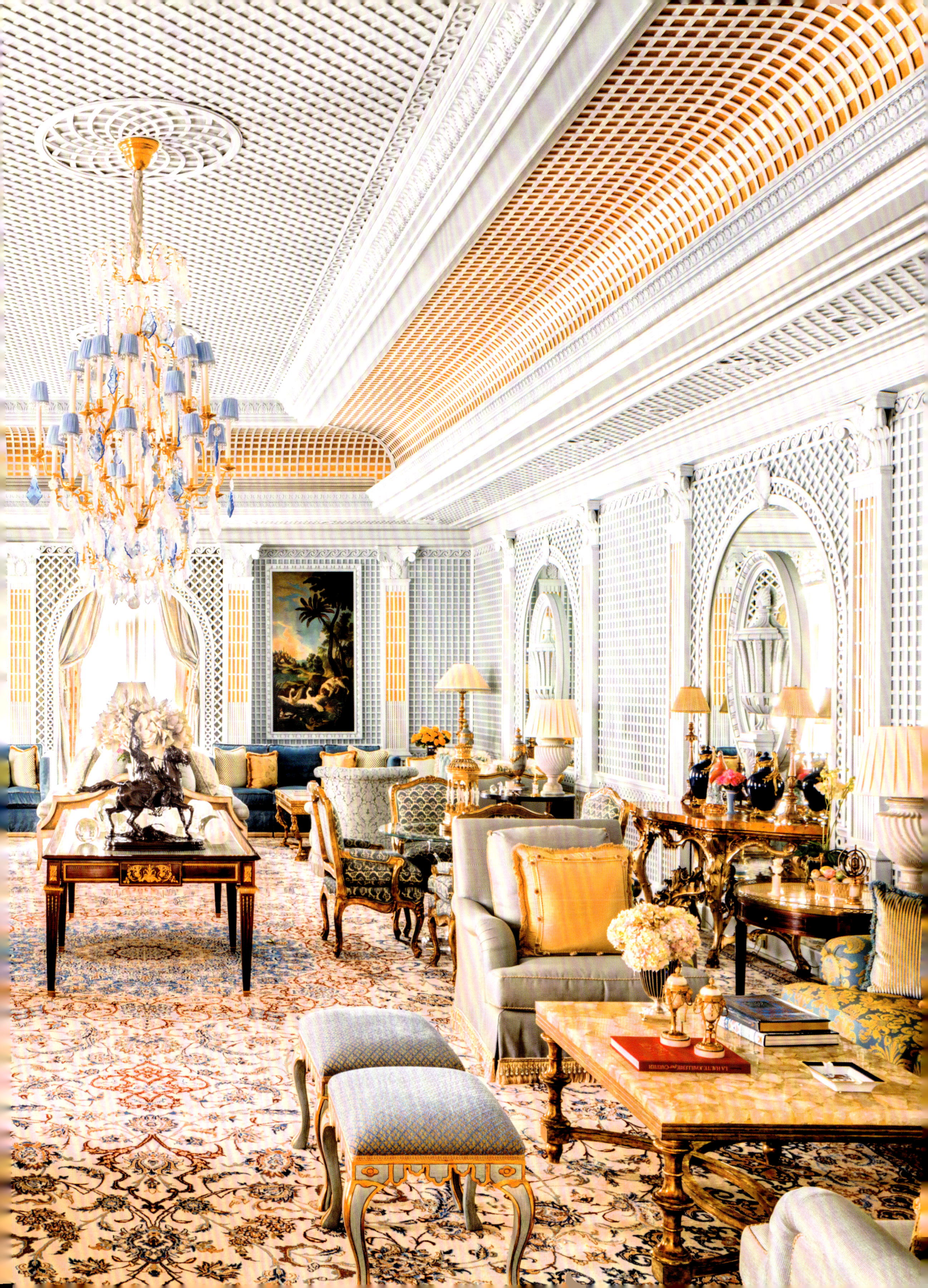

LEFT: The stone floor in the dining room is inlaid with a decorative border, and the fretwork of the wainscoting is backed with mirror; the wallpaper is hand-painted. OPPOSITE: The marble console was made in India, and the mirror is eighteenth-century Italian.

school of fish by Yorgos Kypris, and the room is fitted out with a trio of custom light fixtures depicting schools of fish circling endlessly. The soft, sandy tones are offset with white furnishings and blue upholstery and accents that turn this room into the ultimate cooling respite from the desert sun.

The complex includes both beach and pool cabanas, which gave us the chance to be playful and more contemporary. The pool pavilion is draped in navy fabric with white trim to give it a nautical effect. A separate indoor pool is a seaside fantasy inspired by my love for the paintings of Raoul Dufy.

This particular castle in the sand was designed to encompass the family's full range of activities, everything from formal receptions to intimate dinners to, yes, children playing on the beach. It functions on several levels without ever losing sight of its location or its most important function—helping a family to gather together for relaxation and enjoyment.

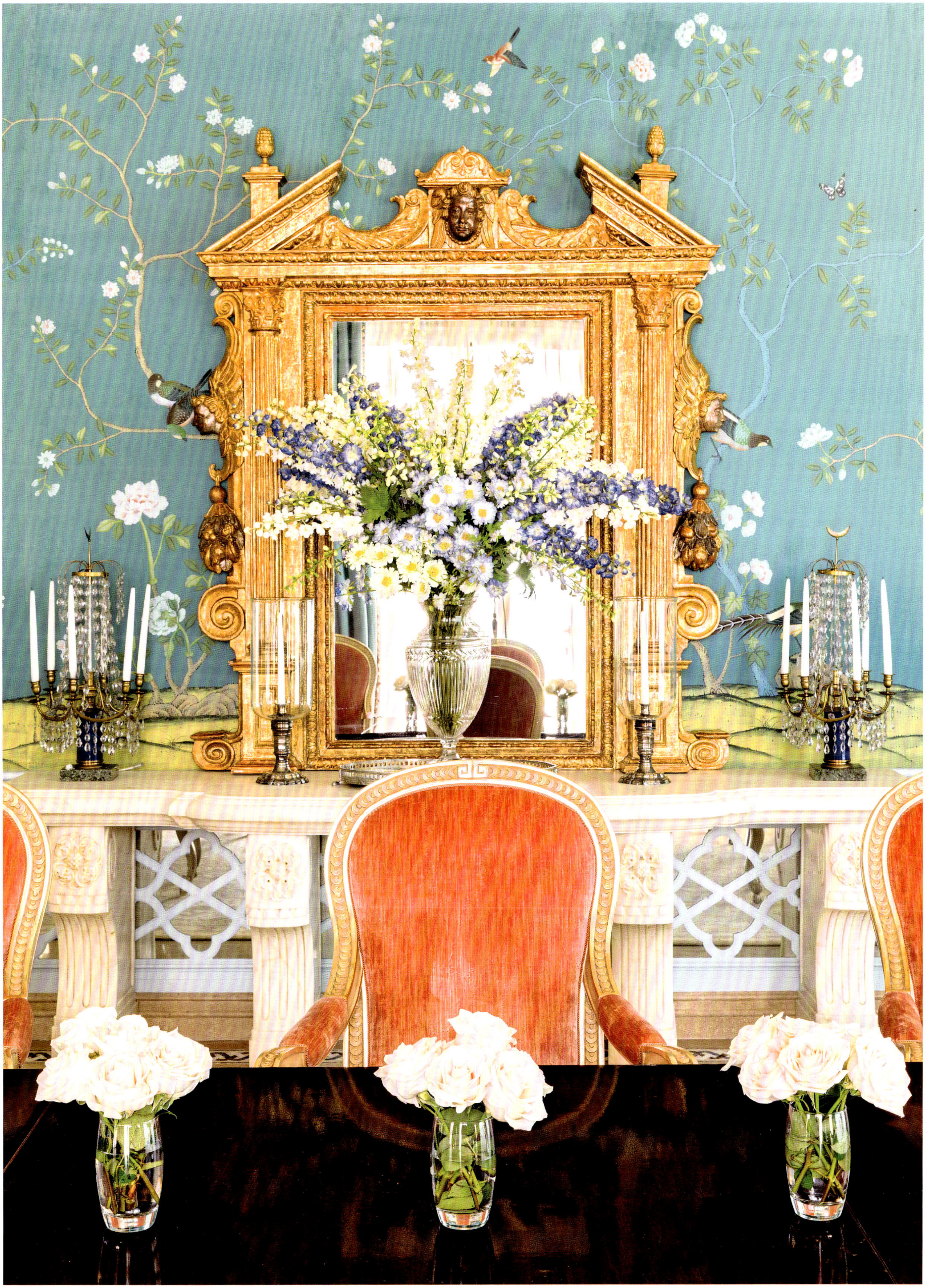

The lounge and games room features custom paneling and bookcases. The rug, cocktail tables, and sixteen-foot-long sofa were all designed for the room. FOLLOWING PAGES: Matching beachside living rooms flank the rotunda entrance; each has a custom wood starburst ceiling and walls embellished with subtle murals of palm-tree shadows.

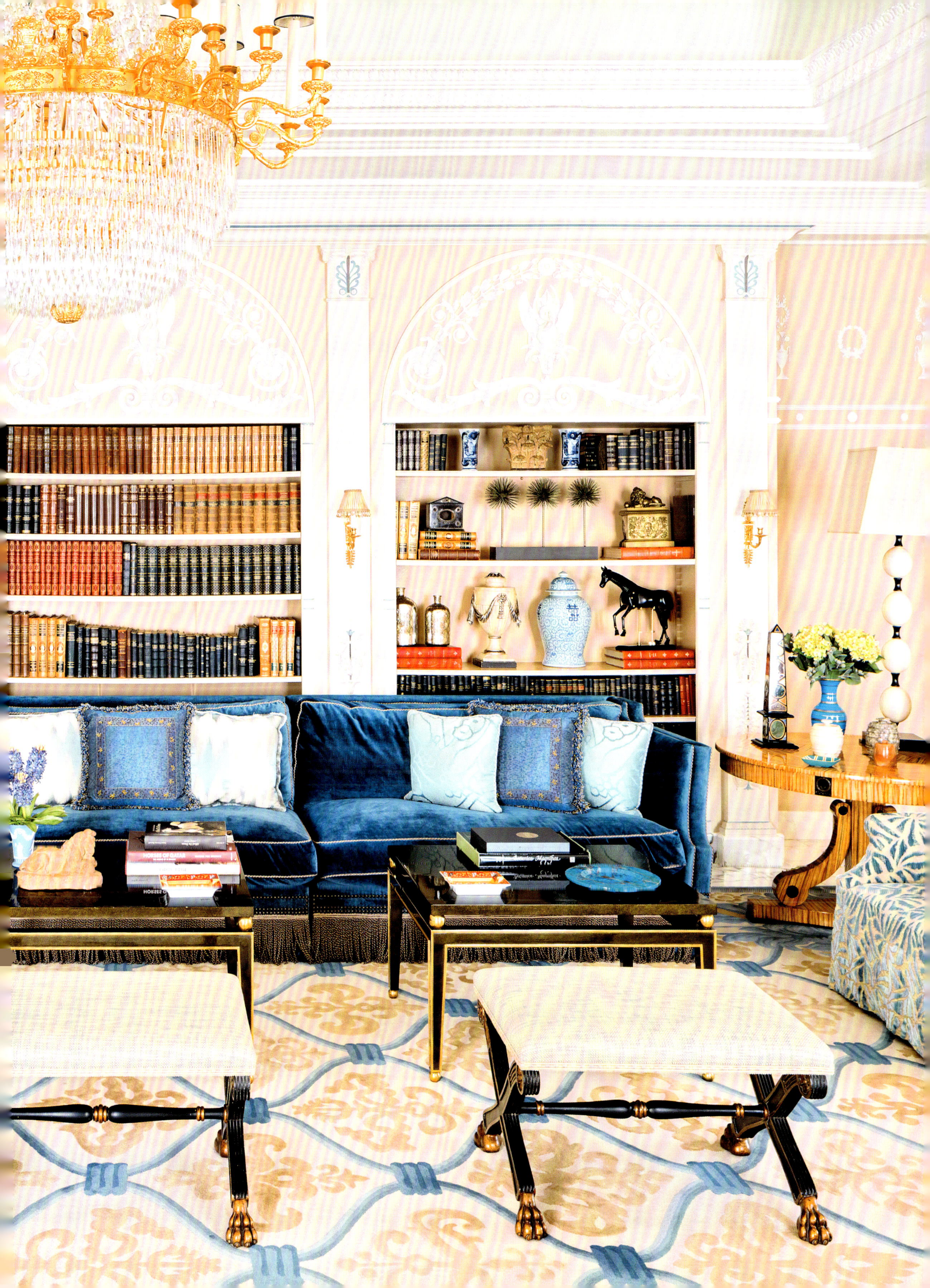

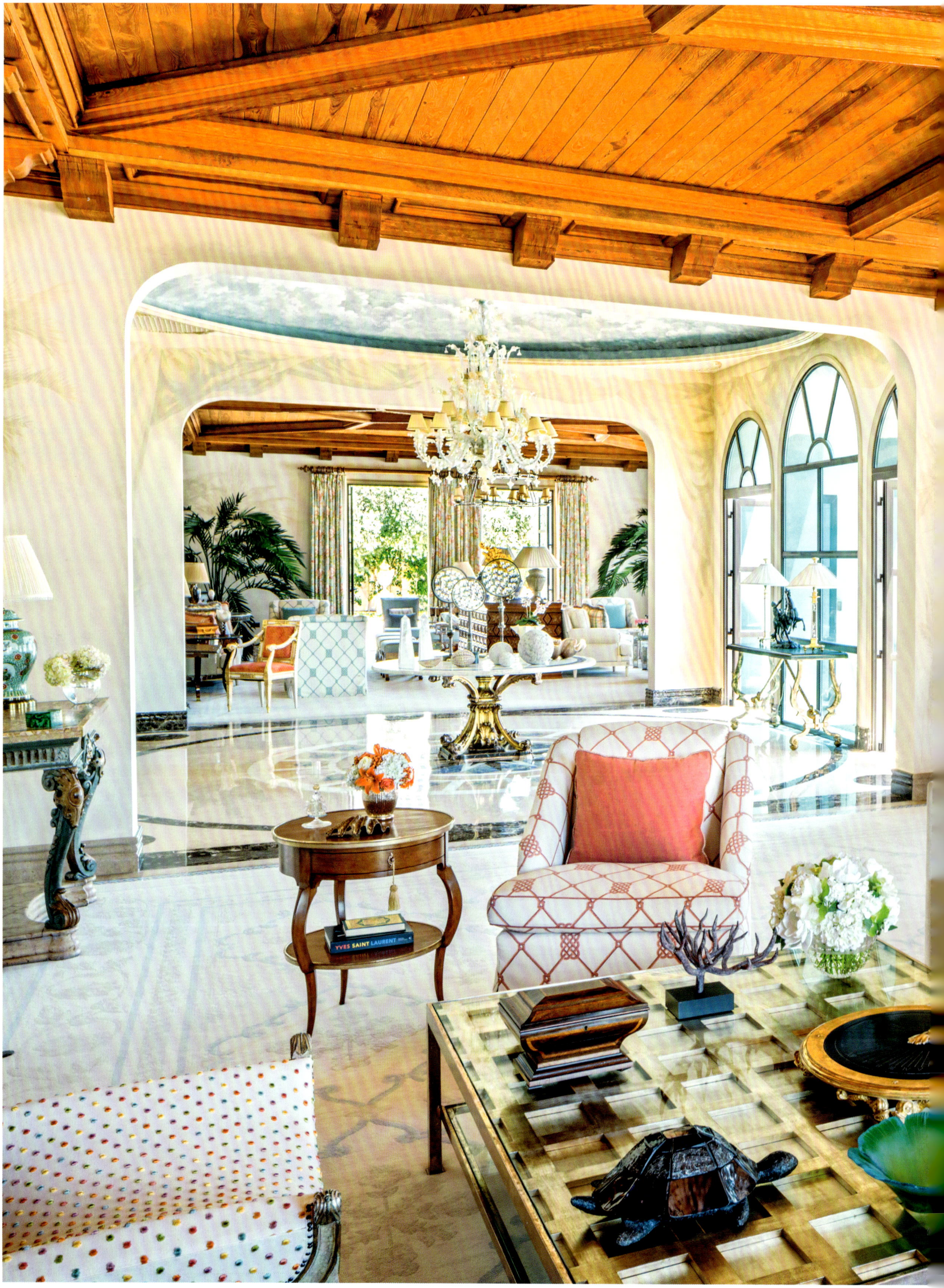
YVES SAINT LAURENT

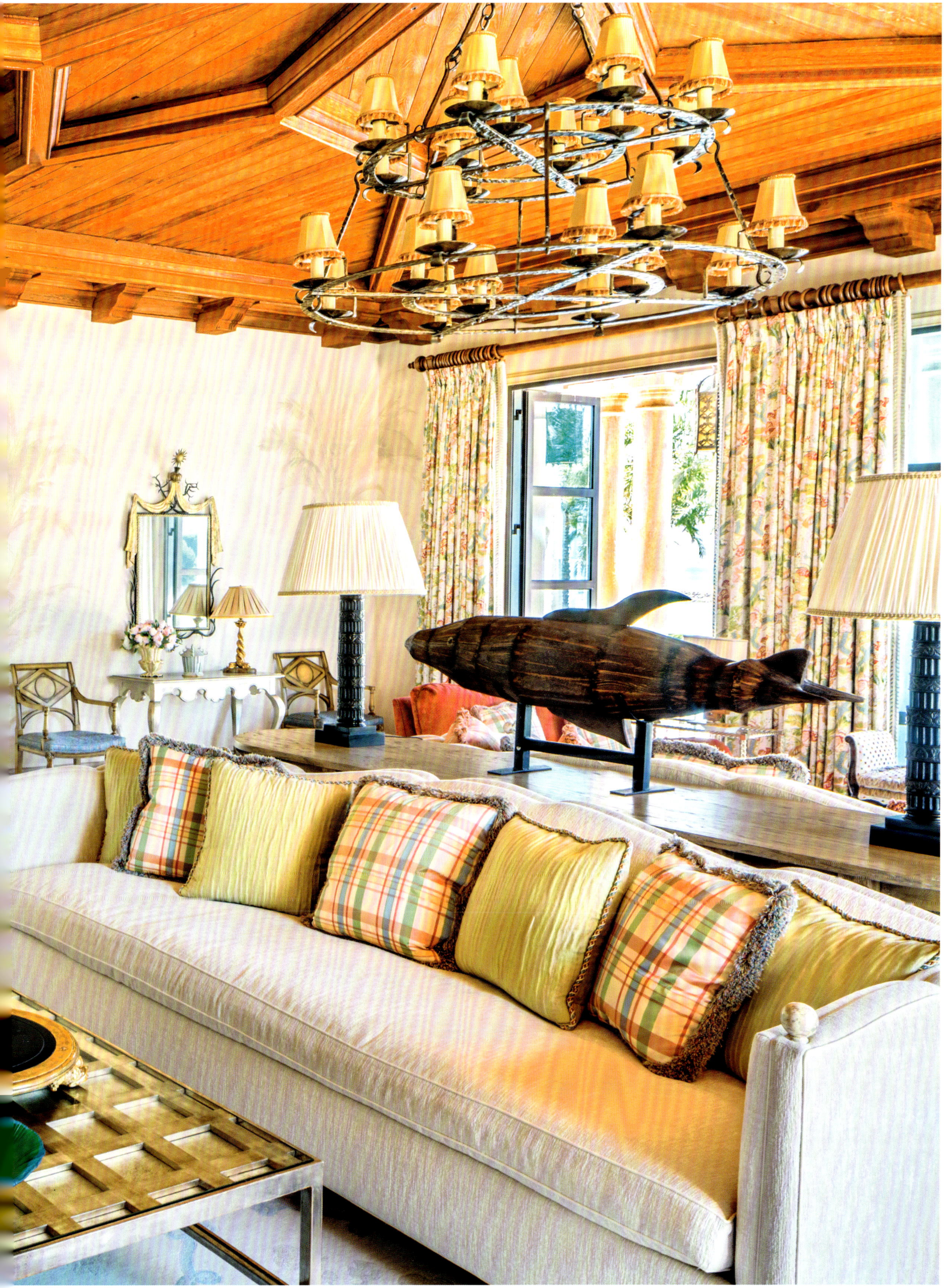

ABOVE: The family kitchen centers on an oversize island with a vivid blue countertop.
LEFT: The family room seating area features outdoor fabrics and an indoor-outdoor rug.
OPPOSITE: The marble table is inlaid with a rope motif, which is reiterated in the white gold–leafed carved-rope detailing on the cabinetry. Outdoor fabrics and rugs are used throughout for practicality.

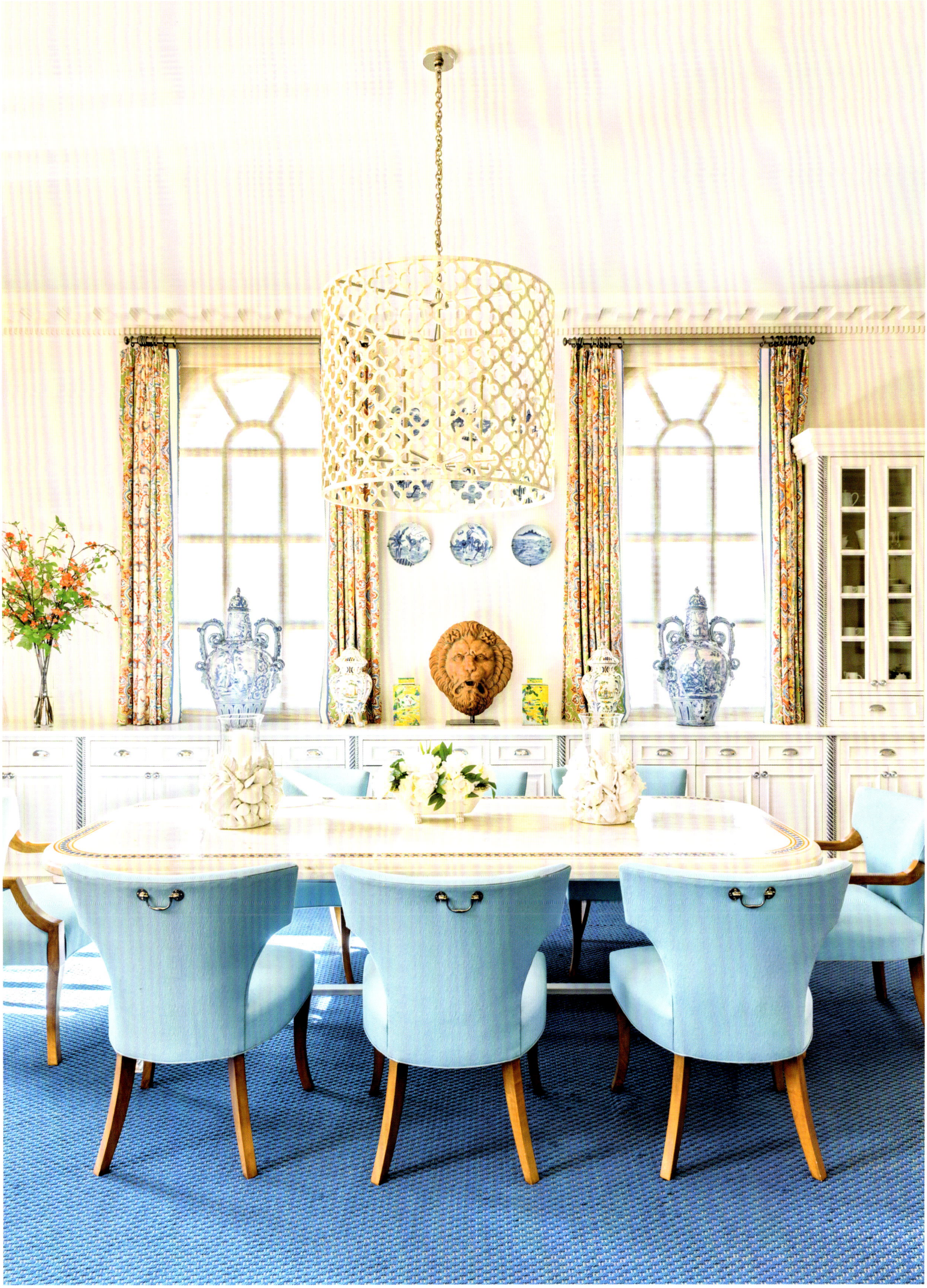

ABOVE: In the sitting room of the master suite, the walls and ceiling are embellished with contiguous coffered paneling that is painted to create a subtle ombré effect, fading from pale blue to cream at the top.
OPPOSITE: The Jerusalem stone floor and columns provide a vivid contrast to the cool, pale palette.

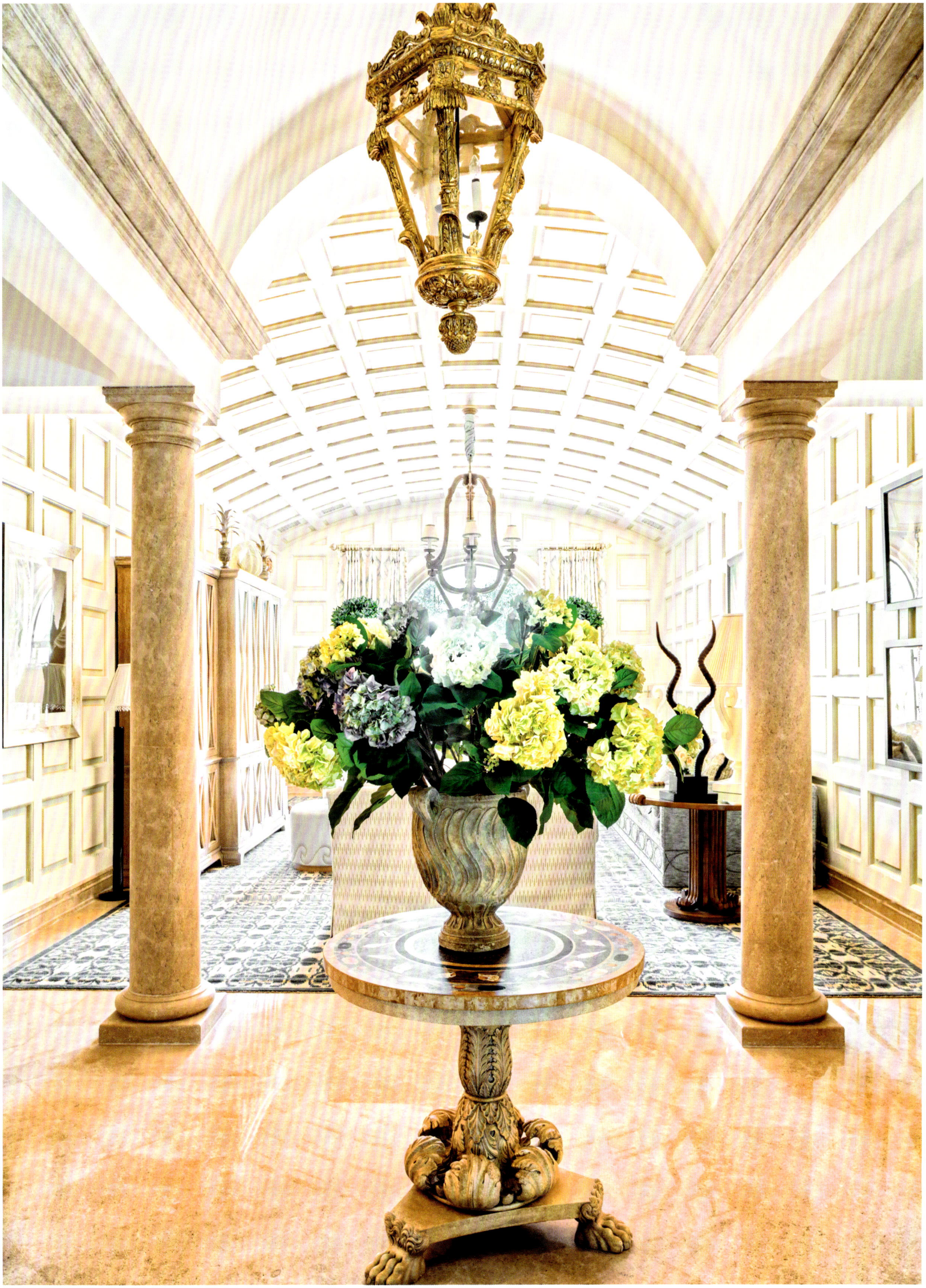

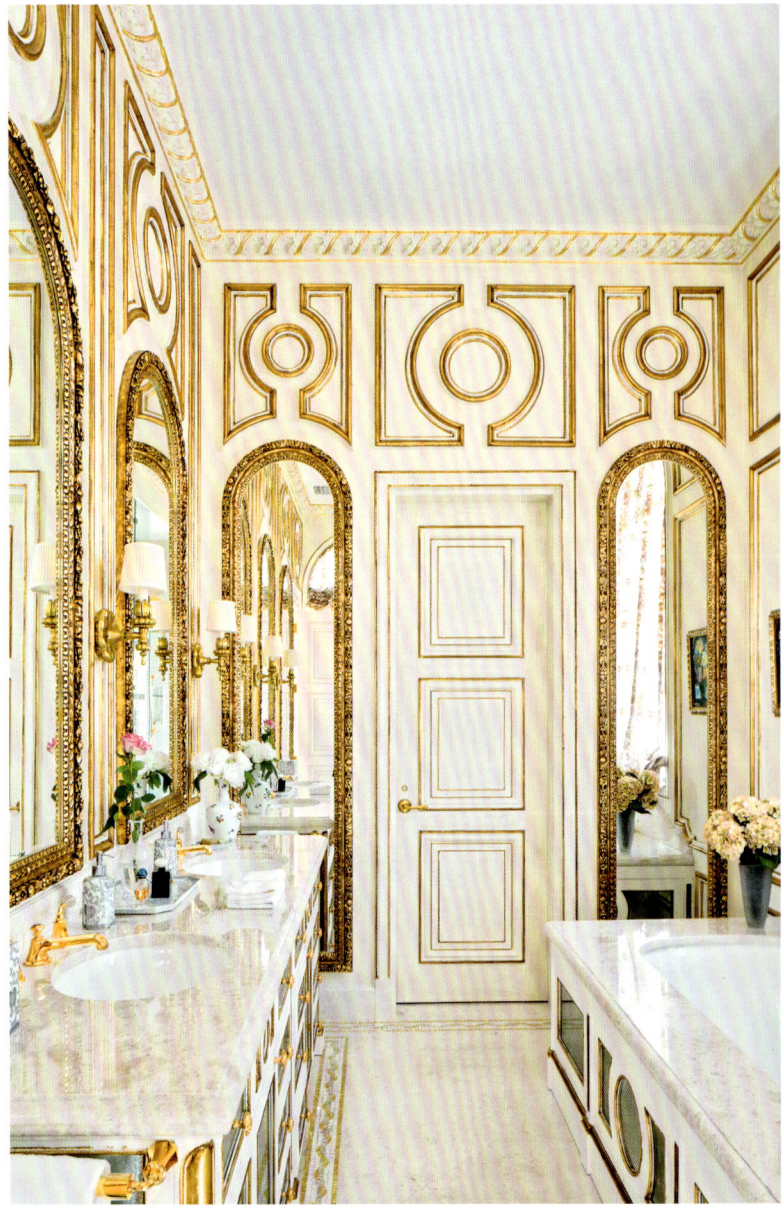

ABOVE: A guest room bed juxtaposes a traditional gilt headboard with a contemporary steel four-poster frame. RIGHT: In the wife's bath, hand-carved and gilded wood paneling edges the arched mirrors and creates a circle-and-rectangle motif that is reiterated in her bedroom. OPPOSITE: Her bedroom is embellished with carved detailing on the ceiling and walls.

100 THE NEW ELEGANCE

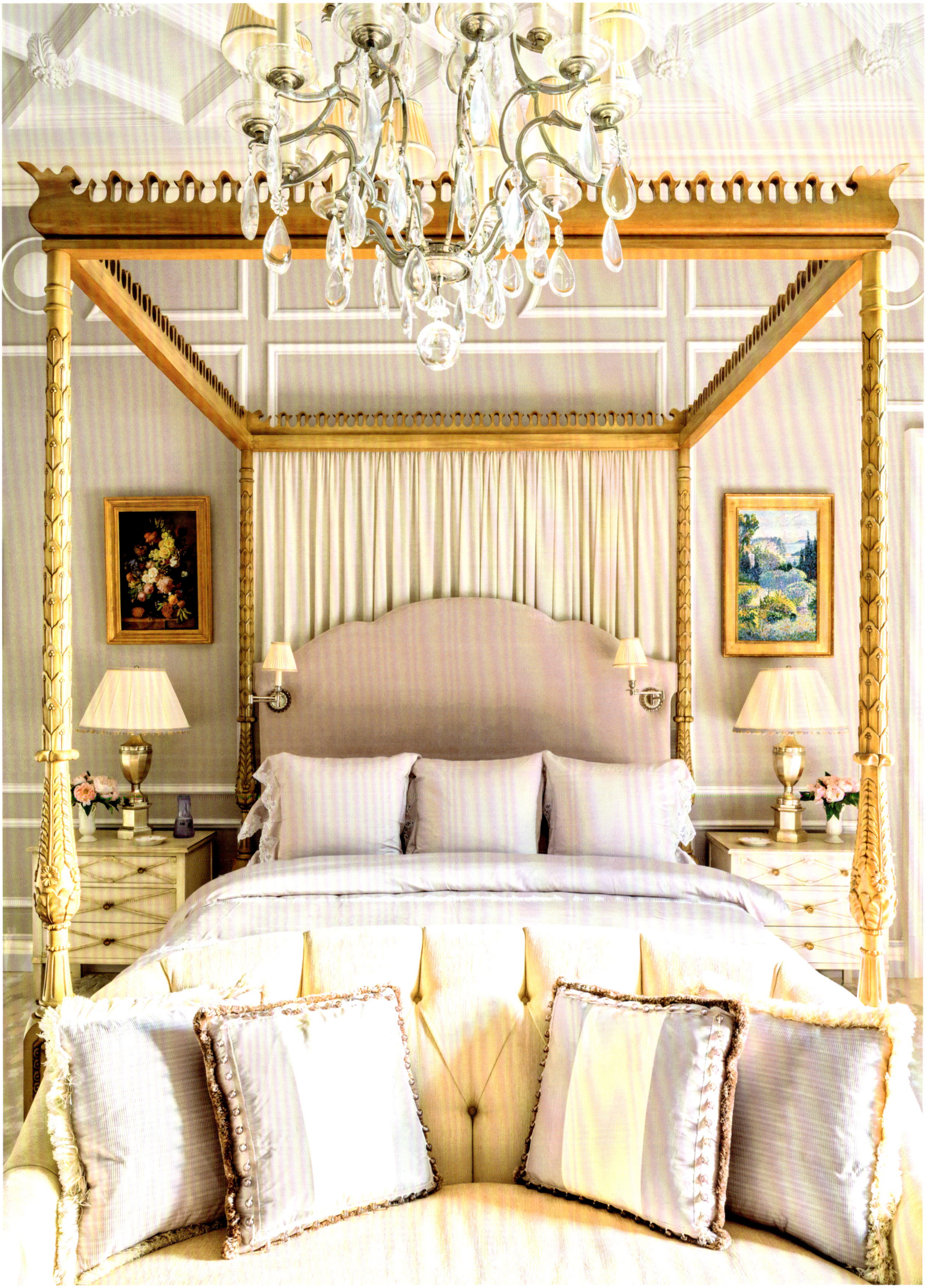

ABOVE: The walls of the elliptical media room are covered in a wood-veneer wallpaper cut and applied to create a patchwork effect; the curved sofa and rounded lines of the cocktail table echo the shape of the room, and the wall sculpture of a school of fish and porcelain fish light fixture, one of three, were commissioned for the room. OPPOSITE: One of the two beachside pavilions; the walls are draped in an outdoor fabric by Perennials, and the floor is fitted with an outdoor rug.

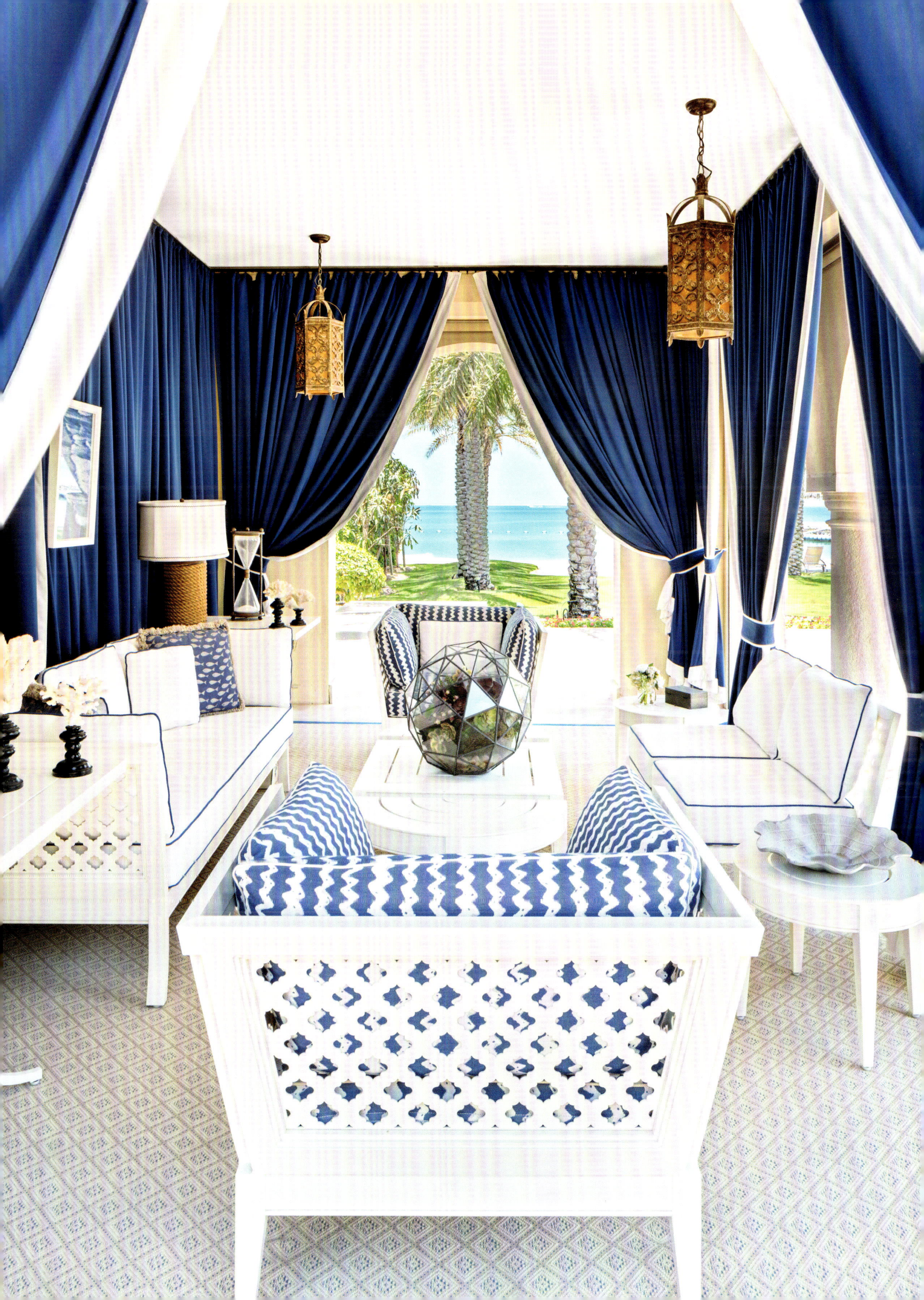

INTERLUDE
IMPACTFUL SURFACES

Have you ever walked into a room and sensed something was missing? All the components are there, but the room somehow feels boring. Often the missing element is an impactful surface.

Walls, floors, ceilings, tables, and consoles can all impart texture, visual weight, balance, and interest to a room. There is no reason to confine yourself to painted drywall and simple floors. Paneling, stone, textiles, wallpapers, specialty murals, or tile can take a room from sedate to spectacular. Impactful surfaces can range from bold gilt bronze to the background softness of old, worn wood furniture. Paint techniques such as *faux-bois* or ombré effects will all bring drama to a room.

Sometimes effects that reveal themselves over time—soft shadows painted on a wall, the gleam of a light fixture lined in mother-of-pearl, the shadowy shimmer of silver leaf—have the most impact. A great room should not reveal all of its secrets at once.

Shiny surfaces reflect light and bounce it around a room, whereas matte or heavily textured surfaces absorb light and soften it. Honed marble, for example, has a far different effect than polished; a glossy floor responds to light very differently than rubbed or waxed parquet.

Furniture, counters, floors, and ceilings can all be a source of delight—or potential solutions to a problem. Glossy paint on trim will highlight architectural elements in a room, whereas a flat- or matte-finish paint will soften lines and create a more enveloping atmosphere. Any surface that can be made to attract the hand or the eye will add richness and depth.

1

The black, gray, and gold color palette of this guest room in Beverly Hills was inspired by a glamorous Art Deco bathroom. To make it as cosseting as it is dramatic, the room is a symphony of luxurious fabrics. The walls are upholstered in a Schumacher fabric that evokes the Deco period, while the daybed is covered in velvet and crowned with a gold-trimmed baldachin and draped in a variety of rich fabrics and trims. Even the club chair is gold, right down to its fringe. This fanciful room is a sheltering jewel box where any guest would be happy to be tucked away for a night or two.

2

A great example of how a wallcovering can totally transform a space is evident here in an entry hall in a Beverly Hills mansion. This wallpaper, which I designed for Fromental, was inspired by a seventeenth-century Gobelins tapestry interpreted in a modern way. The overscale design and fluttering red drapes add a sense of depth and movement to the room.

3

To enrich this master bath, we paneled and gilded the walls, and then created a fanciful mosaic of glass set into marble that we used on the floor and on the wall behind the bathtub. Reflected in the large expanse of mirror and the mirror panels set into the cabinetry, this golden pattern becomes an active presence in the small space.

4

Fabrics are a vital element in bringing visual richness and texture to a room. Here, an entire room is draped in my Hedgerow Trellis fabric for Schumacher, with artworks hung on top. This adds quiet and softness and creates a cozy, enveloping atmosphere in what is an otherwise grand room. Wallpaper on the ceiling adds a sense of architectural detailing and formality.

1

2

3

4

5

In this entry hall in Paris, we brought some of the beauty of the garden inside. The softness of paneled walls painted to look like limestone blocks plays against the gleam of real marble floors. The doors are painted a soft sage green to stand out and lift the eye to the ceiling, which has been covered with a custom design by Iksel depicting a blue sky edged with a fanciful green treillage. The effect is like looking up to the sky through a garden gazebo or folly.

6

To bring glamour to this bath, we commissioned panels of eglomise (reverse-gilded and -painted glass) to be set within the cabinetry, amplifying the golden touches and bouncing light around the room.

7

To add richness to what was a banal dining room with walls of flat, characterless drywall, I found some eighteenth-century painted panels that had formerly been incorporated into a wood-paneled room. We then set them into new paneling made of English knotty pine. To enhance the room further, we added plaster molding to the ceiling so that the visual interest extends to every surface. The romantic landscapes create a magical atmosphere, a perfect setting for a festive meal.

8

When we started with this dining room, it was in a very formal French style. Our clients wanted a much more casual Italian farmhouse feeling. To give the room a more rugged appeal, we used recycled wood and stone, installing a dark wood-beamed ceiling and covering the walls in an irregular pattern of rough stone facing.

5

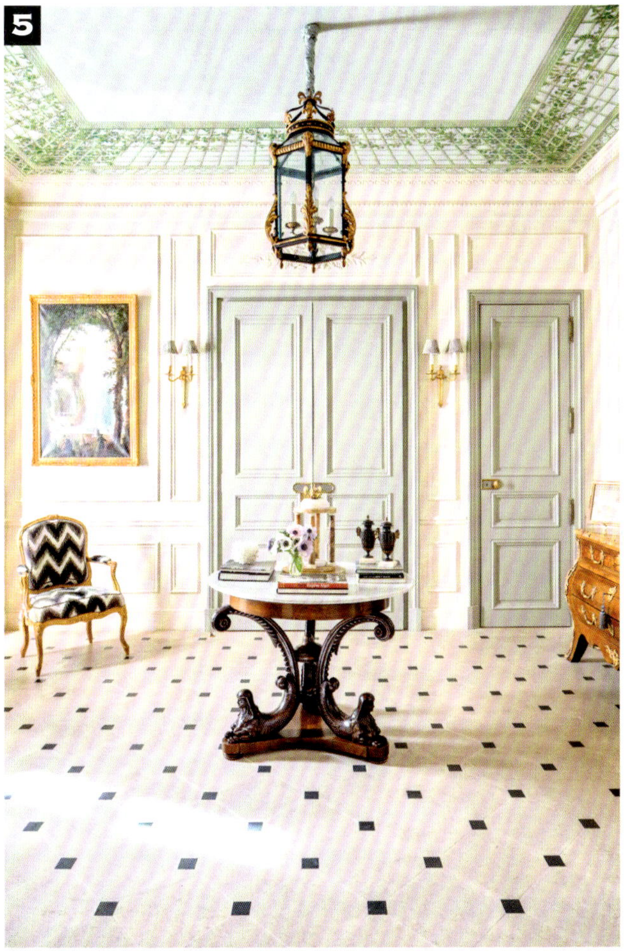

6

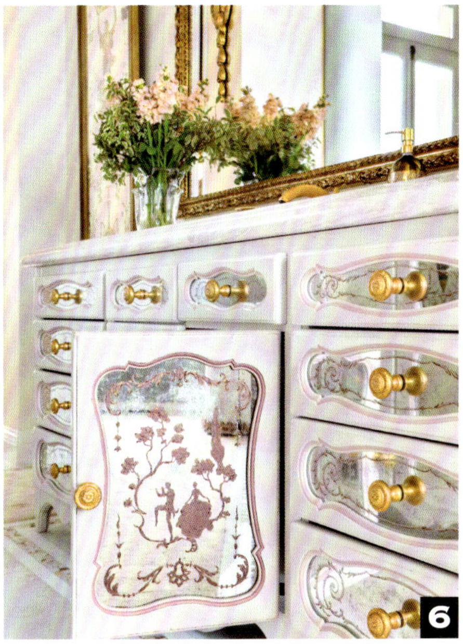

7

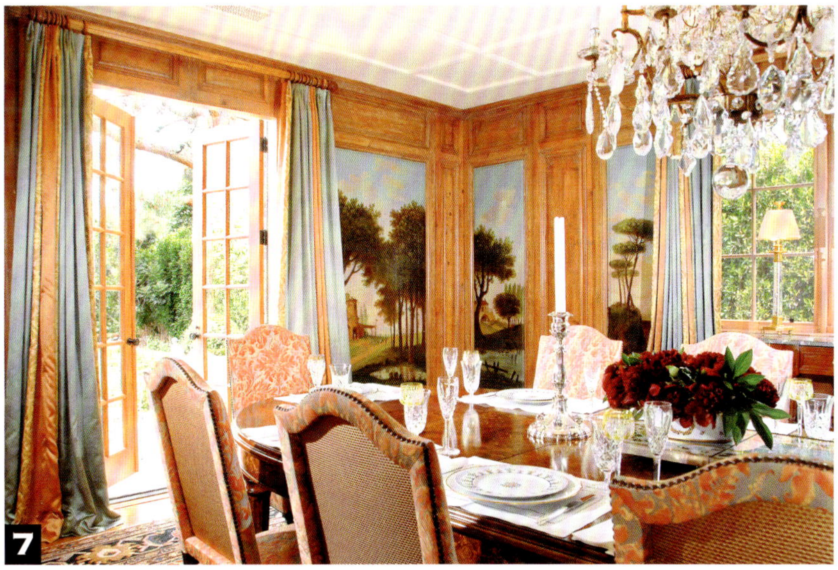

8

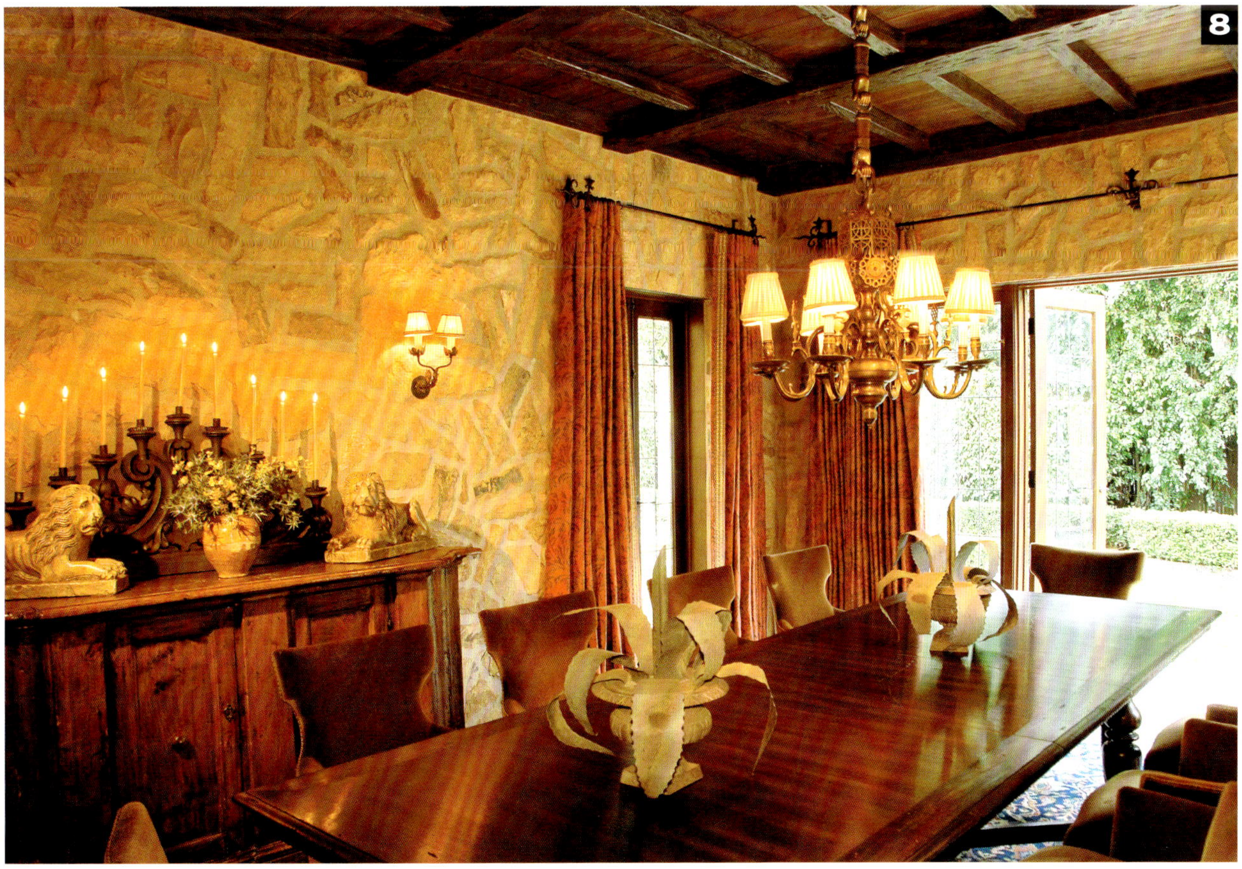

California Colonial

Apologies to Thomas Wolfe, but the fact is, you *can* go home again—at least for a while. This house in the Hancock Park neighborhood of Los Angeles is where I lived with my parents from the ages of seven to eleven, and then again for a little more than a decade beginning in 2006. But of course, Wolfe's larger point is true. When I returned, nothing was the same; the house and its surroundings had changed significantly, and I was certainly very different as well. But did that mean we couldn't come to an accommodation and live together again happily?

The house was built in 1923 in the severe and symmetrical Georgian Colonial style. And many of the elements of the structure that I loved as a child still appealed to me—its foursquare American simplicity and elegance and its central hall plan, with all rooms on the main floor opening off the hallway, which leads directly to the family room with five expansive windows overlooking the back garden. So when I heard the house was on the market, I sent the owners a photo of myself as a child, splashing in the pool, and asked them to please let me come home.

When the house was constructed, the area was a suburb of Los Angeles, almost rural in feeling, so much so that the house originally had stables. But that was certainly no longer the case—Hancock Park had become a high-end enclave of gracious and imposing homes and beautiful gardens, not far from the center of the city. And the once quiet street, like so many in Los Angeles, had become filled with traffic.

There is always a question when you move into an old house: Do you conform your life to the house, or do you reconfigure the house to work for your life? Usually, the solution is a bit of both, and that was the case here. I wanted to adapt the house I had loved as a child to make it functional, yet not lose any of its richness or elegance. Because the place had such good bones, it could easily absorb the many artworks, furnishings, and accessories I had acquired over decades. It wasn't only nostalgia that led me to buy the place—I felt it could become the perfect backdrop for the way I lived and entertained and for all the many treasures I loved.

The house, though handsome, sat squarely on a plot of lawn, exposed and somewhat forlorn. Even the walkway to the front door was awkwardly oriented to the driveway on the side of the house. So to give the front entry a sense of procession and formality, we constructed low brick walls, topped with an elegant white wooden fence and an arched gate. You climb six steps, pass through the gate, and face a wide

To create a more welcoming aspect to my house in Los Angeles and to make the connection to the garden stronger, I changed the color of the doors and shutters from black to dark hunter green.

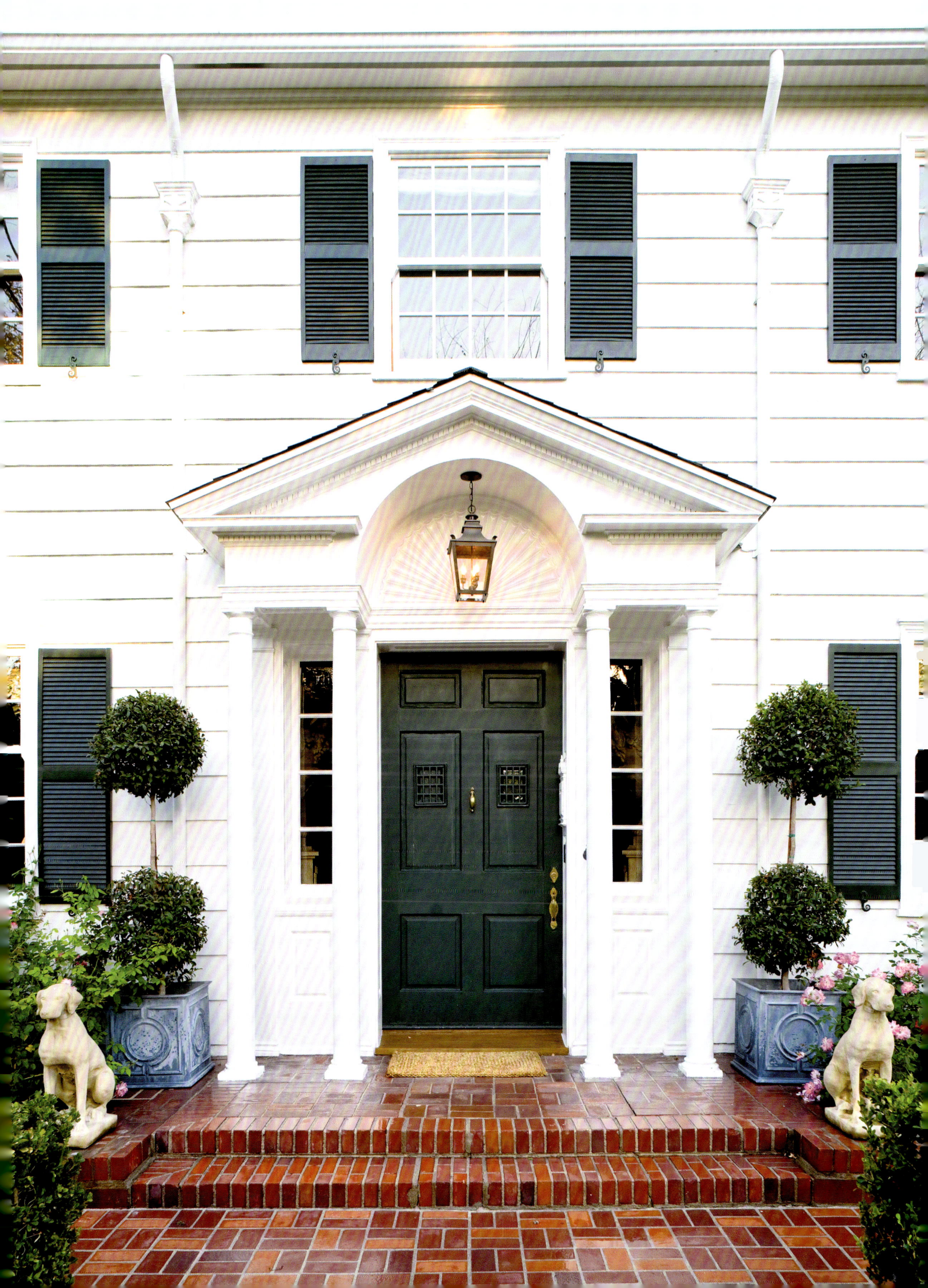

brick walkway flanked on either side by two green "rooms"—lawns outlined in precisely clipped box hedges. The hedges are inset with white-painted trellis screens and stone benches on either side, and in the center of both lawns are perfectly symmetrical brick-edged rectangular pools with bubbling jets of water and columns topped with classical eighteenth-century busts.

All this greenery and architecture not only created a sense of arrival, it also muffled the street noise and softened the severe lines of the house. Even before you entered the house, these many layers—of materials, of spaces, of textures—made you feel cosseted, enclosed, and protected.

The architecture of the foyer is impressive, with a sweeping staircase and a handsome archway that frames the entrance into what was originally the dining room, but it was a bit dark. We brightened the stairway by adding a custom skylight, which also bathes the upper hallway in light, and then enriched the detailing of the wainscot's raised paneling by painting it in two shades of cream, to heighten the shadow effect and subliminally increase the sense of architectural solidity.

Because this house was to become a repository of all the many objects and paintings I loved, I wanted to keep the spaces simple and the detailing refined. I actually narrowed the entry to the living room from the hall to make the room feel more enclosed and make it easier to lay out the furniture in a welcoming manner. I added understated crown moldings and fanciful plasterwork on the ceiling. But the walls are pale, the upholstery fabrics are neutral, and the majority of the color and drama come from the accessories and the paintings, which include a vividly colored nude by Carolus-Duran. I based the design of the coffee table on a richly inlaid seventeenth-century box (which rested atop it), but to keep the table from seeming too formal, I had the piece coated in a glossy protective marine varnish that makes the surface resistant to watermarks and stains. You can even put your feet up on it. Off the living room was my study,

ABOVE: In front of the house, I installed reflecting ponds flanking the walkway, each centered with a column topped by an eighteenth-century Flemish bust and backed by mirrored trellis arches. OPPOSITE: The moldings in the entry hall were highlighted with two shades of cream to add depth and make them appear more sculptural.

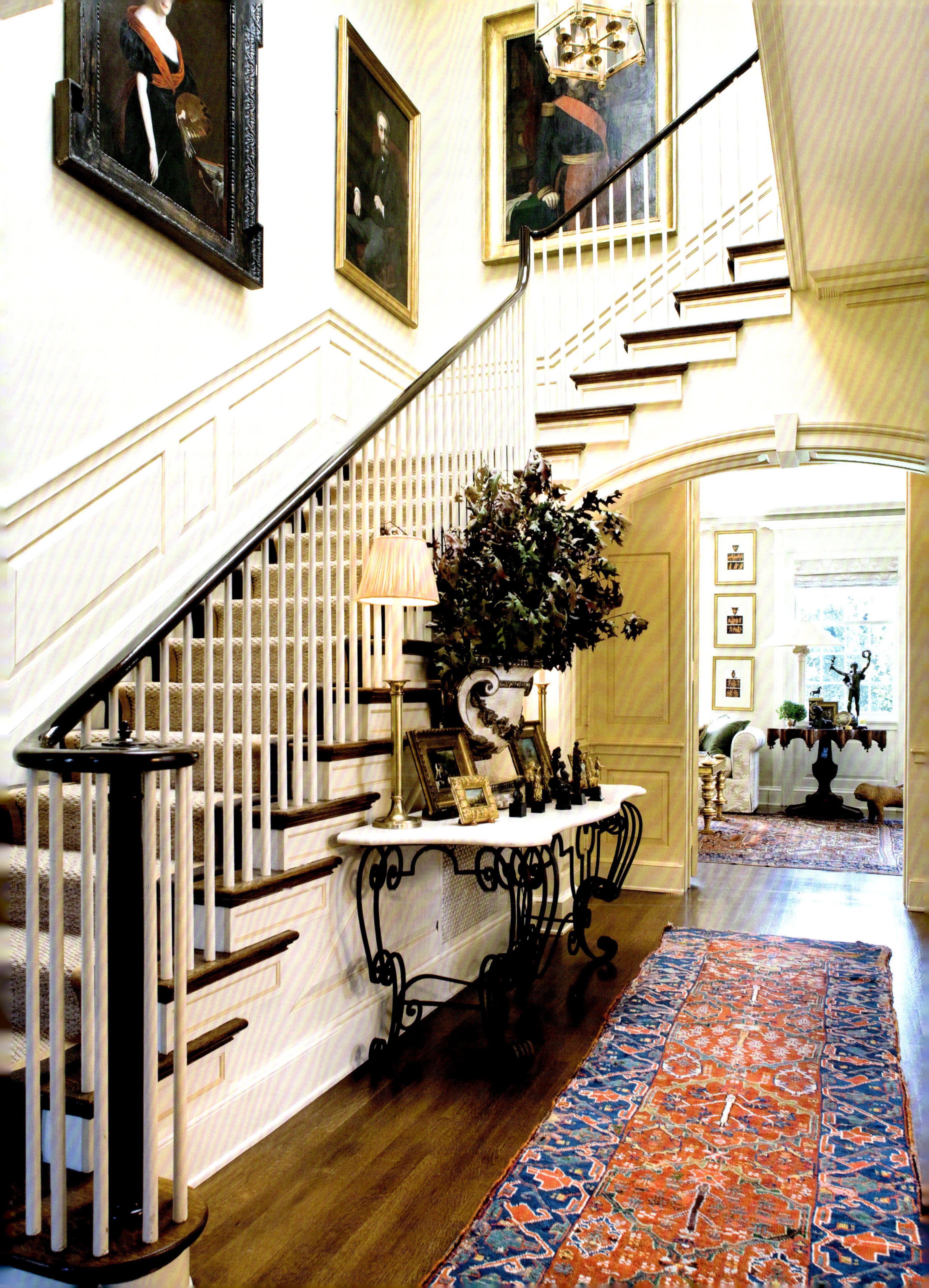

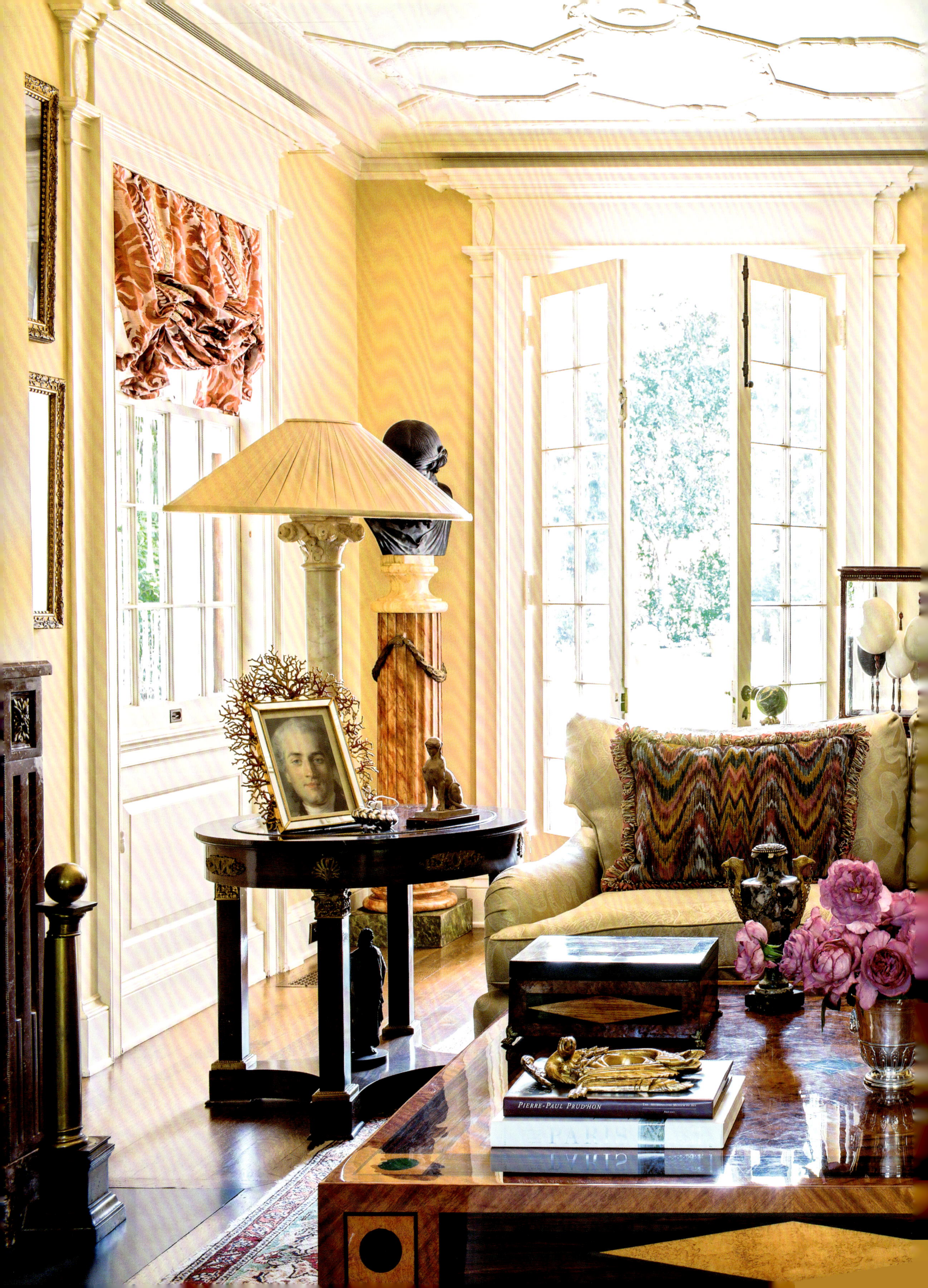

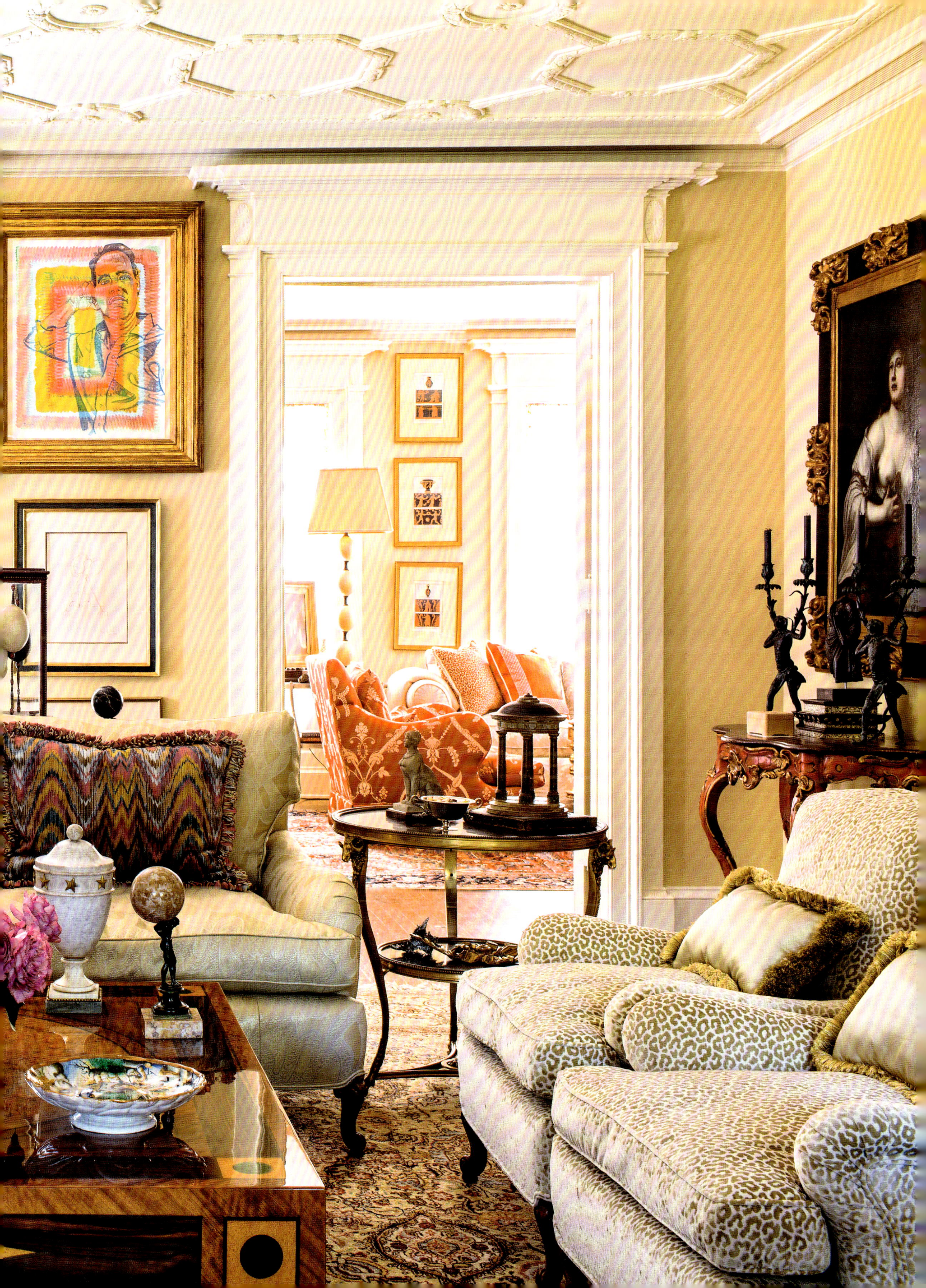

a small space that I fitted out with a cabinet, inset with bisque porcelain intaglios that once belonged to Catherine the Great, a Charles X desk, and a contemporary chandelier.

The dining room, on the opposite side of the entry hall, had served as a library when my parents lived here, and it still retained two paneled walls of bookcases at each end. To brighten the space, I removed one of these, sheathed the walls in a vivid hand-painted spring green de Gournay silk wallcovering, and hung eighteenth-century Italian mirrors on facing walls. Because this was a room used most often at night, I wanted to increase the glamour, so I had the ceiling clad in squares of gold leaf, from which a 1940s French chandelier hangs.

I decided to use what had originally been the dining room as the family room, since it is a much larger space and opens onto the kitchen. Like the stairway, the family room was hung with formal portraits that I have collected by artists such as Jacques-Louis David and Baron Gérard, and an array of neoclassical prints. But it retained a casual feel, with a comfortable, overstuffed sofa, ideal for

PREVIOUS PAGES: In the living room, I added the plaster detailing on the ceiling. The upholstery fabrics are from my collection for Schumacher, and my portrait is by Don Bachardy. The cocktail table was inspired by the box that sits on top of it and was finished with marine varnish to make it more durable. ABOVE: The trumeau mirror over the mantel is from the eighteenth century. OPPOSITE: The chest of drawers is eighteenth-century Italian, the eighteenth-century clock is German, and the painting by Jacques-Louis David is a study for his work *Leonidas at Thermopylae*, in the collection of the Louvre.

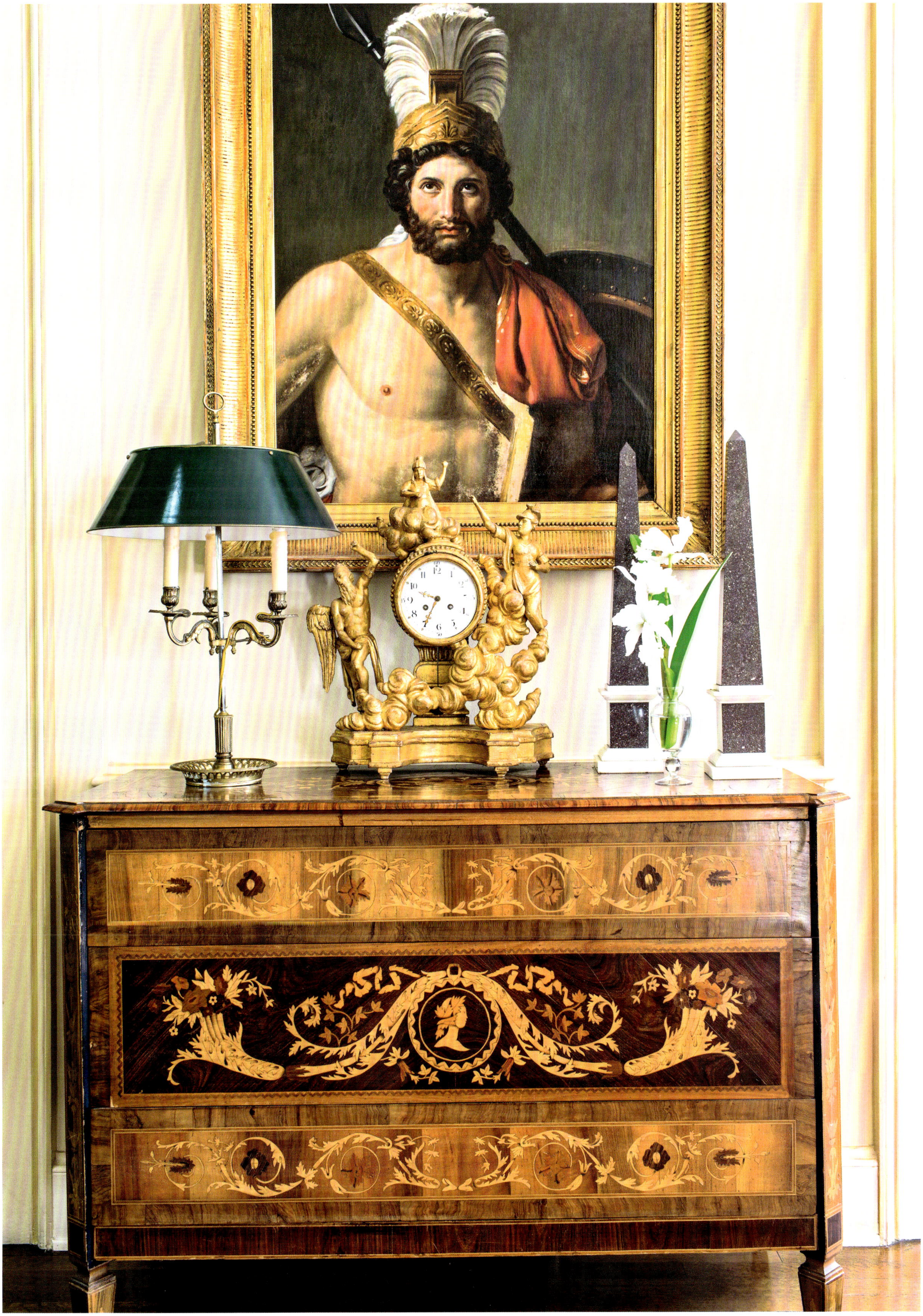

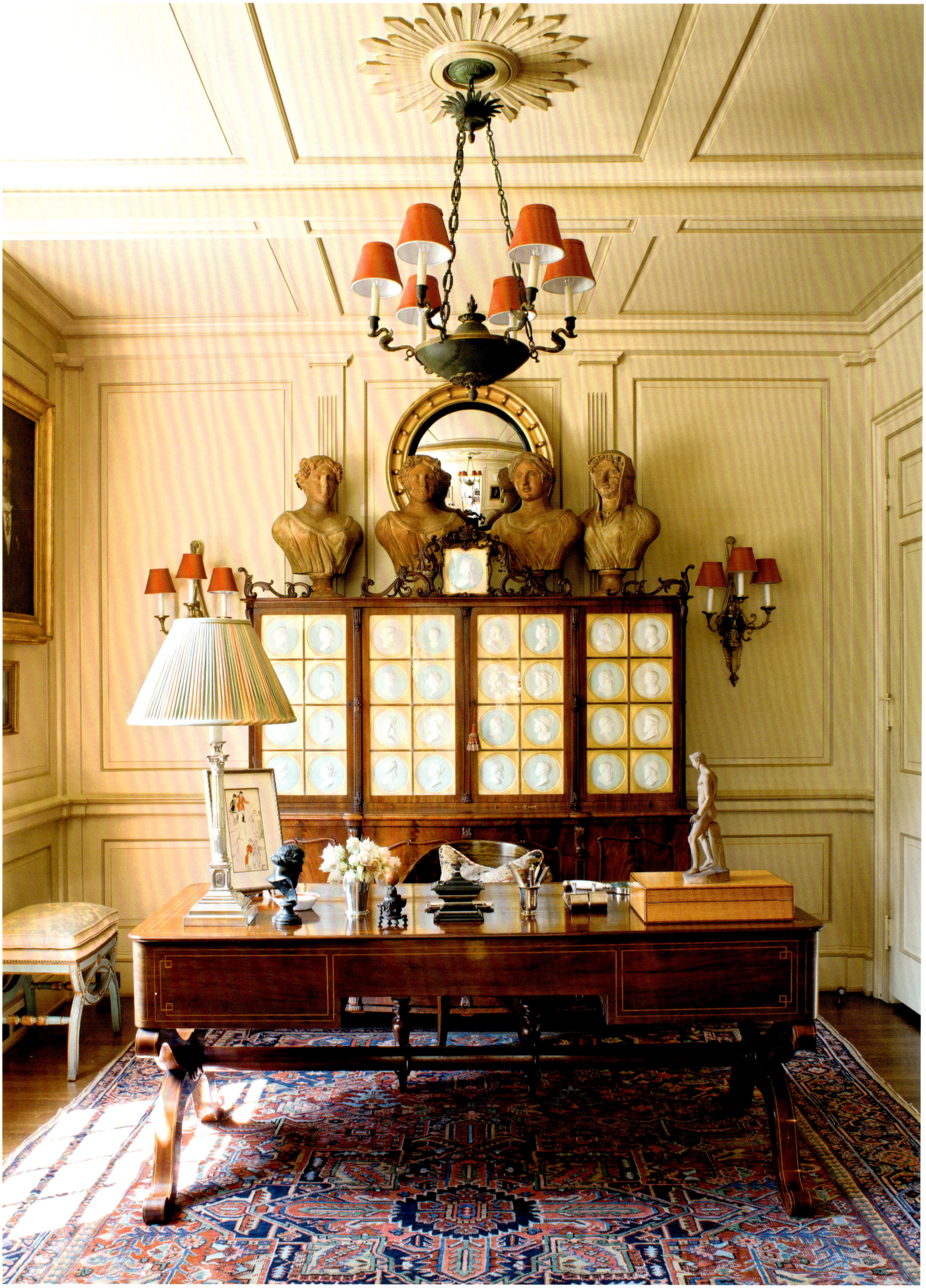

naps, that once belonged to Doris Duke. It contains pairs of chairs by T. H. Robsjohn-Gibbings and André Arbus, but because the room overlooks the back garden, with the fountain and swimming pool visible, the air of relaxation and comfort is palpable.

The kitchen and service areas adjacent to the family room would really only have worked for a family of fifty years ago, with a tiny kitchen, a maid's room and bath, a butler's pantry, and a back stair. I renovated these areas completely, combining them all to create an expansive kitchen and breakfast. Touches of color come from an array of Mexican pottery and a patterned Oriental rug. I actually find antique Oriental rugs perfect for kitchens—you can get them for very good prices, they are virtually indestructible, and their dense, multicolored patterns hide most spots and stains.

Upstairs, the master bedroom featured a gracious fireplace and abundant light, thanks to windows on all four walls. But that created the issue of where to place the bed. As a solution, I upholstered the walls, to give the room a warm and secluded feel, and then installed bed-curtains that cover one window. On the opposite wall, I designed bookcases

OPPOSITE: Wood paneling integrates the walls and ceiling of the ground-floor study. The cabinet with intaglios, which once belonged to Catherine the Great, is topped with nineteenth-century terra-cotta busts representing the four seasons. ABOVE: The display case was made in the eighteenth century for a collector's array of eggs from Asia.

THE NEW ELEGANCE 117

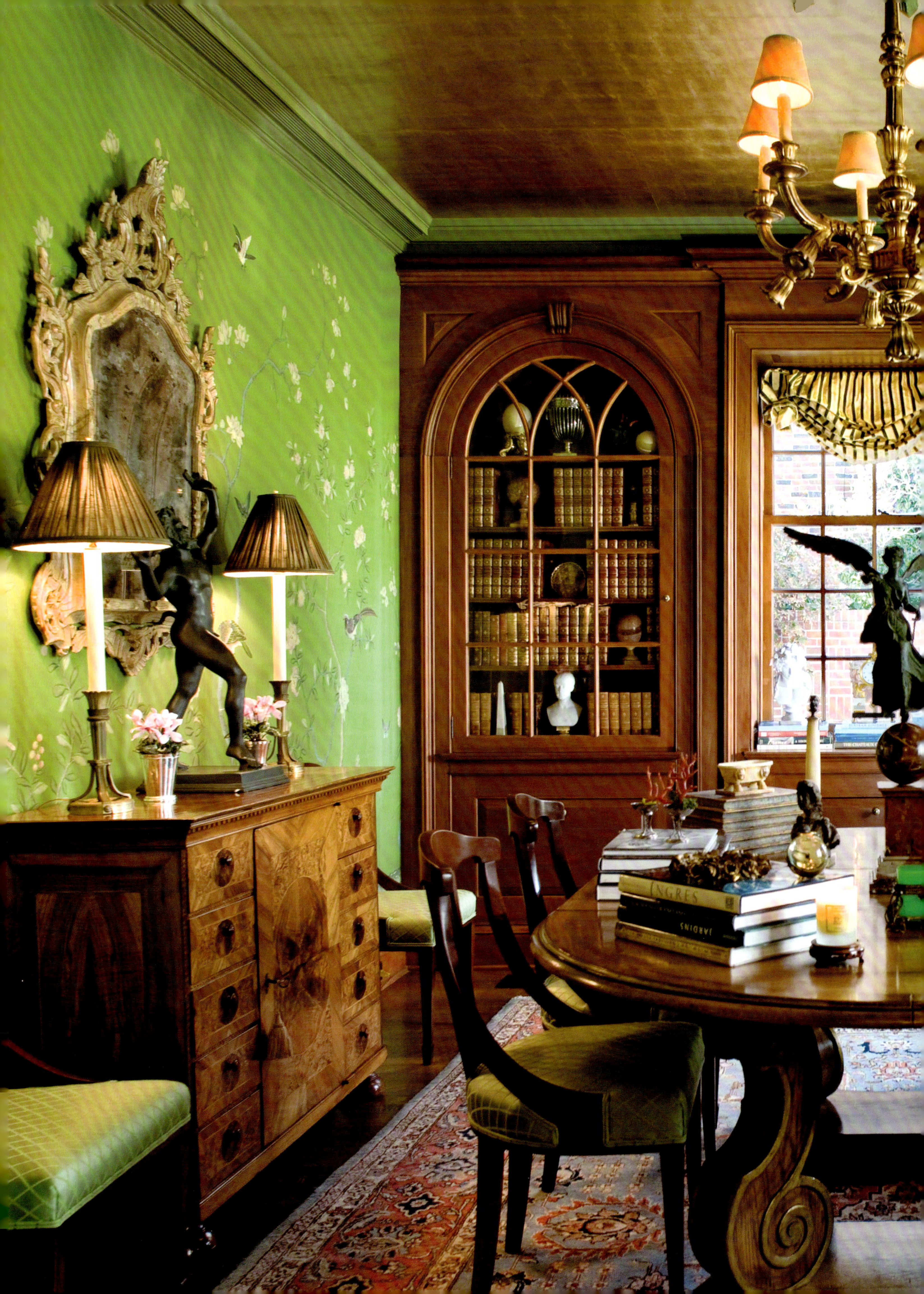
INGRES
JARDINS

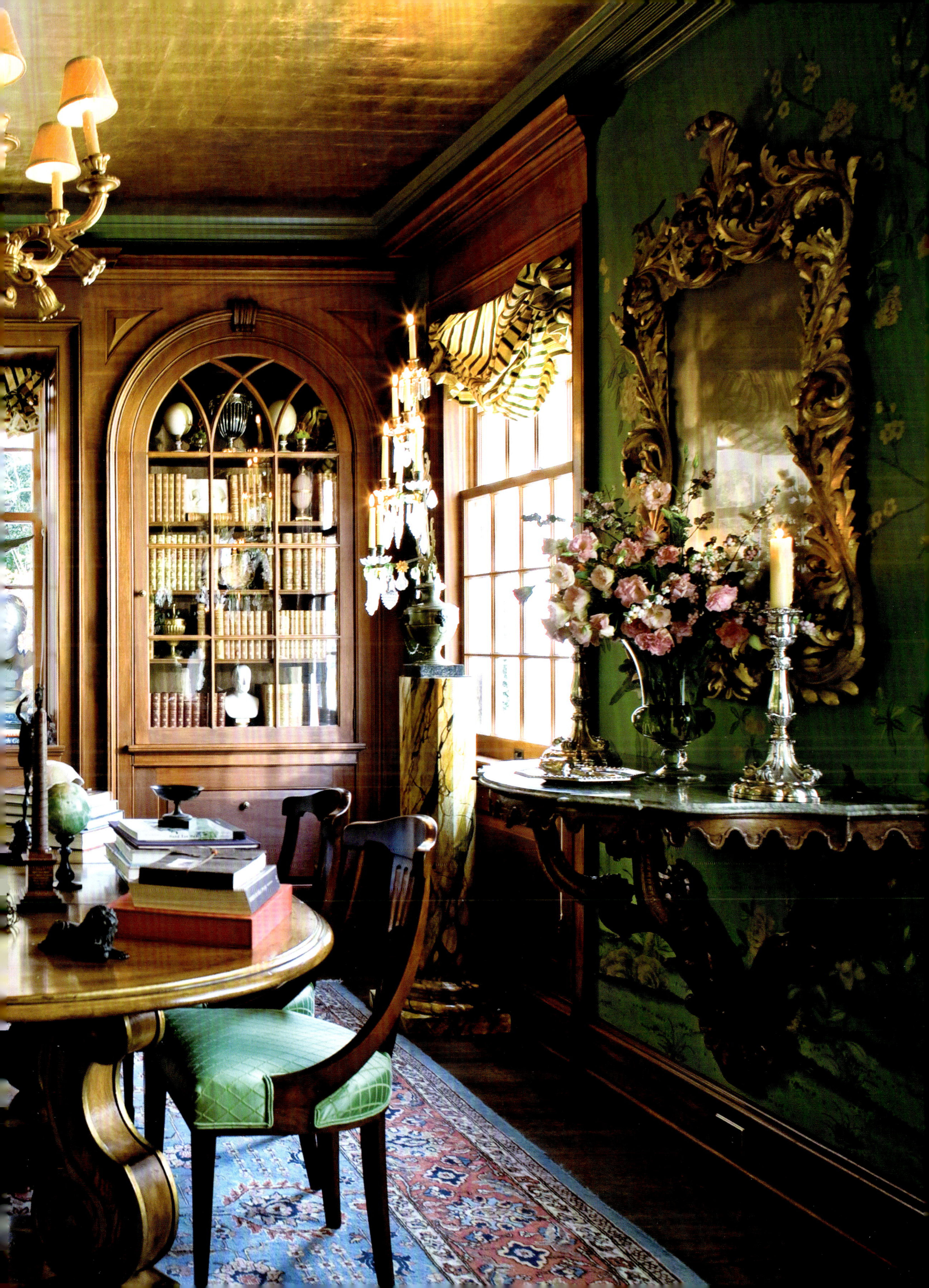

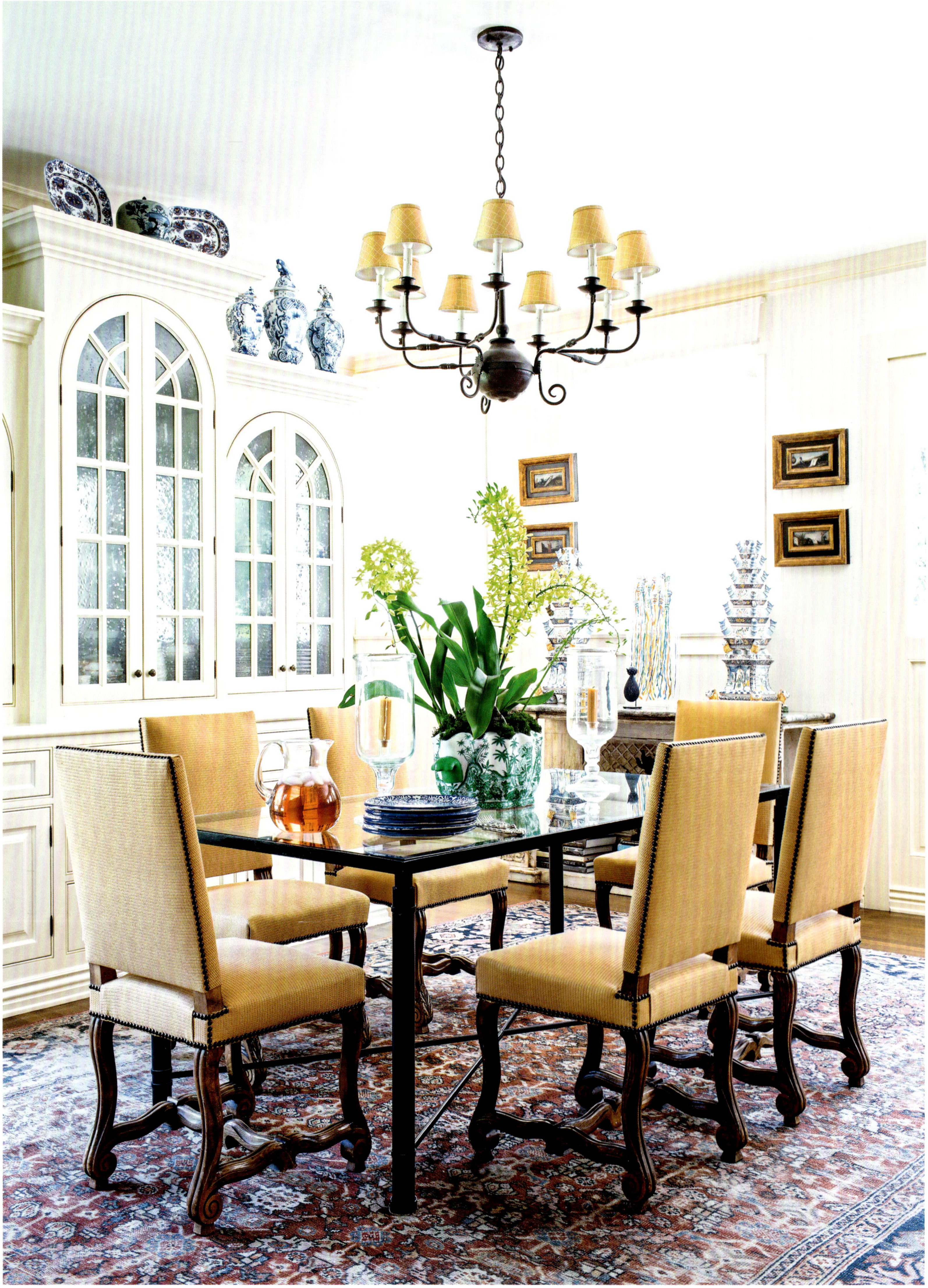

PREVIOUS PAGES: To transform what had been a study into the dining room, I removed some of the bookcases, gilded the ceiling, and added hand-painted wallpaper. The green palette was chosen to create a link to the garden and the kitchen.
OPPOSITE AND ABOVE: What had been four small service spaces were reconfigured to create an expansive kitchen and breakfast area; the center island is painted a vivid green to contrast with the classic white cabinetry.

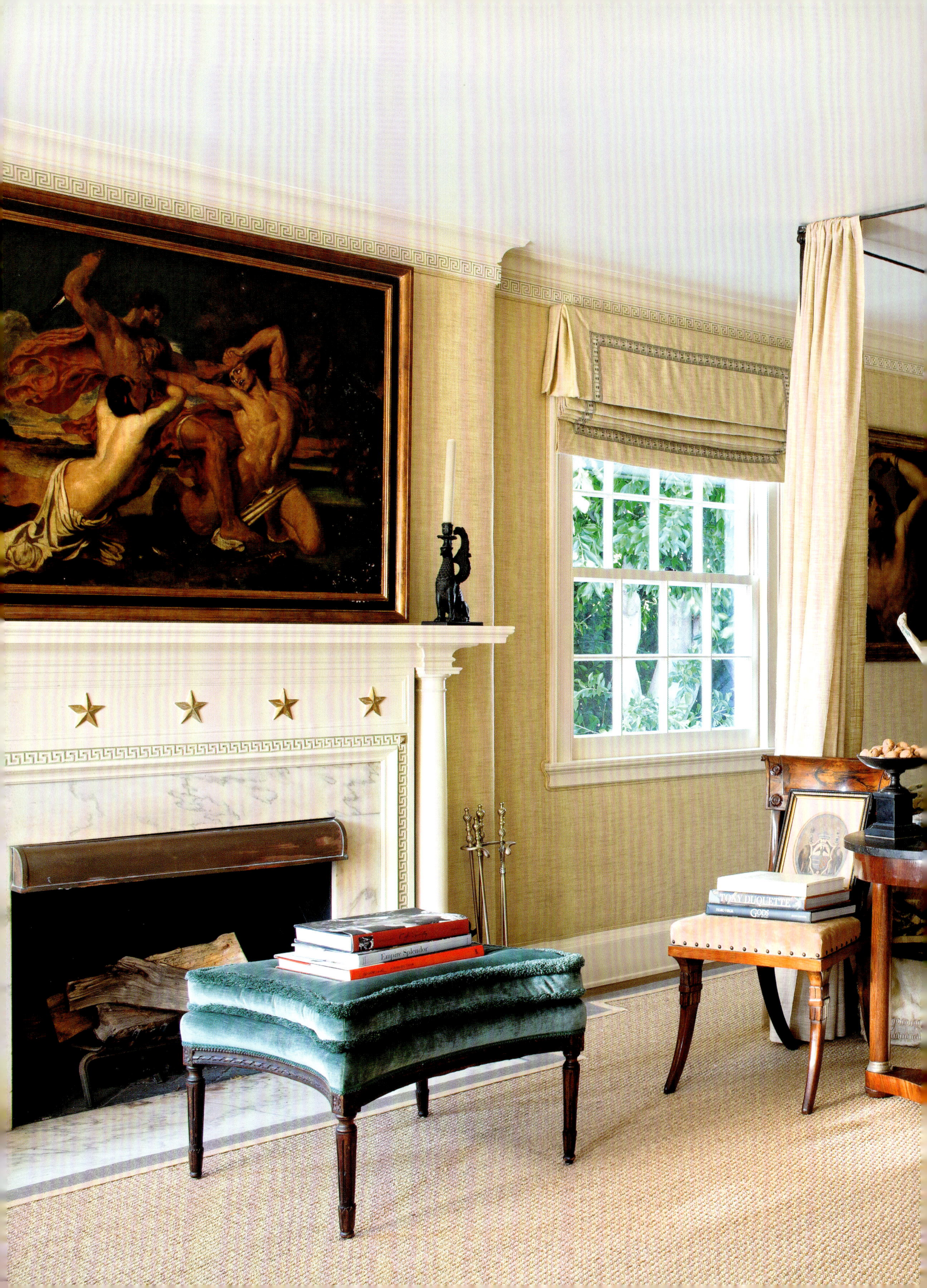
Empire Splendor
TONY DUQUETTE
GODS

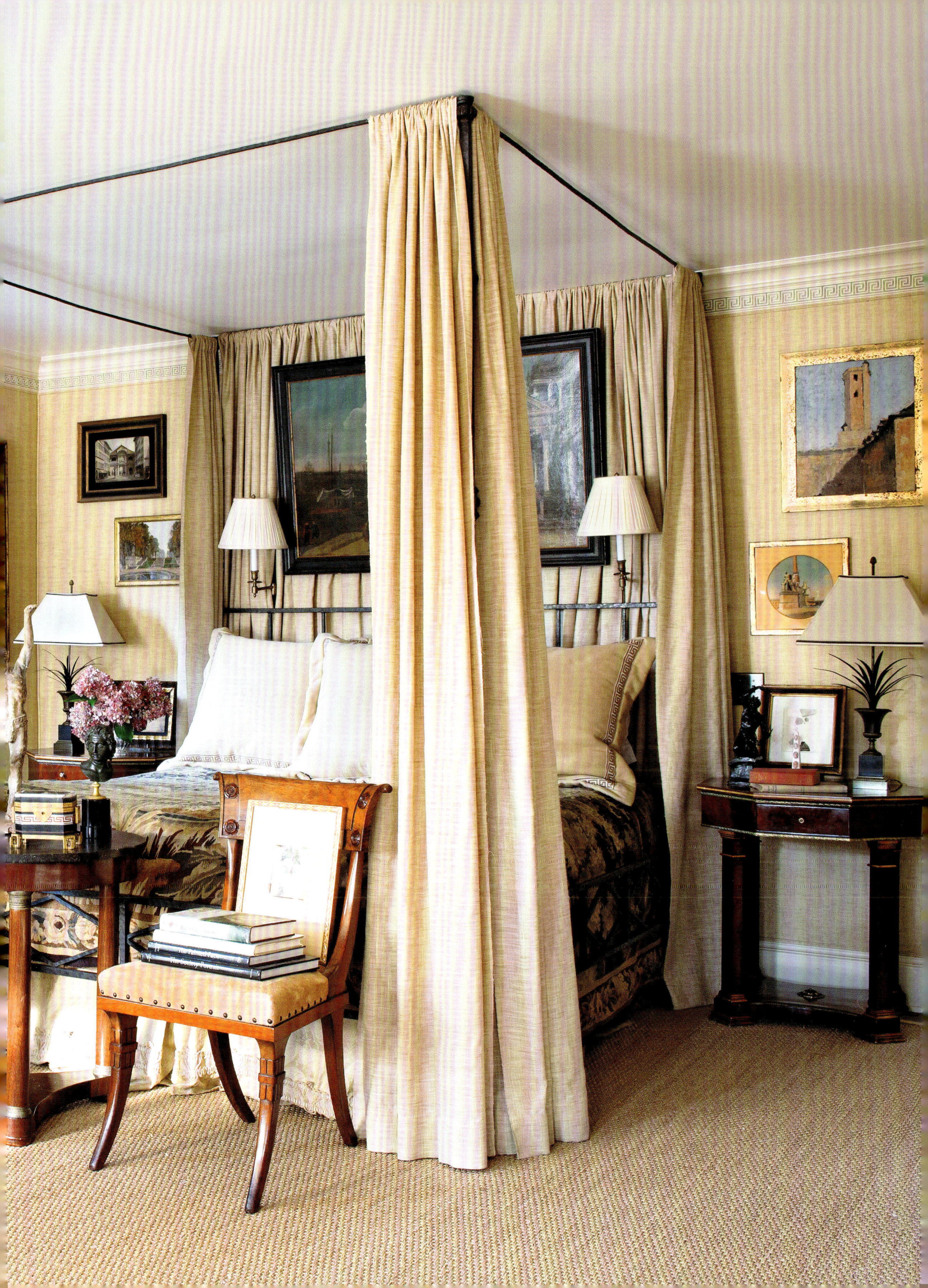

that wrap around the windows. This is where a portrait of my great-great-great-grandfather hung. The other three bedrooms in the main house were more colorful, but also cosseting and supremely comfortable.

When I adapted the house, I wanted it not only to meet my functional needs, but also to serve as a reflection of my passions and to showcase the beauty that I have been lucky enough to surround myself with throughout my career. I have acquired too many remarkable pieces over the years to be able to put them out all at once. I like to change and move around accessories, rugs, and paintings, and the house, flexible in style and palette, beautifully accommodated all of them. I have always found that if items stay static in a room for too long, you stop appreciating them, or even noticing them. I like to rotate pieces, discovering them anew each time they are retrieved from storage. While I lived there, the house and its contents formed a kind of autobiography, and it gave me great pleasure to share its stories with the people I love.

PREVIOUS PAGES: The master bedroom walls were upholstered to create a cozy, secluded feeling, with bed hangings of the same fabric reinforcing the sense of enclosure. A Greek-key motif runs throughout the room, on the mantel, the moldings, and even the bed linens. ABOVE: I installed new bookcases in the master's sitting area; the side tables are from my Timothy Corrigan Home collection. OPPOSITE: The master bath floor is Thassos marble edged in granite. The watercolor study for a poster was found in Italy, and the Greek-key motif reappears in the mirror frame and towels. FOLLOWING PAGES: To create the sense of a secluded grotto by the pool, I hung a chandelier from the pergola.

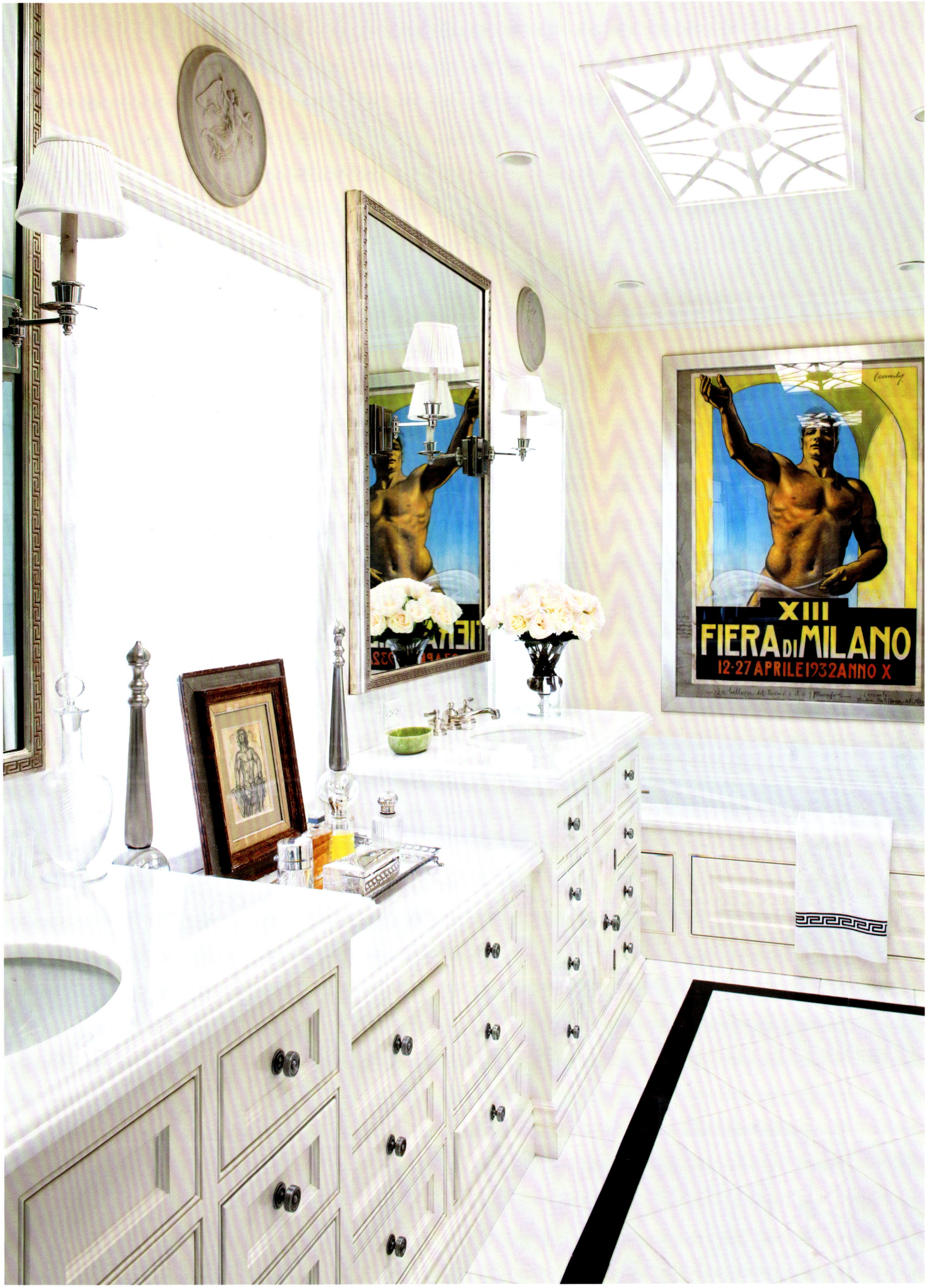
XIII
FIERA DI MILANO
12·27 APRILE 1932 ANNO X

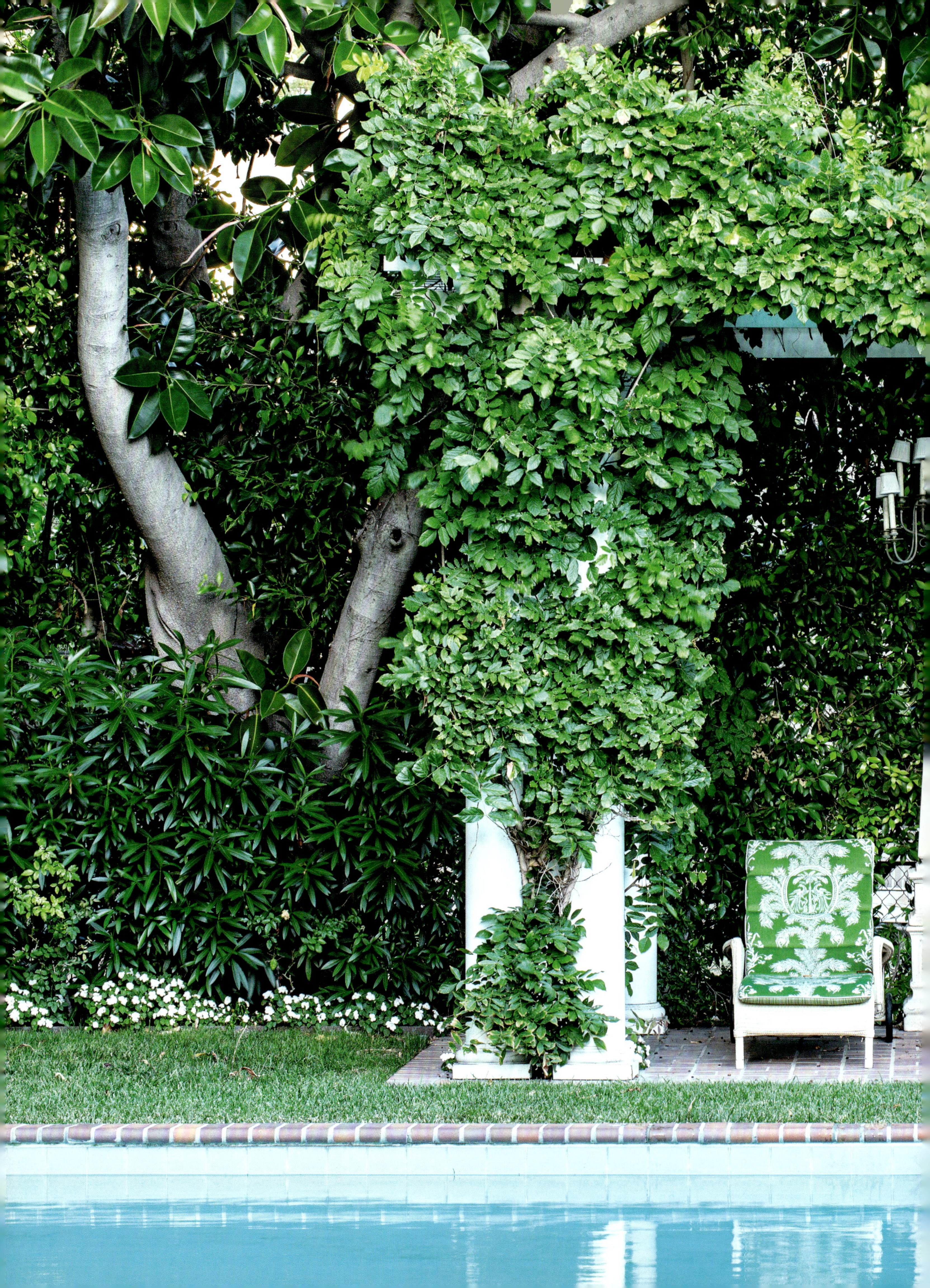

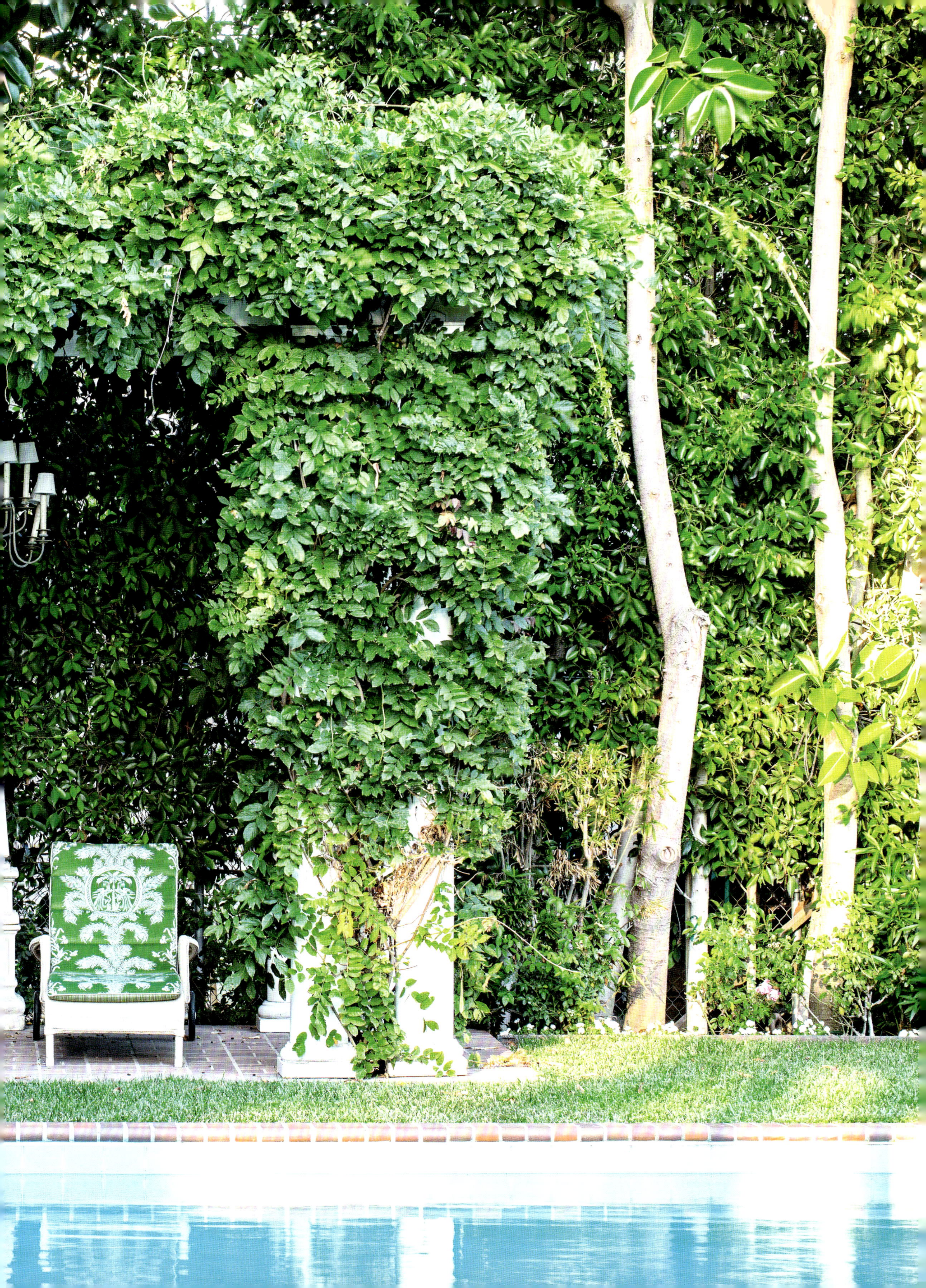

INTERLUDE
THE LAYERED LOOK

As this book makes clear, I prefer rooms that are richly layered and filled with objects—books, lamps, artworks and mirrors, sumptuous fabrics, pillows, flowers, and more. Yes, I admire minimal rooms, those kind of precision machines where every element counts and one perfect item is all you need or want. But I know how hard those kinds of rooms are to maintain—and how cold perfection can be. Minimal rooms may be calming to look at, but they are not soul-enhancing. And they are not for me.

The rooms I create, and the rooms I prefer, are more forgiving. They don't have to be neat and tidy every second of the day, they don't cry out to be straightened up every hour, and they don't ask to have all signs of life, of occupation and use, swept away. The kind of room I love, and strive to create, welcomes the stray drink or mug of tea and even provides a place to set them down. To me, the best rooms allow you to surround yourself with objects that you love, not to mention people. These objects reflect your life, your passions, your experiences, and your memories, and thereby enhance it.

But just because these rooms encompass so much, that doesn't mean anything goes. They may not be haiku, like those minimal rooms that rely on only three items, but they are composed, and every syllable counts. So there must always be order and clarity beneath the plethora of objects. Rooms should be welcoming and relaxed, but not busy or messy.

1
This bedroom in London is an example of layering by color. Here, all the accents amplify the rich blue of the wallpaper, such as the plaque over the lamp, the lampshades, the piece of blue coral, the lining of the bed draperies, the vivid tieback, the upholstery of the headboard, and the bedding itself. The deep brown of the bedside cabinet and the gray of the upholstery fabrics provide enough contrast to prevent visual boredom, and the slight shifts in the shades of blue provide richness and depth.

2
In the entry of a home in Brentwood, the array of books, a bust, and a number of unusual decorative items laid out on a neoclassical table lets you know immediately that you are in the home of people with varied interests—people you want to know better, who are not afraid to share their tastes and passions. The small bouquets of flowers are the final touch, showing a love for color and nature.

3
The busts on this table in Los Angeles range from 300 BC to the eighteenth century. The diverse faces and styles play off one another and form a kind of conversation between personalities, including an ancient Egyptian wife and the musical genius Mozart. The busts' richness of texture and form is amplified by a hefty Indian silver ankle bracelet, and the table they rest on is placed next to a sofa, where they are within easy reach, their tactile pleasures close at hand.

4
In a Brentwood living room, a mix of eras and provenances make for a refined and restful space. The mirror by William Haines, one of a pair, reflects both eighteenth-century and contemporary pieces, dark wood antiques, and designs by Rose Tarlow. The upholstery fabrics are kept to pale neutrals to set off the richly patterned antique Oriental rug and to enhance the view of the garden beyond.

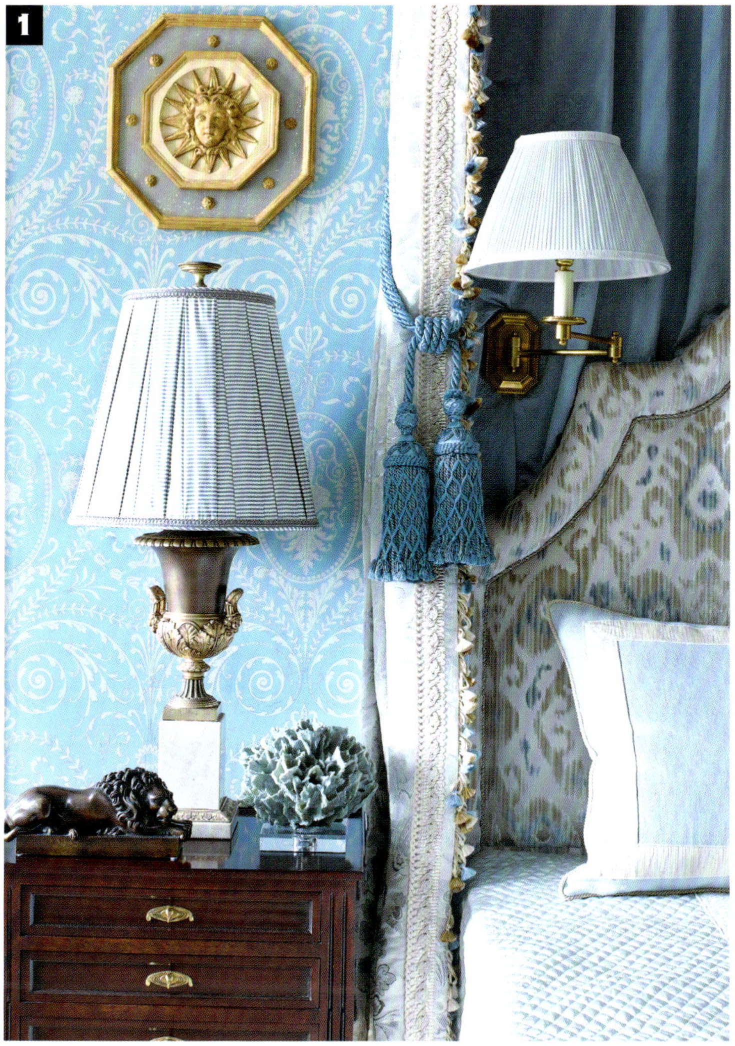
1

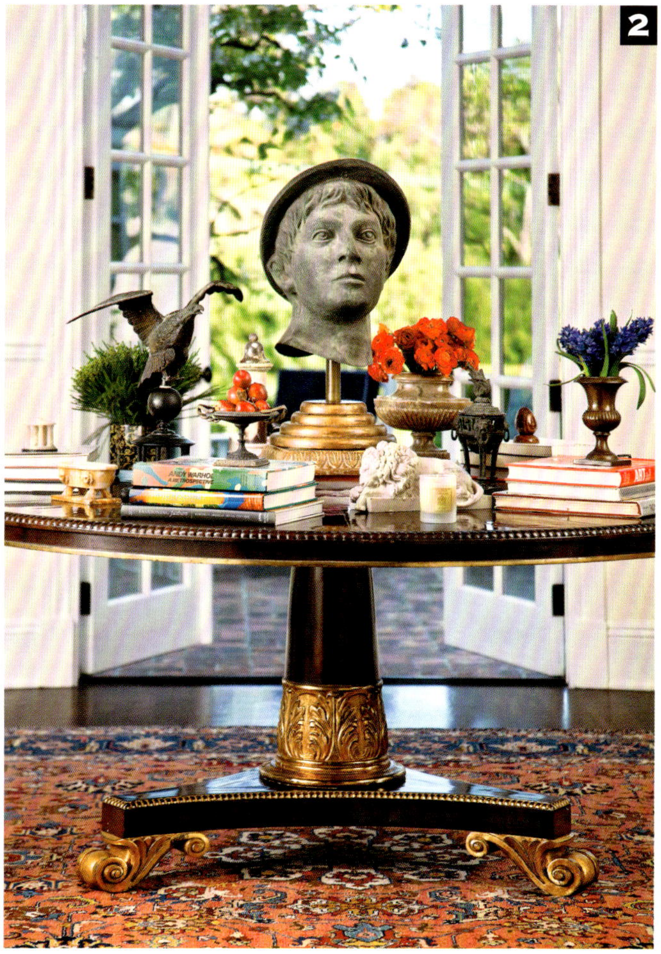
2

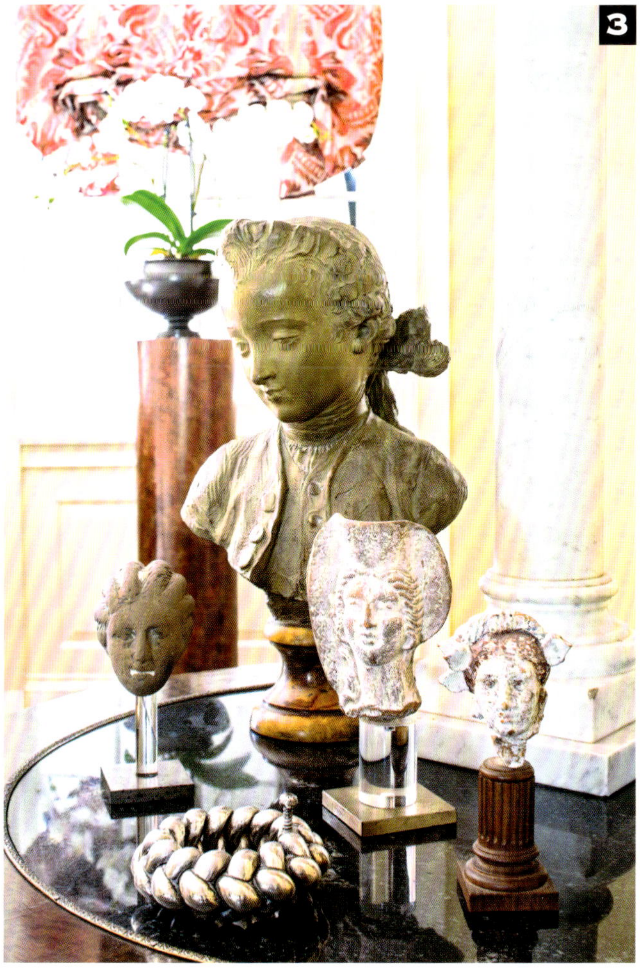
3

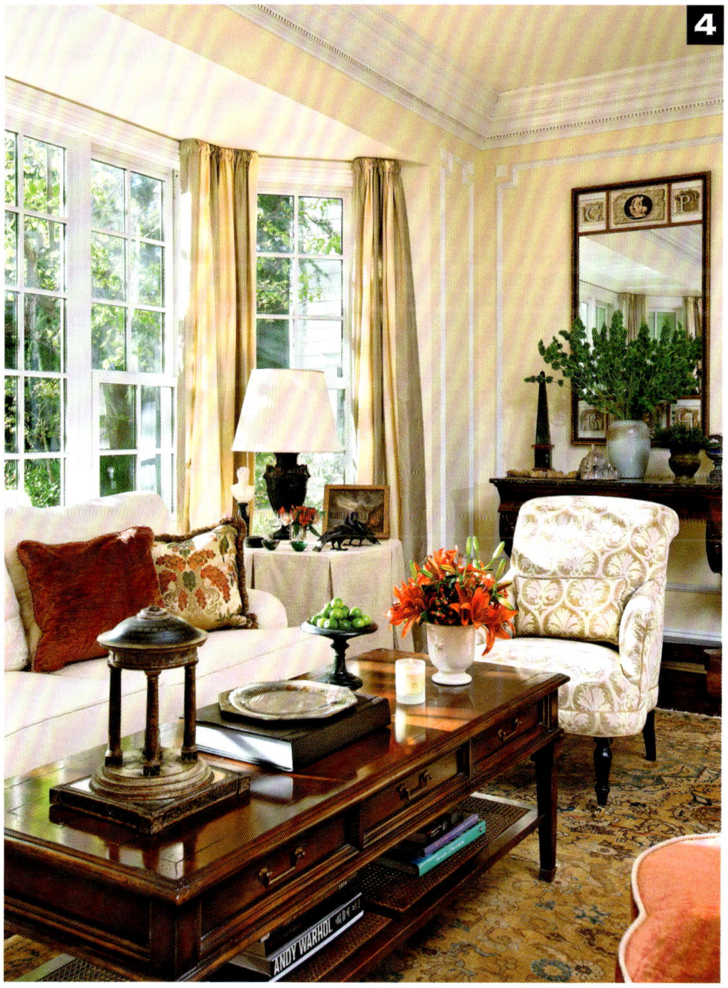
4
ANDY WARHOL

Shoreline Sophistication

As we get older, many of us long for a simpler life. But is it possible to live smaller without sacrificing style, comfort, or elegance? I think so. As Coco Chanel famously said, "Elegance is refusal," and while moving to smaller quarters can be painful in that it necessitates forgoing many favorite and familiar items, the result can be a stronger and clearer sense of who you are and how you really want to live.

This apartment is proof that downsizing can be liberating, and that a space with clean lines and expanses of glass need not be minimal in style or lacking in warmth. The client, with whom we had already worked on two other homes, is a noted philanthropist, devoted to art, education, and medical research. She was moving from a large contemporary townhouse to a new apartment building several blocks away in downtown Chicago. The apartment she selected was on the thirty-sixth floor, with floor-to-ceiling windows that provided sweeping 180-degree views of both the Lake Michigan shoreline and the city skyline.

But the drama of the views was undercut by the banality of the building's interior. Although the architecture was bold and modern, with elegant detailing on the exterior, inside there wasn't a single pleasing surface or detail. It all needed to be stripped away. So essentially the challenge became to create a home for a sophisticated, art-loving woman within an empty shell of glass and steel. That meant new floors, new kitchen and baths, and new architectural detailing throughout. We wanted to evoke the comforts of a traditional home but still have the apartment fit within the modern style of the building.

Her art collection served as an inspiration and a touchstone throughout the design. It encompasses an array of colorful pieces by modern artists including Jasper Johns, Frank Stella, Joan Mitchell, Robert Motherwell, and many more. She also has a strong and intriguing collection of pottery and ceramics and an array of pre-Columbian figures she has collected over the years. Because so many of the artworks are colorful, we decided to opt for a neutral backdrop, with the walls painted in various shades of white and the upholstery fabrics confined to pale, watery

To create architectural interest, depth, and texture, as well as a sense of procession, in what was a characterless apartment in a contemporary building, we installed moldings, overdoors, and paneled doors and frames. The table is Art Deco, and the print is by Robert Longo.

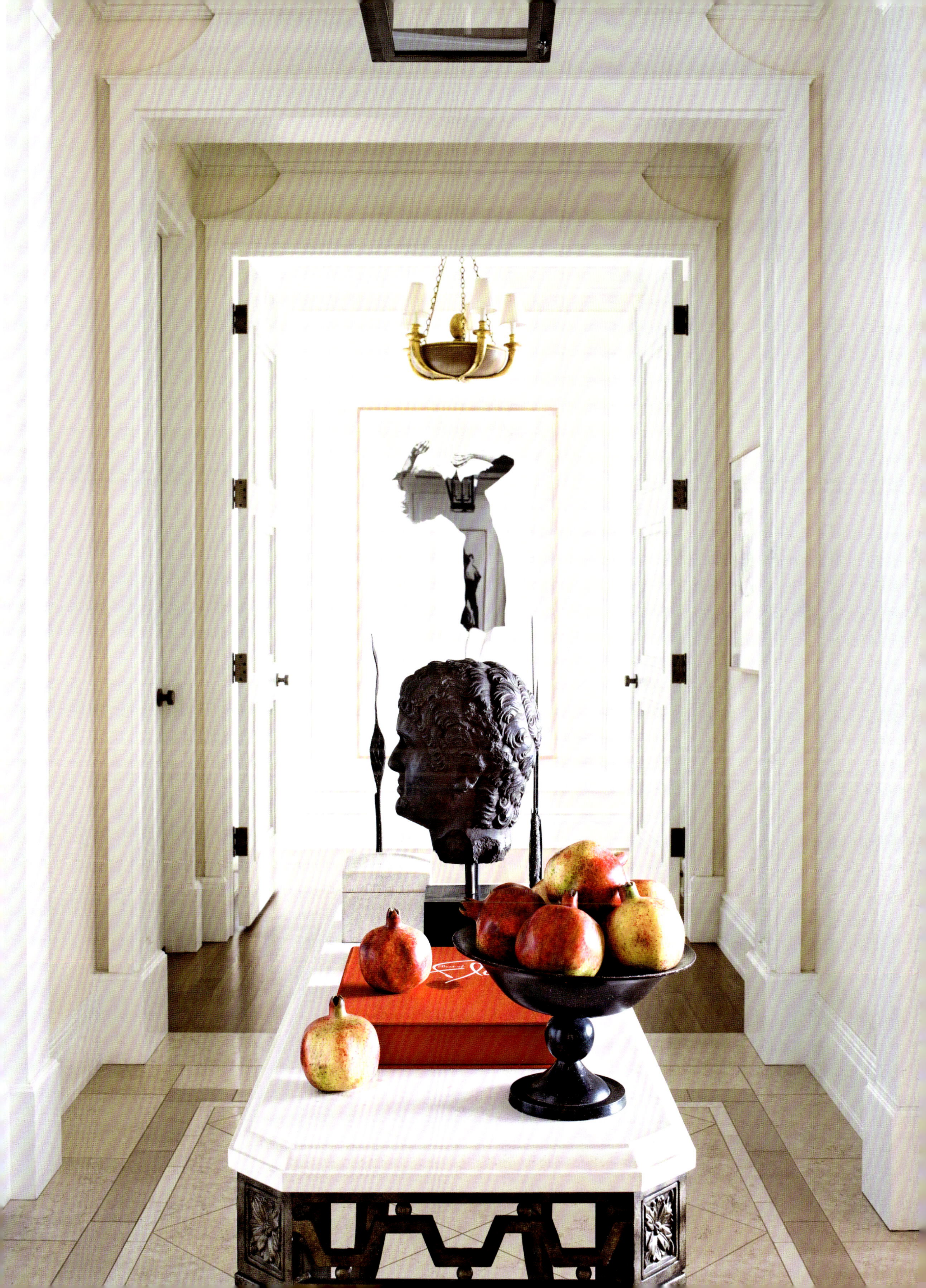

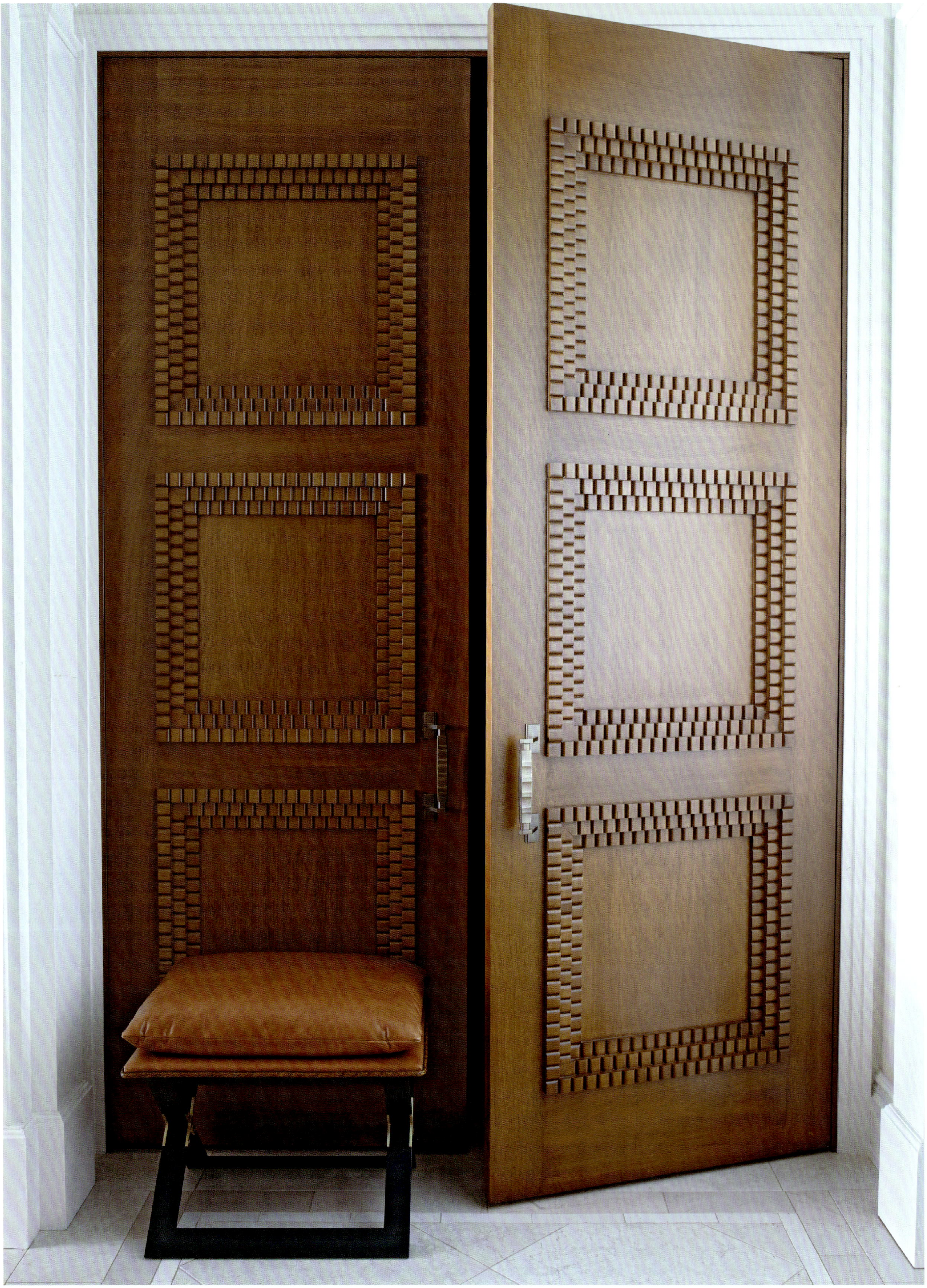

colors of cream, gray, blue, and taupe, but in a rich variety of textures, contrasting with richly patterned antique rugs that are another of the client's passions.

The tone is set at the entrance with a forty-foot-long gallery that is studded with works by Helen Frankenthaler, Robert Longo, and Picasso's famous Bull series. An Art Deco table of bronze and marble and an oversize hanging lantern hint at the elegance within, while antique Tabriz rugs add graphic complexity and color to the space.

As you move from the enclosed gallery to the living room, with its wraparound floor-to-ceiling windows, the dramatic views take center stage, day or night. A pair of white sofas anchors the room, and the furnishings range from an early-eighteenth-century Italian console to a 1940s French cabinet, interspersed with numerous pieces I designed, including a bronze-and-eglomise cocktail table that reflects the sky. The adjacent small sitting area is centered around the fireplace, with a custom ottoman-cum–cocktail table and an antique Tabriz rug; an arrangement of early geometric Frank Stella prints is the focal point. In the adjacent dining area, a custom round table of palisander and bronze is surrounded by dining chairs covered in a hand-embroidered fabric with a monochromatic foliage pattern.

OPPOSITE: Flanking the entry are two sets of doors inspired by ones that Émile-Jacques Ruhlmann showed at the 1925 decorative-arts exhibition in Paris.
ABOVE: In the powder room, the walls are upholstered; a custom vanity of wood and bronze is topped by a hand-carved and hand-gilded mirror by Vandeuren Galleries.

This kind of subtle detailing allows the strong artworks by John Mitchell and Jasper Johns to star but reveal themselves slowly to both eye and hand, enriching your experience of the space.

The kitchen is the most minimal room in the apartment. The cabinetry was designed with no visible hardware; the walls and the backsplash, which are covered in reverse-painted glass, gleam in any light. The slab stone counter on the island appears to float above its base, and the elements are as precisely fitted as a puzzle. This carefully calibrated aesthetic plays off a wall of shelves filled with

THE NEW ELEGANCE

The color scheme of the living room was chosen to complement the sky and the waters of Lake Michigan, visible in the distance. The cocktail table is a custom design of verre eglomise and pyrite panels with bronze detailing.

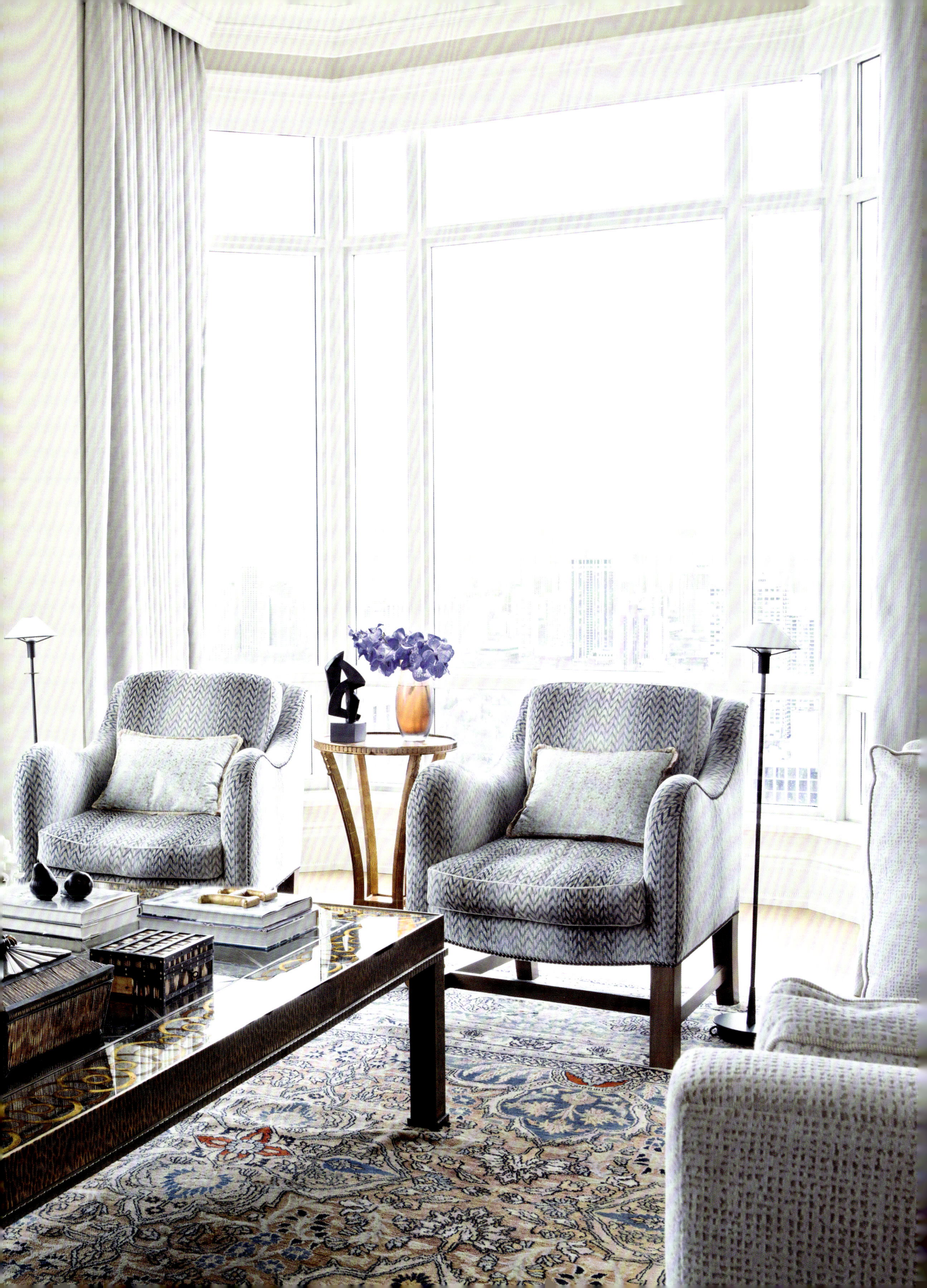

The owner's extensive collection includes, from left, works by Jasper Johns, Robert Motherwell, and Frank Stella, as well as a collection of pre-Columbian figures from Peru.
FOLLOWING PAGES: The eighteenth-century Italian console was specifically chosen to highlight the array of Picasso ceramics; the print is by Robert Motherwell. The dining room table by Promemoria is surrounded by chairs with a subtle hand-embroidered motif on the back. The artworks on the walls are by Joan Mitchell, left, and Jasper Johns.

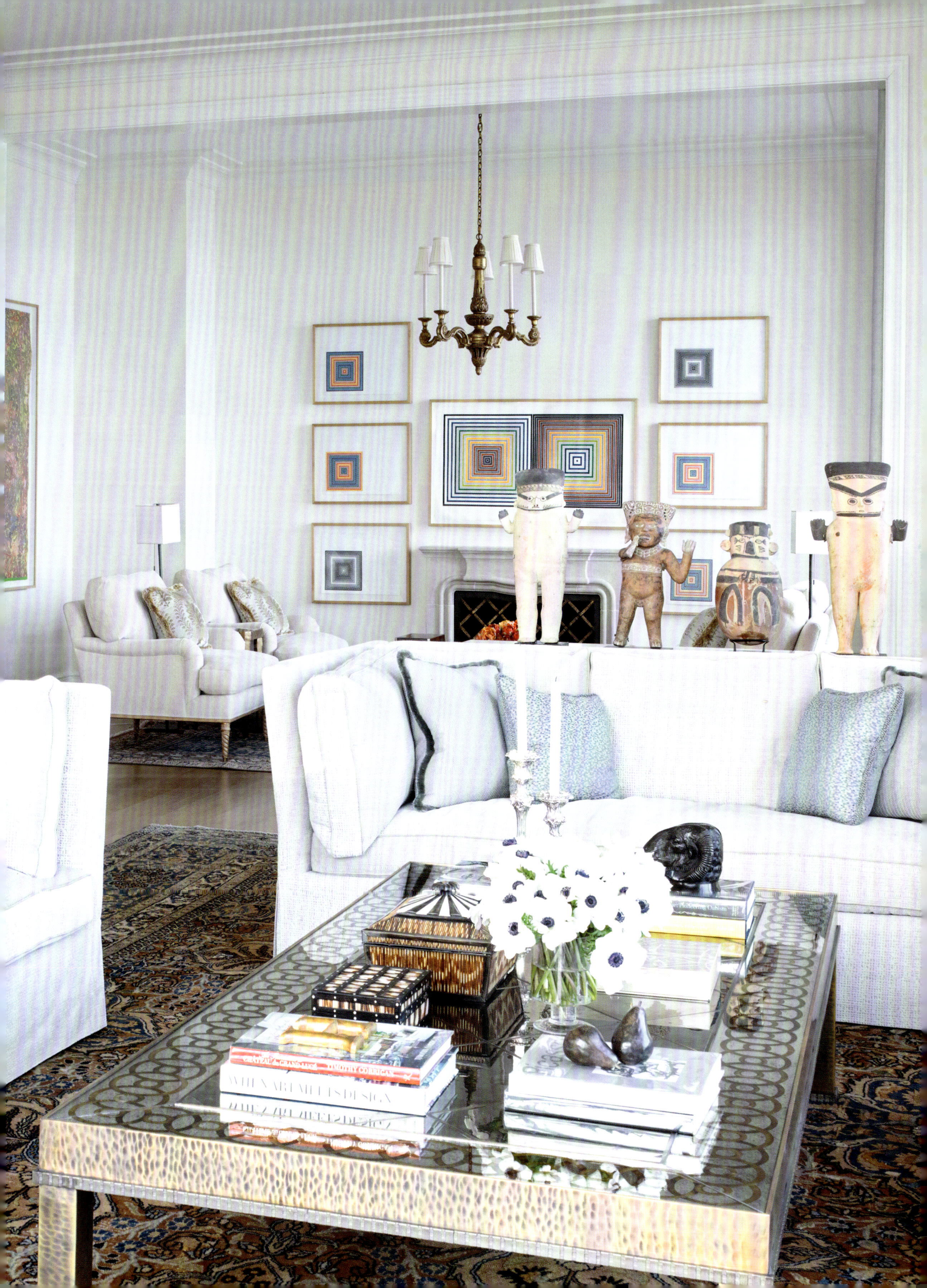

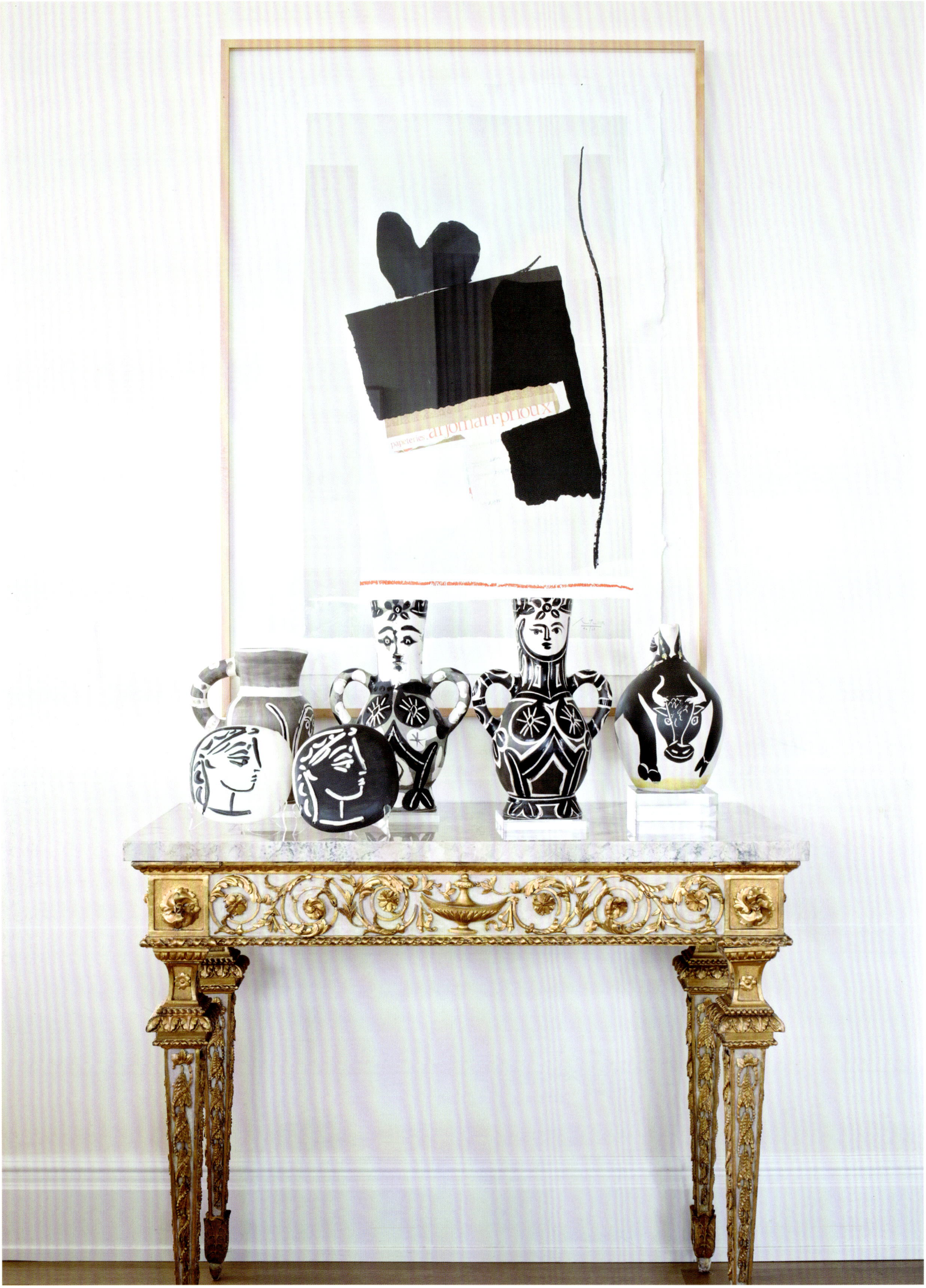
papeteries arjomari-prioux

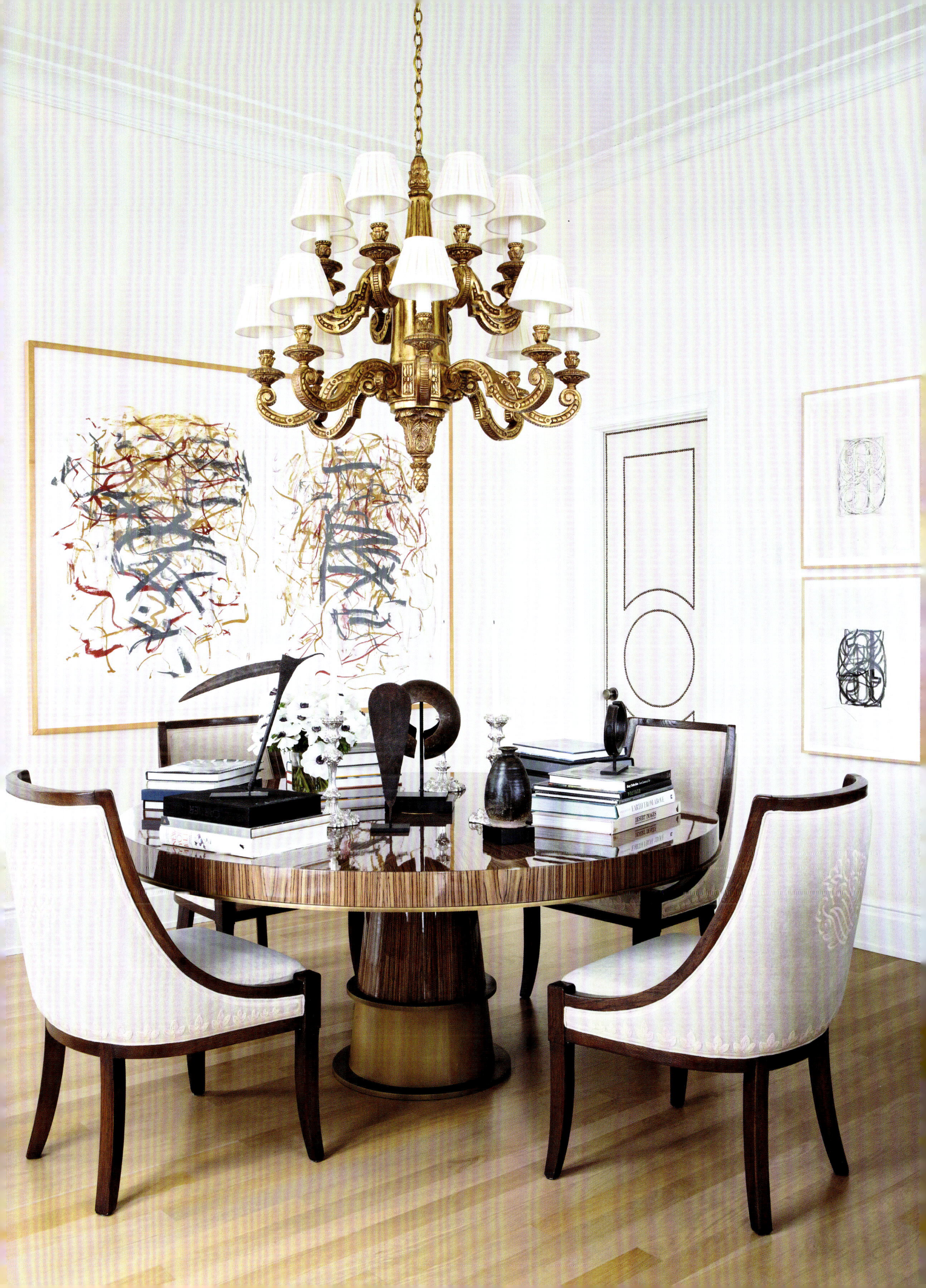

nineteenth-century French pottery confit jars and rustic, woven dining chairs from Italy. These elements bring a tactile element of craft and add a bit of rough texture to this sleek and functional space.

The library and the powder room also contrast with the light-filled main rooms. The library is entirely paneled in golden oak, complete with a traditional dentil molding, carved scallop-shell details, and pilasters to create the feel of a scholarly yet luxe retreat. Here, cerebral works by Jasper Johns hold sway. Modernity is brought into play with a fifteen-foot-long sofa upholstered in a vivid blue and an intricate coffee table of wood veneers inset with semiprecious stones.

The powder room is also paneled, but here the wood is contrasted with inset panels of embroidered fabric, and a fluted demilune vanity is fitted with a bronze counter and topped with an eighteenth-century inspired mirror. The effect is like being in an exquisite jewel box.

The master suite, at the opposite end of the entrance gallery, consists of a sitting room, bedroom, bath, and dressing room, all done in shimmering shades of cream and gold. The sitting area has floor-to-ceiling shelves flanking a fireplace imported from France and a gilt-wood chandelier. The upholstered headboard fits flush into a wall of leather panels and is surrounded by small-scale artworks that are particular favorites, while the master bath contrasts white Thassos marble with hand-carved gilt-framed mirrors. The entire space is feminine yet has an elegance and rigor suitable to the building and to the owner's new life in this pared-down yet richly detailed space.

ABOVE: The study is hung with a series of works by Jasper Johns; the banquette is a custom design, and the light fixture is by Charles Edwards. OPPOSITE: More works by Jasper Johns are featured in the library with a nineteenth-century French side table.

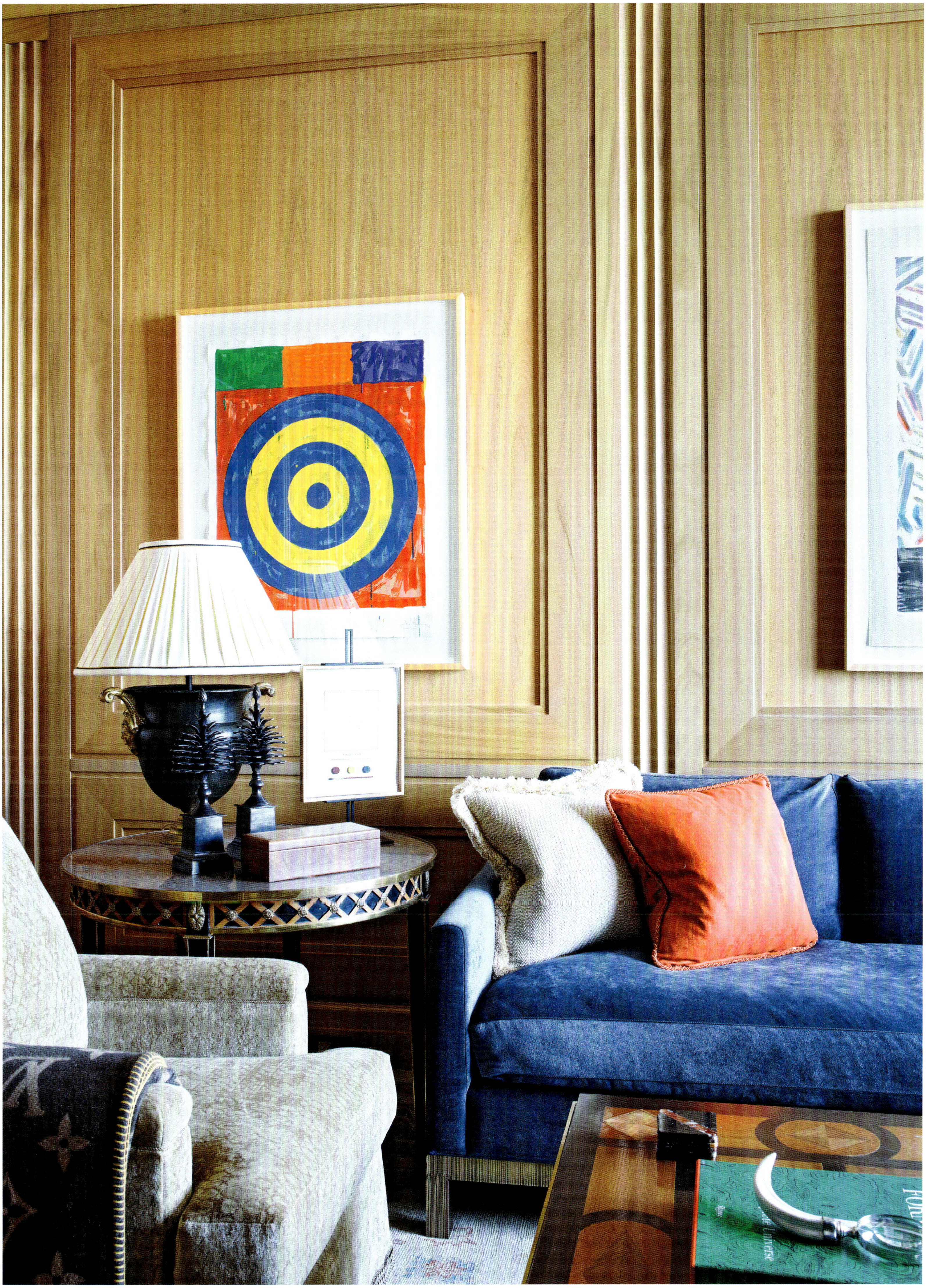

The library was paneled in wood to evoke tradition, but in a more clean-lined, contemporary style, with deliberately oversize fluting; the cocktail table is a custom design.

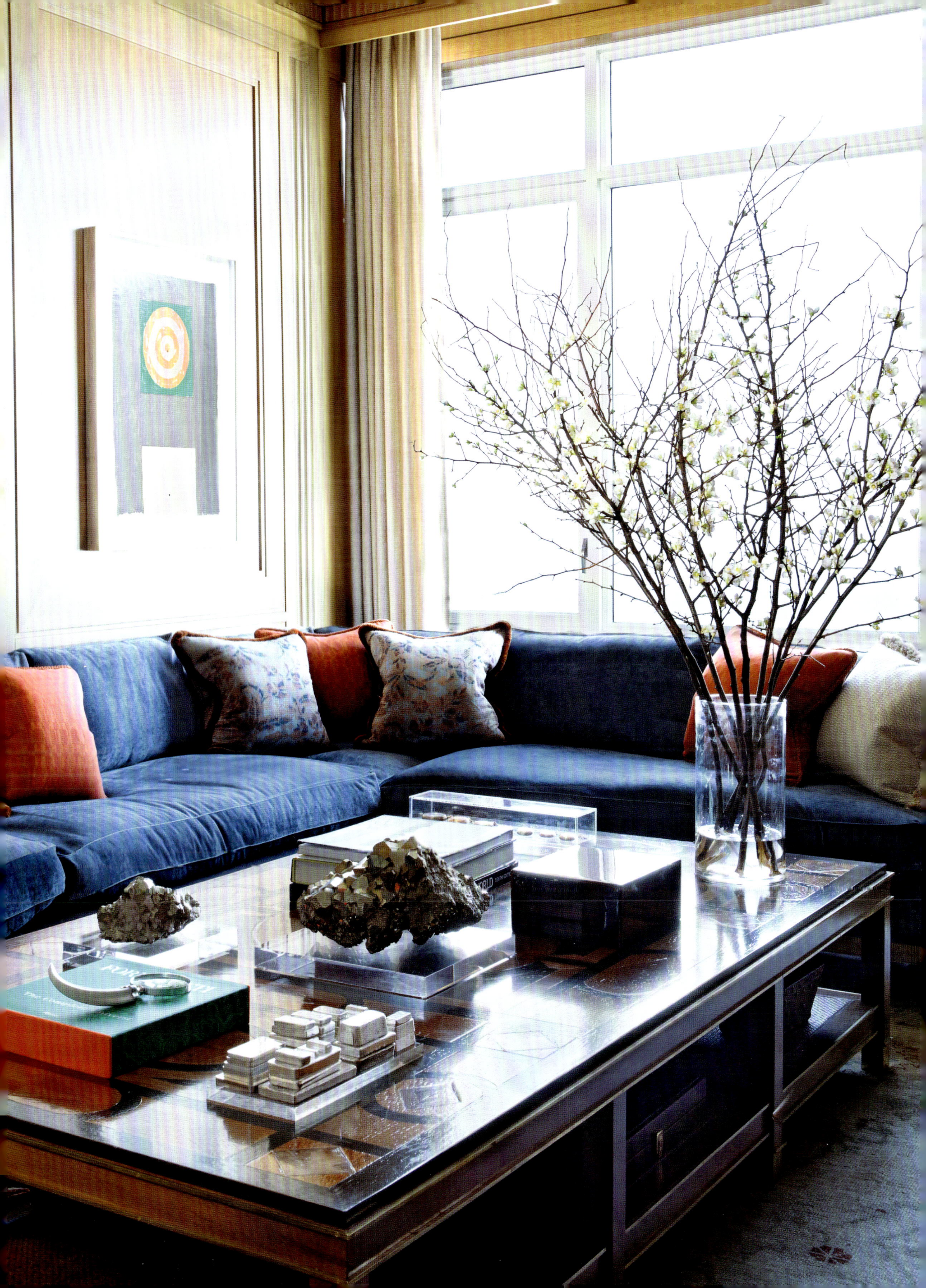

ABOVE: The kitchen cabinetry was inspired by Jean-Michel Frank and has no visible hardware to keep its lines as sleek as possible. OPPOSITE: The custom oak kitchen table has inlaid chrome detailing; the nineteenth-century French confit pots were found at a Paris flea market, and the sculpture of a mixer is marble.

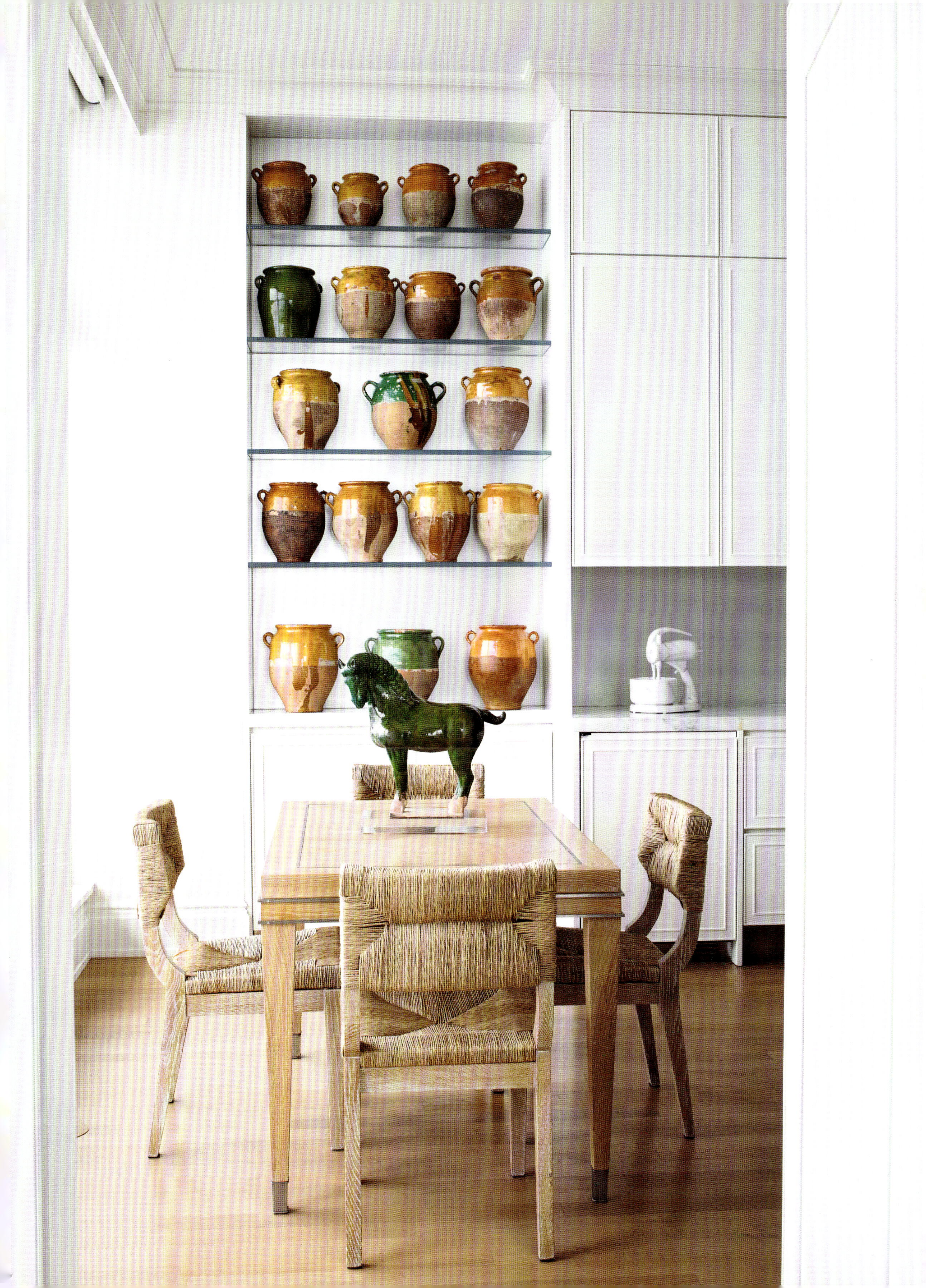

ABOVE AND OPPOSITE: In the master bedroom, the sitting area features custom bookcases flanking the fireplace. The custom bed is inset into the leather-paneled wall; the artwork over it is by Jasper Johns, and the drawing on the nightstand is by Picasso.

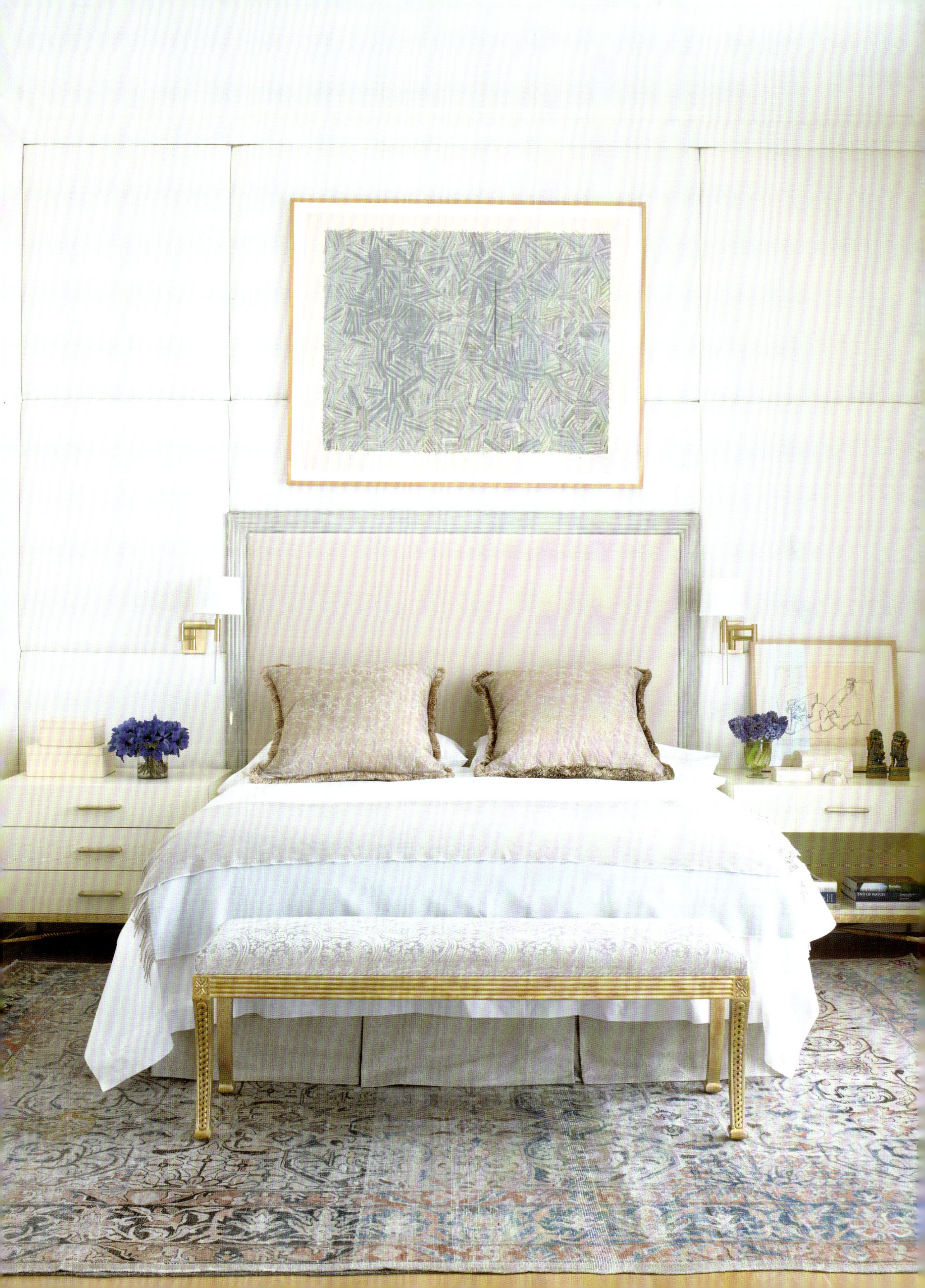

ABOVE: In a guest room, a print by Frank Stella hangs over the custom bed, the nightstand holds a work by Christo and Jeanne-Claude, and the curtain fabric is by Veronese. OPPOSITE: Custom beds and benches flank an early-nineteenth-century Swedish chest; the artworks are by Roy Lichtenstein, left, and Frank Stella.

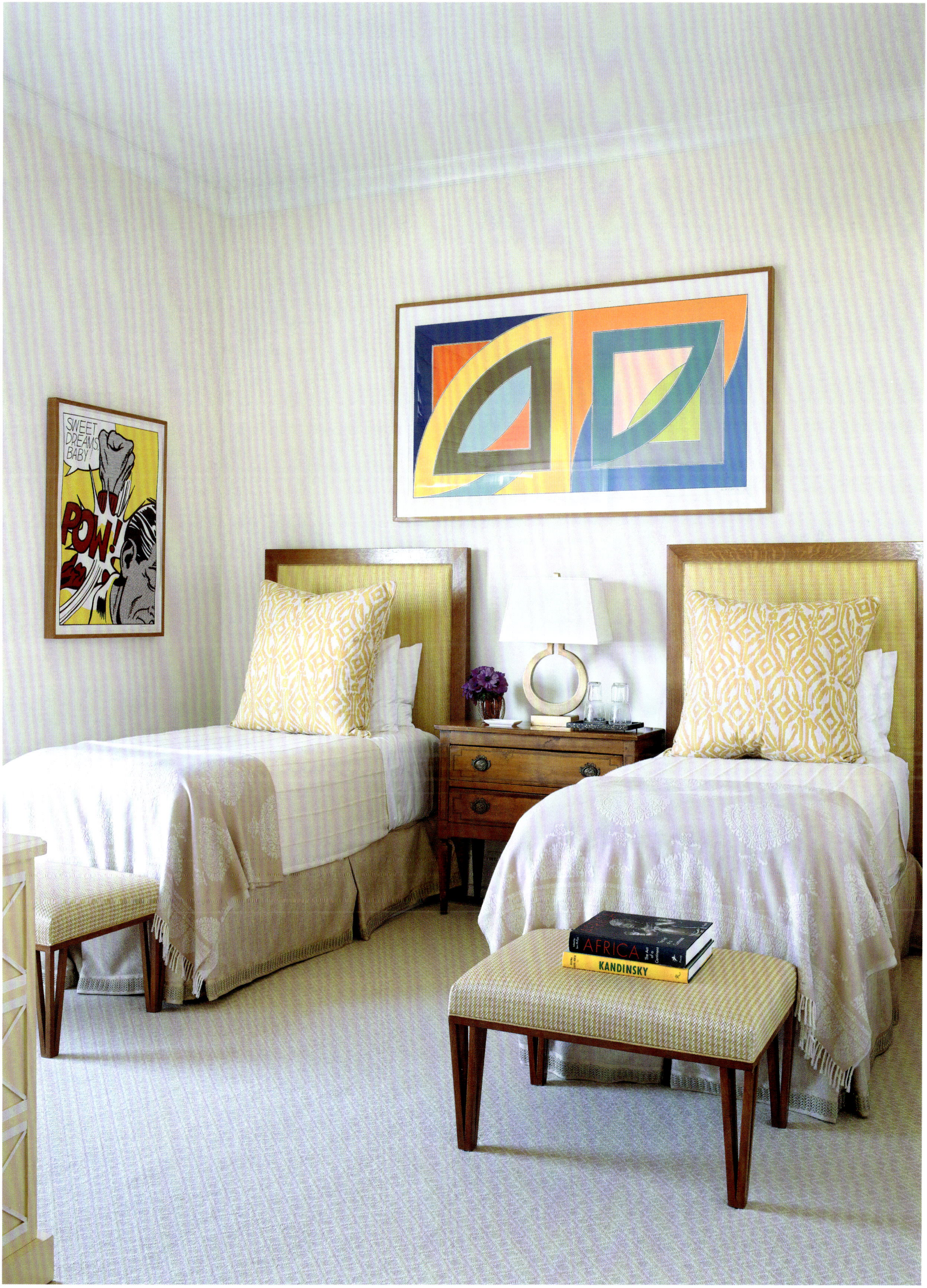
SWEET DREAMS BABY!
POW!
AFRICA
KANDINSKY

INTERLUDE
ART AND MIRRORS

It always surprises me how many clients don't understand the importance that walls play in creating a finished, comfortable, elegant room. Any large expanse of empty wall is likely to make a room feel incomplete or cold. Walls cry out for adornment.

You don't need great works to make a great room. I personally think it is better to showcase a poster of a work you love than to live with bare walls. Don't think about art as an investment, but as an expression of your interests and your tastes. Good works can be had at a variety of price points. I often find lovely works for very little money at auction houses, and the internet has made buying and bidding for art online easy.

Mirrors are a great way to dress up a wall and add depth. Outside the bathroom, mirrors are not about vanity. They open up a room, add interest, expand light, play with reflections. In fact, I often position mirrors high on the walls, or angled to reflect up to the ceiling. I will hang mirrors as a kind of faux window opposite an actual window. In fact, there are few places where a mirror won't work. And mirrors are a fantastic way to highlight a beautiful frame.

There are any number of other ways to add richness and depth to your walls. Hang a length of beautiful fabric, a vintage suzani, a tapestry, a flatweave rug, or a piece of needlework. Place a beautiful illustrated book on an easel to serve as a freestanding artwork. Group smaller works together to fill a wall. What is important is that artwork and mirrors work with the scale and furnishings of the room and that they enhance and complete the desired effect.

1

This Paris apartment is proof of the power of mirrors multiplied. There were too many openings in the entry hall, so we closed off a deep doorway and turned it into a dramatic niche. I removed the door casing, framed it in gold, and backed the opening with a sheet of mirror. I then hung another mirror on top—in this case, a seventeenth-century showstopper found at auction. The eighteenth-century French console is mounted directly to the mirror. The mirror makes the niche seem far deeper than it is, and because you can see through the legs of the console to the reflection behind, it seems to be floating. Thus the liability of an excess of doors becomes a prominent design feature.

2

This entry in Los Angeles is an example of letting art be the star. The clients have an outstanding contemporary collection, including several works by Sam Francis, which we showcased here. But modern art does not demand spare white walls. Here, we painted the traditional paneling and moldings in three shades of blue-gray so that they would recede, letting the artworks be the focus. The exuberant Irish console makes a suitable companion, its sweeping curves and carvings echoing the active, energetic forms of the artworks.

3

In this dining room in France, I hung a seventeenth-century tapestry as a focal point. I love the depth and texture a tapestry brings to a room. I favor old ones for their faded colors and textures, but there are many beautiful modern tapestries as well, and they are often affordable. I hang them from a pole, which gives a softer, more rippled effect, or staple them to a wall for a more tailored effect—fortunately, their fibers are very forgiving. And because they are so unexpected, they often have greater impact than a painting or photograph of a similar size.

4

This bedroom hallway in Beverly Hills is an ode to the power of reflection—and of shimmer and shine. Here, a three-dimensional mirrored wallpaper is amplified and refracted by a custom Cubistic mirror and matching console. The angles are many, and every one is covered in mirror, each reflecting the light in a different direction. This mirror is definitely not for looking at yourself, but it is the ideal centerpiece for a playful, energetic, and contemporary vignette, with just a touch of golden glamour.

150 THE NEW ELEGANCE

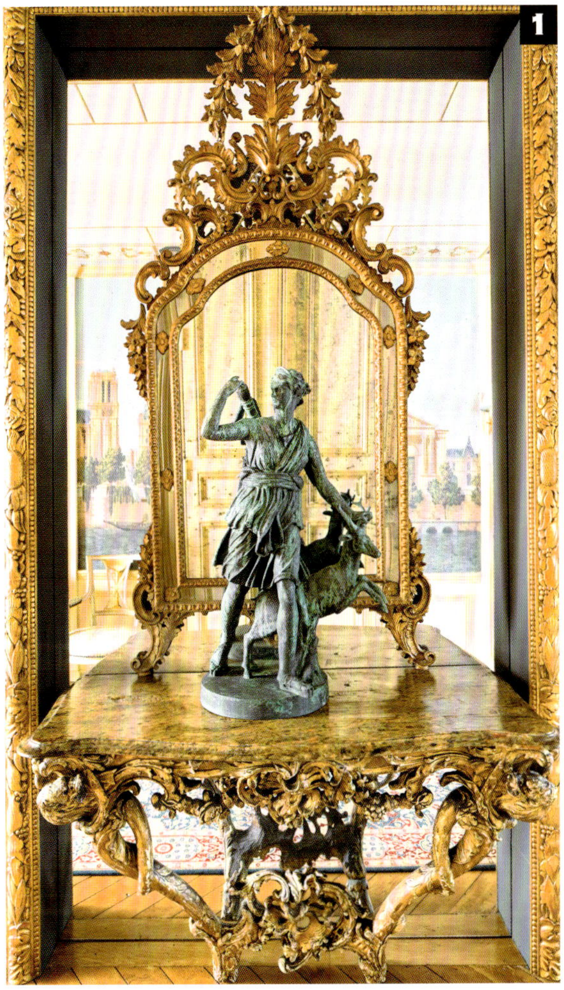

1

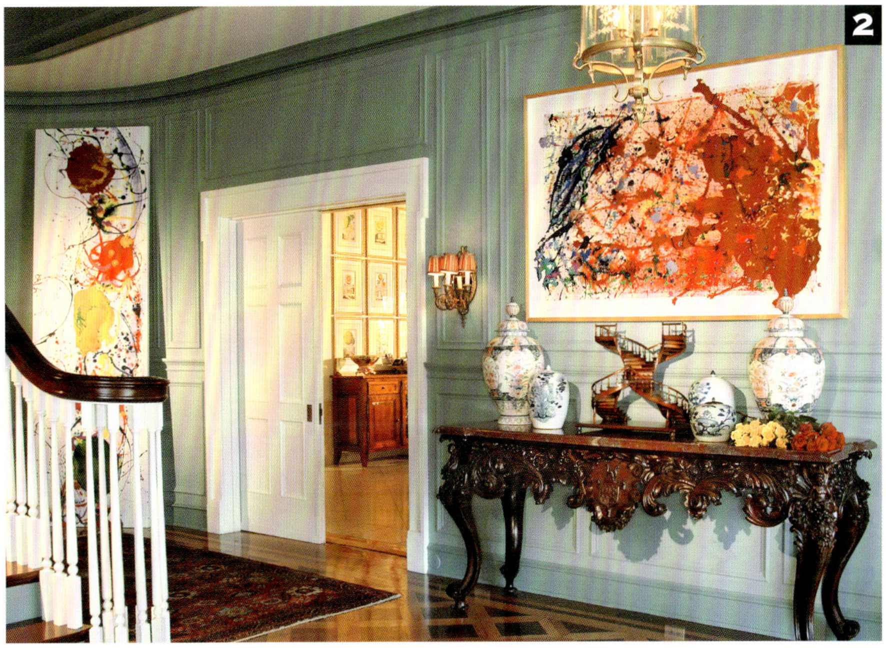

2

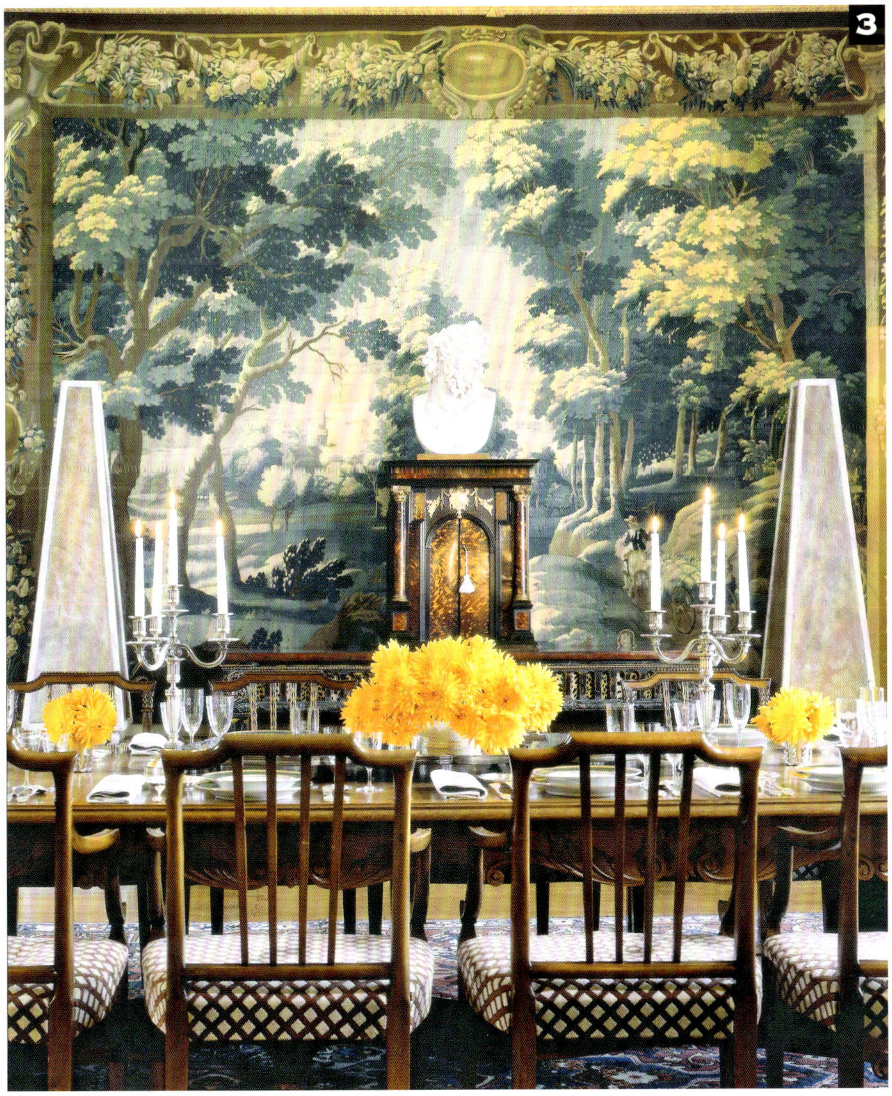

3

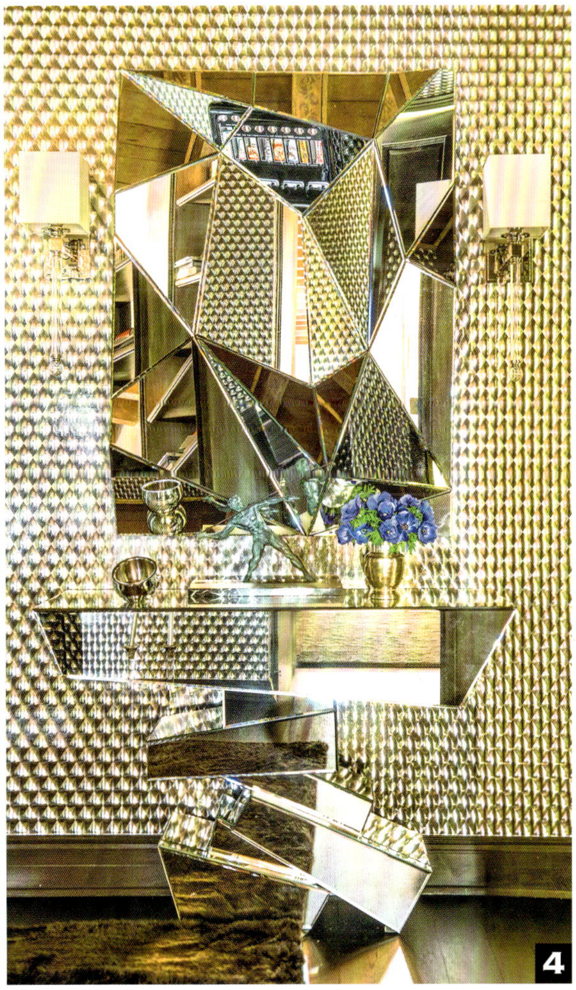

4

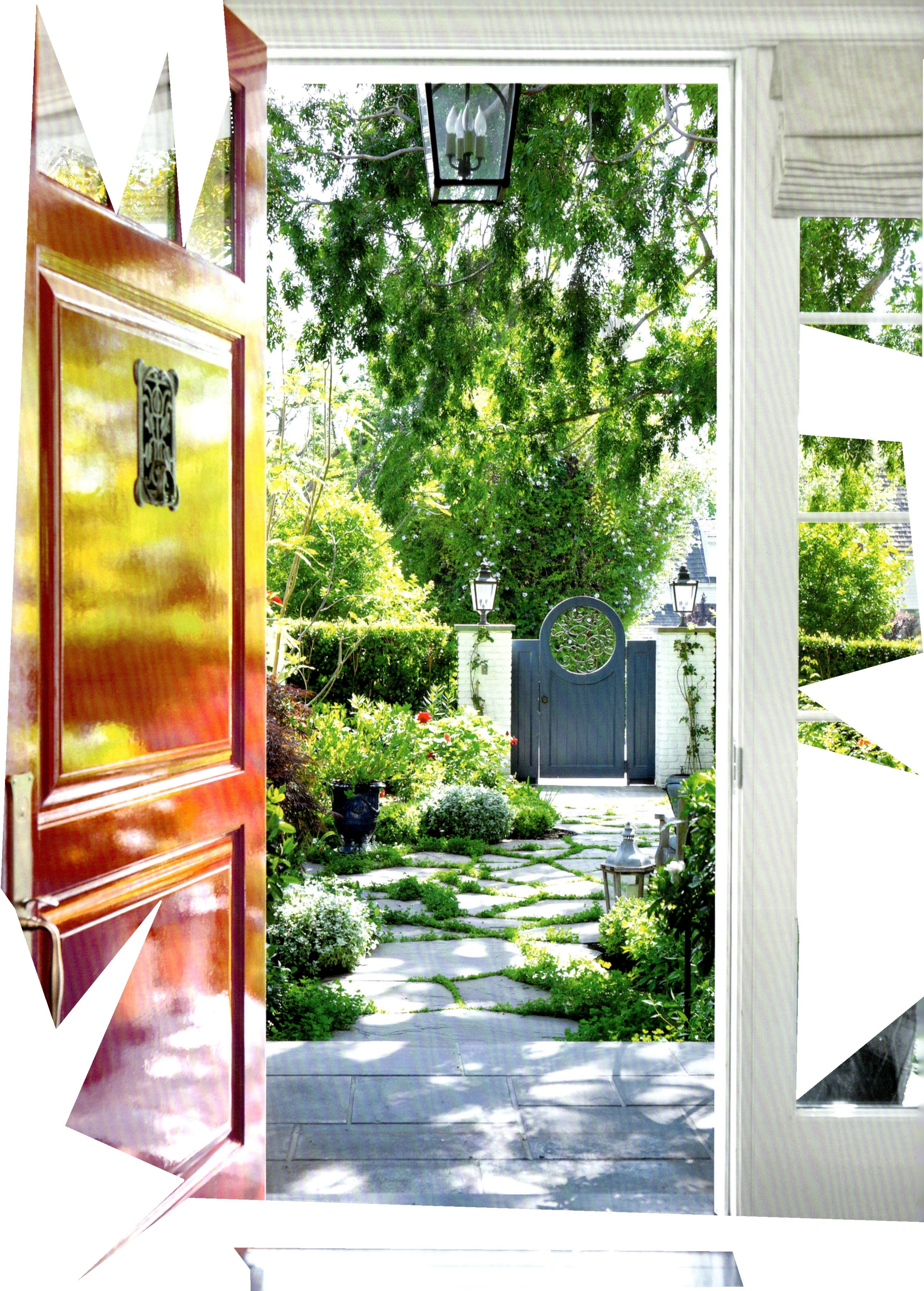

Family Hangout

The classic white American house, the kind with dormers and shutters, a welcoming front door, a picket fence, and a garden gate, remains a potent ideal for many of us. But none of us live in a storybook these days, and it isn't always easy to adapt a classic structure so that it fulfills all of a contemporary family's needs while retaining its essence and charm.

This colonial-style house, newly constructed in the upscale Los Angeles neighborhood of Brentwood, is a perfect case in point. To start with, it was neither unique nor distinctive, but it was large and capacious and had great potential. The clients, one an attorney and the other an author/human rights advocate, have three children and a passion for literature. They love to entertain and host weekly dinner parties, as well as film screenings and frequent gatherings in support of their favorite causes and charities. They wanted a home that, while classic, would also reflect their personalities and their high-energy approach to life. The answer turned out to be color.

That color makes itself felt even on the exterior, starting the minute you approach the gate. The gate and shutters are painted a rich Mediterranean blue, while the front door is a glossy tomato red by Benjamin Moore, a color agreed upon only after countless trials. The blue is reiterated further in the cushions on a bench and in the glazed pots that hold a variety of plants.

Color is a strong element throughout the interior of the house, as well, in ways both big and small. But it is always offset by expanses of white in spaces that are infused with light. This is immediately evident in the bright entry hall, which features a custom-designed grille over the skylight that floods the serene and welcoming space with sunlight. The central stair rises gracefully to the second floor, but at the landing the expected railing is replaced with two panels of glass that allow even more light from the skylight at the top of the stairs to suffuse the house.

The walls of the living room are white, but here the color acts as a background for bold reds and blues, especially from the wall of books, which is accented with black-and-white photographs of writers, making it immediately clear that this house belongs to a literary couple. The backs of the shelves are lined with mirrors to multiply the colors and provide even more sparkle. The comfortable furnishings are covered in rich blue and cream linen velvets, contrasted with a pair of stools upholstered in a red cut velvet to add a bit of punch. The room is lively without being overwhelming, a place

We painted the garden gate of this classic Brentwood house a rich blue and then contrasted it with a vivid red door—a shade that took several attempts to perfect—to signal that this is a colorful, eclectic home owned by fascinating people.

ideal for spirited conversations with guests or an hour or two curled up alone with a book.

The dining room is more dramatic, with its red walls, blue wainscoting, and dramatic early-nineteenth-century japanned sideboard. The blue is repeated in the leather dining chairs and in the velvet-covered banquettes at either end of the custom walnut dining table, which make the room more versatile while avoiding the visual monotony of too many identical chairs. The final flourishes come thanks to a vibrant overscale Persian rug and the nail-studded blue leather door that leads to the kitchen.

The kitchen's big surprise is the vivid green island and matching pendant lights that sit in the midst of the traditional white cabinetry. Everything is reflected in the glossy, dark-stained wood floor. This spacious room is used frequently, as the owners are passionate cooks, so it was important that it be not only functional but also pleasant to spend time in, and the green really energizes the space. The adjacent family room picks up the greens in the armchair upholstery and in a variety of pillows strewn across the sectional sofa. That piece, where the family gathers more often than anyplace else, is covered in a practical but plush outdoor velvet. Both rooms feature luminous white-painted board ceilings, which amplify the already abundant light.

In most houses, the downstairs public rooms are the formal spaces, while private bedrooms and baths upstairs are more relaxed and less decorated. Here, we reversed that rule, because the couple entertains so frequently, and the upstairs rooms, private refuges, are the most elegantly finished in the house. The tip-off comes in the upstairs hall, which we fitted out with an elaborate antique English gilt-wood eagle console topped by a custom gold-leaf mirror. The master bedroom, which is accessed though a lacquered paneled hallway, is a composition in blue and white, with a fanciful chandelier, a velvet headboard backed by white drapery, and blue and white–striped armchairs.

On the lower level, a games room is fitted out with an early-nineteenth-century drum table and chairs, with bookshelves backed in a graphic red-and-white wallpaper with a circular motif that seems to radiate energy into the room. The adjacent screening room is a seraglio of red, with authentic Art Deco sconces and an architectural motif from the period printed in gold on the scarlet fabric that envelops the room. Even the back stairs immediately signal that this is a house that is playful and lighthearted, with a vivid striped runner and treads carpeted in a range of blues and greens—plus one bright shot of red.

That relaxed atmosphere extends to the outdoor loggia, where comfy wicker seating gathers around an outdoor fireplace overlooking the pool, all of it surrounded by lush foliage and gleaming blue and lime green pots. Inside and out, it is a house that is laid-back but never dull, relaxed but energized by shots of colors and the client's abundant joie de vivre.

The entry hall is brightened by a custom skylight whose graphic lines are echoed by a light fixture found at JF Chen.
FOLLOWING PAGES: To give a relaxed feel to the living room, we installed colorful upholstered pieces and wall-to-wall bookcases backed with mirrors, transforming the space into a cozy library; photos of favorite writers hang on the bookcases.

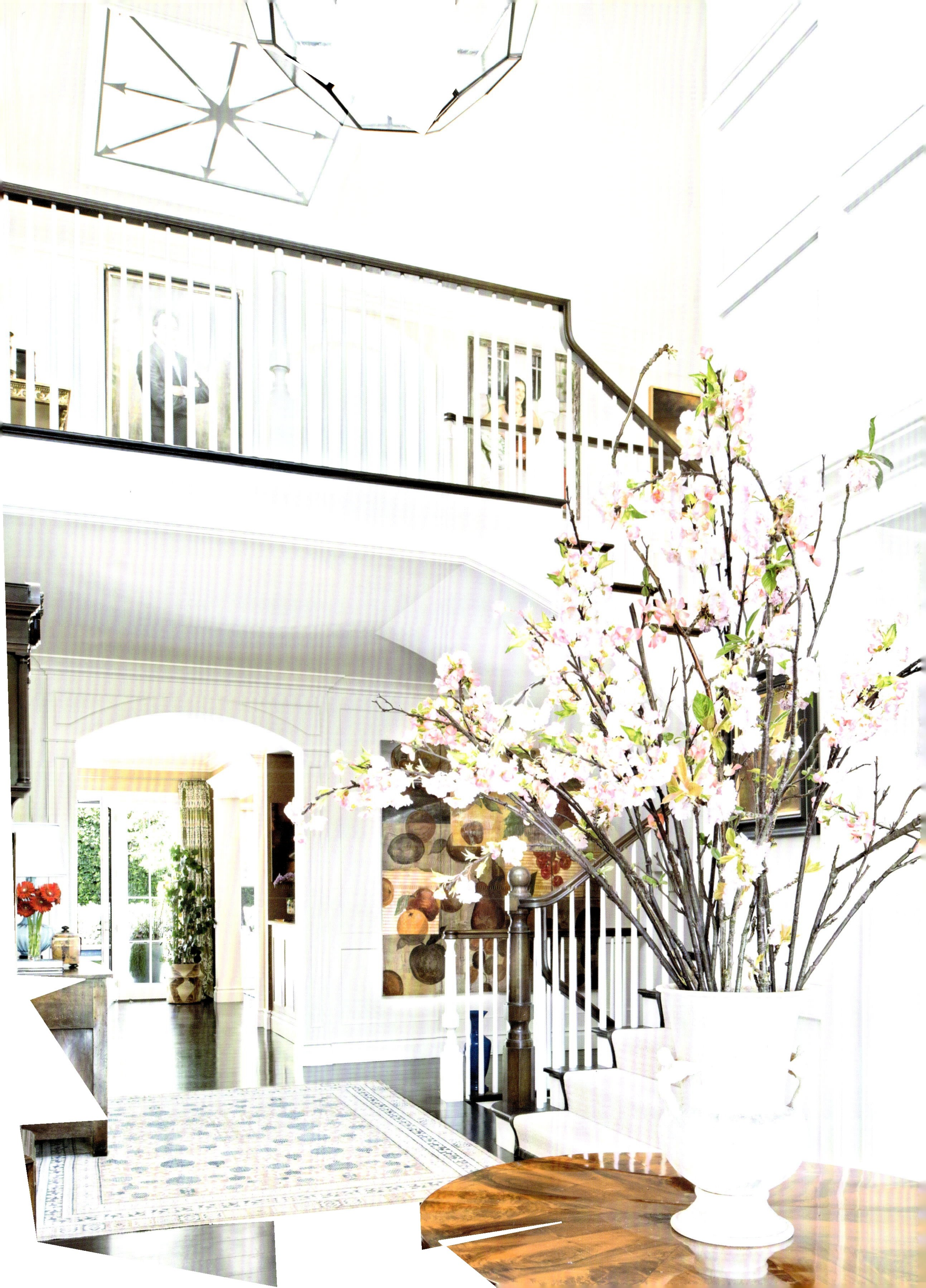

CENTUR
DELUXE ILLUSTRATED ATLAS OF THE WORLD
THE PLANETS
The Library
REZA WAR+PEACE
ART WORLD
American Stories

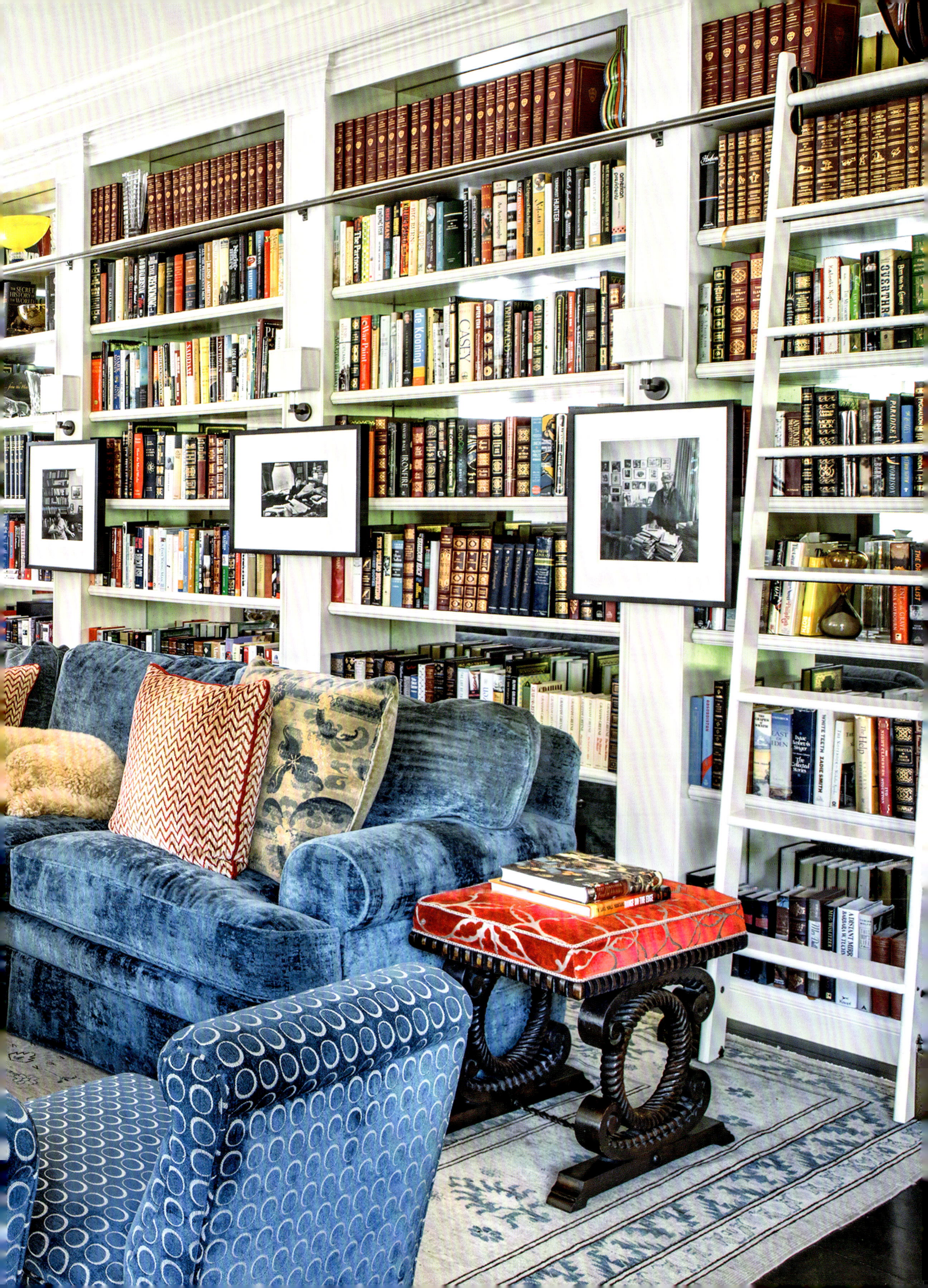

The strong colors of the dining room echo those of the entry gate and front door. The walls are covered in a strié wallcovering, the door is upholstered in leather, and the light fixture is by Fuse Lighting.

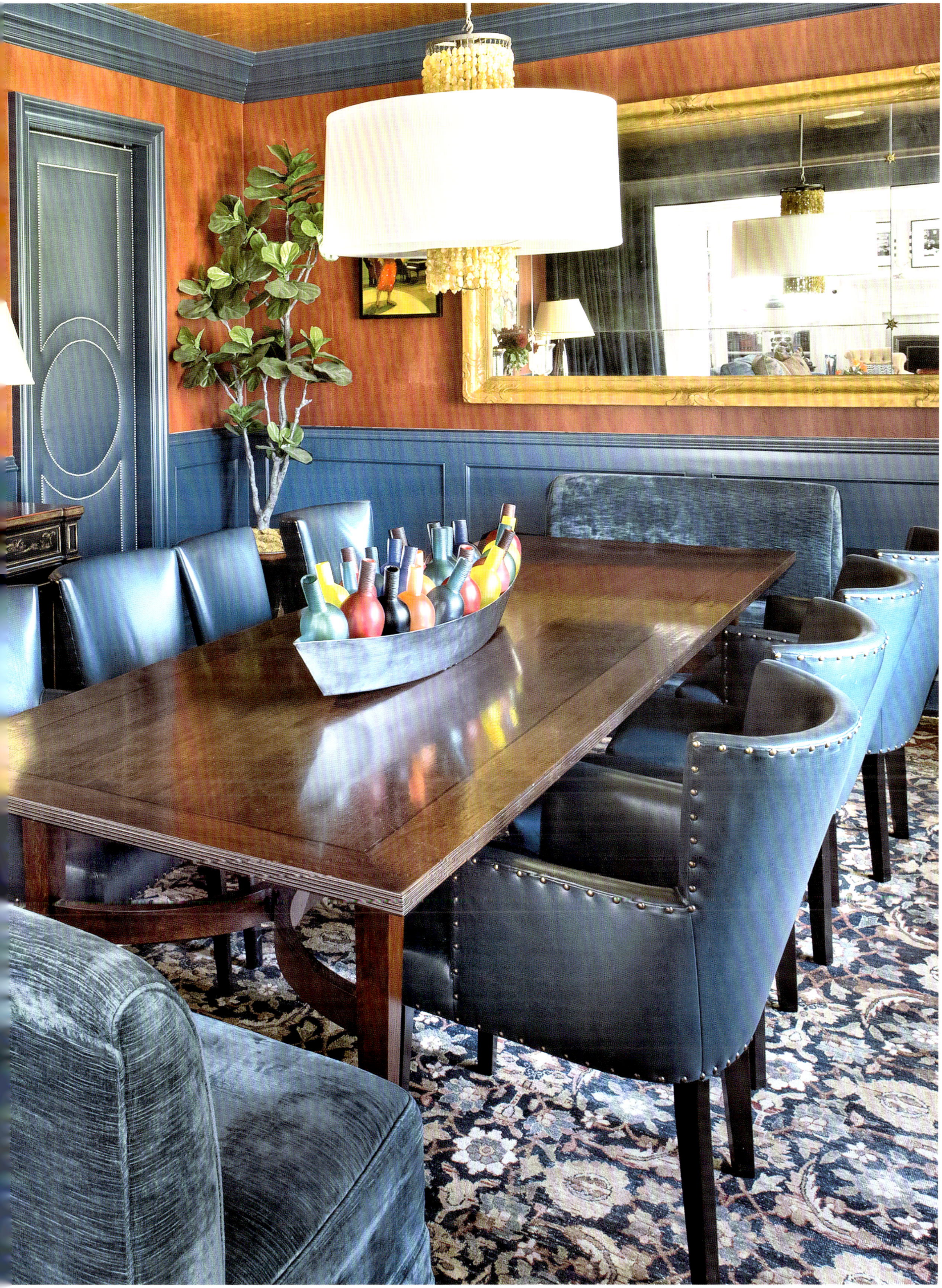

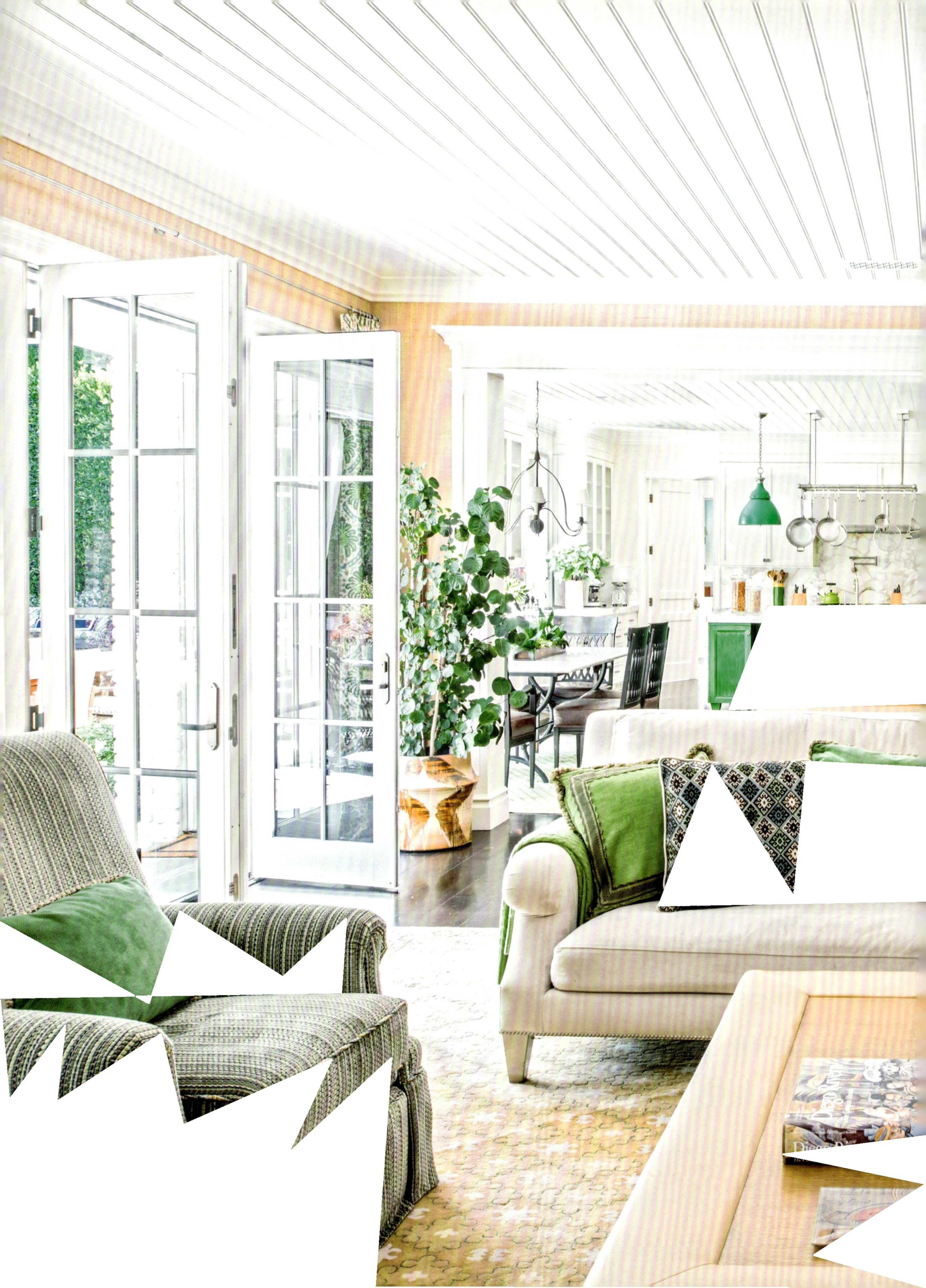

ALL ACCESS
LUXURY PRIVATE ISLANDS
FLOWERS CAROLYNE ROEHM
LEIBOVITZ AMERICAN MUSIC
VINTAGE FASHION COMPLETE

PREVIOUS PAGES: The family room leads to the kitchen and an outdoor living space. The sectional sofa is covered in an outdoor fabric, and the cocktail table is edged in a faux leather to encourage people to put up their feet. RIGHT: The kitchen island is topped with marble and painted a vivid green to link it to the garden just outside; the matching pendant lights are from Ann-Morris.

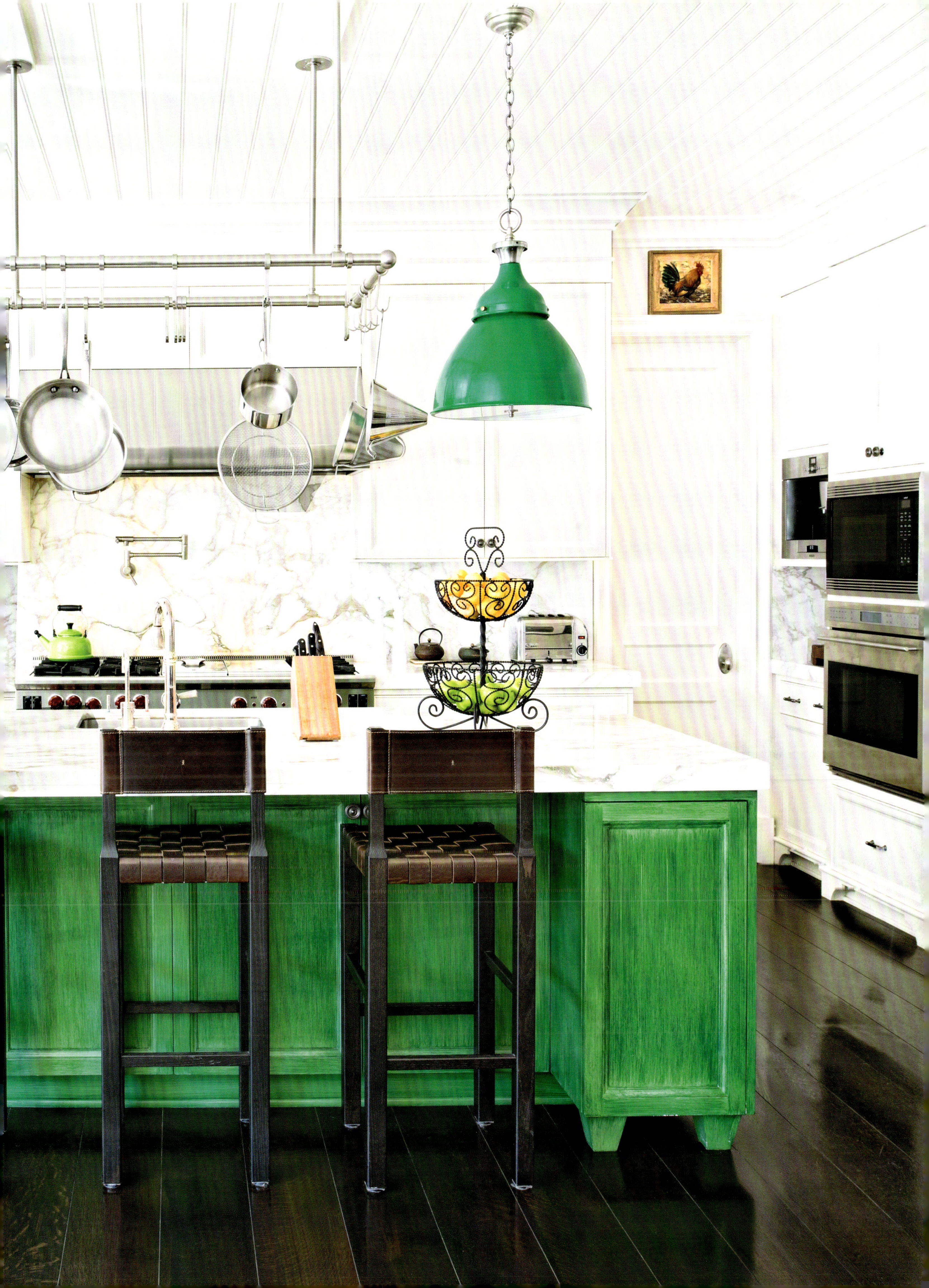

ABOVE: The back stairs are carpeted in a playful runner that unites the three primary colors of the house. RIGHT: The daughter's bedroom contrasts white with emerald green. OPPOSITE: We chose a strong blue as the accent color in the master bedroom; the chandelier is by Formations.

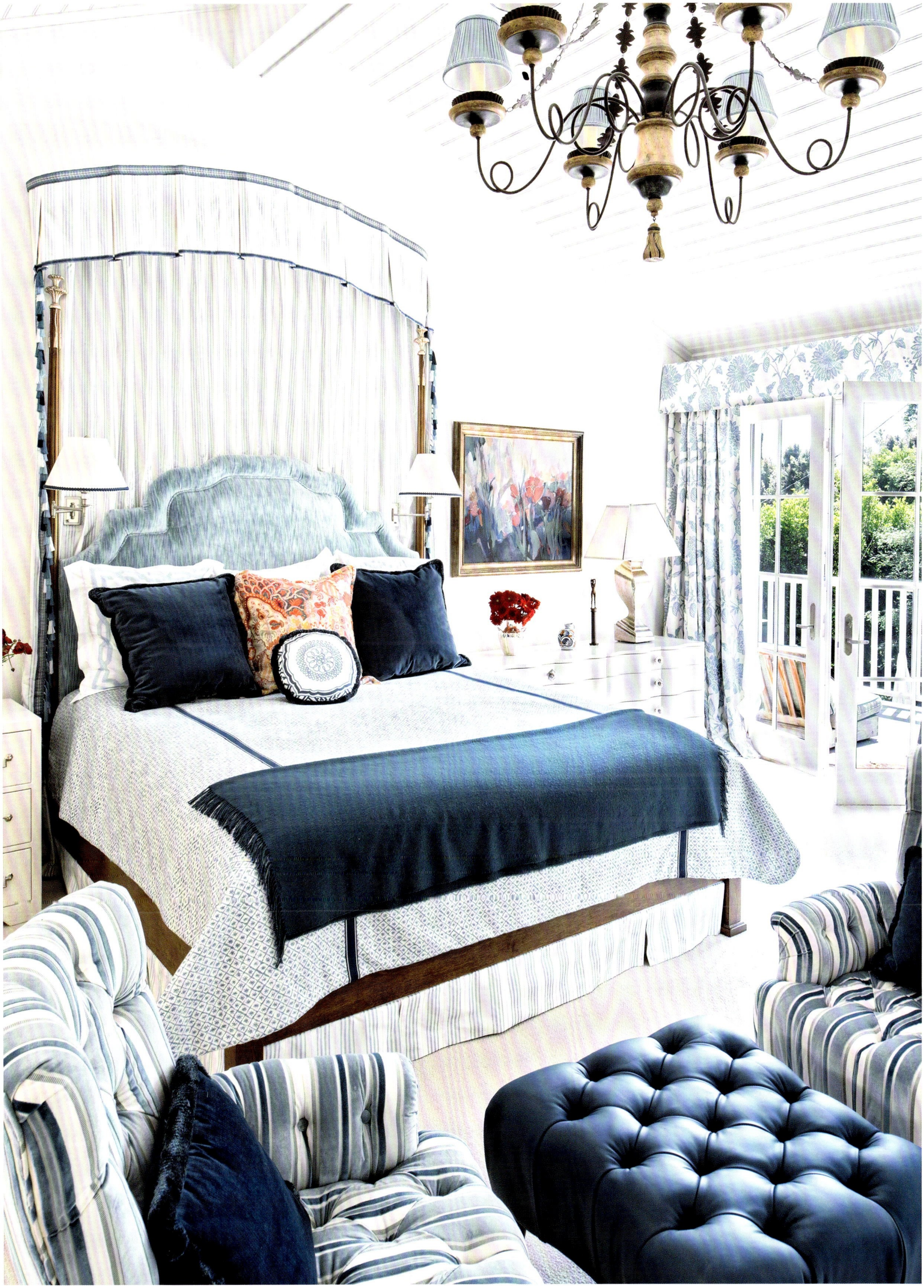

The outdoor space off the kitchen and family room reiterates the green-and-blue palette; Balinese dancing figures strung on wires preside over the scene.

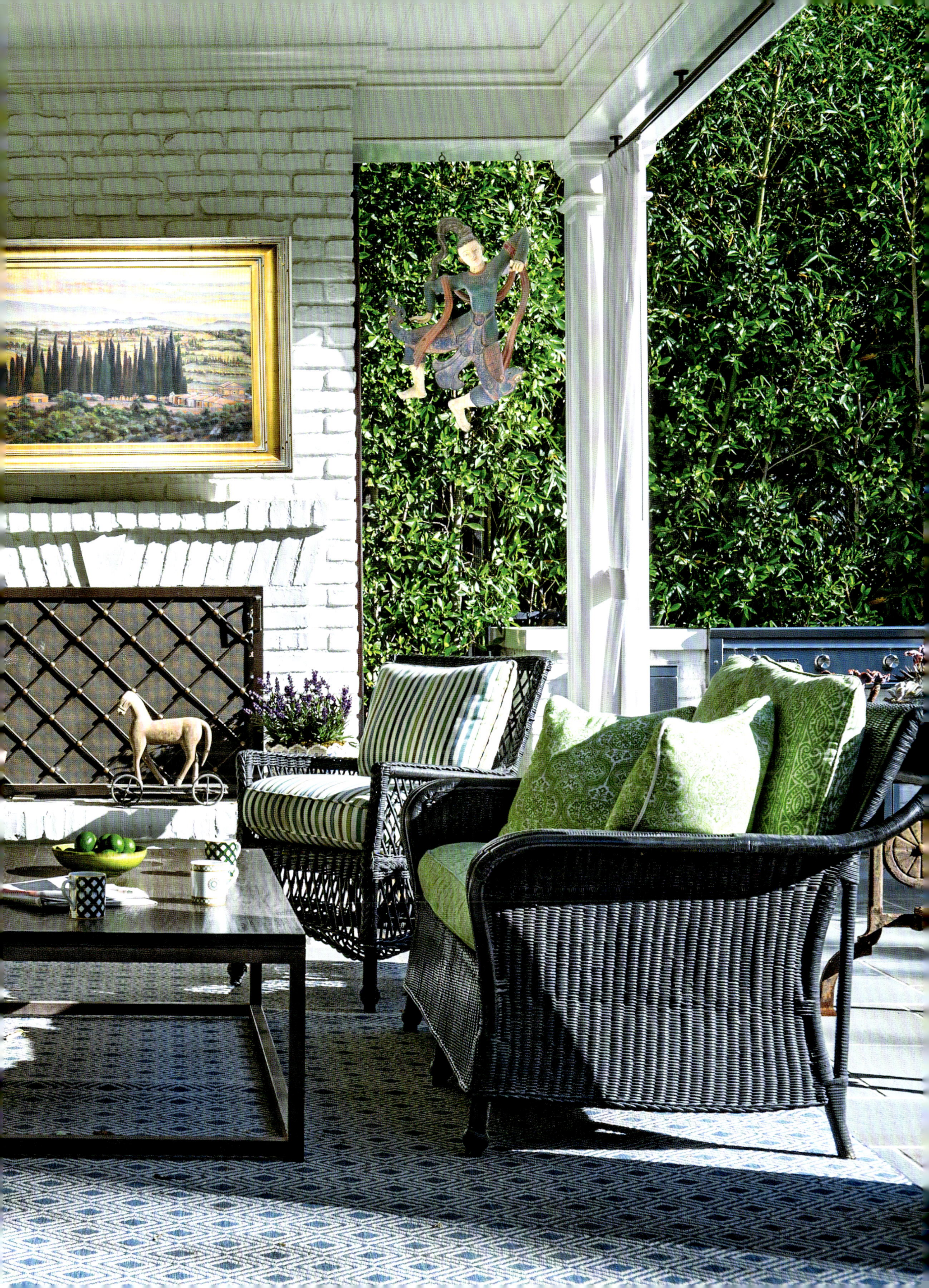

INTERLUDE
THE POWER OF COLOR

Color is one of the most powerful tools a designer possesses, because it literally has the ability to influence moods and thoughts. For example, red raises a room's energy, yellow communicates sunshine and happiness, and green has a calming and restful effect. Color will also influence the way we perceive the shape and size of furnishings within a room and even the room itself. Light colors are perceived as airy and expansive and make rooms seem larger; dark colors feel intimate and cozy.

Because it is so powerful, color can also be easily misused—or overused. For example, while red is energizing, it has been shown to increase heart rate and raise blood pressure. So you probably wouldn't want to use it in a bedroom. While yellow equates with sunniness, too much of it seems to increase frustration and anger. People lose their tempers more often in yellow rooms, and babies cry more.

Whatever color you choose will be affected by light—natural and artificial. Colors change depending on the light, sometimes drastically. Gray can appear blue; cream can turn gray or yellow. Light in a city is far different from that at the seashore, and sunlight in the country takes on a different cast than in the city due to all the greenery. Electric light can vary drastically from warm to cool depending on the choice of bulb, and there are numerous kinds now on the market. So always try to look at color samples in a variety of lights, throughout the day and in the evening, before choosing.

Whichever palette you select, try to limit colors within a room to no more than three or four—too many can make a room seem crowded and chaotic. By using different shades and values of those colors, you can create all the variation you need to make sure that a room is rich and engaging.

1

In a traditional, heavily paneled, and somewhat dark entry hall in Los Angeles, I used bold, saturated colors to add youthful energy including shocking pink curtains and a wallpaper by Fromental with vivid blues and pinks. The unexpected color range immediately signals that this is a house for today, and that its mood is upbeat and positive.

2

This room in a Beverly Hills mansion opens to the pool, and we wanted to reiterate the connection to the outdoors and give the space the feel of a country-club cabana, so we chose a range of greens and used outdoor fabrics to make the space relaxing and low-maintenance. The carpet is actually Astroturf, and the leafy wallpaper plays up the garden feel.

3

We traditionally think of certain colors as feminine—pinks, pale peaches—and others as more masculine—deep blues, browns. For this lady's bedroom in Hancock Park, we wanted to break the mold, contrasting bright spring green with a rich pink, all against a pale green wall to create a room that is undeniably feminine, but brighter and more playful than might be expected.

4

This is clearly not your grandfather's billiards room, and it is color that makes that immediately apparent. We replaced the traditional green felt of the pool table with a shocking pink and then reiterated that color throughout, in the leather on the chairs, in the bubble-wand light fixture, and, most amusingly, in the deep fringe of the pendants. But the gray carpet and walls, the aggressive angularity of the chairs, and the strong classical features of the room ensure that in this case, pink is a masculine hue.

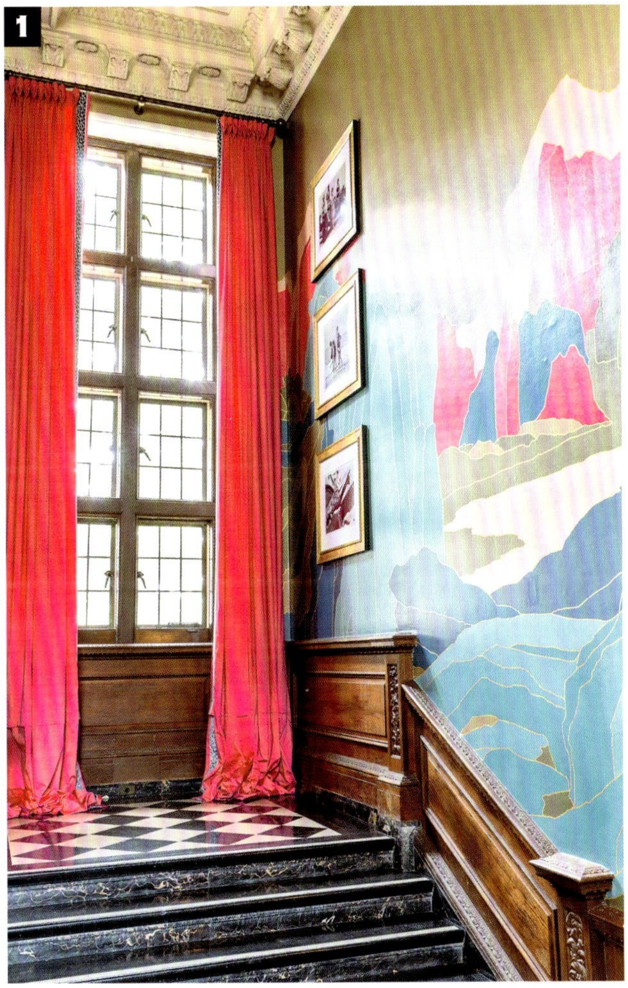
1

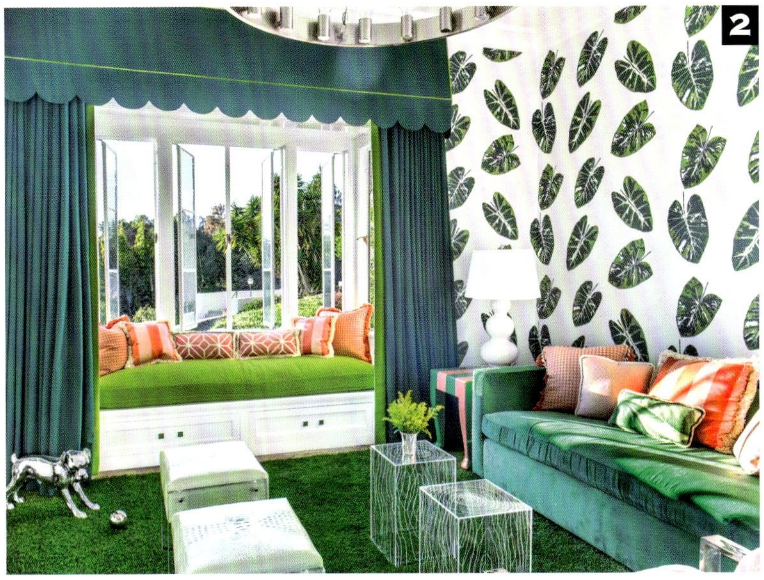
2

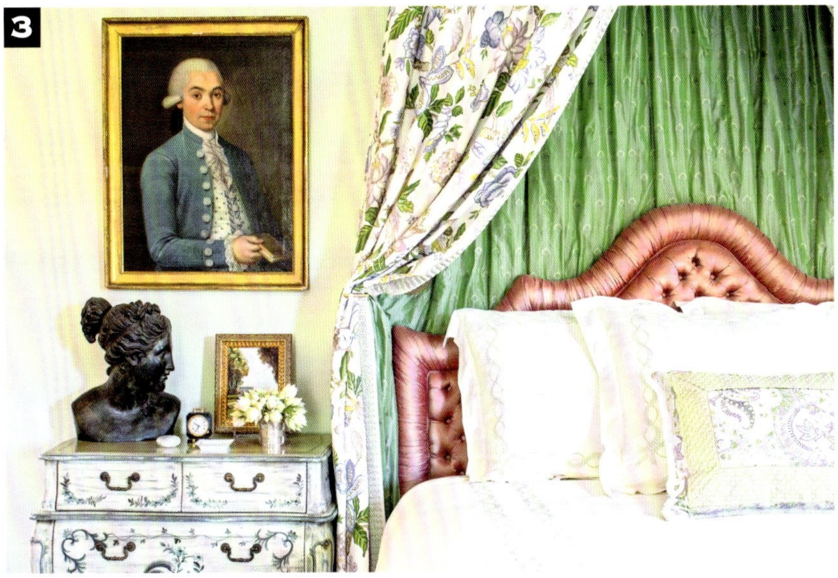
3

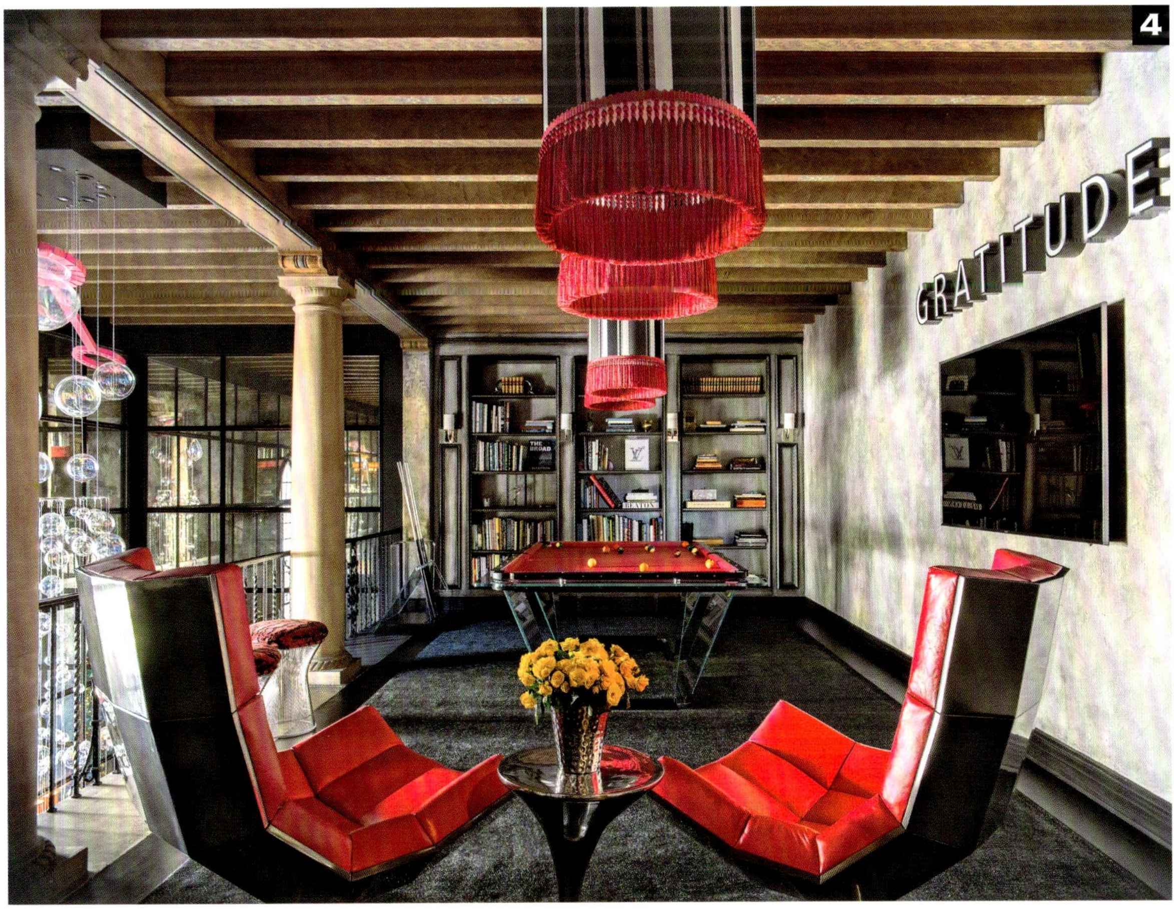
4
GRATITUDE

5

No color combination is more classic than blue and white, and its appeal is global, as the popularity of Chinese porcelains and Delft tiles proves. The pairing is (almost) fail-safe and always appealing, works in both urban and seaside settings, and can evoke all-American energy, Asian exoticism, or French formality and elegance. Here in this living room, two of my fabrics for Schumacher are used to create a modern take on the combination, Mandeville on the walls, and Huntington Gardens for the curtains and skirted table. Tried and true combinations (black and white is another) are popular for a reason—they work in so many situations.

6

Small spaces can be ideal for bold colors. The less time you spend in a room, the more over-the-top and colorful it can be. This tiny powder room is in a house near the beach, so we wanted it to feel sunny and bright, despite the fact that it had no windows. So it was the perfect place to use this chartreuse-and-dark brown wallpaper. A pattern and color as bold as these are difficult to work with in a larger space, but here they provide drama, glamour, and interest and provoke a response the moment you step through the door.

7

In this room, we contrasted two shades of gray on the dado paneling and door with a vivid red-orange. The upper wall is covered in wallpaper, and the settee is upholstered in damask. Gray is such a strong neutral that it can offset these bold colors. I didn't want to use the same shade on the walls and settee, because any place that contains too much matching color or pattern soon becomes dead to the eye. The variations in the color also create the sense that the space evolved over time and give it a more nuanced effect.

8

Often, the most unexpected color combinations prove the most interesting and inspiring. We wanted to bring new interest to a classical room, so we contrasted the walls, which were painted celadon, with intense burnt-orange curtains and bed draperies. Unexpected colors in traditional rooms immediately make them seem more approachable and more modern. Just as it is desirable to mix midcentury furnishings with antiques or contrast old master paintings with contemporary artworks, unusual color combinations bring a fresh perspective to the past.

171

Packing a Punch

Los Angeles is a city of dreams and fantasies, a place that has incubated elaborate visions ranging from Walt Disney's *Fantasia* to James Cameron's *Avatar*. It is a city that rewards unfettered imagination and freewheeling daring, and it is full of creative people—actors, musicians, directors, stylists, and set and costume designers—who are encouraged to dream big and bring their wildest visions to fruition.

Except, as the clients who commissioned this project pointed out, when it comes to interior design. The vast majority of homes in the city are somewhat conventional and safe, pretty but predictable, and that is the last thing these clients were interested in. They challenged me to make this house a canvas for creativity at its most unbridled, to unleash my, and their, most outlandish impulses.

And this 1922 mansion in Beverly Hills was no small canvas. One of the largest private estates in the city, it sits high above Sunset Boulevard, with expansive gardens and sweeping views of L.A. below. The house was designed by one of California's leading architects of the time, Gordon Kaufmann, who mixed Spanish Revival elements with the glamour of Art Deco—all on a very grand scale.

The idea here was not to play up traditional grandeur, but to undercut it. We wanted to acknowledge the traditional elements of a grand mansion, while simultaneously endowing them with humor and surprise. Yes, the entry has marble floors, but here the marble is polka-dotted rather than the conventional squares or rectangles; inset within the floor are circles of glass that allow you to peer down to the room below. A dramatic chandelier hangs down the center of the sweeping iron staircase, with a cascade of glass "bubbles" that appear to be emerging from a giant pink bubble wand, evoking a favorite moment of everyone's childhood. The adjacent grand hall of mirrors is lined with a custom-made runner that conjures an Argentine moss garden, overhead crystal light fixtures are alight with multicolored butterflies, and leather-wrapped torchieres light the way.

In the living room I was again inspired by Josep Maria Sert, but here the silvery architectural murals are offset with renderings of peacocks, and the room itself is a sea of peacock blue, including a custom carpet and a central pouf upholstered in velvet and sporting a gleaming chrome-and-cut rock crystal sculpture of a floral bouquet. Yes, there is a paneled library, but here it is a library of liquor, with refrigerated brass-fronted wine cabinets

To brighten the entry of a historic Los Angeles estate, we worked with the architectural firm Poon Design to remove a wall and flood the three-story space with light. The custom bubble light fixture extends the full length and is topped with a pink bubble wand.

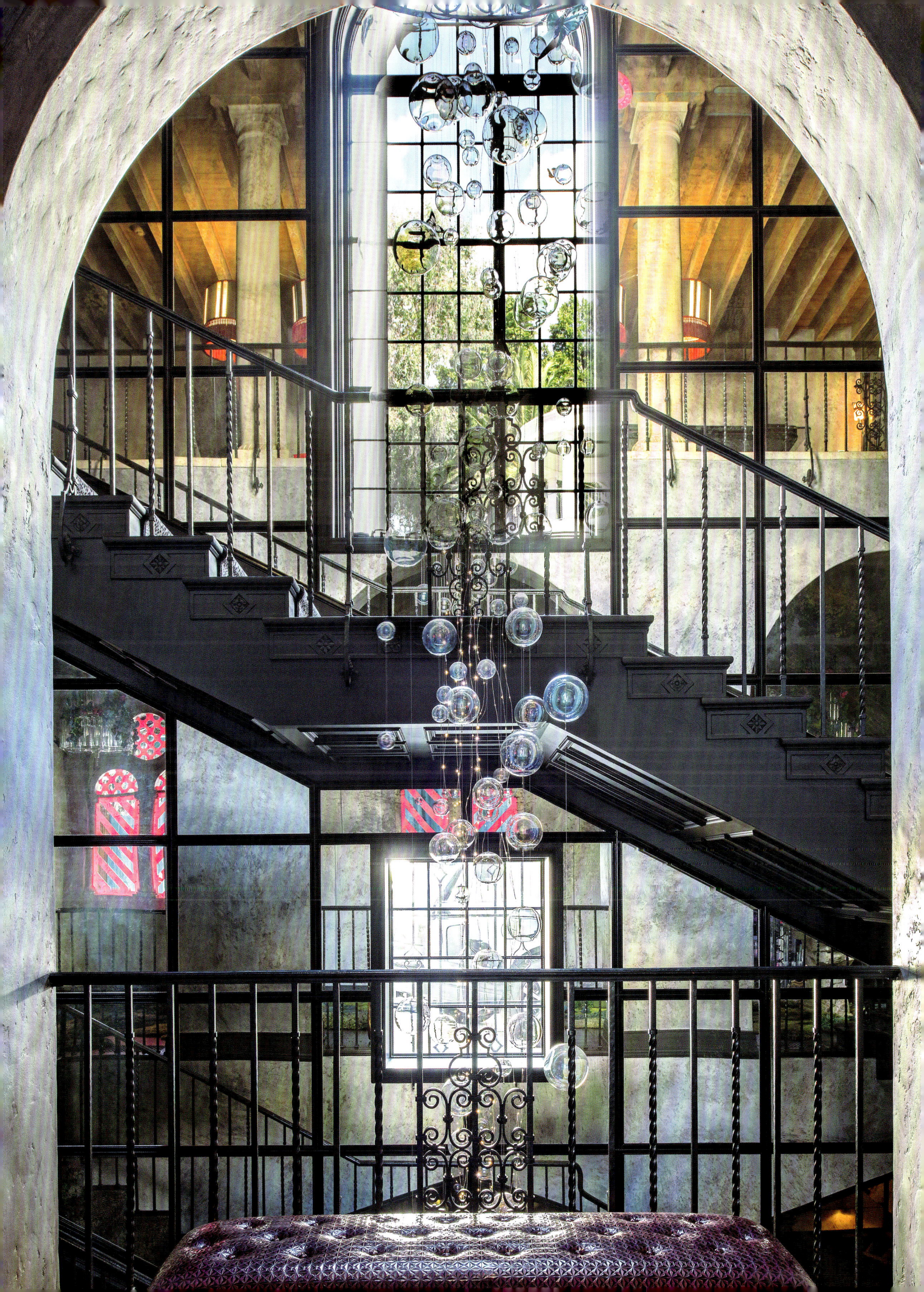

rather than books, the traditional wood paneling inset with dramatic tortoiseshell. In the center stands a sunken bar, illuminated from within. The original plaster ceiling, lacquered a glossy, reflective black, is the perfect showcase for the room's pièce de résistance: a superhero of glowing rock-crystal beads soaring overhead.

In the dining room, eighteenth-century Italian chairs surround a glass-topped table that sits on fanciful bases that appear to be wrapped in gold cord, and the walls are lacquered peacock blue and gold, with curtains embroidered in iridescent peacock colors and adorned with real feathers. The breakfast room is tented in fabric covered with actual leaves from South Africa, preserved in glycerin, so they remain soft to the touch and their lush green never fades. Coffee is served on a table of the same leaves under glass, but with a gold-leafed tree-trunk base, a reminder that this forest is nothing if not magical. The kitchen is dark and masculine, with gleaming black-lacquered cabinetry, ceiling arches of black tile contrasted with antique "charred" wood beams, and an enormous island with a zinc top. Even the game room surprises with a vibrant pink pool table rather than the expected green felt—with matching pink leather chairs, and even pink fringe on the light fixtures.

And this riotous creativity continues in the private spaces. The master bedroom suite contains a sitting area, where dark panels of wood are offset by gleaming chrome strips, and a printed and embossed paper by de Gournay makes the whole bedroom seem as if it has been enveloped in swags of rose velvet. An ornate gilded headboard is enclosed within a severe brass four-poster bed. The black-and-white master bath takes an almost cartoony play on classical motifs, invoking the classic Miami mansion Vizcaya, in Coconut Grove, with an oversize Greek-key frieze in marble, bold geometric flooring, a glass tub, and mirrors everywhere. The guest room features an elaborate crown over a Napoleon III daybed,

ABOVE: For the long central hall, we created a custom rug that evokes moss and grasses and installed a series of light fixtures bedecked with decorative elements evoking nature.
OPPOSITE: The formal living room is enveloped in real and faux draperies made of velvet, plaster, and trompe l'oeil painting; the rug is one of my designs for Patterson Flynn Martin.

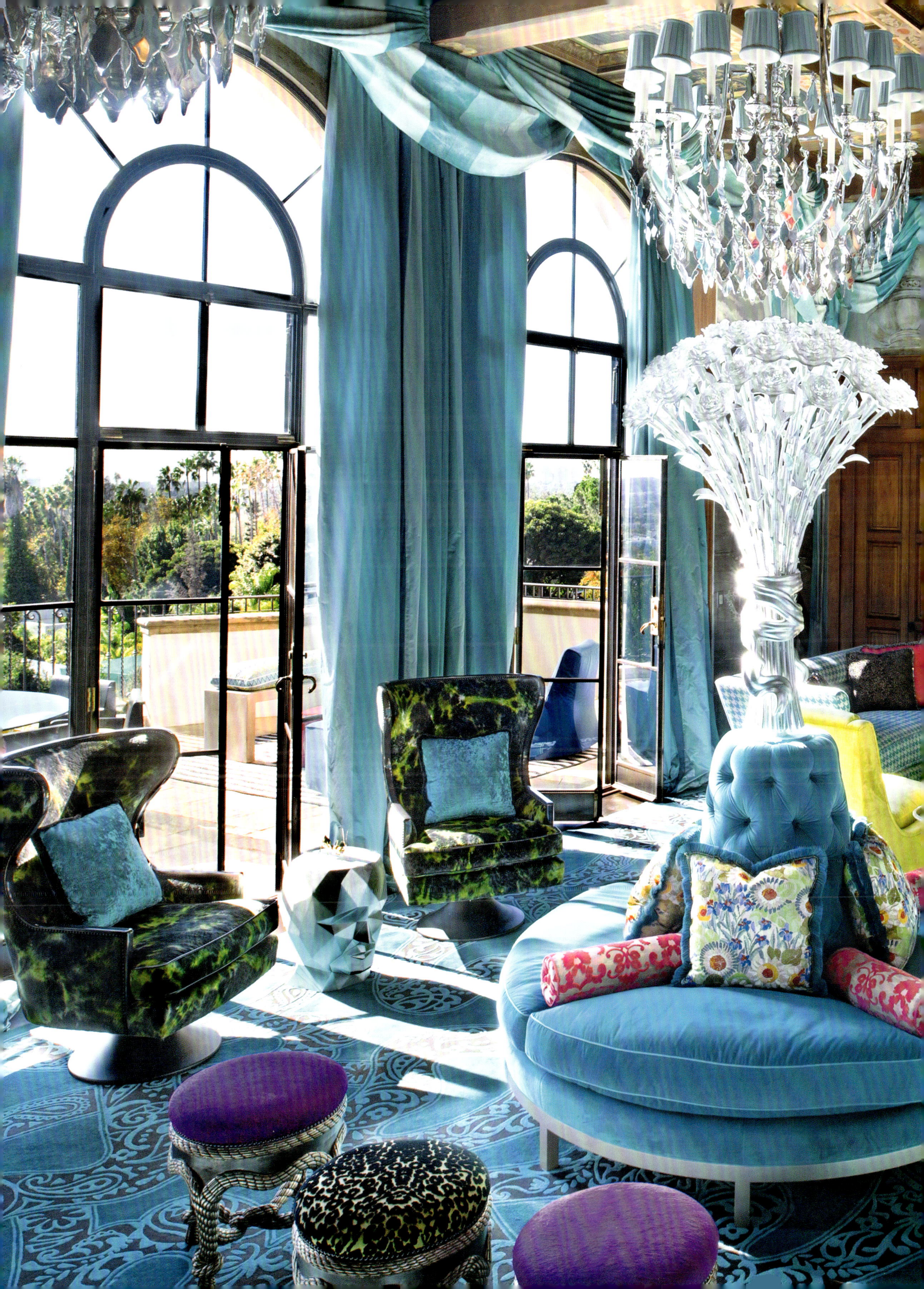

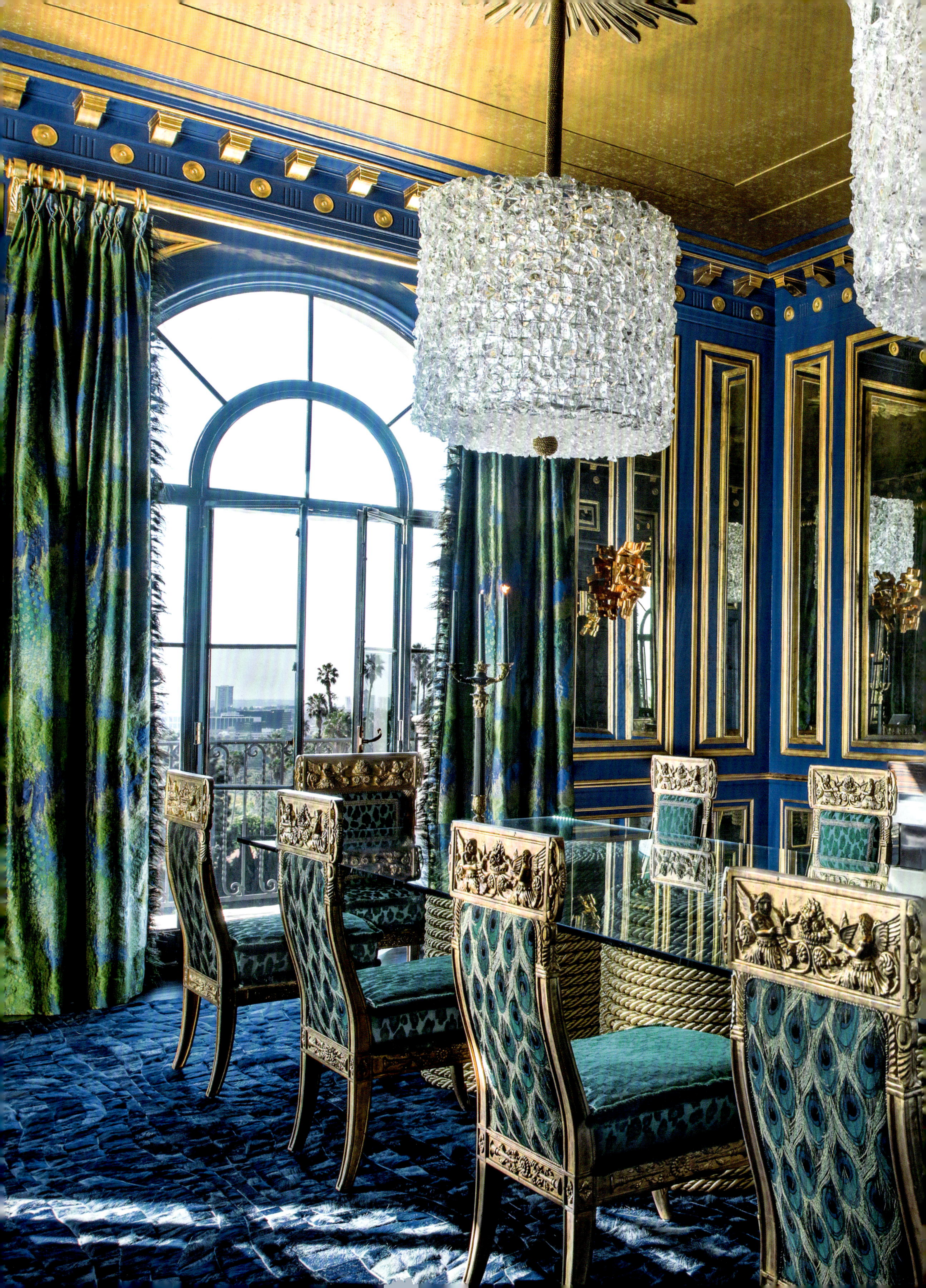

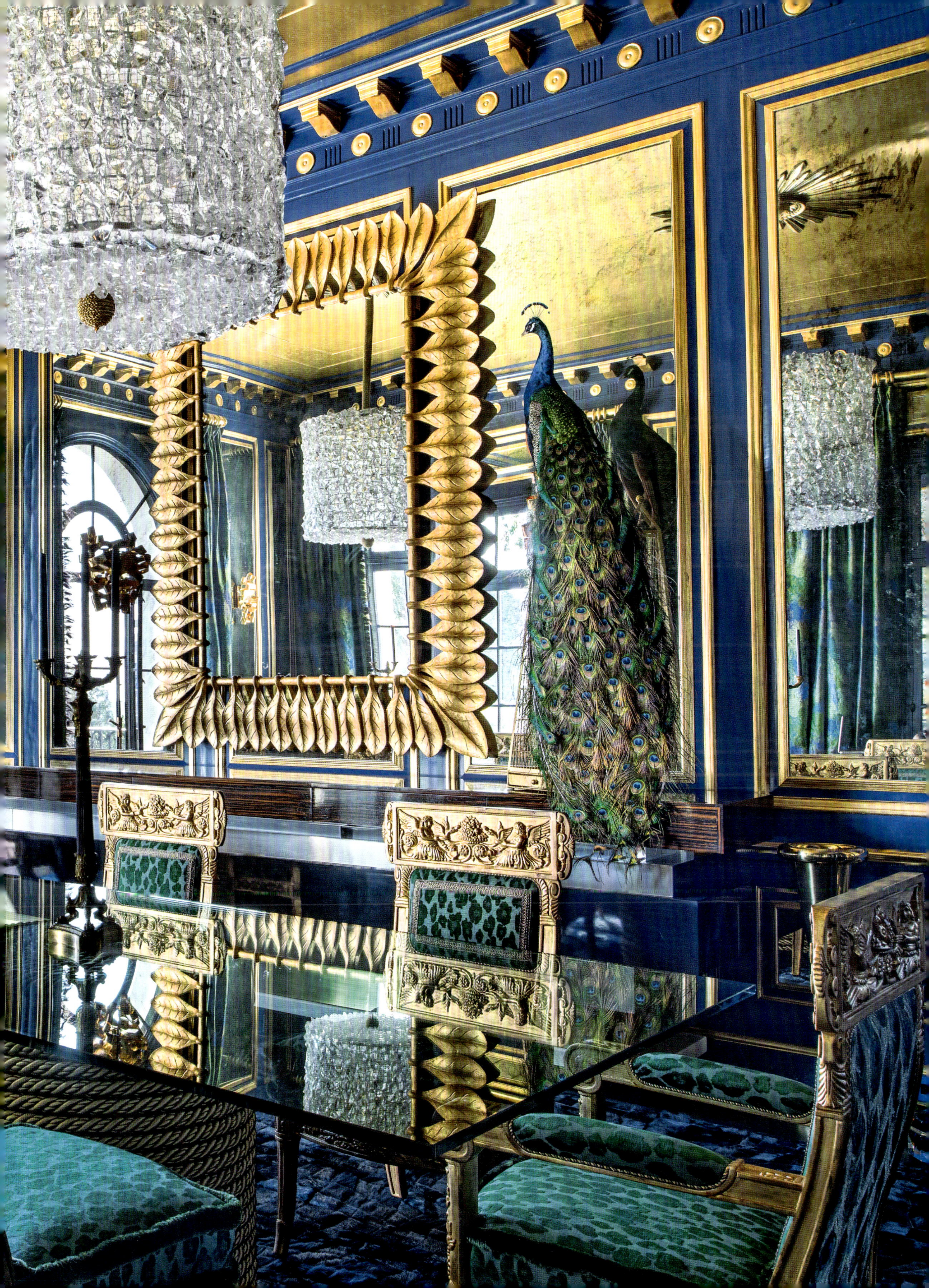

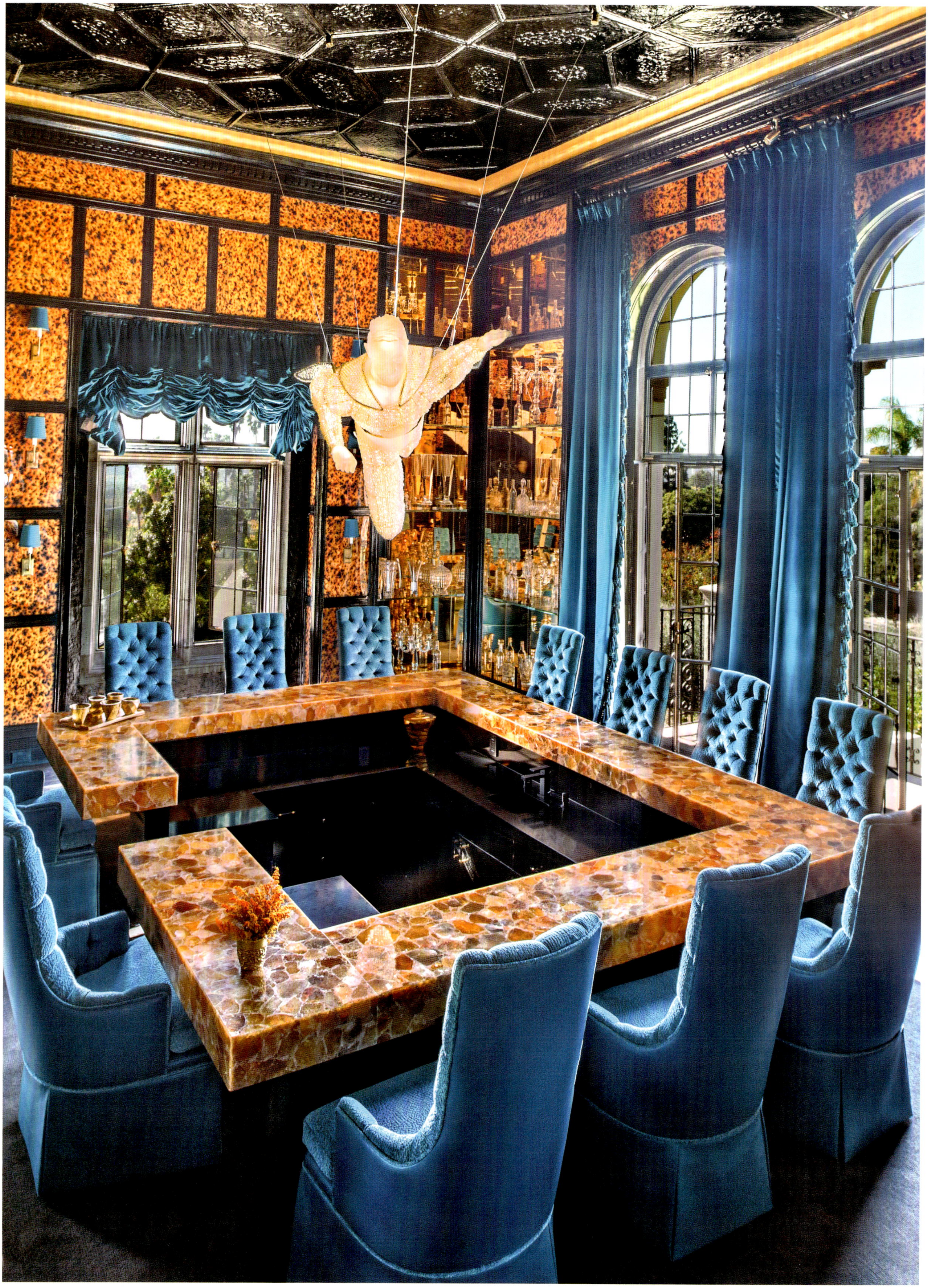

all surrounded by a wallpaper of budding trees and leaping gazelles, a reissue of a classic Art Deco pattern by Schumacher. Even the home office exhibits an offbeat flair, upholstered with lime green leather squares rather than the traditional paneling, with a bronze desk and animal print–covered guest chairs.

The attitude that inspired the decor may have been playful, but the attention to detail and the care with which we crafted each room never wavered—from the hologram wallpaper and Cubist mirror in a hallway to the room off one of the two swimming pools, which is carpeted in faux turf and where the playful window treatments evoke the awnings at 1950s country clubs.

The house is theatrical, extravagant, and even a touch decadent. But it also functions for the clients and accommodates every need of daily life, from exuberant parties to teleconferences. The artifice is elaborate, but practicality never suffers. And as the clients requested, it is never boring or conventional. This house and these clients offered me the opportunity to run wild and indulge my—and their—wildest fantasies. And even in Los Angeles, that opportunity doesn't come often.

PREVIOUS PAGES: A peacock theme enriches the formal dining room, evident in the embroidered backs of the eighteenth-century Italian dining chairs and the curtains; the cowhide rug is by Kyle Bunting. OPPOSITE: What had been a library is now the liquor library, with walls of faux tortoiseshell created by artisans at Warner Brothers; the Superman figure flying overhead is made of rock crystal and crystals. ABOVE: The breakfast room curtains, and the ceiling and wallcovering, are made of real leaves preserved in glycerin; the chandelier is a custom design.

The master bedroom walls are covered in a custom Fromental wallpaper of velvet imprinted with a swag pattern, and the ceiling is covered in gold leaf. OPPOSITE: This master bath, one of two, was inspired by a bathroom at Vizcaya in Miami and is fitted out with a floor and wall panels of marble.

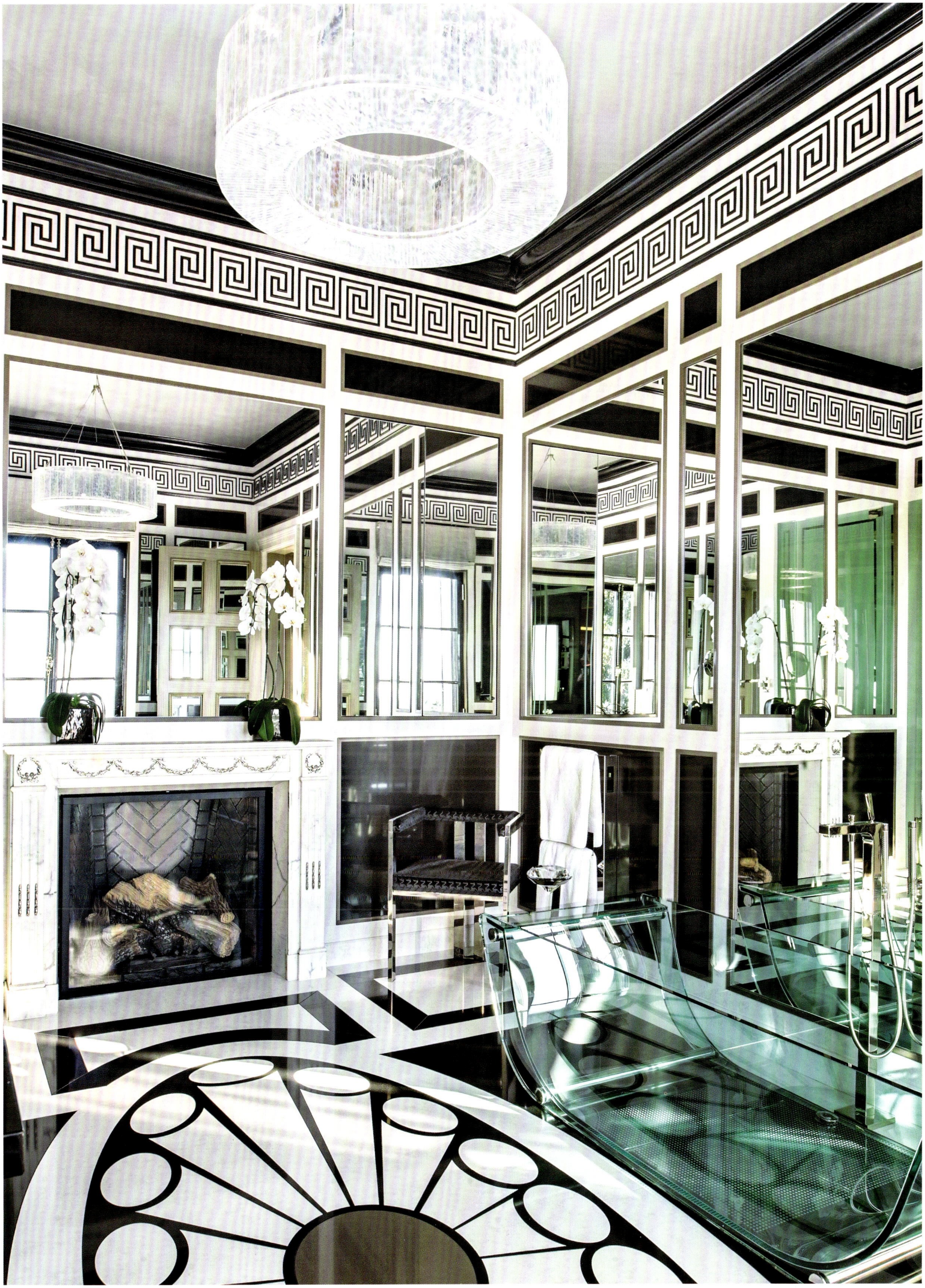

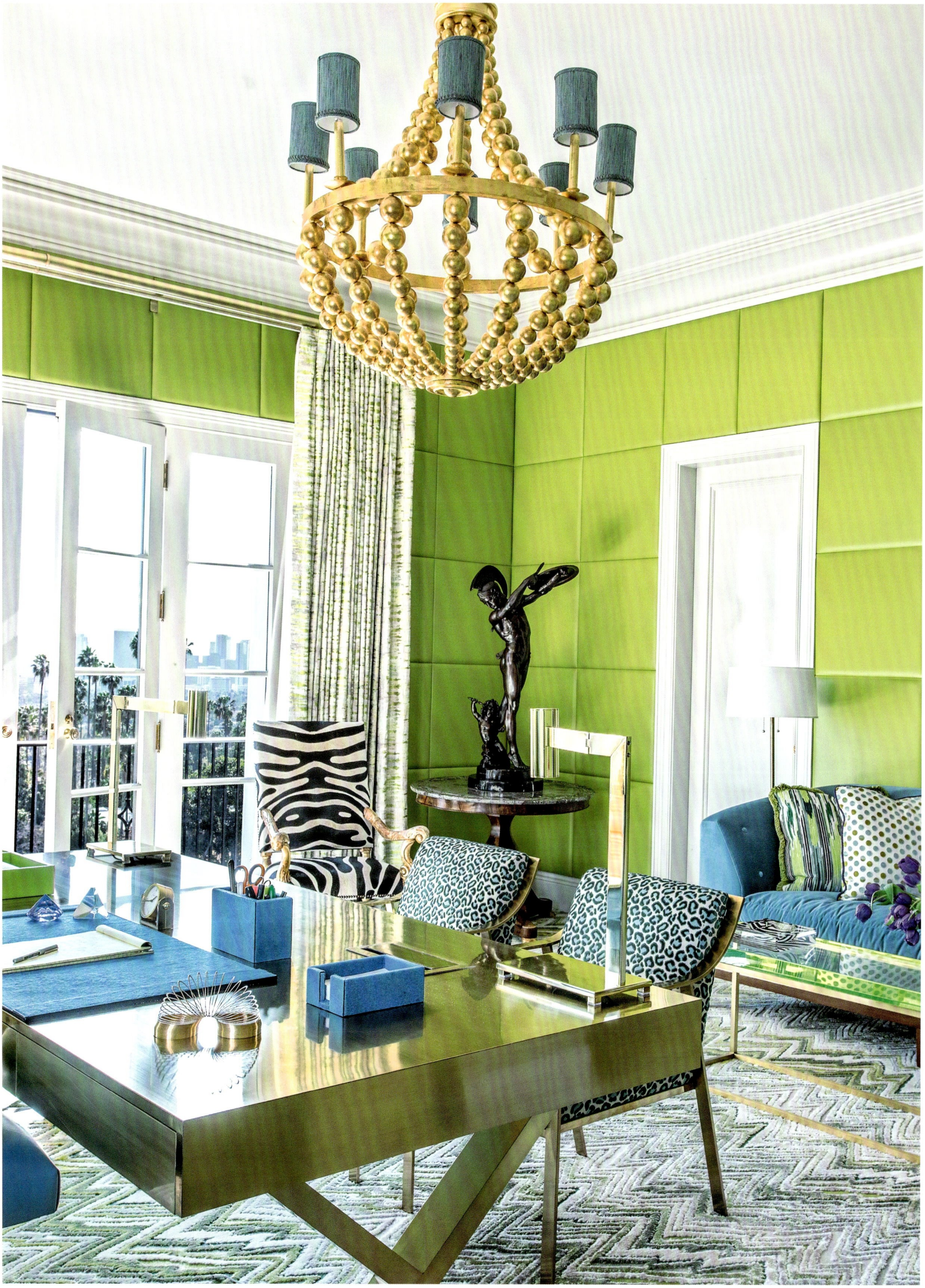

OPPOSITE: The walls of the study are paneled in a vibrant spring-green leather; the brass desk is a custom design.
ABOVE: In a guest room adjacent to the pool, outdoor fabrics are used on the walls, curtains, and upholstery. The rug is also suitable for the outdoors, making the room virtually indestructible.

A breezeway was enclosed to create the artist's atelier. The custom desk does double duty for both creating drawings and dealing with paperwork.

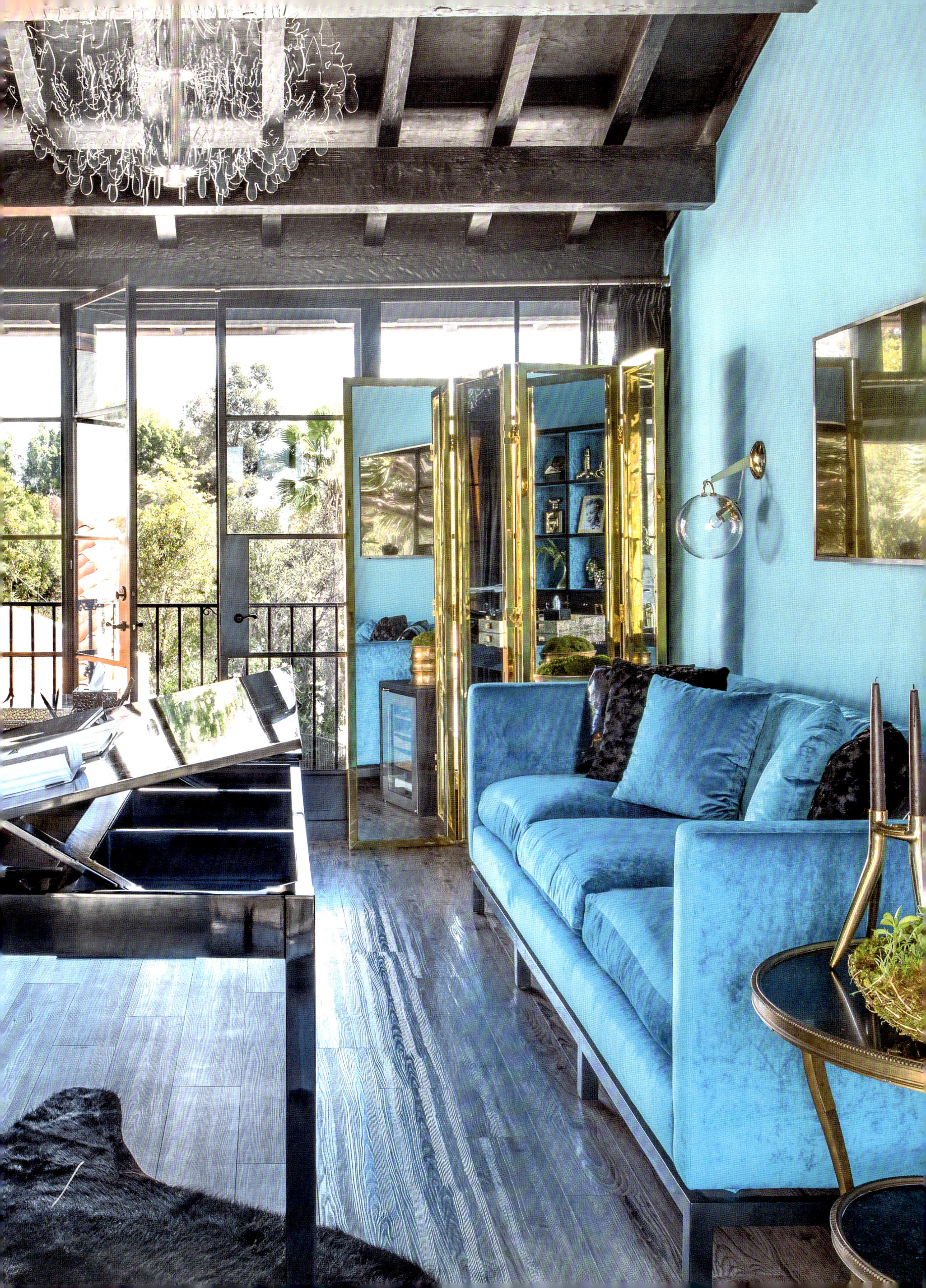

INTERLUDE
DRAMA AND SURPRISE

Where would we be without an occasional dose of drama and surprise in our lives? No one wants to lead a boring or routine existence. Stability is important, of course, but sometimes you need to break out of your routine, do the unexpected or unexplained, indulge in a bit of whimsy or humor, or make a grand gesture or two. The same is true for interiors. If a home is totally predictable, too consistent or one-note, it loses out on joy and spontaneity. At the same time, just as in our lives, too many surprises can be irritating and exhausting.

So how do you strike a balance? I always tell my clients that the three best places to go all out for drama are the entry hall, the powder room, and the dining room. What unites these disparate spaces is that they are all places that we tend to move through and not linger in, or, in the case of the dining room, spend at most a few hours. Unlike our living rooms or bedrooms, these are not the rooms we turn to for sanctuary or relaxation. Because our interactions with them are limited, they can be dramatic, colorful, exuberant, spectral, mysterious, or playful. Like spices in cooking, they add flavor and color to a home and make it far more appealing.

1

The lattice ironwork of this outdoor dining area evokes turn-of-the-century Paris, but it would only work in a climate as mild as that of Los Angeles, since there is no glass involved. But this folly is actually used often by its owners who love to entertain outdoors. The chandelier surrounded by wisteria adds another fanciful touch, and allows dinners to go on late into the night.

2

The hallway in this home in Beverly Hills was impressive but also rather awkward. It was a strongly vertical space—the ceilings are fifteen feet high—and the passageway between the windows and the stair railing was quite narrow. I designed a brightly colored rug of cowhide with strong diagonals that pull the eye to either side, making the floor seem wider. The classic bust of Nero is offset by two whimsical aluminum chairs upholstered in red leather that reiterate the bold color of the curtains, adding a bit of fun to this formal space.

3

The surprise in this home in Bel Air came about after the clients confessed that they never used their living room. The thought of a room sitting idle and unused made me ask, "What would inspire you to use it?" It turned out they were oenophiles and loved collecting wines and sharing them with friends and family. So I suggested we move their wine cellar to the living room. By installing walls of refrigerated wine storage encased in elegant woodwork, we turned an underutilized space into the hub of family life.

4

This grand Brentwood living room reveals its surprise at the touch of a button. A screen descends from the pelmet of the window on the right, covering the window seat. The chairs swivel and recline, making this the most comfortable place to see movies or binge-watch the latest hit series. The elegance of the room is never compromised, but it is now used for far more than just formal gatherings.

5

The dining room in this Hollywood Hills home was an awkward space with a pitched ceiling that had been added on, and doors were seemingly everywhere. My solution was to turn it into a magical Arabian-style tent. We hand-painted the fabric, draping it over the ceiling and edging it with a vivid green, a color we also used for the window frames. A mirrored table reflects the antique crystal chandelier that hangs overhead, and Art Deco sconces add another note of drama. The eighteenth-century Italian chairs are upholstered in a sumptuous velvet, and a matching green rug sports a bright orange border. Now when the owners sit down for dinner, they are guaranteed a couple of hours of magic.

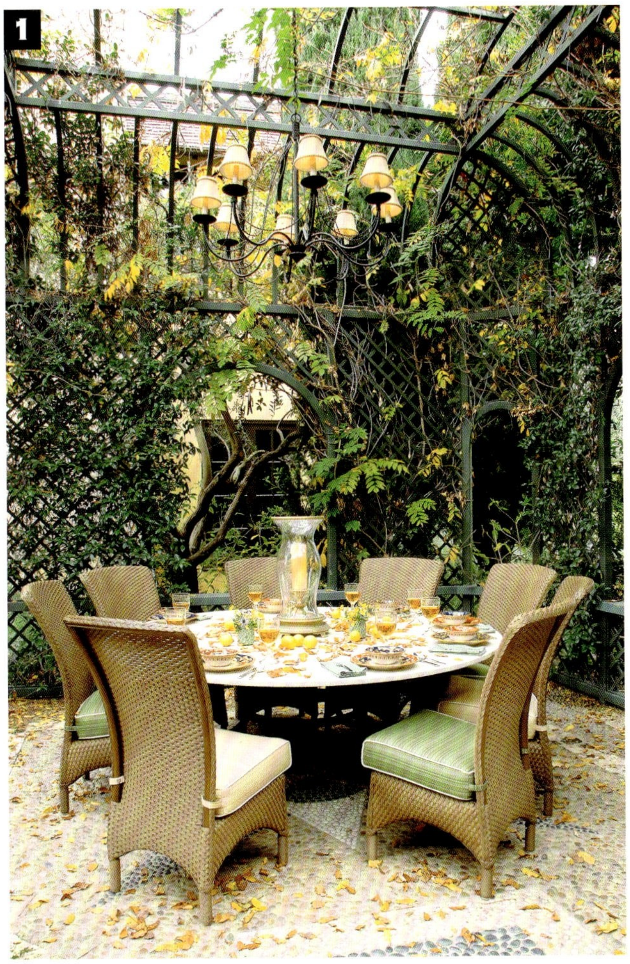
1

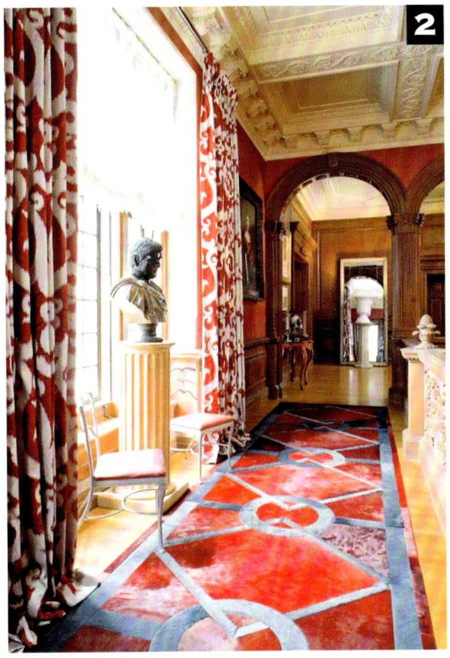
2

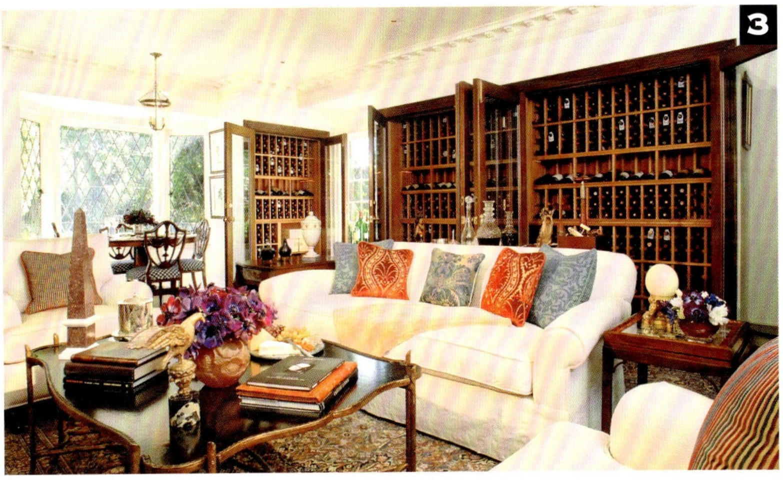
3

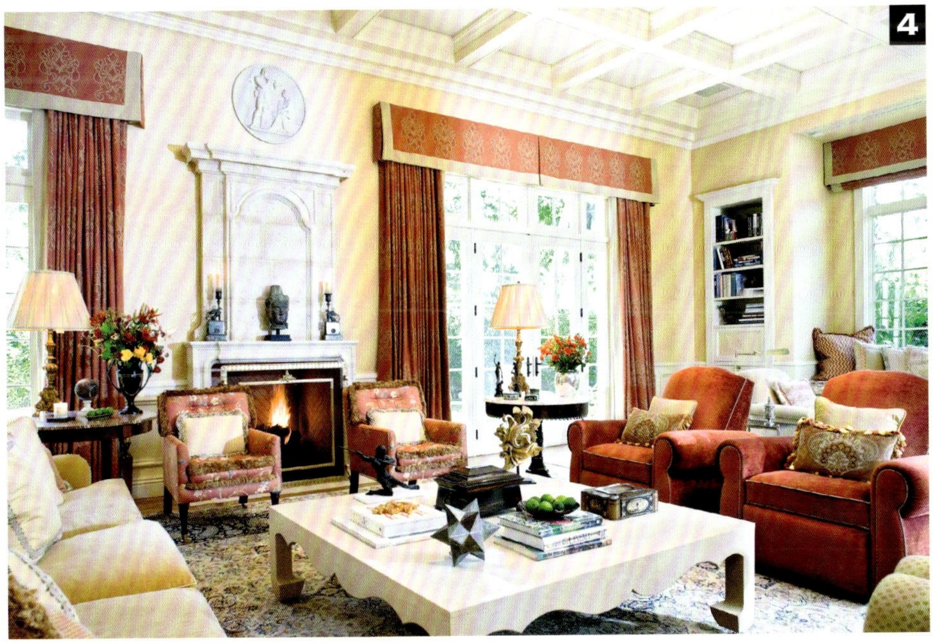
4

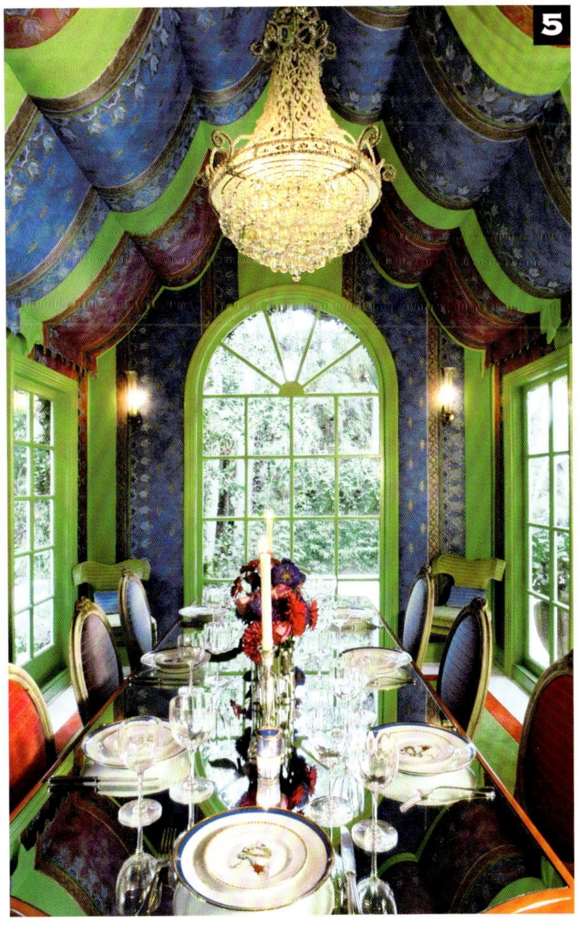
5

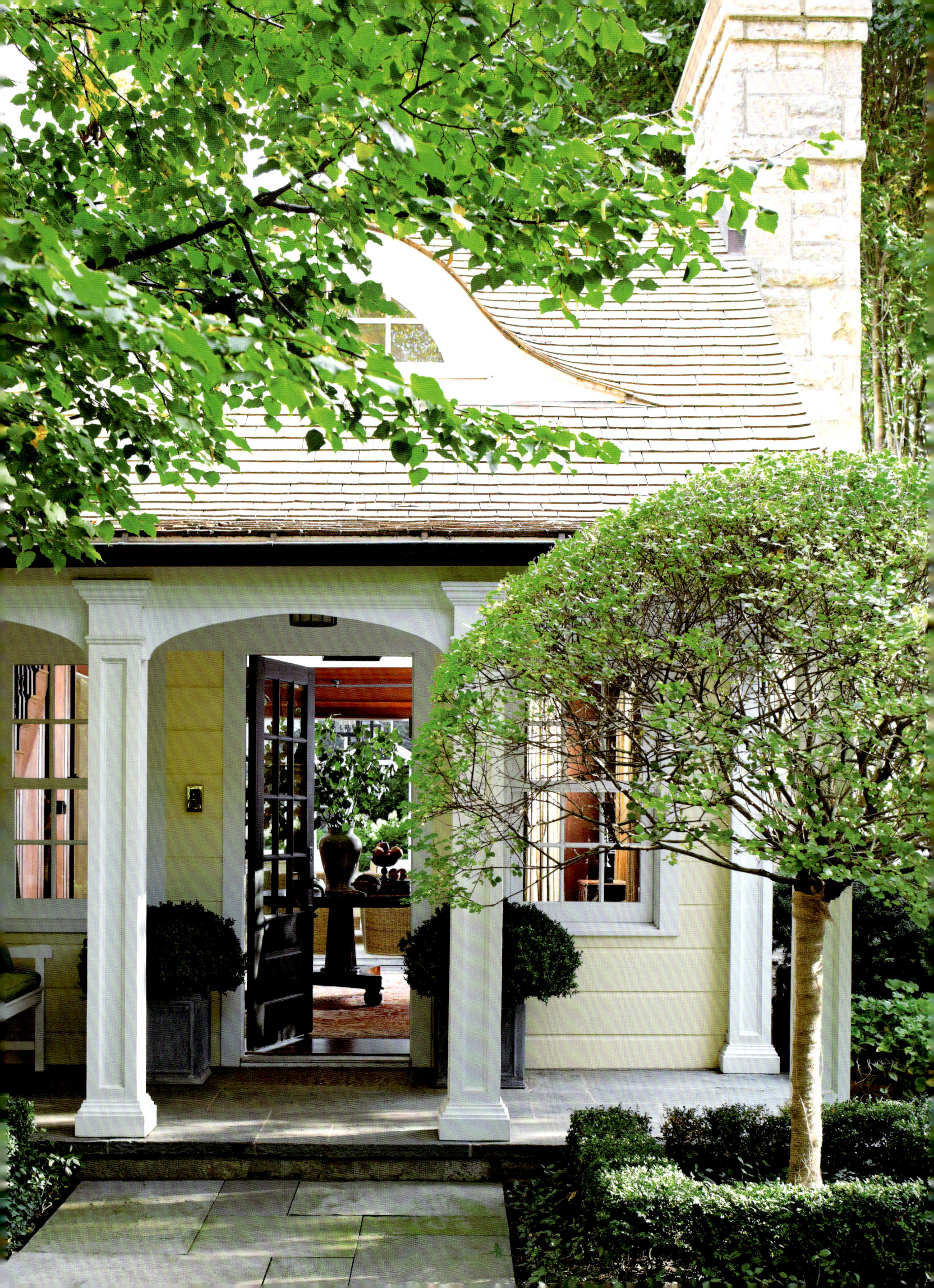

Country Cosmopolitan

In this age of the super house, of 40,000-square-foot mansions that incorporate everything from basketball courts to gift-wrapping rooms, there is something charming about a small house. Less can be more, especially if every element of the less is considered and curated.

For their weekend retreat in the Chicago suburb of Lake Forest, a couple who had been looking at classic David Adler estates finally decided instead on a gardener's cottage that had once served as part of a much larger property designed by the Arts and Crafts master architect Howard Van Doren Shaw (who gave Adler his first job). The cottage had been added onto over the years, but it was hardly large or sprawling. However, what the place lacked in size, it more than made up for in charm, with its fairy-tale gambrel roof and white-pillared exterior, gracious layout, and attached greenhouse. Plus, it had the advantage of being surrounded by expansive lawns and beautiful old trees.

This couple was willing to not only adapt to a different scale of living, but also adopt a different style as well. In the city, they lived in a large but spare contemporary home, with the kind of white-box rooms that they felt created an ideal backdrop for their extensive modern art collection. But in search of a weekend place where they could entertain their children and grandchildren, they embraced a softer style—hardly rustic, but certainly more eclectic than their urban abode.

They asked me to create a home for them that reflected the surrounding bucolic area and the age and period of the house, but also a place where their more contemporary artworks would be at home, since they could not imagine living without art. The challenge was to respect what was there yet add ease and modern elements. We decided we should retain the footprint of the house, but we changed how the rooms were used. This ended up making all the difference.

We transformed what had originally been the living room, right off the front door, into a gracious, double-height, skylighted entry by removing a bedroom that was situated immediately above it and installing wood paneling that gave it a warm and welcoming air. The living and dining rooms are essentially one large area divided by a pair of symmetrical columns. Both rooms were painted a creamy, warm white, and the array of comfortable upholstered furnishings recalls the classic ease of an English country house—but in a more edited and restrained way.

The dining room originally had a cabinet on one side of the central mantel, which I

We retained the look of a traditional country cottage at this weekend home in Lake Forest, Illinois, as a deliberate contrast to the sophistication within.

THE NEW ELEGANCE 189

wanted to replace with a bookcase and install its twin on the other side. However, I was stymied by the fact that the area to the right was too shallow to incorporate the full depth of a bookcase. But I realized that a bit of trompe l'oeil here would be worth the effort. We installed a narrow matching bookcase and then fitted it out with antique books that we had cut down by a third in depth. This is something I normally would never do, but none of the books were valuable, and the symmetrical effect was worth it. We then reiterated the classical feel of the room with klismos-style dining chairs by Michael Taylor.

We retained the warm pine paneling in the library, but removed the varnish and applied a colored French wax, so it serves as an effective backdrop to a suite of Frank Stella and Jasper Johns works. We opened the room up to the expansive kitchen and breakfast rooms, both of which feature simple white cabinetry, to create a kind of relaxed gathering place that serves the day-to-day needs of the couple and their family.

We placed the pool on axis with the greenhouse (and the entry hall beyond) and turned it into a sunny cabana, installing air-conditioning (to supplement its original hand-cranked vents) and laying down a heated granite floor. We fitted it out with wicker furnishings and easy-care outdoor fabrics and rugs, so that the room can be used year-round by everyone.

Upstairs the master bedroom is surrounded by windows on three sides and finished with warm beige and cream fabrics and subtle foliage-patterned drapes that reiterate the room's tree-house feel. A red alabaster fireplace surround that I found in Paris adds a touch of color to the room. The guest rooms are bedecked in numerous shades of white with contrasting accents of yellow, green, or tan, and all of them are hung with important artworks. The room that is a favorite of the clients' grandchildren features a Roy Lichtenstein screen print depicting a punch to the face and the words *POW!* and *SWEET DREAMS, BABY!*—proof that good art speaks to all ages and works in all kinds of settings.

ABOVE: The eighteenth-century armillary sphere in the side garden was found in Denmark. OPPOSITE: What had been the living room was transformed into a spacious entry hall; the light fixture is by Formations, and the rug is a nineteenth-century Serapi.

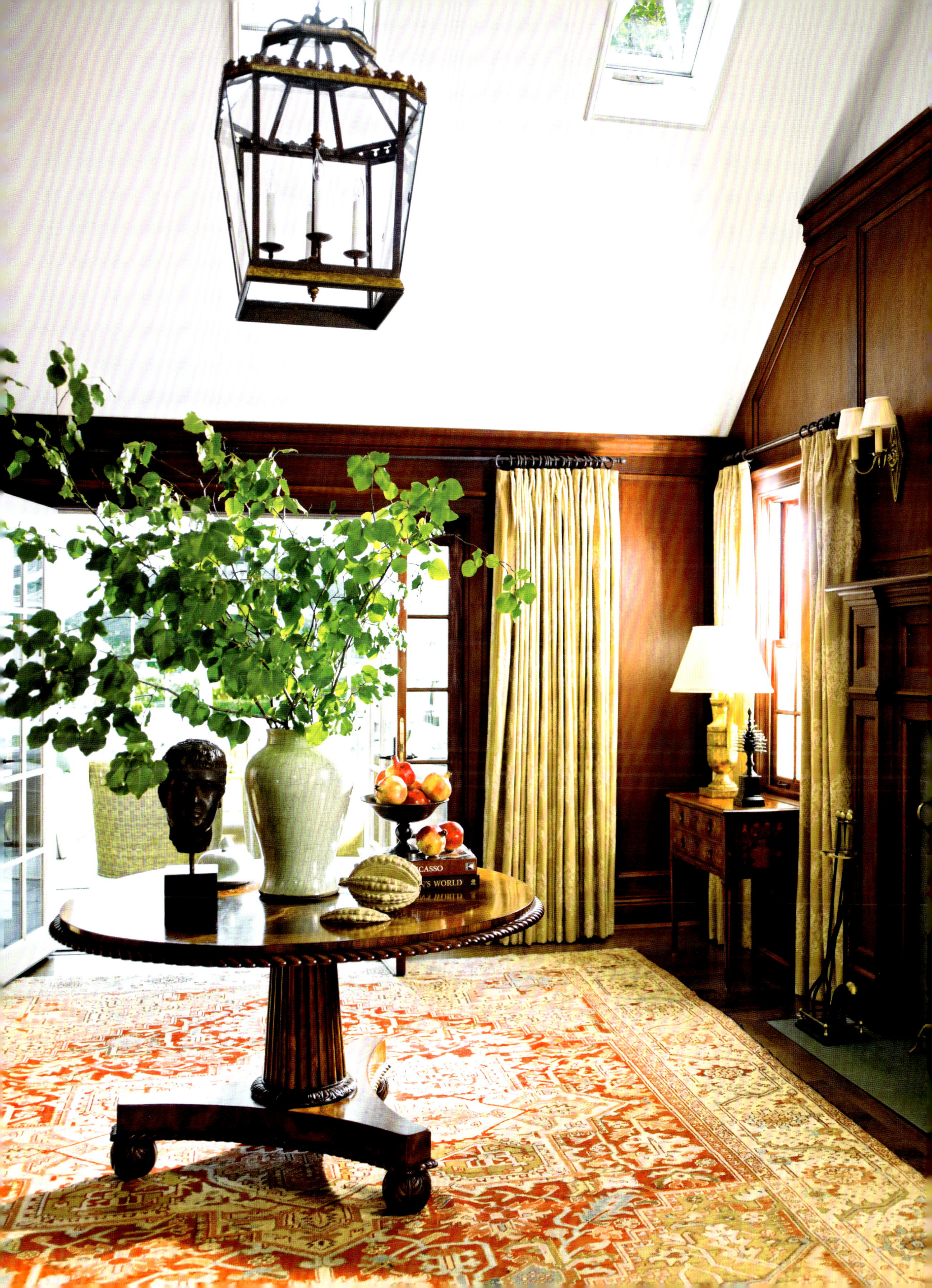
CASSO
'S WORLD

Symmetry reigns in the living room, with a pair of custom sofas facing each other, centered on the mantel; the artworks are by Jasper Johns. FOLLOWING PAGES: In the dining room, we installed a false bookcase, only six inches deep, to create symmetry where it was lacking. The dining chairs are by Michael Taylor Designs, and the light fixture is by Paul Ferrante.

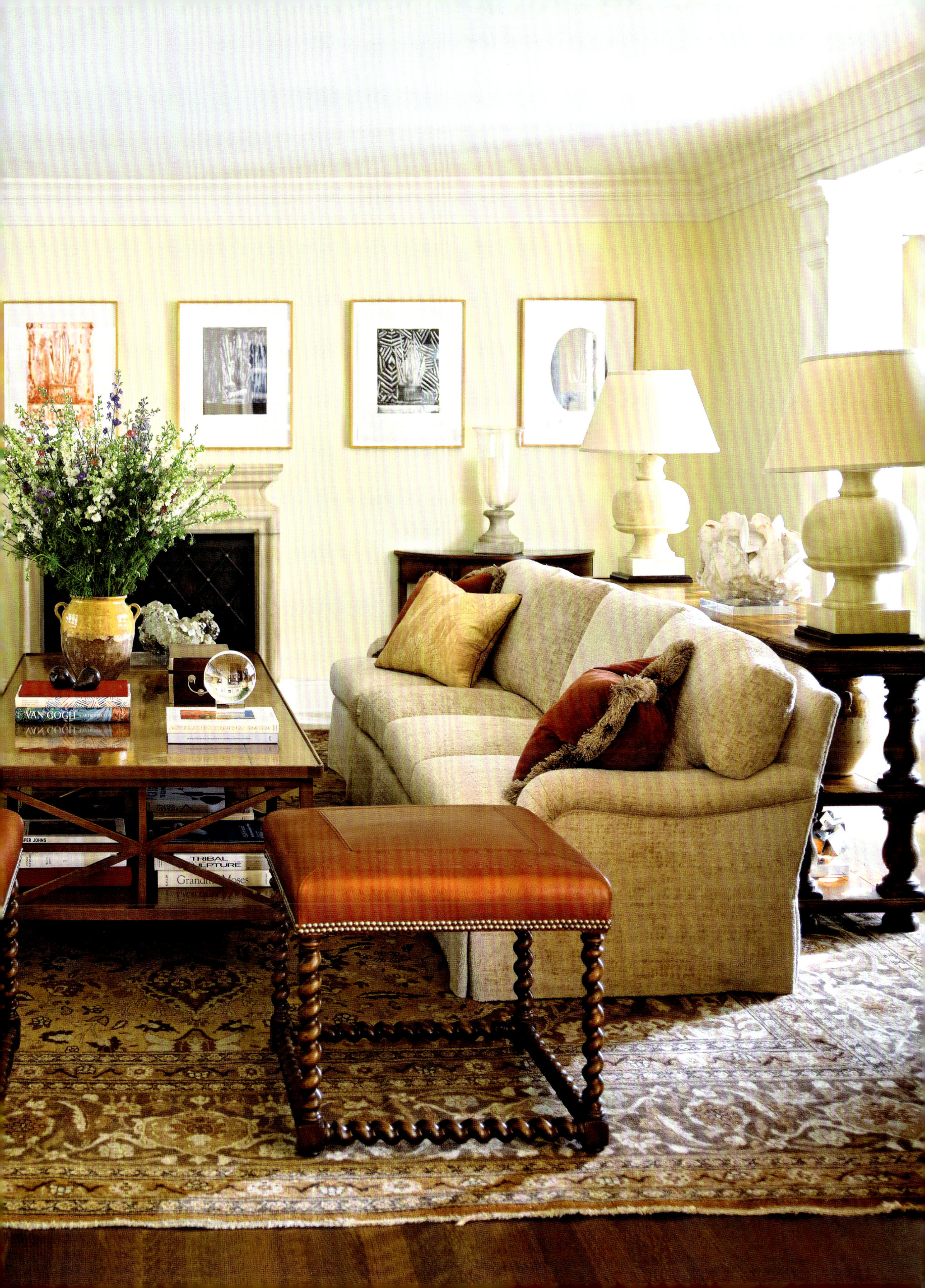
VAN GOGH
TRIBAL

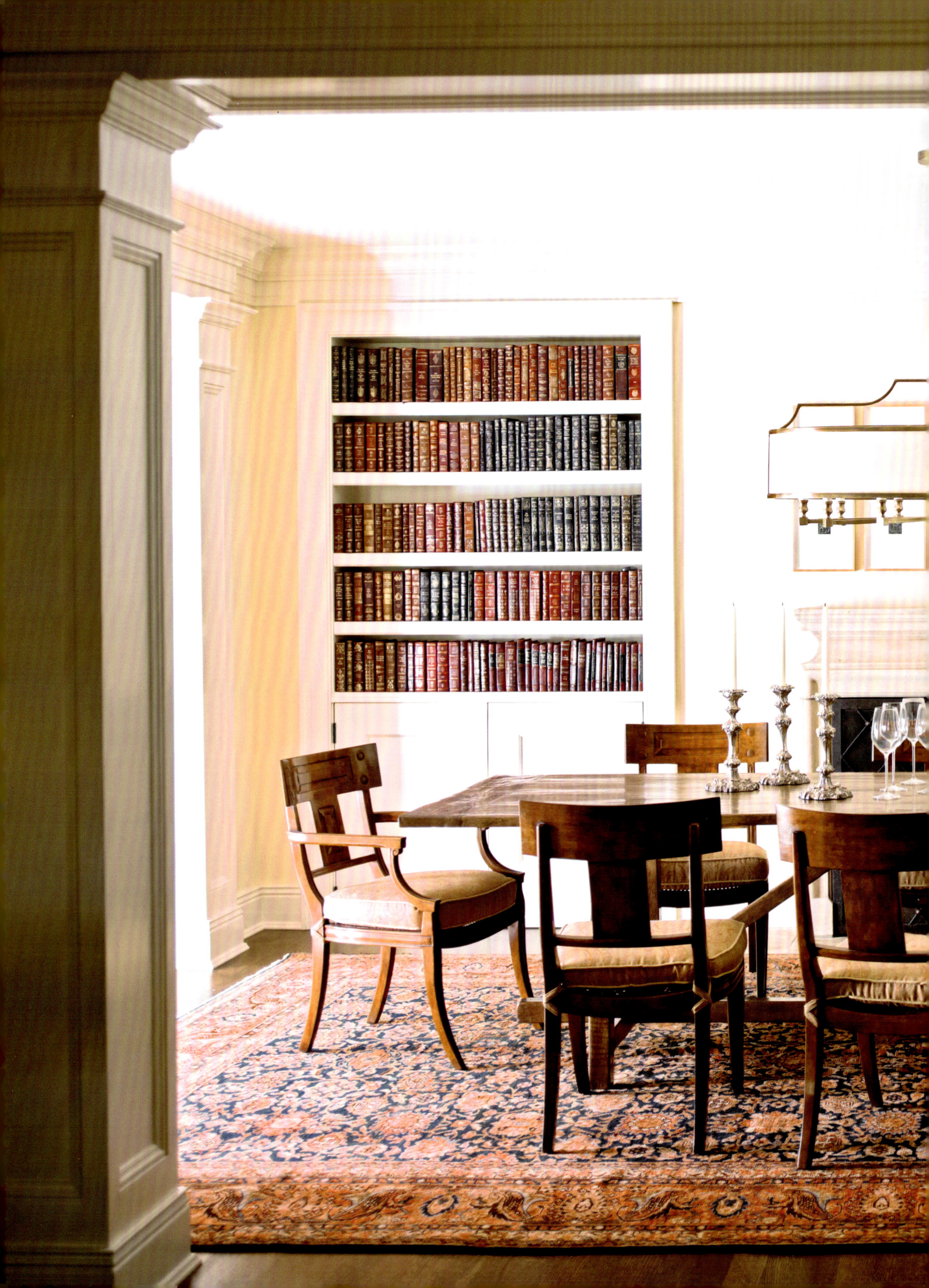

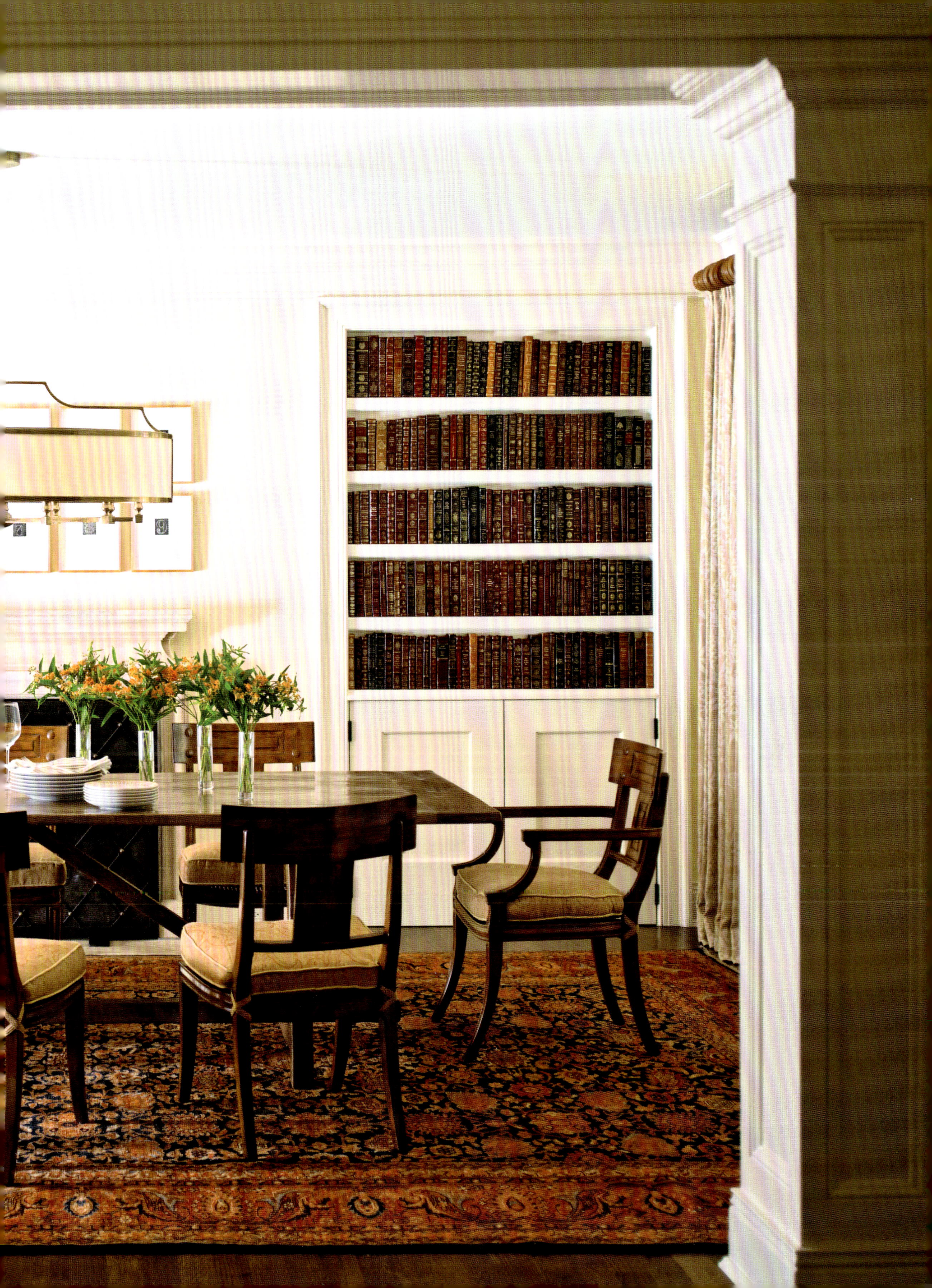

ABOVE: The breakfast room table is by Gregorius Pineo, and the light fixture is a custom design.
OPPOSITE: The island is fitted with a butcher-block top to give the kitchen a warmer feel.

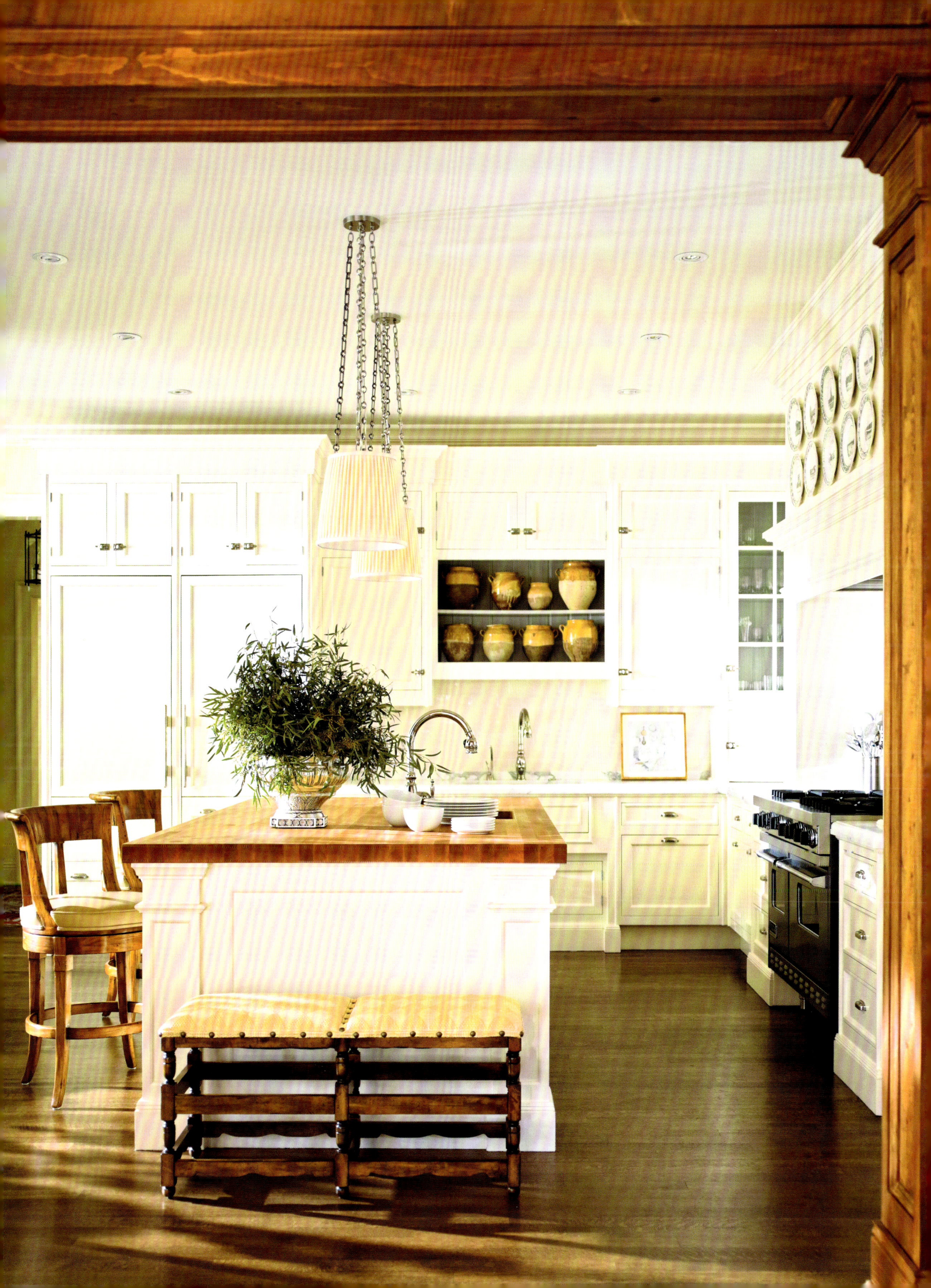

ABOVE: We paneled the family room in knotty English pine and then rubbed the wood with a colored wax from Paris to give it a luminous glow. The artwork is by Jasper Johns. OPPOSITE: A work by Frank Stella hangs above the mantel in the same room; the side table is from the nineteenth century.

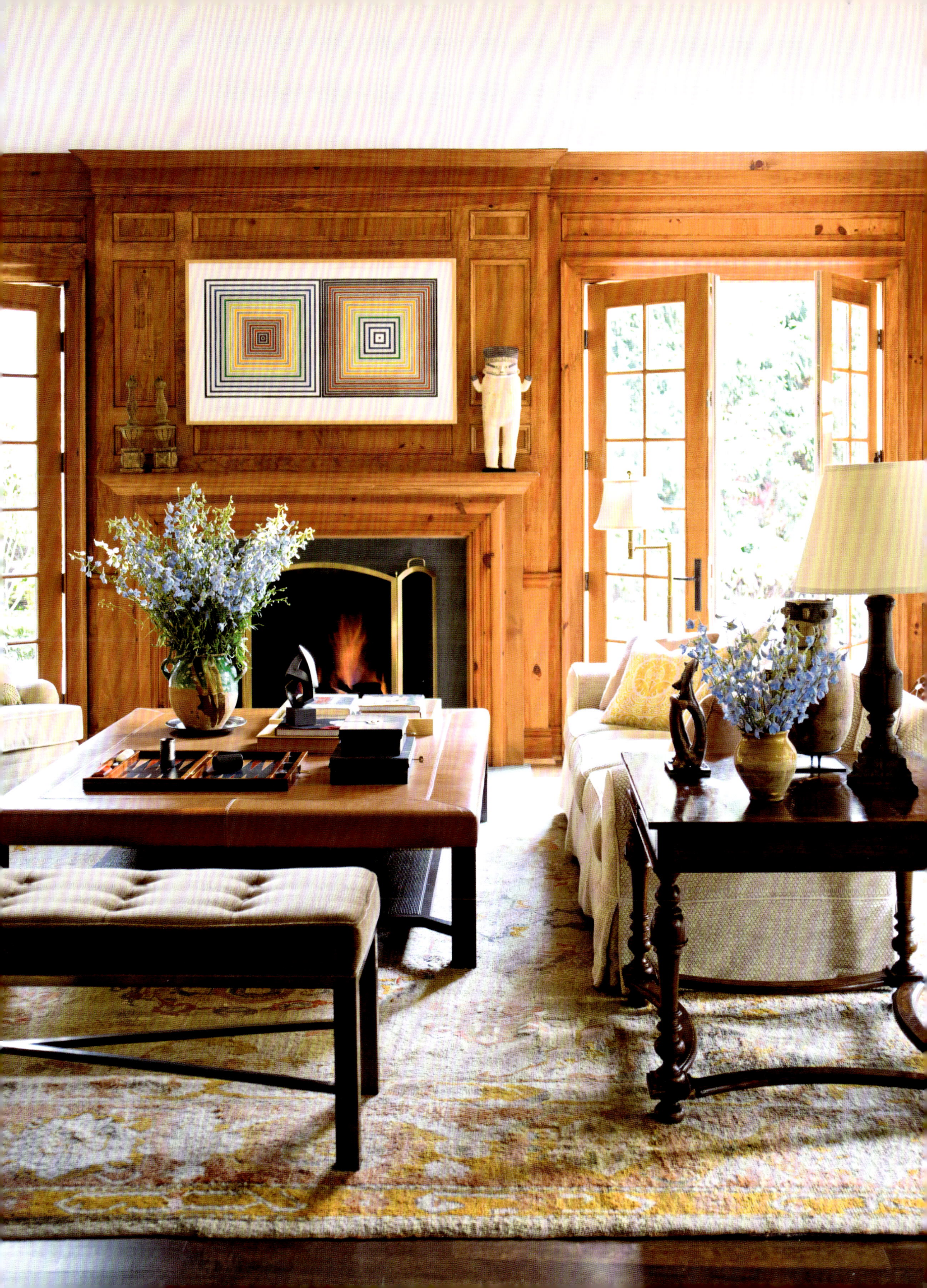

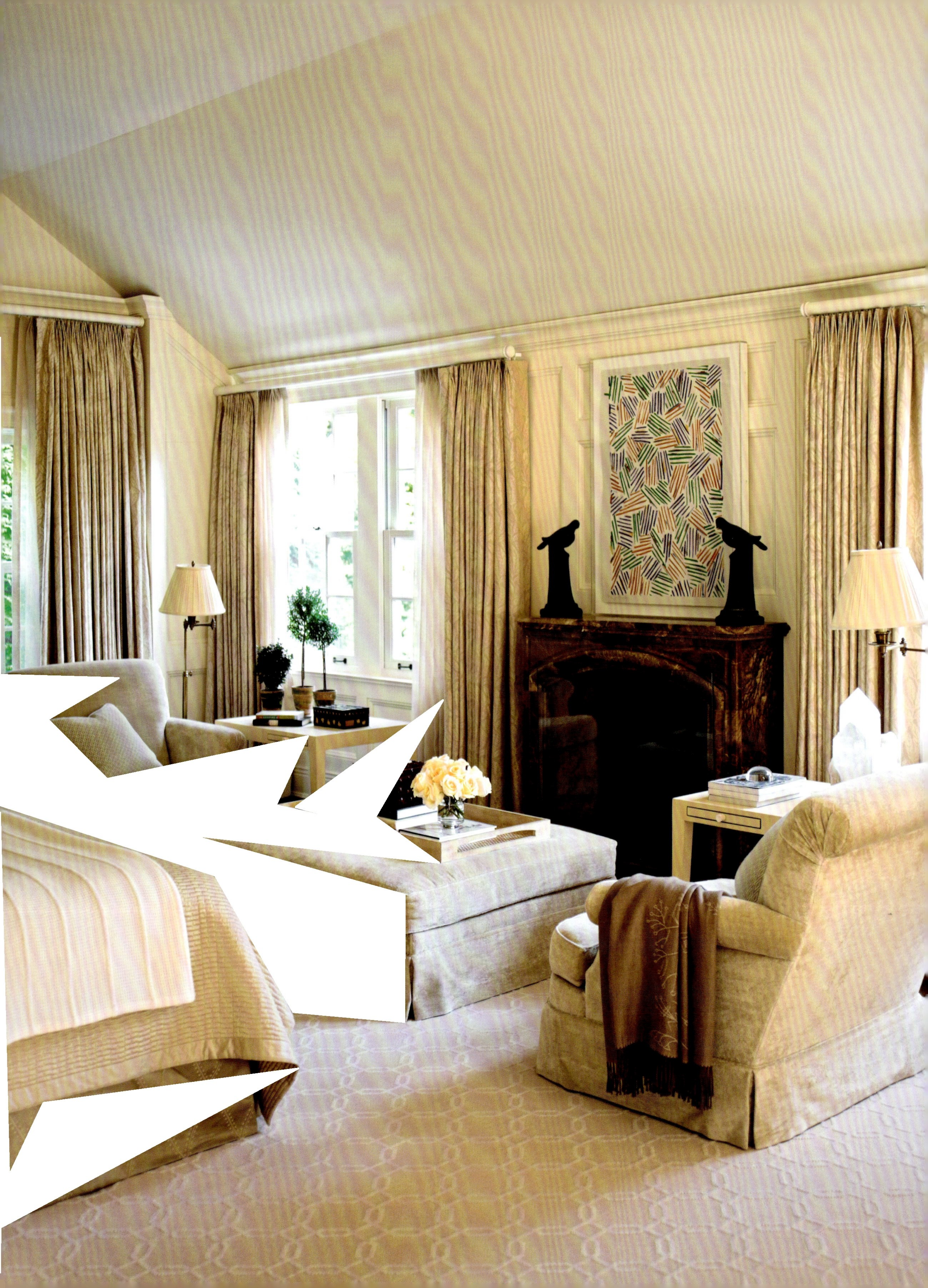

OPPOSITE: The master bedroom has French doors at both ends, which gives it a bit of a tree-house feel. To defer to the greenery outside, we kept the palette warm and neutral; the alabaster mantel was found in France, the artwork is by Jasper Johns, and the rug is by Stark. ABOVE: A guest room is painted in sunny yellow. The furnishings are custom pieces, the artworks are by Roy Lichtenstein, left, and Frank Stella, and the rug is by Stark.

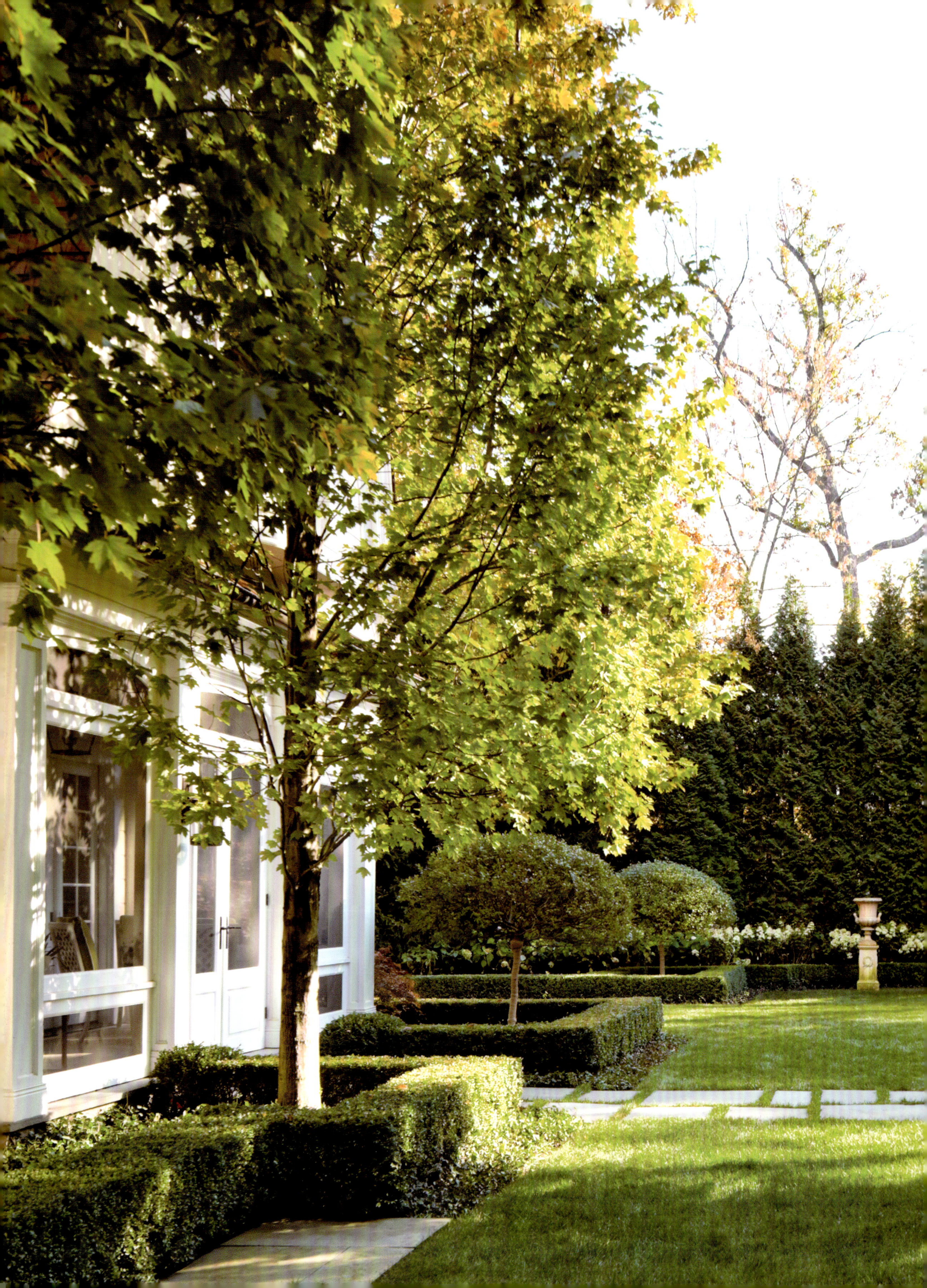

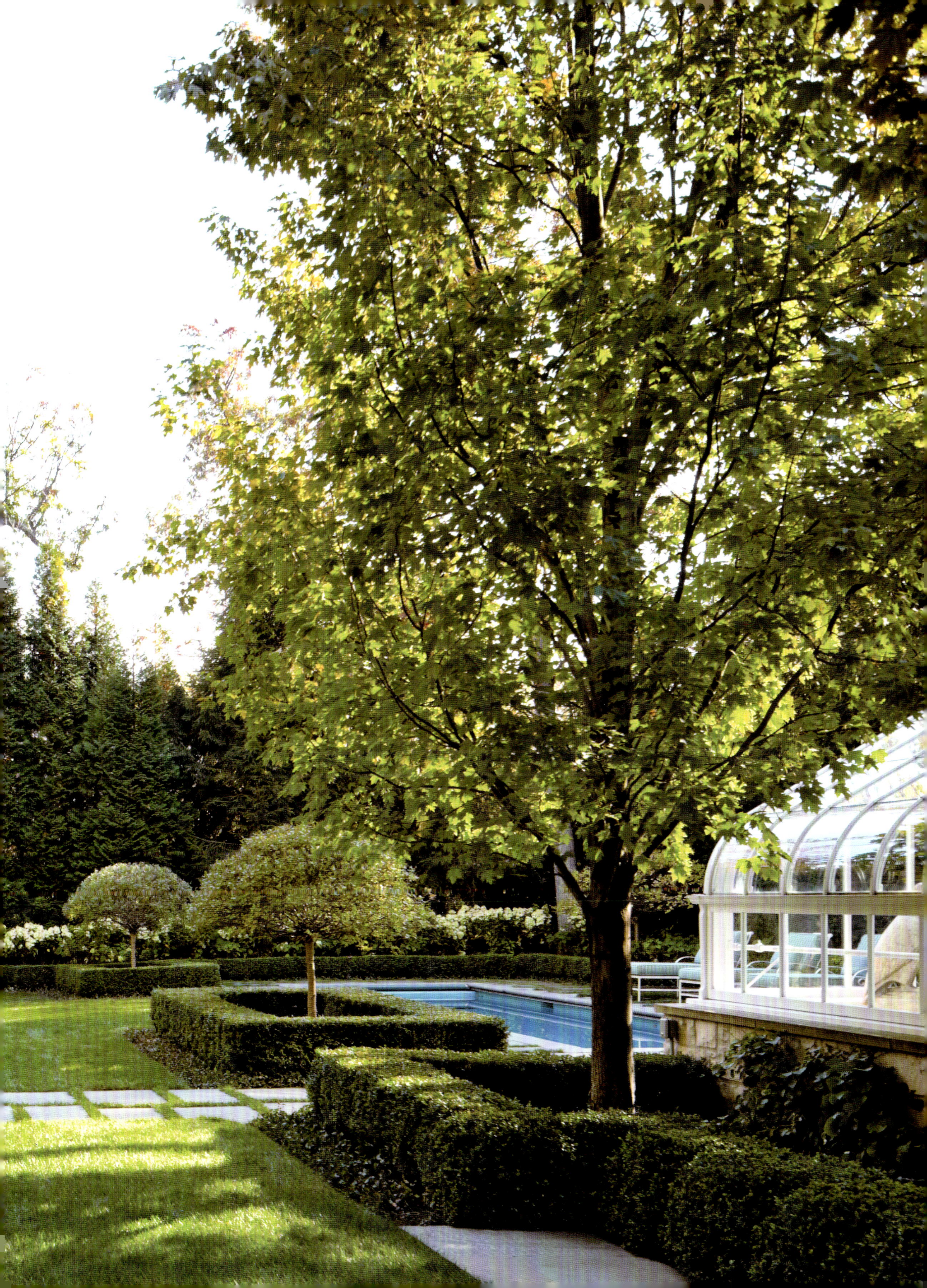

PREVIOUS PAGES: The garden was designed by Scott Byron & Co., and the pool was sited on axis with the greenhouse, which now serves as a lounge. RIGHT: Heating and air-conditioning were installed in the greenhouse, extending its use for many months beyond summer. The wicker seating is upholstered in fade-resistant outdoor fabrics, and the floors are slate.

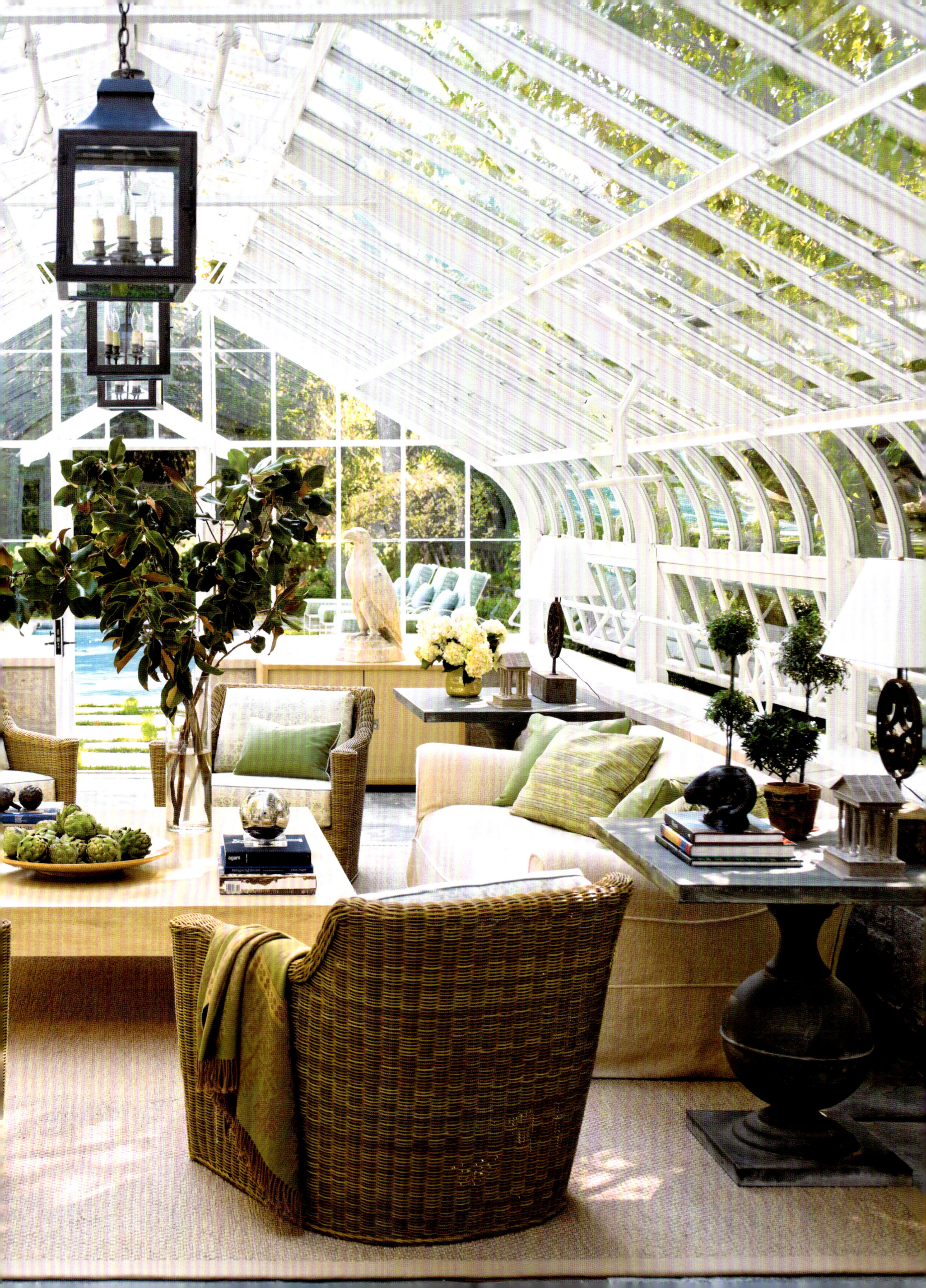

INTERLUDE
COMFORT

Comfort is crucial, but it is also hard to define. One person's comfortable chair can be another's torture implement. And comfort encompasses a lot more than simply our physical well-being. Psychological factors, personal taste, and even spatial harmony are all important in creating a space where we can let down our defenses and open ourselves to pleasure and relaxation.

Beauty alone is not enough. We do more than look at a room. We inhabit it, use it, move through it, and absorb its layout into our muscle memory. Who can relax in what seems to be a museum period room? We have to know that a space is forgiving of our personal foibles and clumsiness. All of us have enough daily stress without having to worry about breaking a delicate piece of furniture or staining an expensive fabric with a drop of wine. Our homes should be cosseting as well as beautiful. The more we feel that a room is comfortable, the more we will use it, and the more familiar and beloved it becomes. No matter how elegant or visually pleasing a room may be, if we don't feel that we belong there, it will never be a room we love or one where we feel at ease.

1

This combination kitchen and family room in Beverly Hills was created for a family with three kids and multiple dogs. It serves as both the center of family life and a portal to the outdoors, where the pool beckons just beyond. The table was coated with impervious marine varnish, and the dining chairs are slipcovered in a washable fabric. The success of the room is proven by the fact that it has held up beautifully for years.

2

I wanted this outdoor space at a home in Beverly Hills to be as relaxing and welcoming as any room inside since, due to Los Angeles's mild climate, it can be used virtually year-round. We created custom upholstered furniture of teak and outdoor foam that can stay outside (today, it is far easier to find outdoor upholstery on the market) and outfitted the space with all the accoutrements of a living room, from curtains to a cocktail table, to encourage lingering, convivial gatherings, and conversations long into the night.

3

This Bel Air family room incorporates many of my favorite devices to bring comfort to a space—an array of outdoor fabrics; a richly patterned Oriental rug; and marine varnish on all the wood surfaces. The clients have four dogs, and they wanted the room to have an intimate connection with the pool just beyond. The husband confessed that he never really felt comfortable in the living room, and after dinner he would usually go off to his office, leaving his wife on her own. So I installed an antique partners' desk, which two people can use at the same time. Now they linger in the room, catching up on business, watching television, reading the newspaper, and just being together. It's proof that the most comfortable room is the one we use and where we feel truly at home.

4

For another house in Beverly Hills, the clients requested a dining room that would not be stiff or formal, a place they could use for all kinds of occasions, or none at all. So I decided to fit it out with a vibrantly colored sofa, then scaled the dining table lower than the standard height so you can sit on the sofa to eat. The wall of mirrors adds sparkle and light, and the large display cabinet is filled with books and personal items, making the room cozy and inviting.

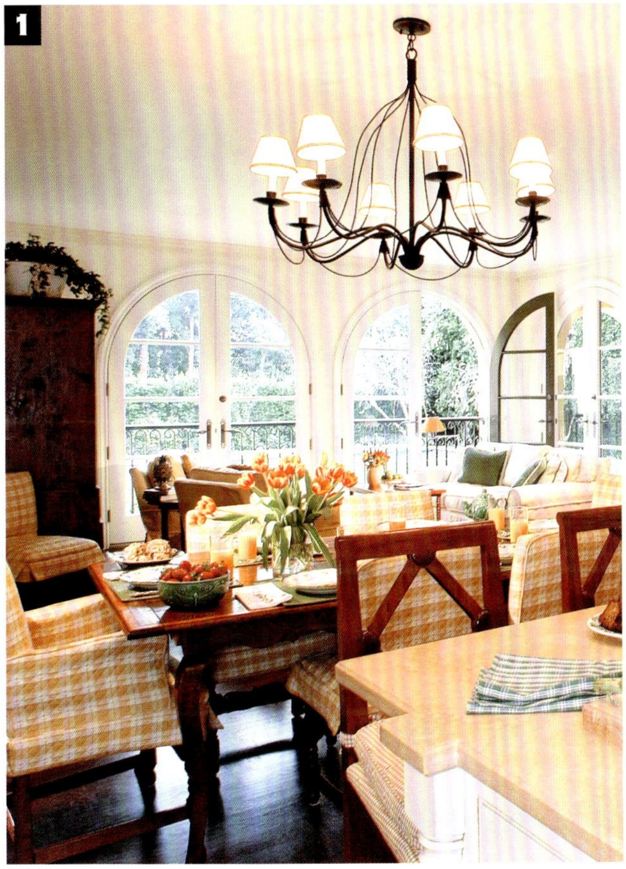
1

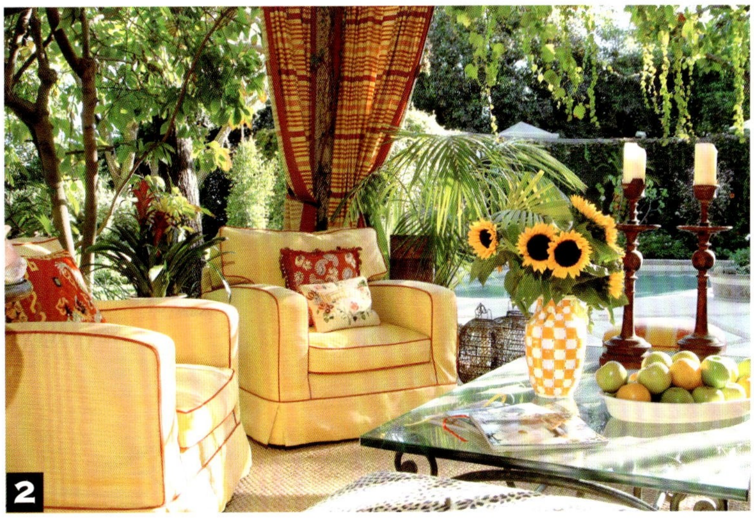
2

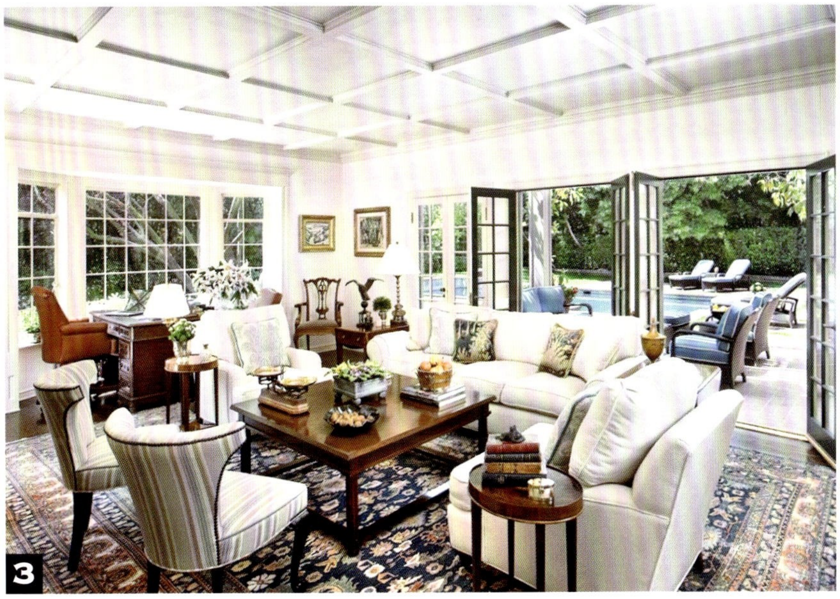
3

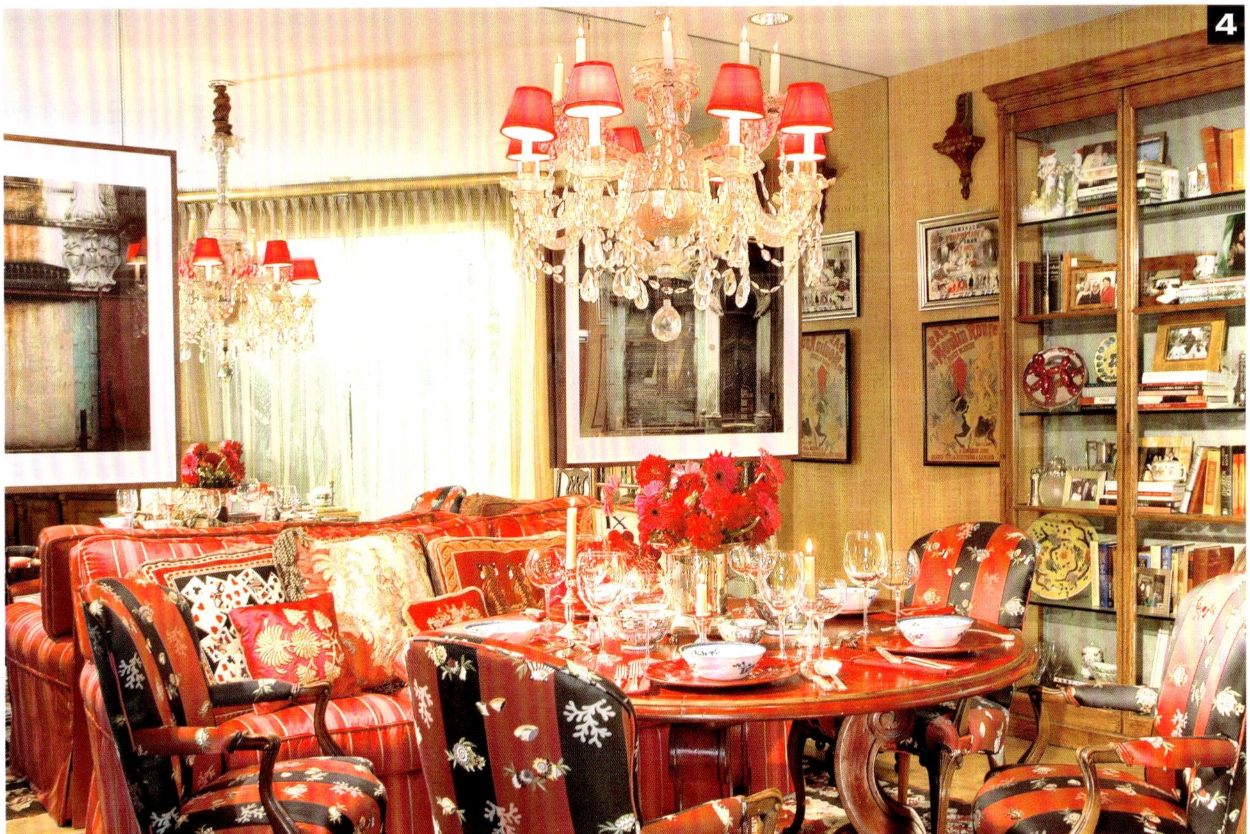
4

Western White House

I am a huge fan of old buildings—so much so that, after I left advertising, I dubbed my first company Landmark Restoration. The best old buildings have a scale, grandeur, and quality of construction that is costly and difficult, if not impossible, to match today. And they link us to the past in the most visceral and immediate way. Who doesn't love to go to Rome and be surrounded by centuries of architecture—ancient Roman, baroque, neoclassical, and modern at all once? That kind of visual richness makes immediate and direct our links to human history and helps us appreciate the incredible diversity and richness of architectural and decorative arts history.

But I also understand that historic buildings have to work for today. Very few people would be willing to undertake the rehabilitation, upkeep, and maintenance of an older structure if it can't be made to satisfy contemporary needs. Old warehouses are practical as offices only if they can accommodate open workspaces, fresh air, high-speed Wi-Fi, efficient elevators, and all the other amenities that firms and workers have come to expect. Gracious old homes will only be saved, and embraced, if they can be adapted to supply what any contemporary home buyer longs for—abundant light inside, spacious and luxurious bathrooms, commodious closets, kitchens that work in an era where big staffs are no longer a reality or even desired, and a close link between indoors and out. No matter how grand, no matter how elegant, no matter how impressive an old house may be, it will not be loved if it does not function well for the way that we live today.

This grand Beaux Arts house in the Windsor Square neighborhood of Los Angeles was certainly impressive. It was built to impress. It is so imposing that many of its neighbors assumed the building was a post office or a public library, rather than a private home. It was designed for a real estate investor in 1913 by J. Martyn Haenke and William Dodd, who would later work with Julia Morgan, William Randolph Hearst's favorite architect and the mastermind behind Hearst Castle. But the house really came to prominence in the mid-1950s, when it was acquired by Norman Chandler, the publisher of the *Los Angeles Times*, and his wife, Dorothy Buffum Chandler, whose extensive philanthropic endeavors are only hinted at by the fact that her name graces the auditorium at the Los Angeles Music Center where the Academy Awards were presented for so many years. She was a prodigious hostess and the house, which she playfully dubbed *Los Tiempos* (The Times), was the scene of numerous parties and fund-raising galas. Over the decades the house welcomed so many U.S. presidents (Eisenhower, Kennedy, Johnson, and Nixon

The entry hall of this historic house in Los Angeles was lightened by stripping the beautifully detailed paneling, columns, and balustrade and then re-waxing the wood so it glows. The center table is from the early nineteenth century, and the bench is eighteenth-century Venetian.

208 THE NEW ELEGANCE

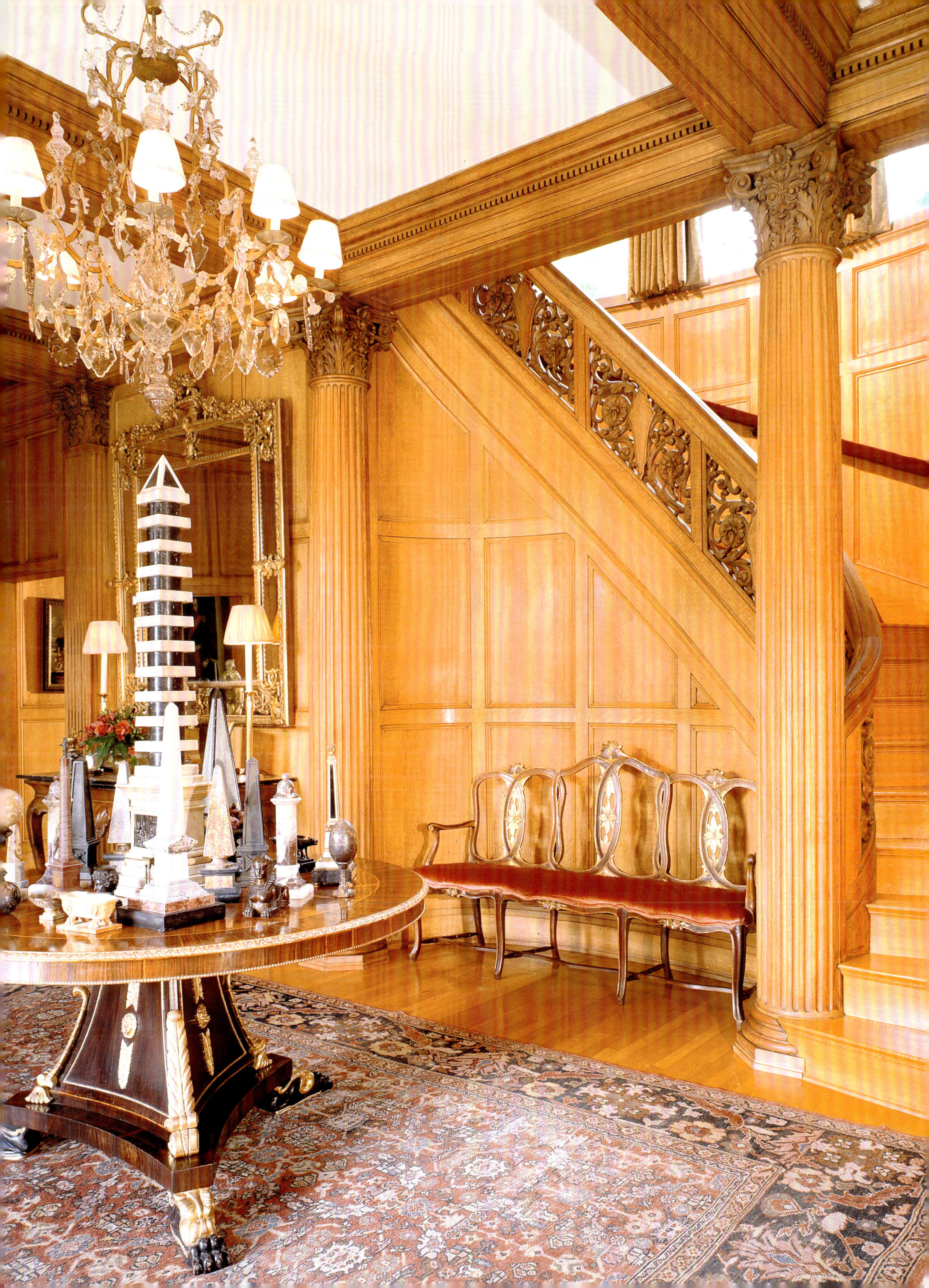

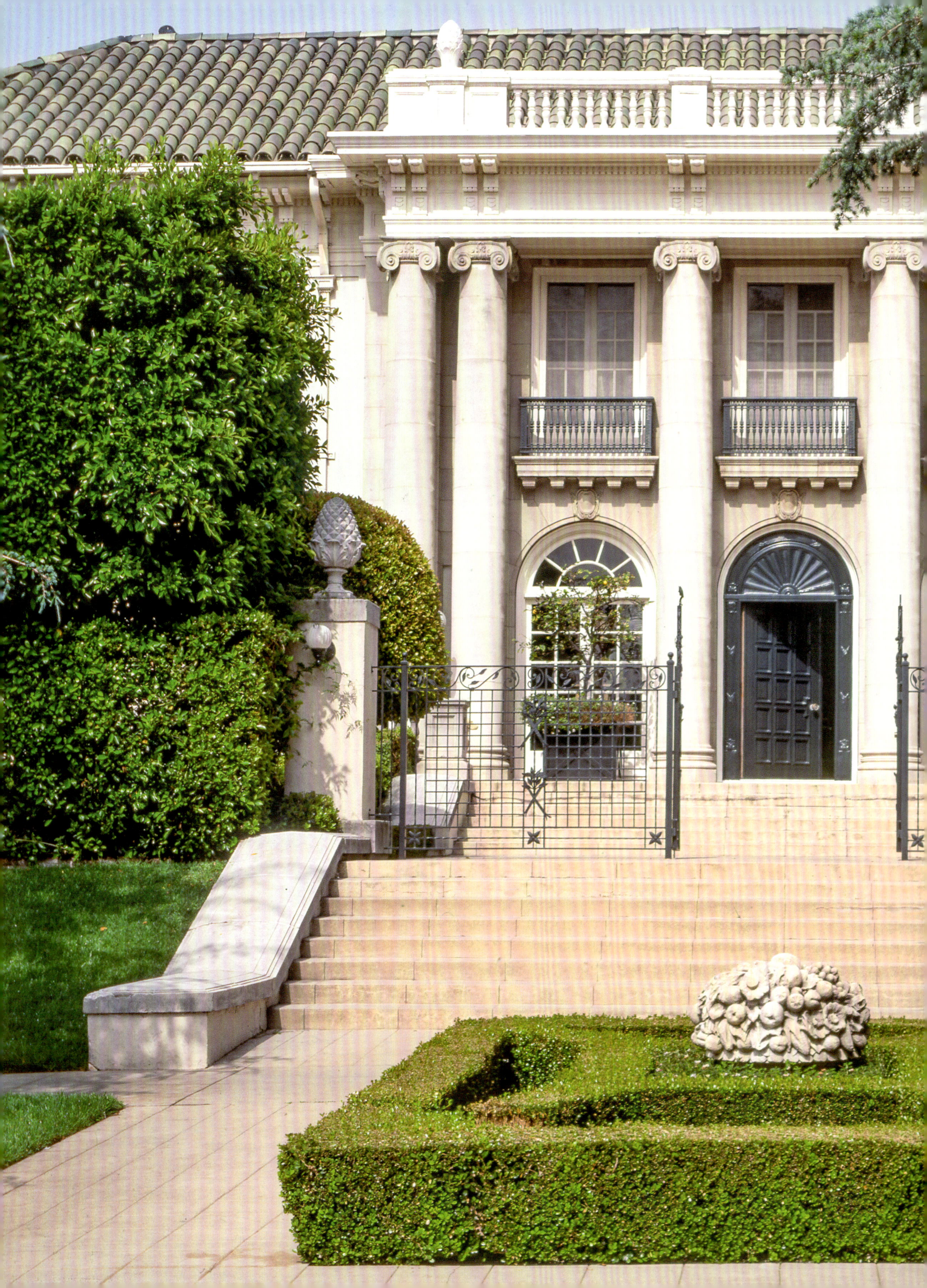

To buffer the front of the imposing house from the street, I planted layers of hedges and trees and installed a set of 1918 gates that had been at the back of the house. A new parterre of boxwood separates the sidewalk from the street, creating a further sense of protection.

211

Another view of the entry hall, which looks into the library. The table holds an array of grand tour souvenirs, and the monumental eighteenth-century terra-cotta urn once belonged to Karl Lagerfeld.

212

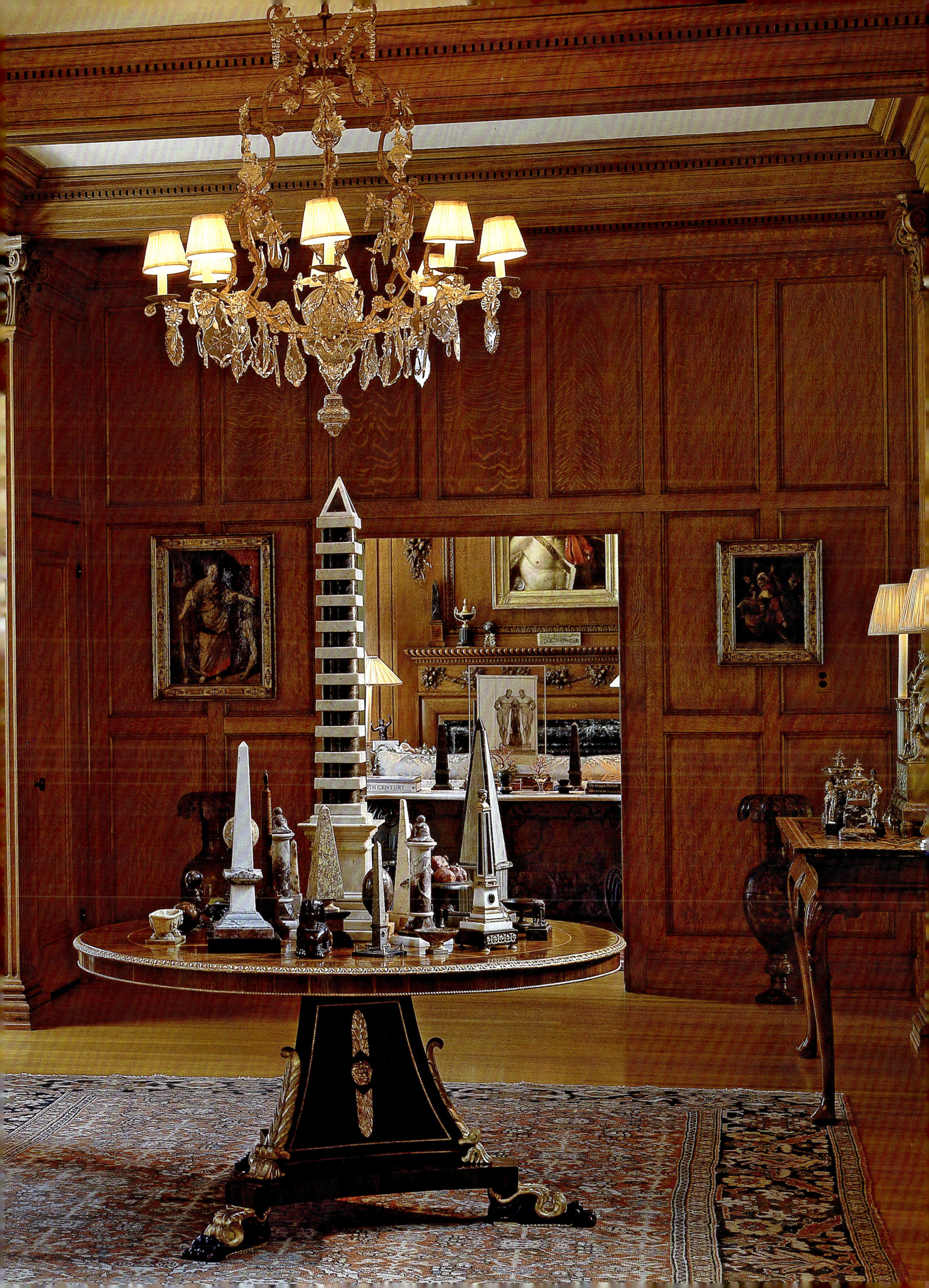

were all frequent guests) that, for a time, it was known as "the Western White House."

The house had long enchanted me. I used to walk by it often when I was young and lived only a few blocks away. It dazzled me with its grandeur, its formality, and its massive Ionic columns facing the street. And when I was eleven or twelve, I was invited to a party there. I always remembered the high coffered ceilings, soaring curved windows, ornate woodwork, and the way the grand rooms flowed one into the other. In 1997, following the death of Dorothy Chandler, the estate was put on the market. I was the first to see the house and immediately bought it, renovated it, and ended up living there for nine and a half years.

Vivid as my memories were when I acquired the house, the structure itself was worn and forlorn, its glory days long past. So the question was, how do you respect the building and its illustrious history while making it functional as well as beautiful? The answer was to restore, not renovate, the house, to make its elegance and scale work for life today, retaining decorative elements but approaching each room in a less august fashion.

That started right out front, where the large set of stairs leading to the columned entry were nothing less than daunting. To soften the effect, I brought some beautiful hand-wrought iron gates that had been in the garden and installed them in the front, reducing the openness so that it was more human-scaled and creating the additional benefit of a front garden area, which I landscaped with topiaries. That softening continued inside, in the grand entry hall. Here we stripped and bleached the dark oak paneling and fluted columns, hand-waxing the wood to give it a soft, honeyed glow. We lost none of the striking carved details of the Corinthian capitals and stair railing, but we gave the space a less imposing, more welcoming presence.

The adjacent library has the feel of a gentleman's lair or a literary salon, with its rich quartersawn walnut paneled walls. I tried to reinforce that feeling with an array of neoclassical paintings and objects that an aristocratic British gentleman might have acquired on the grand tour. The living room is imposing, but it also looks out onto the pool and receives abundant sunlight, which gave me the opportunity to focus on the indoor-outdoor aspects of the space and undercut any possible pretension. To soften the walls, which had been sheathed in travertine, I had the massive stone panels scored into two-foot squares and stained them, so they had the softness of limestone. I laid down seagrass carpets and installed vibrant furnishings in shades of scarlet and emerald (which are fitted with white cotton damask slipcovers in summer). *Faux-marbre* columns that originally came from the Palazzo Mocenigo in Venice demarcate the space so it never feels overwhelming. It is both formal and relaxed, so much so that it was the setting for several movies and an iconic Steven Meisel fashion campaign for Versace.

The painting over the mantel in the library is by Jacques-Louis David; the middle painting on the left is a study by Peter Paul Rubens; and below it is a portrait by Pierre-Paul Prud'hon. The table holds third- and fourth-century pottery, and a bench stripped of its upholstery and fitted with a marble top serves as a cocktail table.

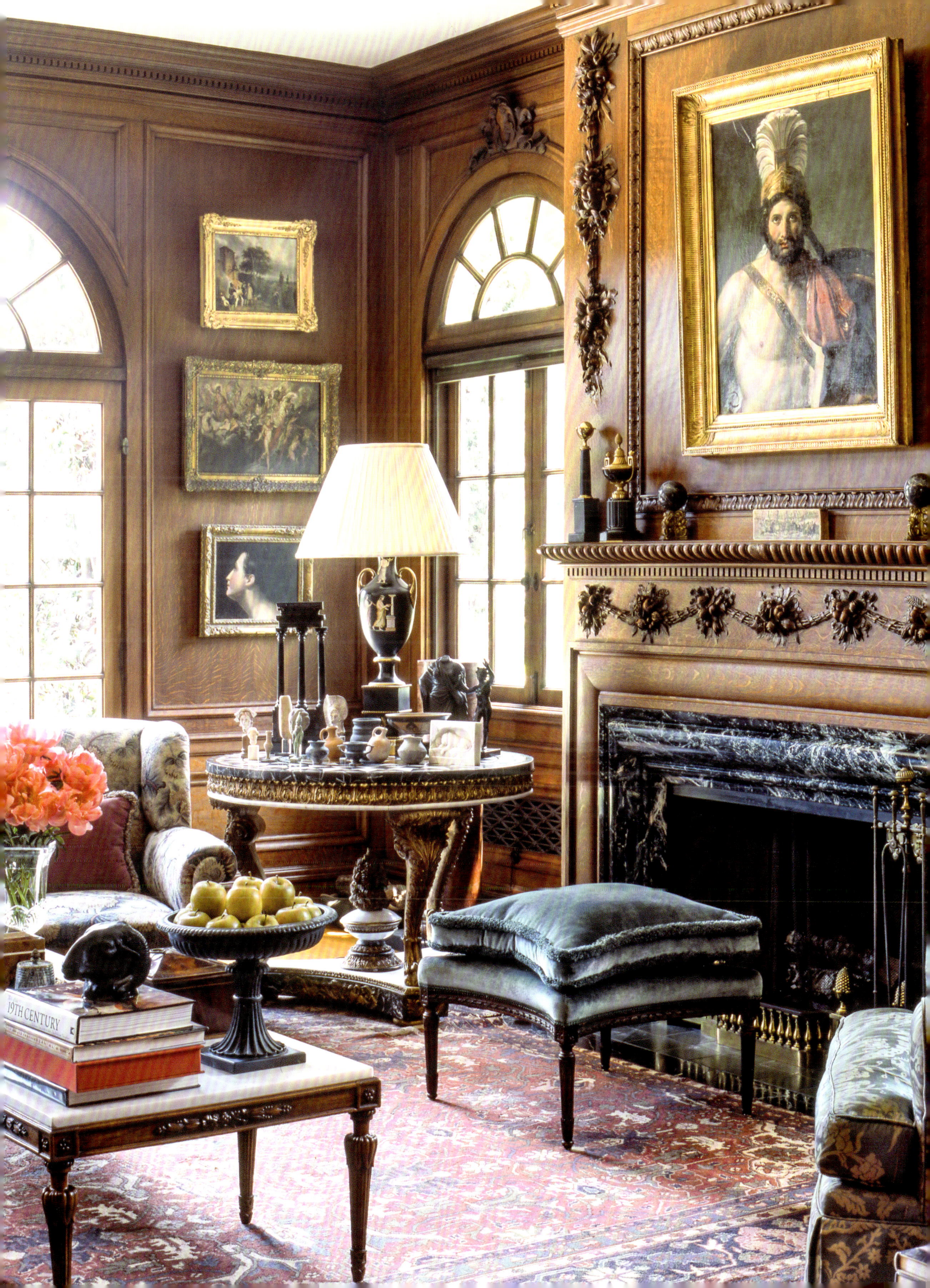
19TH CENTURY

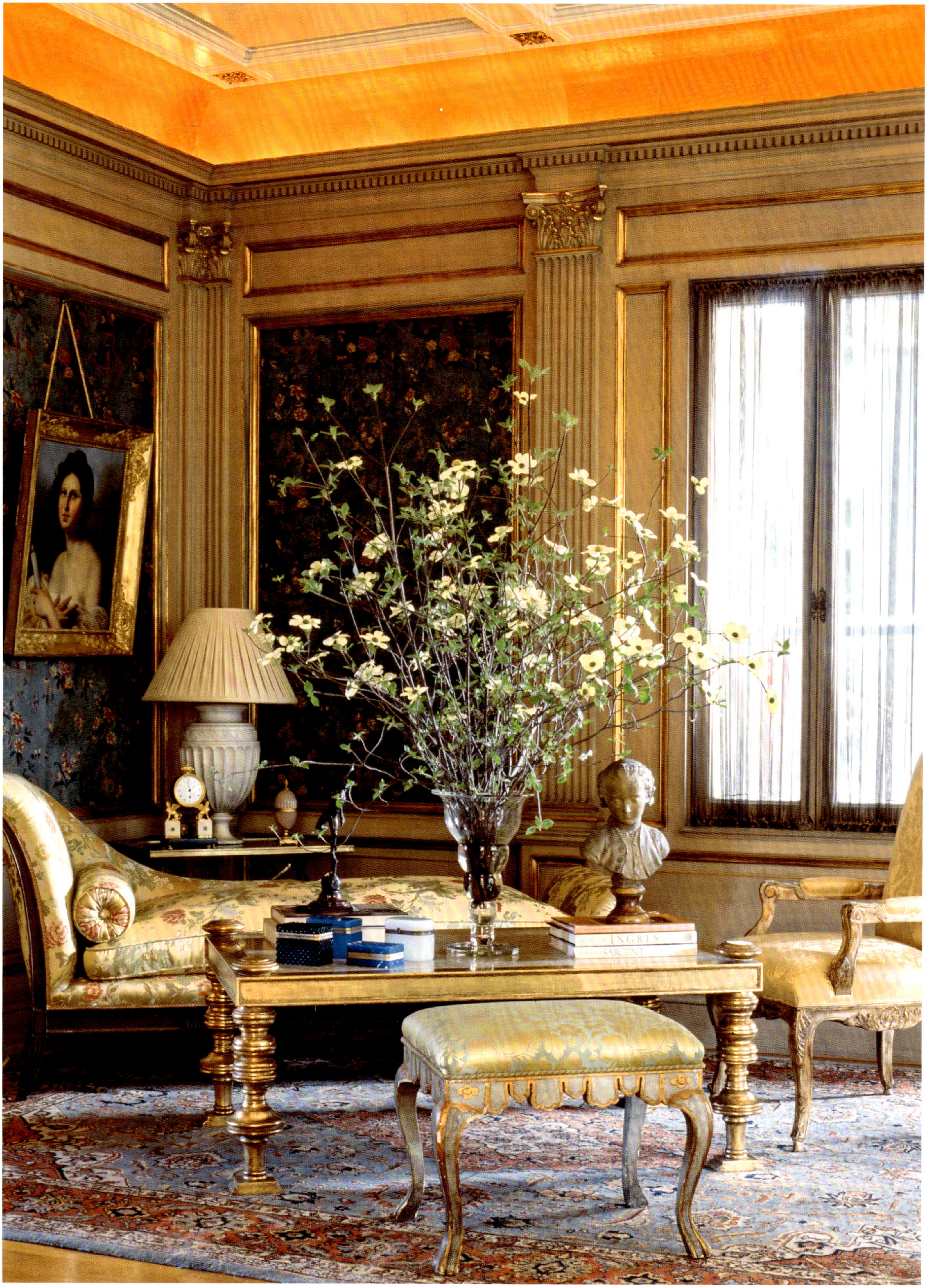
INGRES
SARGENT

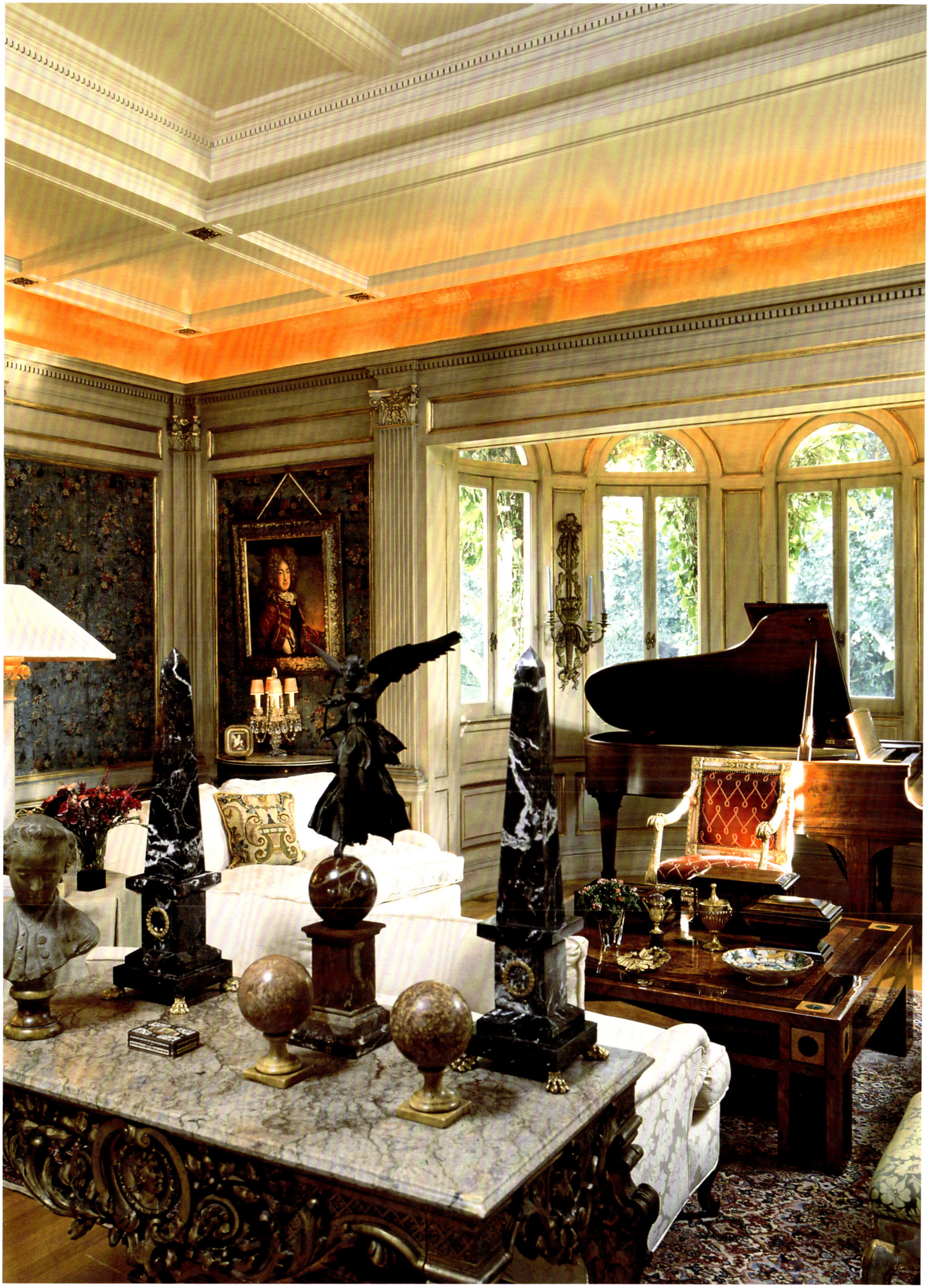

PREVIOUS PAGES: The music room walls are inset with hand-painted eighteenth-century silk panels. The grand piano belonged to the Chandlers and is signed by Sergei Rachmaninoff and other musical luminaries who were guests at the house. RIGHT: Because of the lush landscaping that was added at the front of the house, the French doors facing onto the street in the dining room need no window coverings. The seventeenth-century painting depicts Cleopatra with an asp.

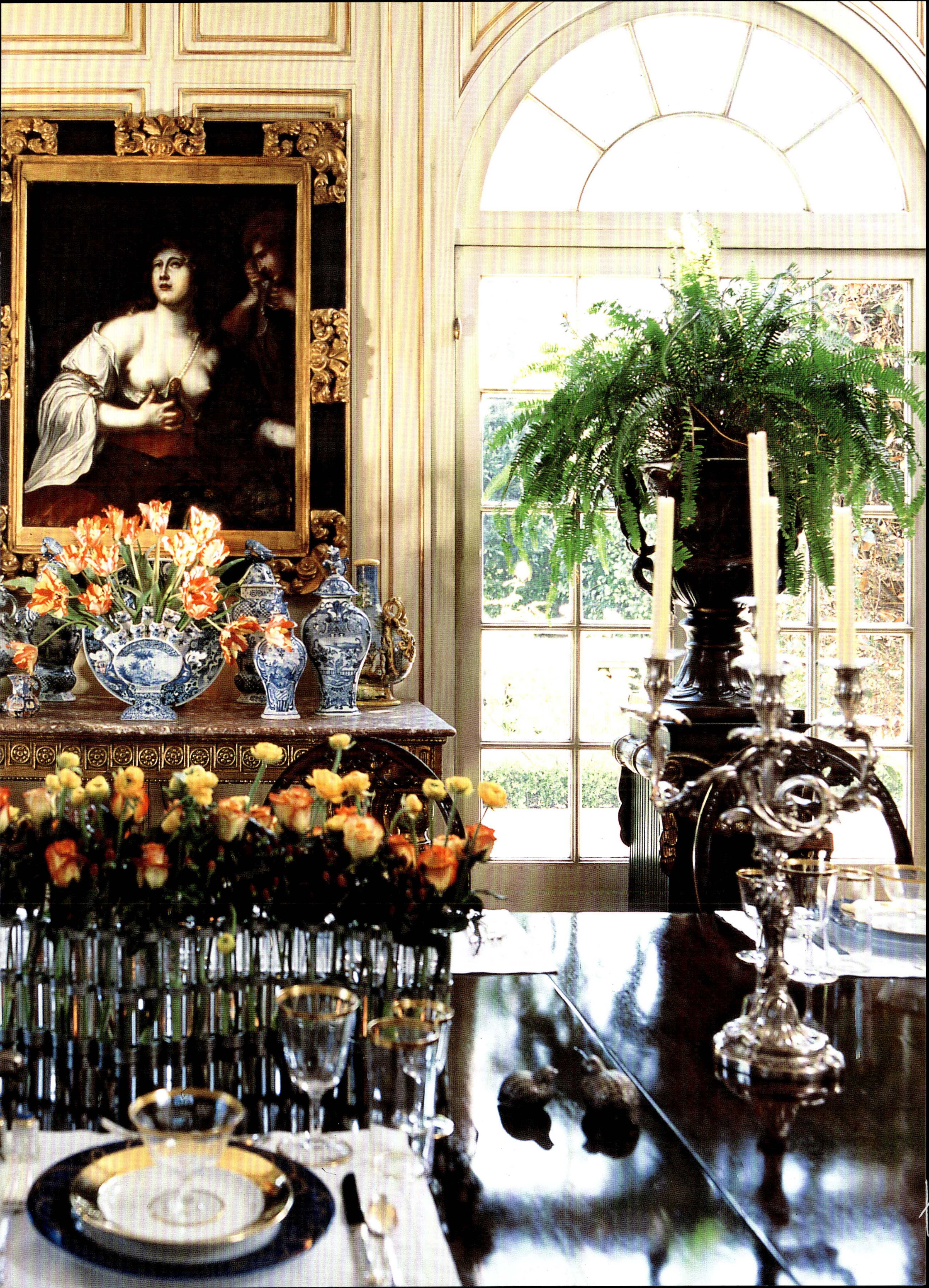

The living room walls are sheathed in travertine, and the columns and light fixtures were originally from Palazzo Mocenigo in Venice. The paneled and painted doors lead to the music room. FOLLOWING PAGES: The master bedroom has terraces on three sides, so the bed seems to float amid the trees. The center table, side tables, and chairs are Biedermeier.

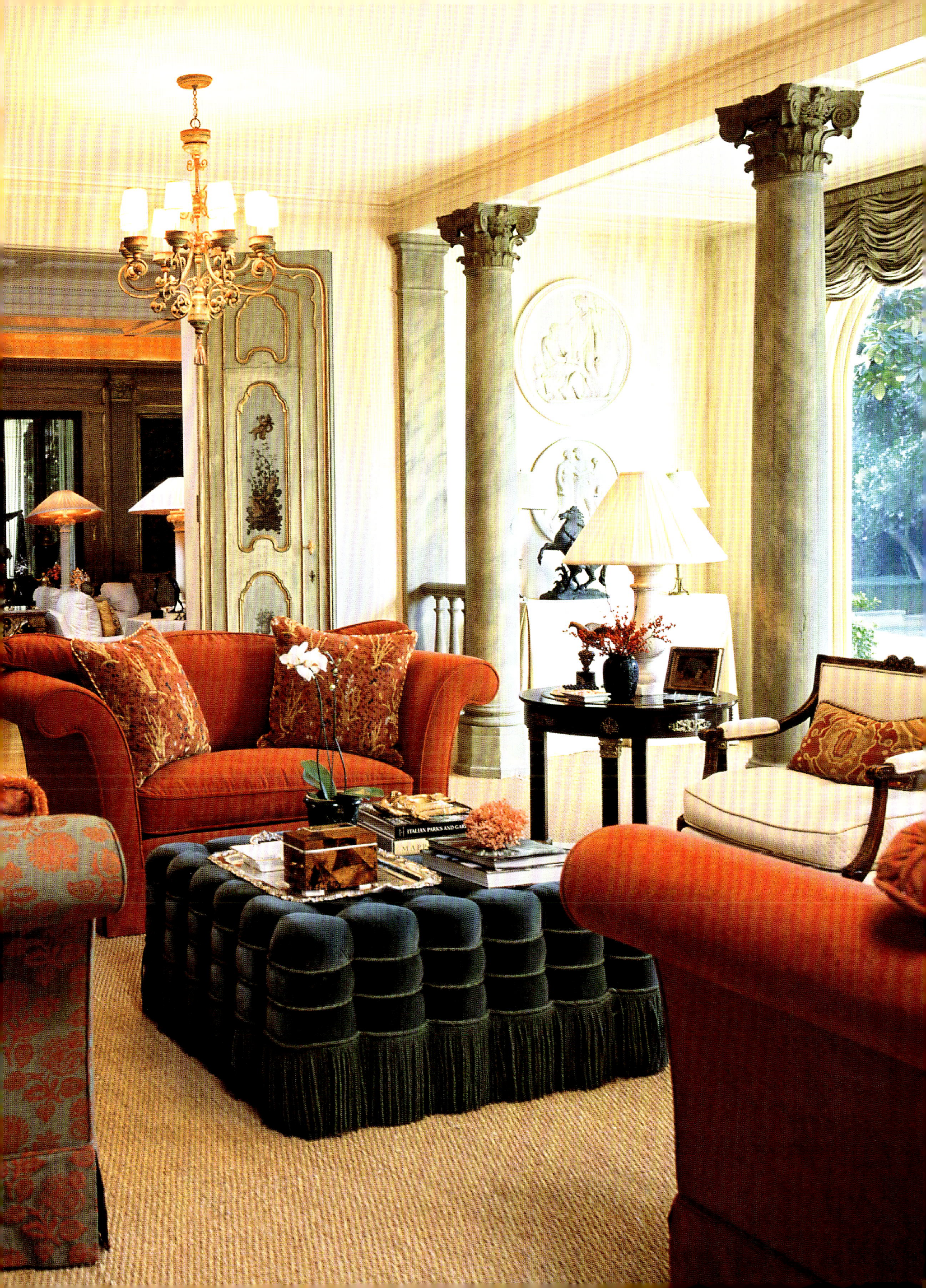
ITALIAN PARKS AND

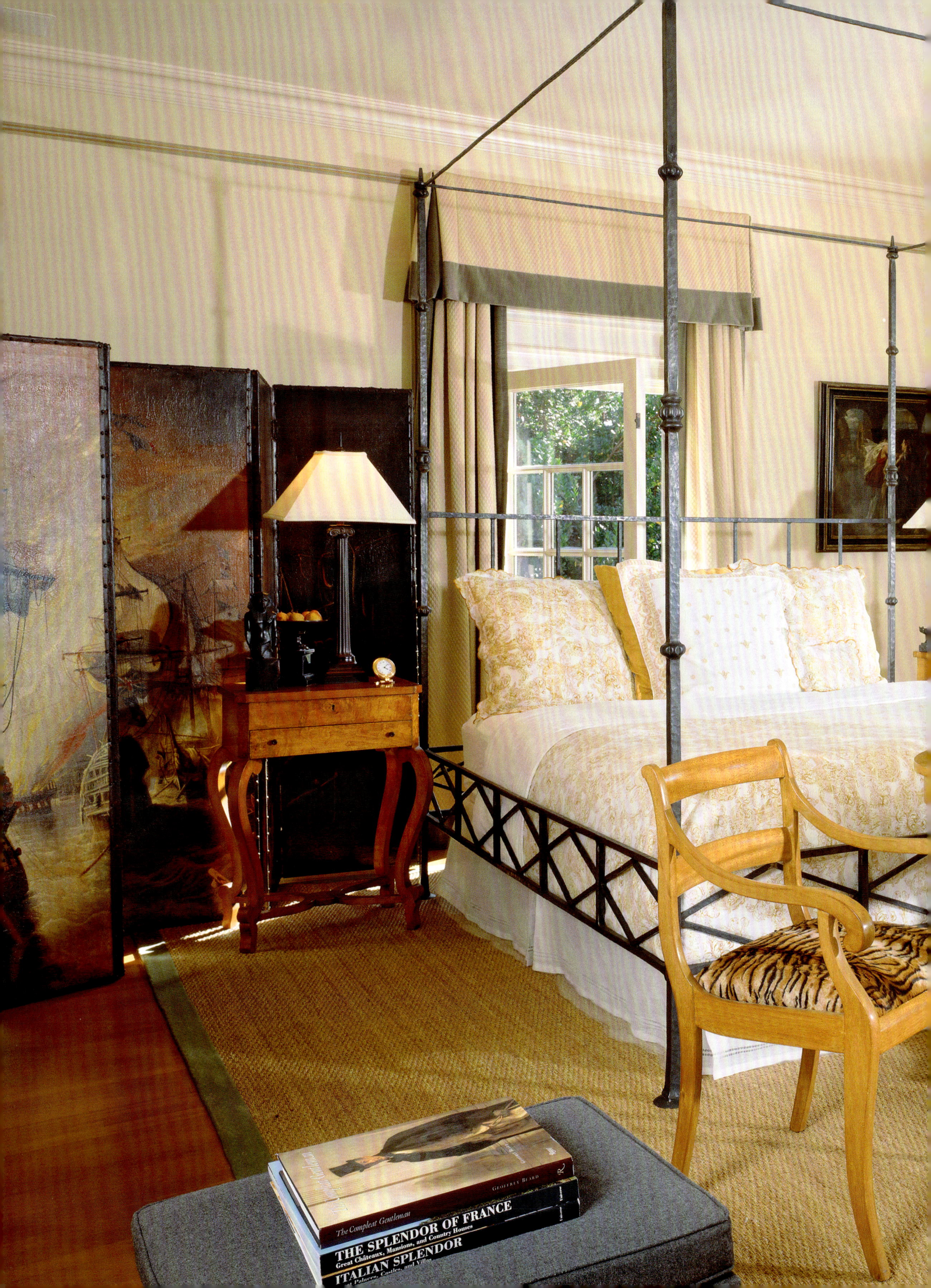

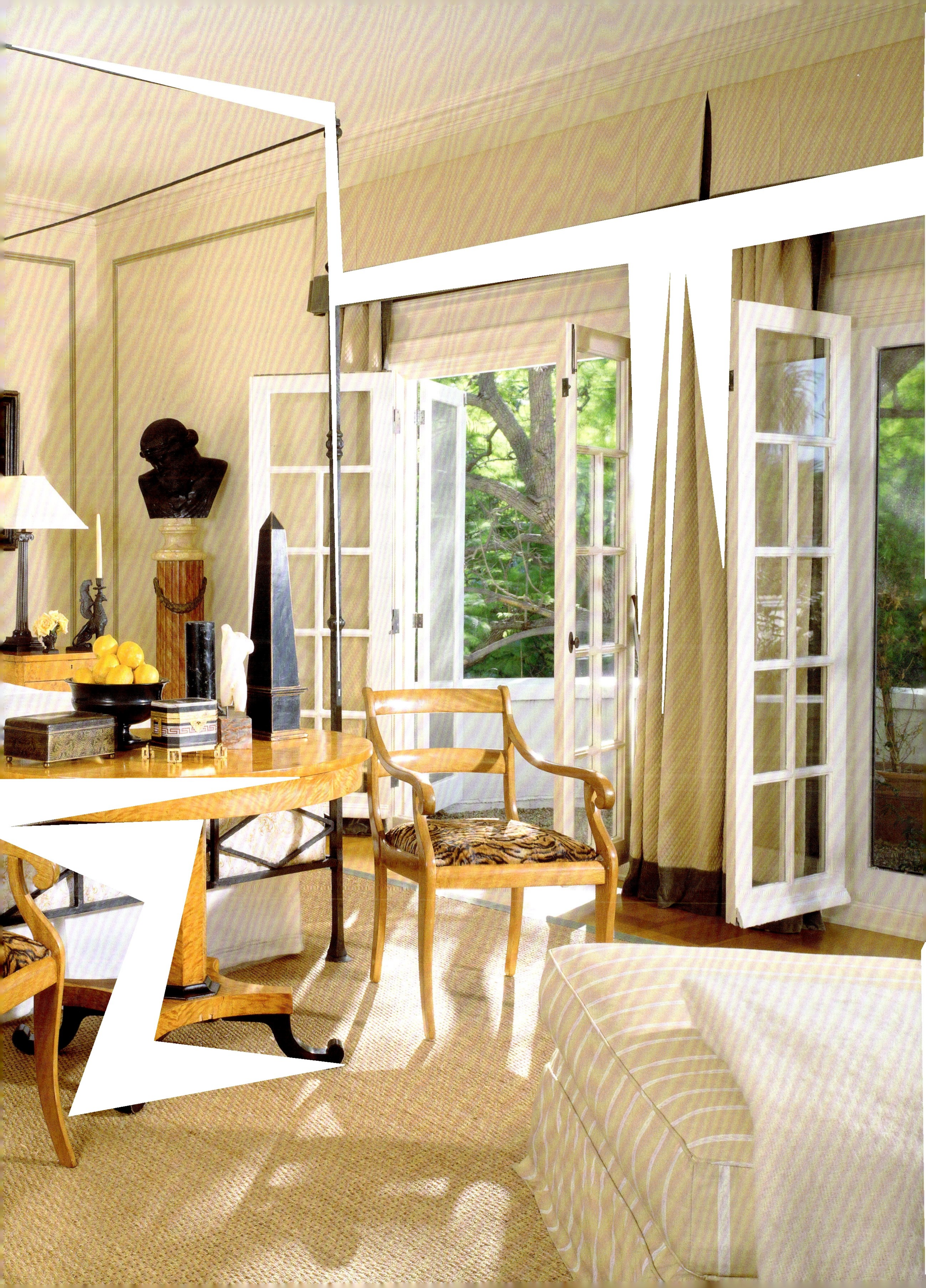

The music room is the largest, grandest, and most historic room in the house. This was a space created for musicales, for glittering gatherings orchestrated to both classical music and Cole Porter, and the room still contains the Chandlers' original Steinway baby grand, signed by both Sergei Rachmaninoff and Van Cliburn. The walls are covered with hand-painted silk panels that originally adorned a room in a castle outside Munich where a young Mozart composed and performed. There was no possibility of underplaying the drama, so we increased it.

The dining room, which seats sixteen, has boiserie taken from a French chateau, French doors that look onto the front garden, and luxe, layered theatrical-style curtains at the end of the room. The windows there provide a view of the reflecting pool, itself a bit of theatrical sleight of hand. When I installed the pool, I used false perspective—it is two feet narrower at the far end and lined on each side with balls of boxwood that are planted progressively closer together to make it seem far larger than it actually is.

But if the public rooms were expansive and welcoming, the staff areas were anything but. The kitchen reflected the era when it was solely

ABOVE: The master bath has three exposures. Frosted-glass enclosures for the toilet and shower ensure privacy and create symmetry. OPPOSITE: In a guest room that was often used by visiting American presidents, a pale blue palette and a nineteenth-century ebony bed establish a serene mood; the lamp is by Jean Royère.

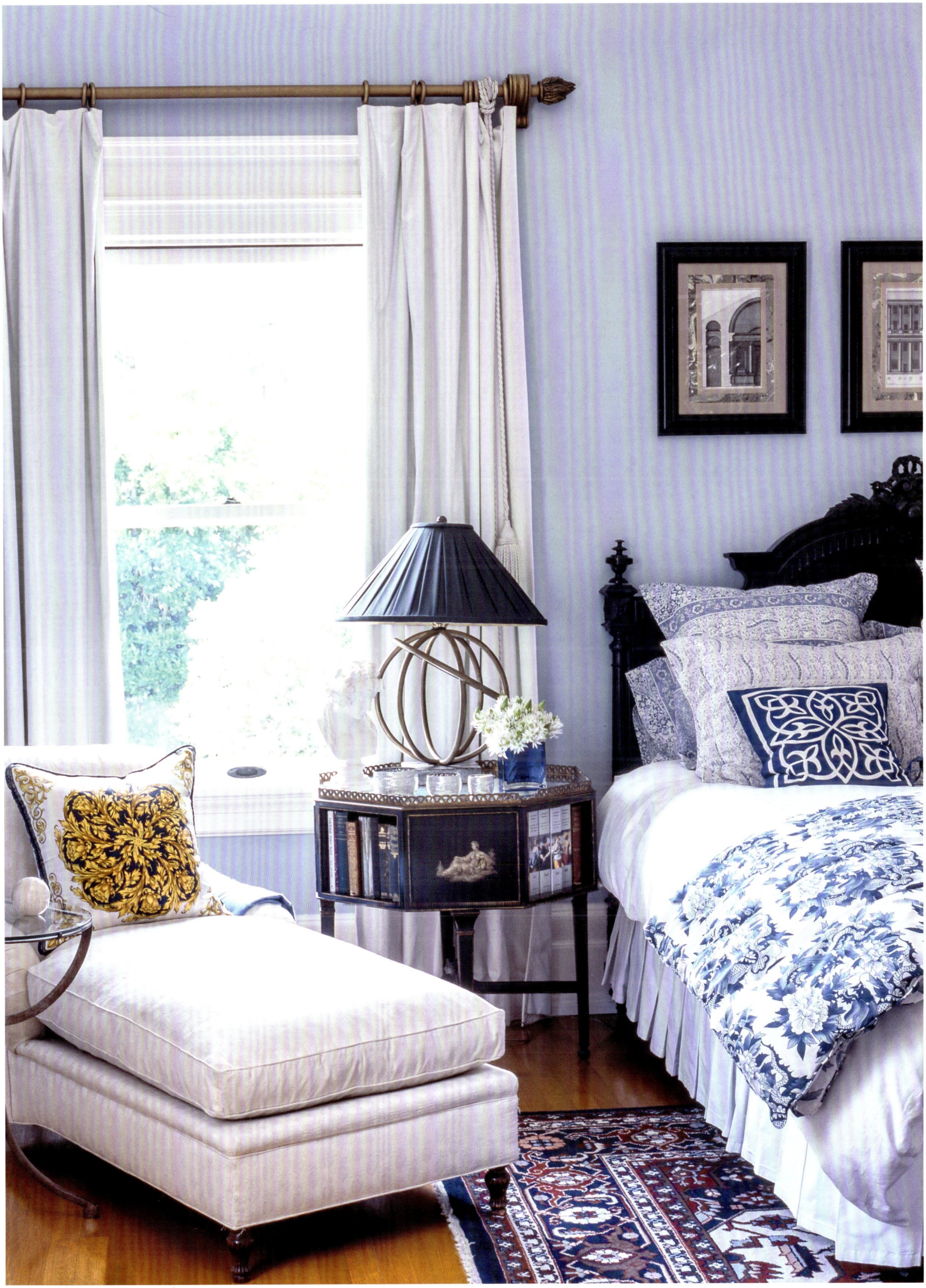

the domain of staff, with a kitchen, a pantry, a silver storage room, and a staff dining area. It even incorporated a functioning dumbwaiter, which I retained. We transformed it into a large kitchen and family room. But all the new cabinetry was inspired by the original in the pantry. Two maid's rooms became a home office, with views onto the garden and the swimming pool.

Upstairs, the master bedroom suite decor is simple, with a pale, monochromatic palette, a simple wrought-iron four-poster, clean-lined Biedermeier furniture pieces, and comfortable upholstered seating covered in white cotton slipcovers. The other three bedroom suites are, in deference to their presidential pasts, slightly more formal, but still welcoming and easy.

The garden and landscaping were a great pleasure for me. The plantings are predominantly lush hedges and topiaries in simple geometric shapes that serve as a soft backdrop to the unadorned rectangular pool. The gatherings in the garden, for iced tea in the afternoon or champagne at twilight, may have been smaller and less grand than the soirees held indoors, but they were no less festive and fun.

ABOVE: To lighten the aura of the semicircular guesthouse, we stripped and limed the floor and used outdoor fabrics for the slipcovers. OPPOSITE: The reflecting pool off the dining room uses false perspective, narrowing at the far end—and with boxwood balls planted progressively closer together—to make it seem longer than it is.

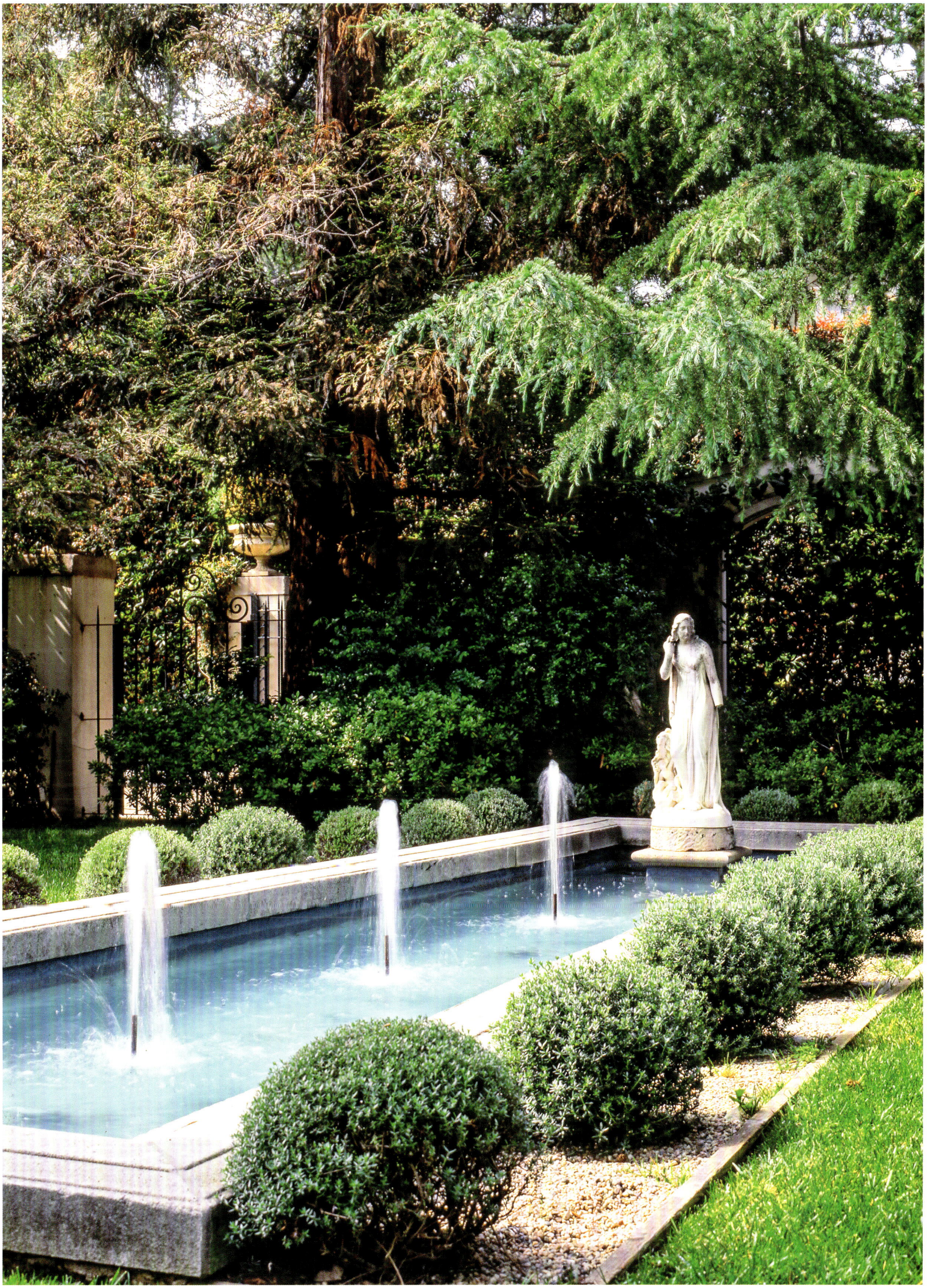

The rear facade of the house at night. The back garden had been covered with stone pavers suitable for large parties but was not conducive to day-to-day enjoyment.

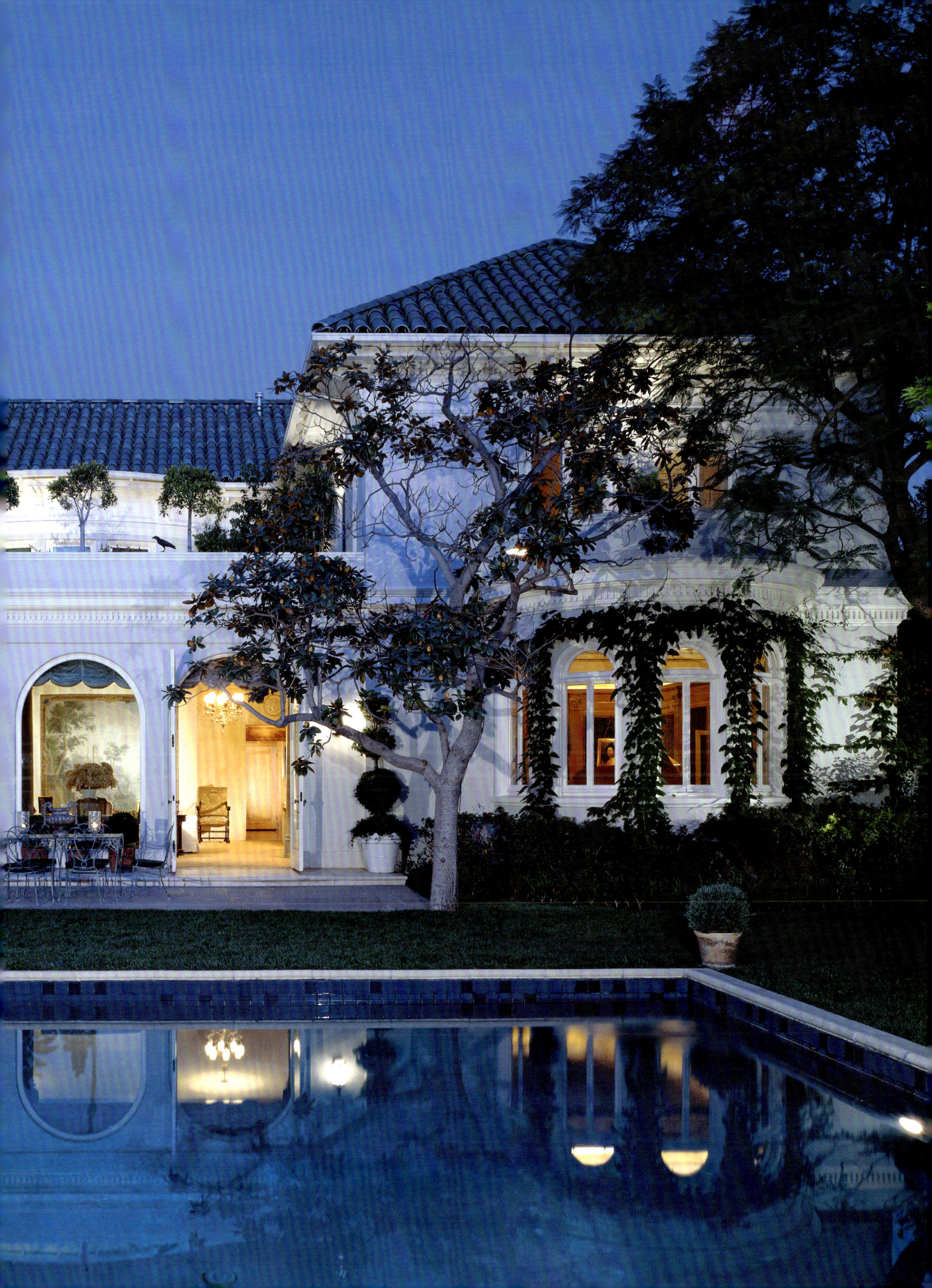

INTERLUDE
MIXING ELEMENTS

All too often, when the term mixing is used in decorating, people think of pattern mixing. And while that is important—and requires real skill—there are many other elements that can be brought together to enrich a space. For me, mixing means contrasting rough with smooth, refined pieces with brutalist ones, luxury items with inexpensive ones, contemporary designs with antiques. I think of putting a room together as a kind of cultural exchange, encompassing everything from artworks, furnishings, and accessories to the wall colors, upholstery fabrics, and furniture layout.

But that doesn't mean simply throwing things together willy-nilly. When disparate items are juxtaposed with no cohesive vision, the result is not decorating but chaos. Mixing elements successfully involves taking into account not only their style, provenance, materials, and function, but also their scale, their utility, and their essence.

It is important to understand the spirit of any item, so you can present it in the best possible way. You might not want to pair rustic pottery with fine porcelain, as neither would be shown to the best advantage, just as you probably wouldn't want to use sterling silver at a poolside lunch. Context counts, and function, style, and materials are all important considerations.

Yet good pieces will work in an amazingly diverse range of settings, and there are no hard-and-fast rules. I once designed a house for a couple whose husband had assembled an impressive collection of antique fishing lures. We presented them in the living room, amid groupings of more elegant accessories, and their presence and impact were similar to that of a collection of eighteenth century enamel boxes.

Mixing elements will add depth and interest to your rooms, allow you to showcase objects you love in a fresh way, and create a home that both functions for your needs and expresses your interests, your sensibilities, and your history.

1

In this Los Angeles home, an entry with white walls and a plain floor becomes a backdrop for small treasures. A collection of tiny sixteenth-century allegorical paintings of Bible stories from Spain surround an intricately carved eighteenth-century console. On top, a bold, modern sculpture by Arman of paint tubes fixed in Lucite is flanked by eighteenth-century Delft *tulipieres*. These also add height, leading the eye to the paintings. Even the books stacked below on the console are decorated with bronzes. This mix of the rare, the unusual, and the unexpected is reminiscent of the *wunderkammer*, or cabinet of curiosities, that has been popular in Europe since the Renaissance.

2

In this house belonging to the newest generation of an old Hollywood family, diverse styles and cultures meet, while deliberately bold colors energize the traditional space. The orange upholstery of the sofa stands out against white walls and the deep, saturated blue-and-teal rug. The nineteenth-century lamps had belonged to the client's grandmother, and we fitted them out with deliberately over-the-top new shades. The graphic Balinese sculpture and woven, patterned chair are unexpected elements, especially when paired with a midcentury cocktail table. Even the green foliage outside enhances the liveliness and appeal of this colorful and inviting room.

3

In this Los Angeles library, the dialogue between contemporary and classic elements makes for a successful room. The traditional paneling acts as a warm background for a modern table with a bold, sculptural steel base, which in turn holds an array of classical decorative items, including an Italian finial, architectural models, and a pair of 1950s mirrored obelisk lamps. But modernity is reiterated in the Lucite-and-leather desk chair and the hair-on-hide patterned rug.

4

This house in Beverly Hills is the second I did for the clients; the first, finished twenty years earlier, was very traditional, but they now wanted a place that was more contemporary, where they could see many of their favorite pieces in a fresh context. We paired their early-eighteenth-century French circular neoclassical painting by Jean-Baptiste Pater with multiple bright Marilyn Monroe portraits by Andy Warhol. Swedish midcentury side tables contrast with late-eighteenth-century English stools. The cocktail table is based on a Pompeian bed, I designed the playful ostrich-egg lamps, and nineteenth-century carved folk-art flowers add charm and color.

1

2

3

4

ROYAL RESIDENCE

For a fan of grand French style like myself, the opportunity to update a classic Parisian *hôtel particulier*, especially one on the Right Bank overlooking the Seine, would seem to be a dream assignment. But sometimes the old adage "Be careful what you wish for" applies.

That was the case here. The home was in a classic Haussmann-style building that dated to around 1865. While the exterior retained its period elegance, the space within had been horribly renovated, chopped into multiple small rooms, and stripped of its period details, with a commercial kitchen full of stainless steel appliances that could not have been more out of place.

The client is a world traveler with a passion for Paris that nearly matches my own. He could not be in the city as often as he would like, so he wanted his time there to be spent in a retreat that was quintessentially Parisian, suffused throughout with the elegance and romance of the City of Light. We both agreed that the purest expression of Parisian elegance was the eighteenth century, and that period became our touchstone in the renovation. But while we wanted to restore the sense of grandeur and occasion, it was also essential that the apartment function seamlessly and efficiently and incorporate the latest technology. So we gutted the whole space, modernizing all its functional systems, and reconfigured the rooms so that they flowed elegantly into one another.

You now enter the house through an octagonal reception room with subtly patterned stone floors, walls painted to resemble limestone, a ceiling adorned with trelliswork and faux vines, and a fanciful landscape painting by Hubert Robert. I wanted to emphasize the transition from outside and evoke the surrounding gardens and the elegance of nearby Avenue Montaigne.

You then proceed literally through a hall of mirrors. I sheathed the hall with aged mirror panels framed in gilt wood, which evoke the glamour of Versailles but also disguise how narrow the hallway and doors are. We added another bit of theatrical trompe l'oeil via a backlit faux skylight, so light bounces off all the surfaces to literally dazzling effect.

The hall leads to a semicircular rotunda, whose shape is echoed by a circular medallion

A view looking from the entry into the living area of a *hôtel particulier* on the Right Bank of Paris. To brighten the space and add glamour, we installed a faux backlit skylight and lined the walls with antique mirrors and gilded trim and sconces.

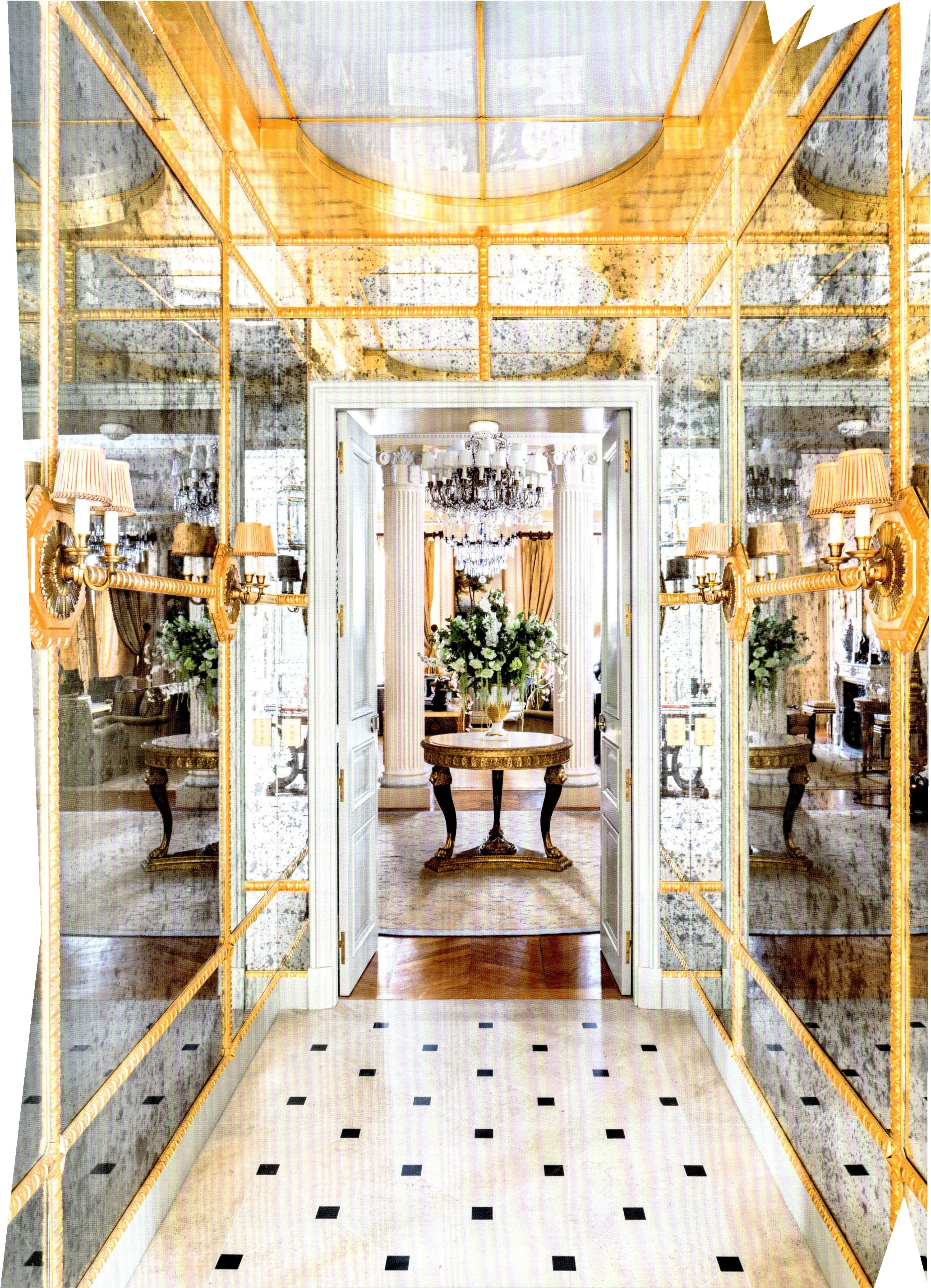

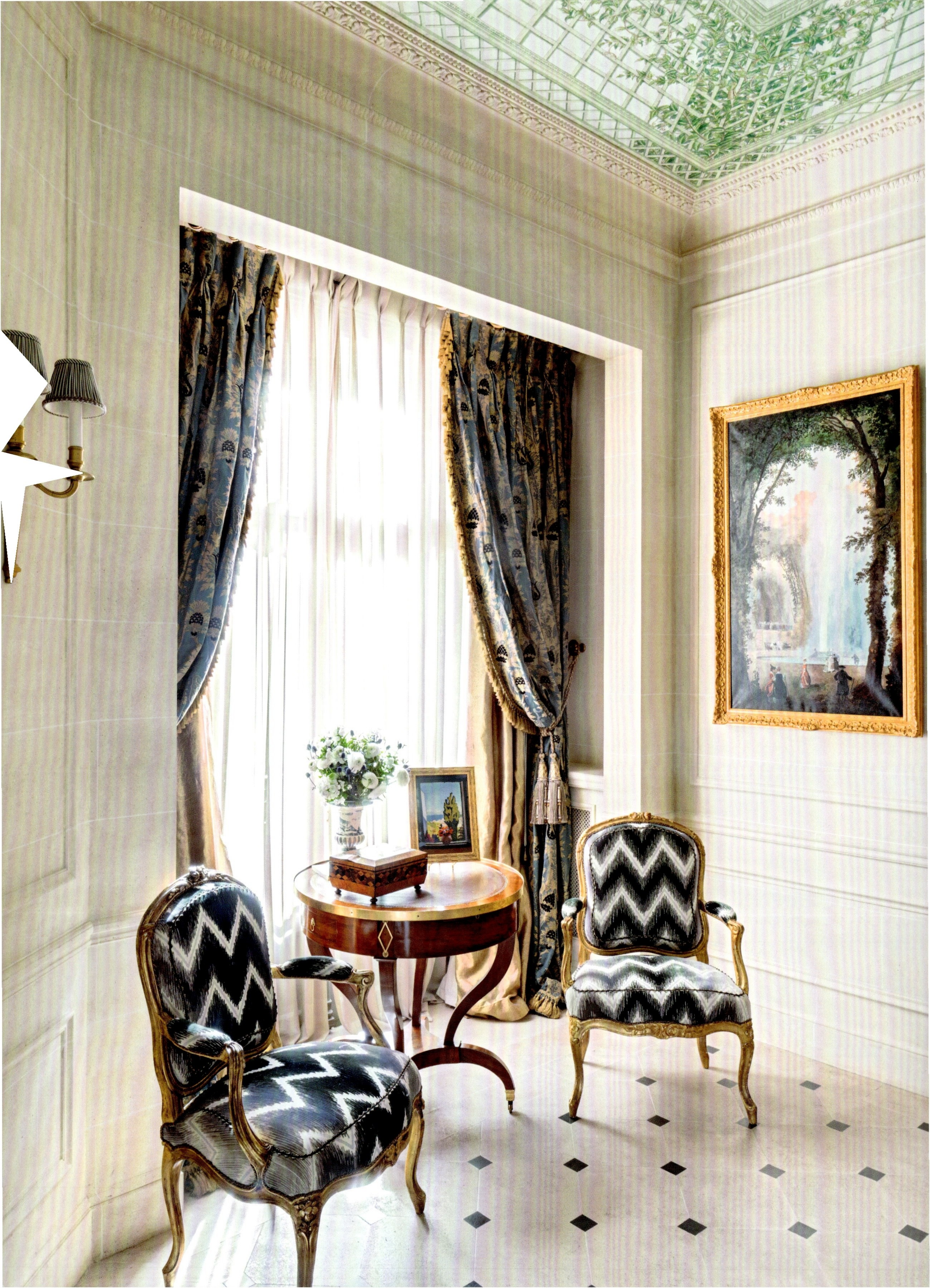

and an Empire center table. On one side of the rotunda is a fountain that had originally been in the lobby of the theater at the palace of Versailles. It was so heavy that we had to reinforce the floor to hold it. The space is further demarcated by a pair of stone Ionic columns that were carved in India.

Visible beyond is the grand salon, which extends the length of the apartment and which looks onto the Seine. These stunning views are framed by curtains in a lush gold fabric. The room is strongly symmetrical, with matching fireplaces and nineteenth-century gilded mirrors at each end, a pair of identical silk velvet–clad sofas in the middle, facing in opposite directions with a ten-foot-long marble console table between them, and matching early-nineteenth-century Swedish crystal chandeliers hanging above. The palette is a warmer, golden variation of the limestone in the entry area, contrasted with an array of jewel-tone blues and greens in the accessories and especially in the landscape paintings by Jean-Baptiste Oudry.

The dining room is more vivid in its colorations and use of pattern, featuring a richly decorative blue rug, paisley silk upholstery on the dining chairs, and sumptuous gold damask for the curtains, all played out against soothing paneled walls painted in a variety of warm creams and beiges.

The small salon is formal as well, but lighter in tone and feeling. Carved gilt decorations enhance the new boiseries, which are painted in the palest of watery blues. The palette throughout is softer and subtle, punctuated by splashes of blue, including the shades on the chandelier. A TV is hidden behind the overmantel mirror, and an overscale leather-topped cocktail table in the center encourages relaxed gatherings or putting your feet up for a nap.

The one major departure from tradition that the client requested was an "American-style" kitchen, so we installed simple paneled cabinetry, a center island covered with a blue rock-crystal counter, and a spacious

OPPOSITE: The entry hall walls are painted to look like limestone blocks, and the ceiling mural by the London firm Iksel depicts an open trellis with the sky beyond. ABOVE: The fountain off the entry came from the opera house at Versailles.

THE NEW ELEGANCE 235

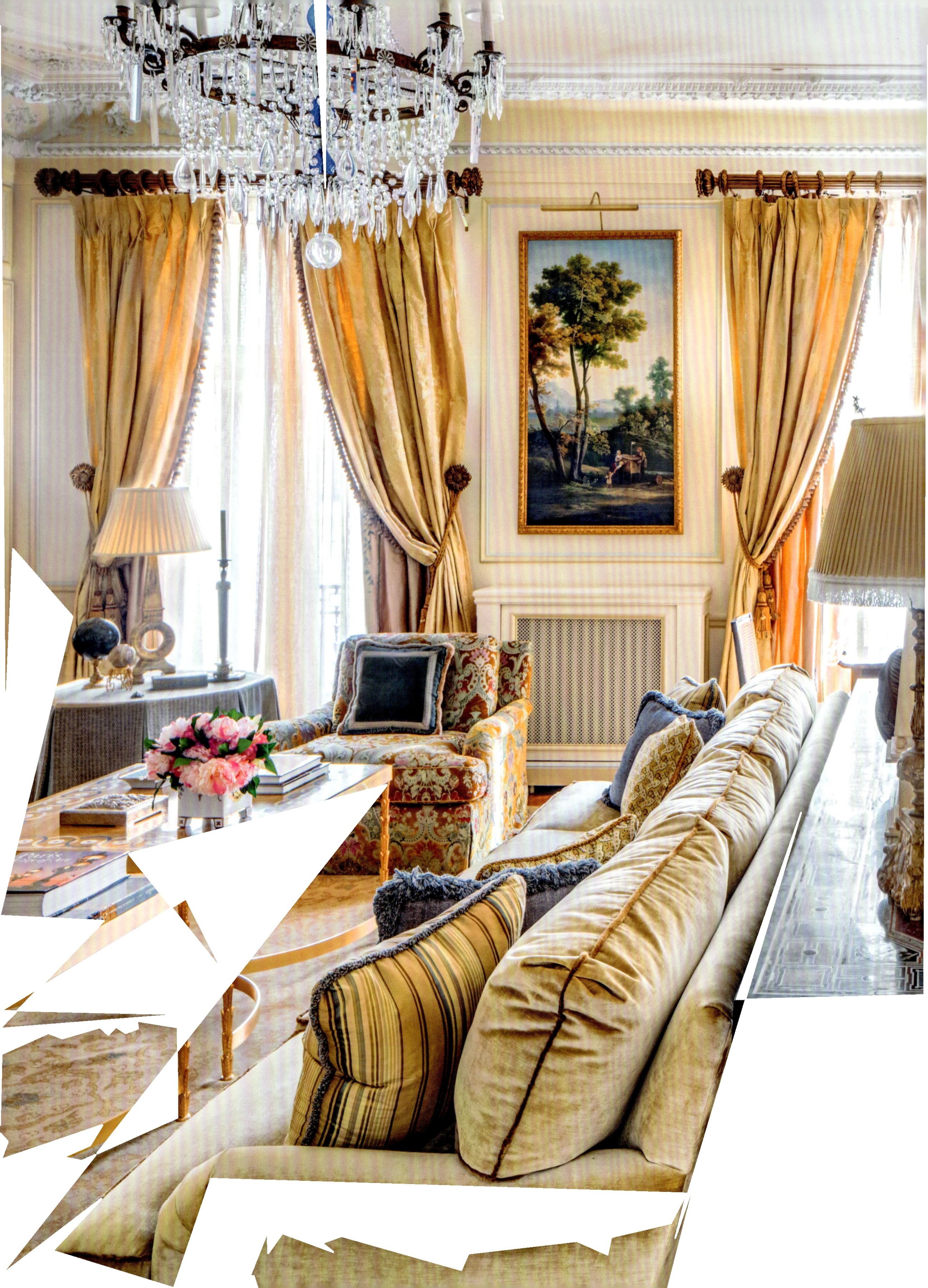

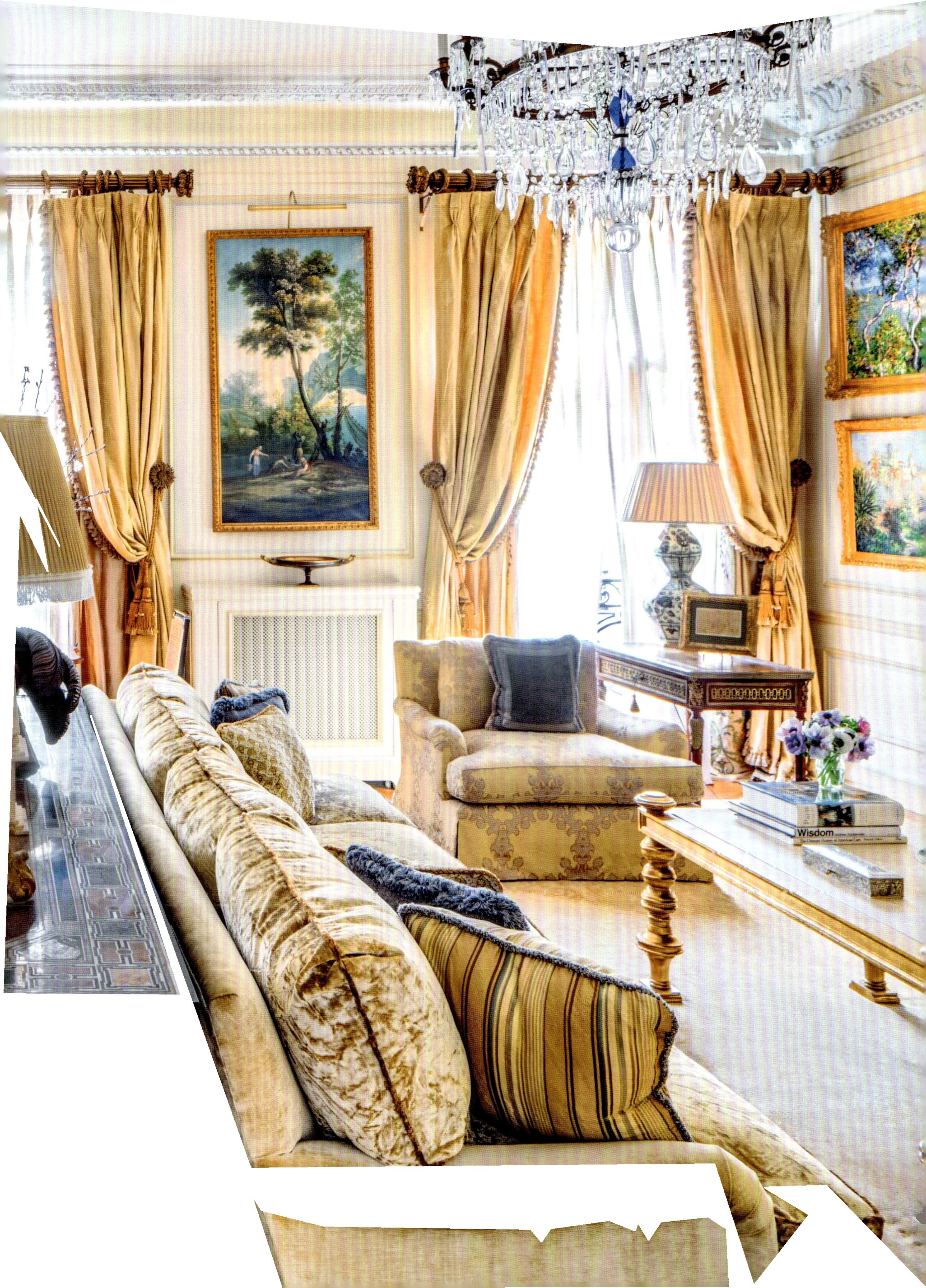
Wisdom

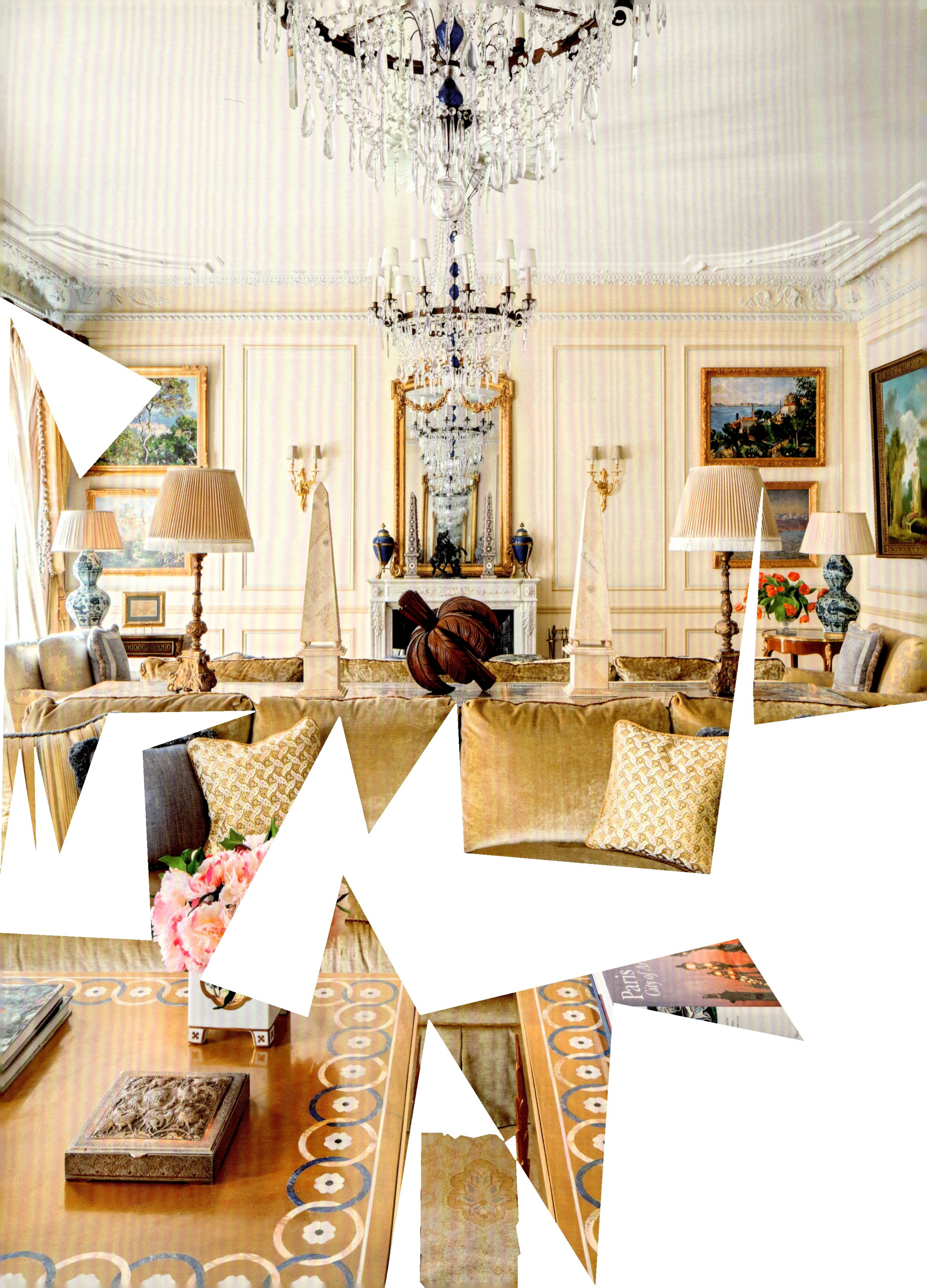
Paris

dining table. But even here you are in no danger of forgetting where you are—the walls are sheathed in a wallpaper depicting the eighteenth- and nineteenth-century monuments of Paris.

For the long hallway that leads to the bedrooms and library we commissioned a mural that depicts the Right and Left Banks, but only as they could appear in your imagination, with fanciful details and a mash-up of periods, so the city appears both familiar and entrancingly lighthearted.

The library is a cozy retreat with faux bois–painted walls, an array of modern French landscape paintings, plush seating, and a silk velvet sofa. The custom rug brings pattern and color to this most private room.

If the library is practical and comfortable, the bedrooms evoke a more luxe and layered vision of Parisian high style. The wife's lavender bedroom is an unrestrained feminine indulgence, with seven shades of lilac silk on the walls, curtains, and bedding, an elaborate gilt canopy crown, embroidered and gold-fringed bed hangings, and custom cream and gilt furnishings. The adjacent dressing room and bath continue the mood, with pink marble floors inset with mother-of-pearl and cabinetry with verre eglomise panels set into almost every door and drawer.

The husband's bedroom is more restrained, a composition in pale blue, where paintings by Claude Monet and Eugène Boudin stand out, but more subtle richness comes via sumptuous silk curtains and a glittering mirrored screen. The streets of Paris hang over the bed, via an antique map of the city, and the pale rug evokes water lapping at your feet—and the Seine flowing by, just outside the windows.

And to me, that is one of the signature successes of this project. The apartment functions beautifully, but most important, the spirit and style of Paris seem to infuse every room, the city's history, refinement, and signature beauty inherent in every detail.

PREVIOUS PAGES: The expansive living room overlooking the Seine was created by merging two rooms and features a fireplace at each end. The center table between the matching sofas was a custom design made in India. OPPOSITE: The chandeliers are early nineteenth-century Swedish. ABOVE: The wood carving on the table came from one of the four corner posts on an eighteenth-century bed.

The intimate dining room gets a luxe feel thanks to dramatic curtains with embroidery by Embroidery Palace. They are topped by panels of a Nobilis damask with Samuel & Sons trim; the fabric on the dining chairs is by Clarence House.

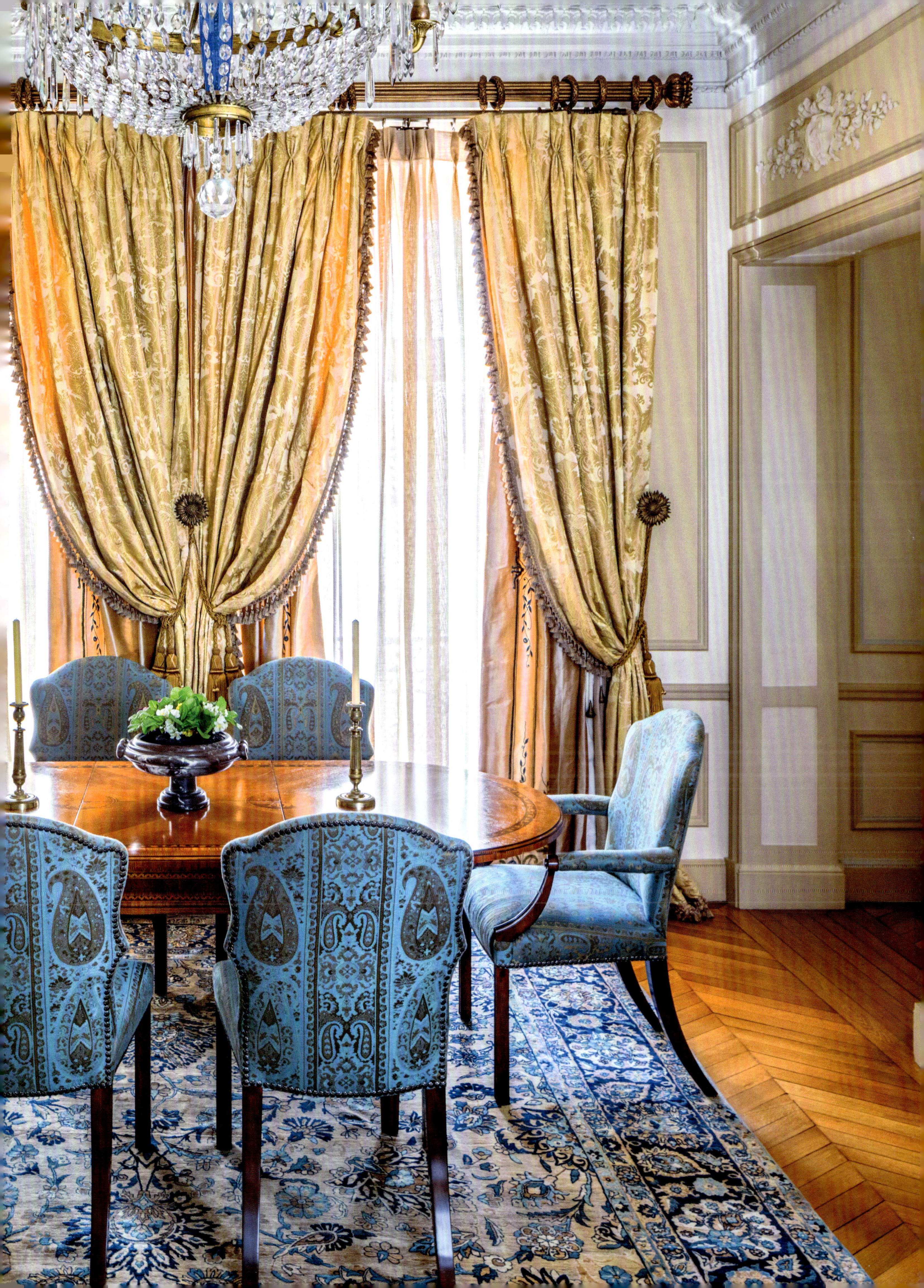

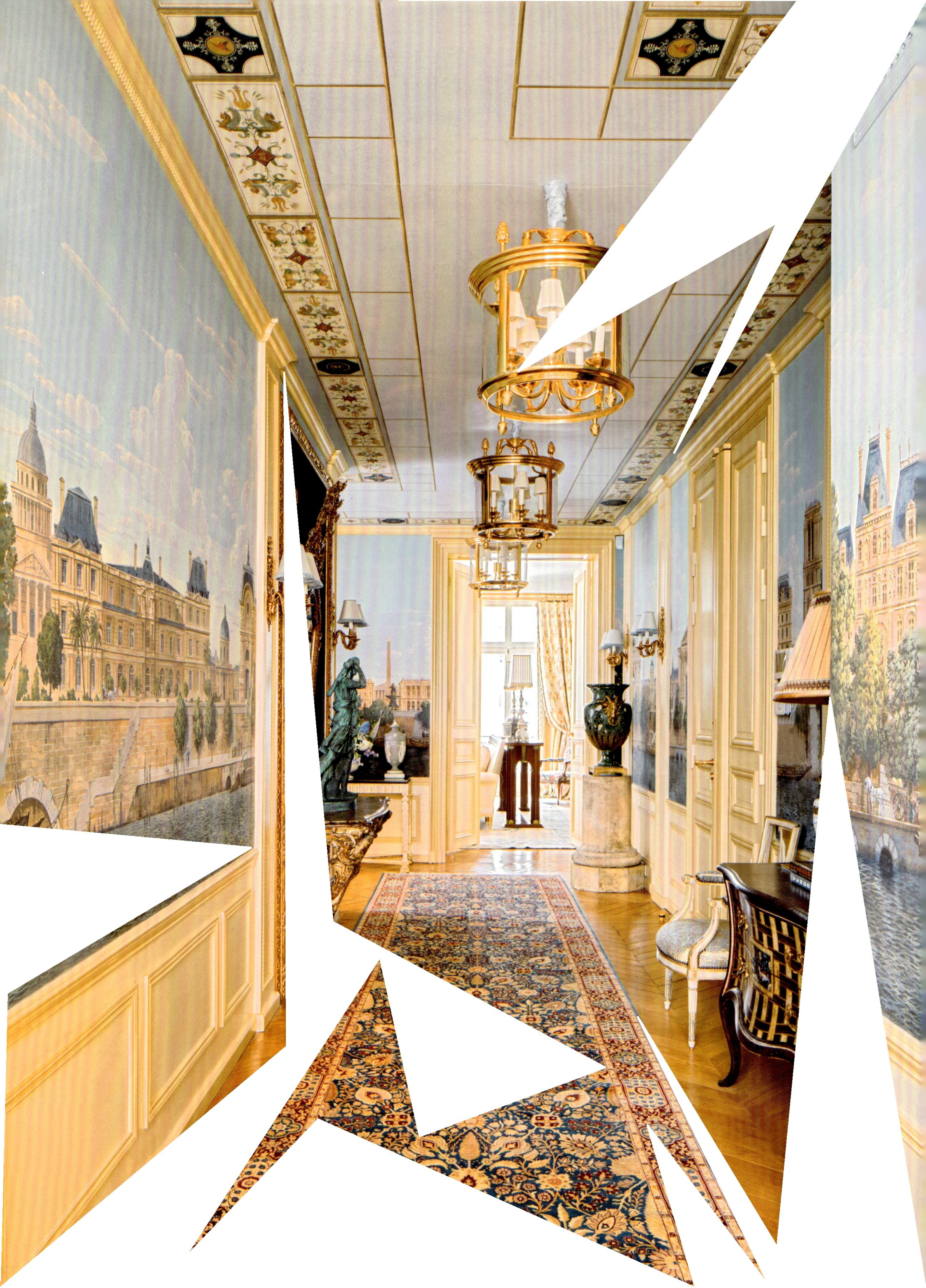

OPPOSITE: The hallway leading from the kitchen to the bedrooms is lined with murals by Pascal Amblard depicting fanciful scenes set on the Right and Left Banks; the ceiling decoration is by Iksel. ABOVE: The library walls were painted by Atelier de Ricou to look like burl-wood paneling; the upholstered ottoman features small pull-out trays to hold drinks.

THE NEW ELEGANCE 243

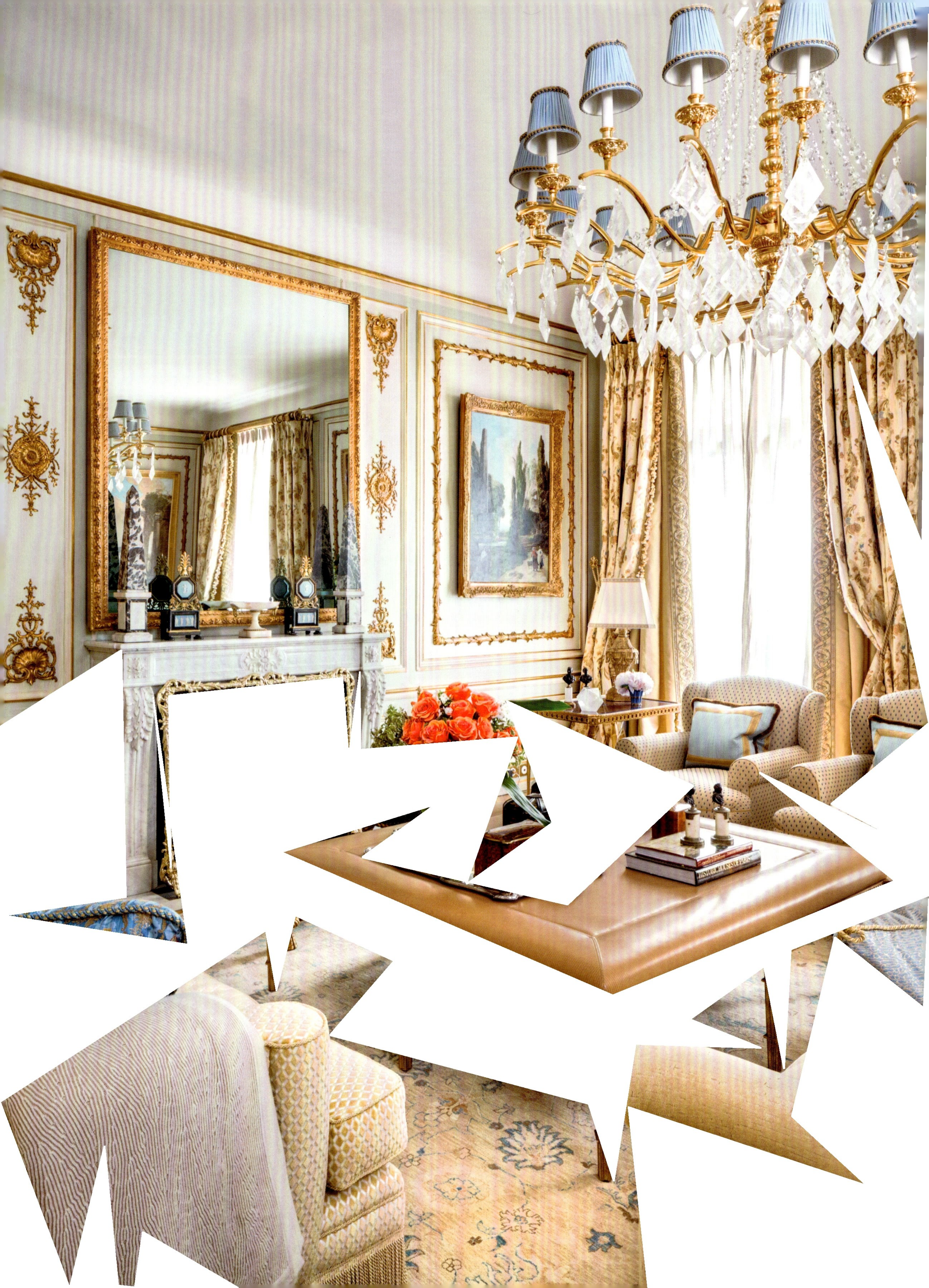

OPPOSITE: The small salon was embellished with gilt boiseries. ABOVE: The breakfast room features a custom table and an island fitted with a countertop of semiprecious stone. The outdoor fabrics and rugs are by Perennials, and the wallpaper by Manuel Canovas depicts the landmarks of Paris.

THE NEW ELEGANCE 245

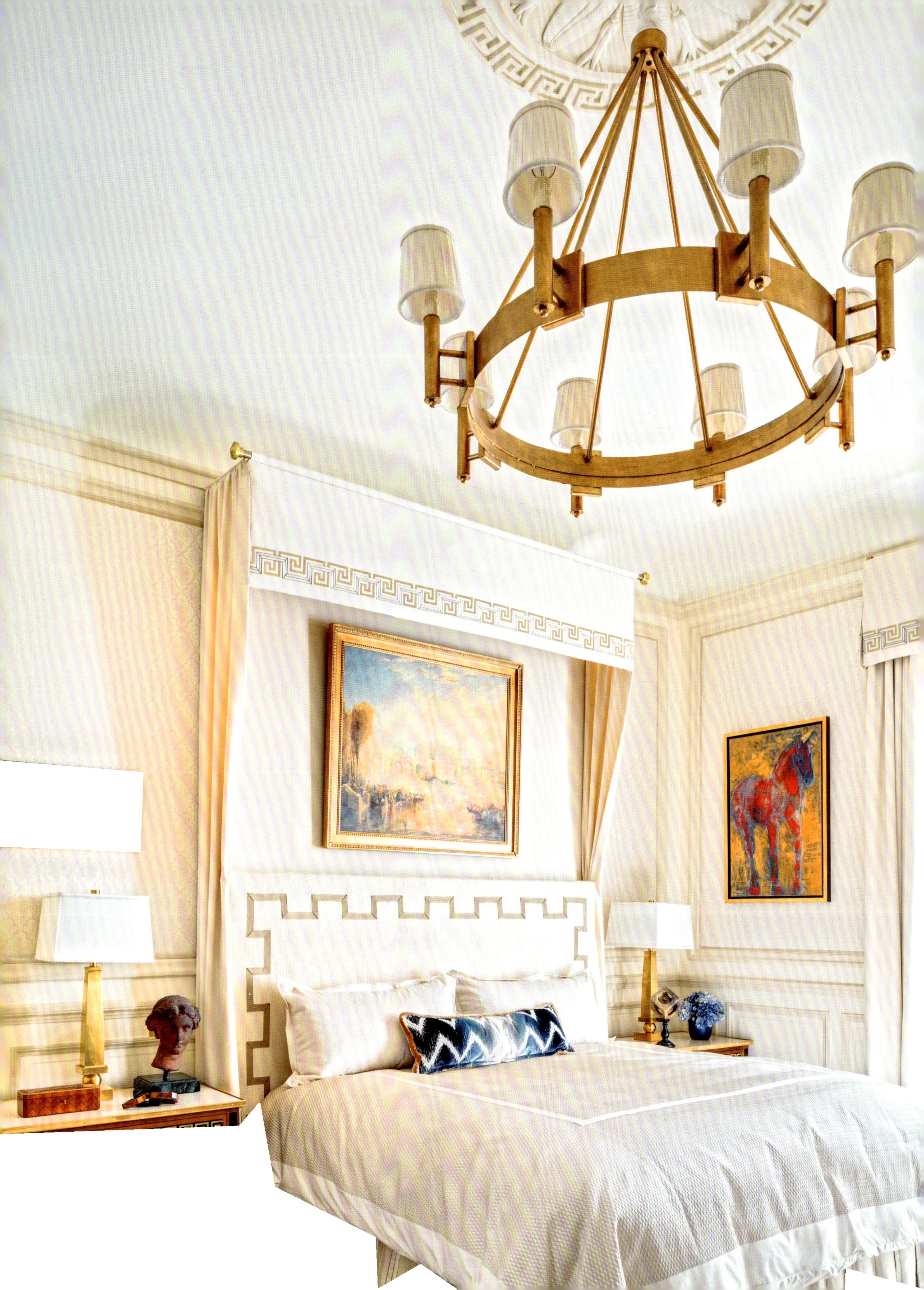

OPPOSITE: The guest room is subtly embellished with a Greek-key motif on the headboard, bed hangings, curtains, and even the nightstands. ABOVE: The wife's bath suite is decorated with framed wallpaper panels by Zuber.

THE NEW ELEGANCE 247

ABOVE: The walls of the wife's bedroom are covered in a paper-backed silk. OPPOSITE: Her bath features cabinets and a vanity inset with eglomise mirrored panels depicting eighteenth-century scenes by Frédéric Monpoint. FOLLOWING PAGES: In the husband's bedroom, an antique map of Paris hangs over the bed. The headboard is by Nancy Corzine, the linens are by the Italian firm Dea, and the rug is by Stark.

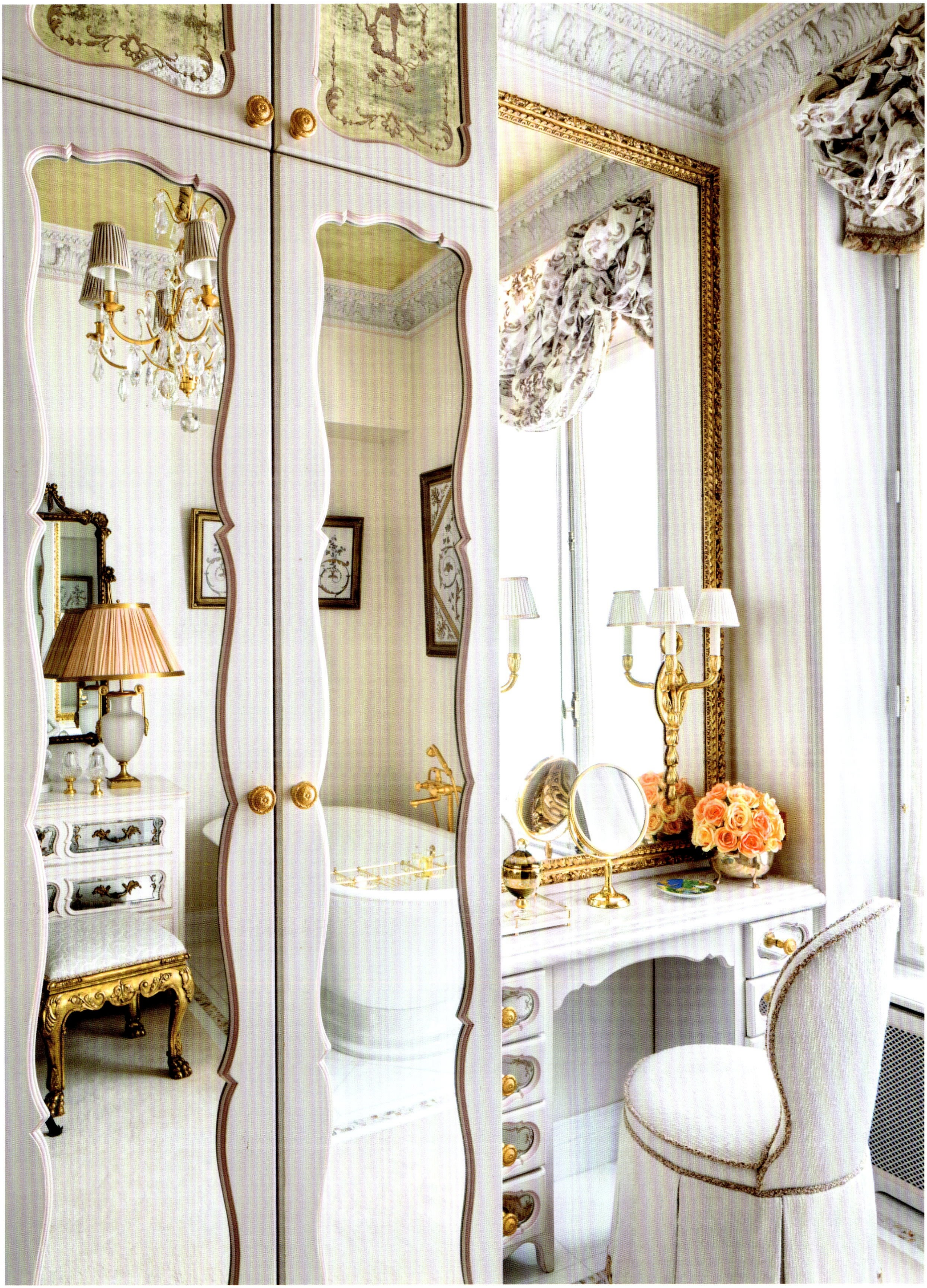

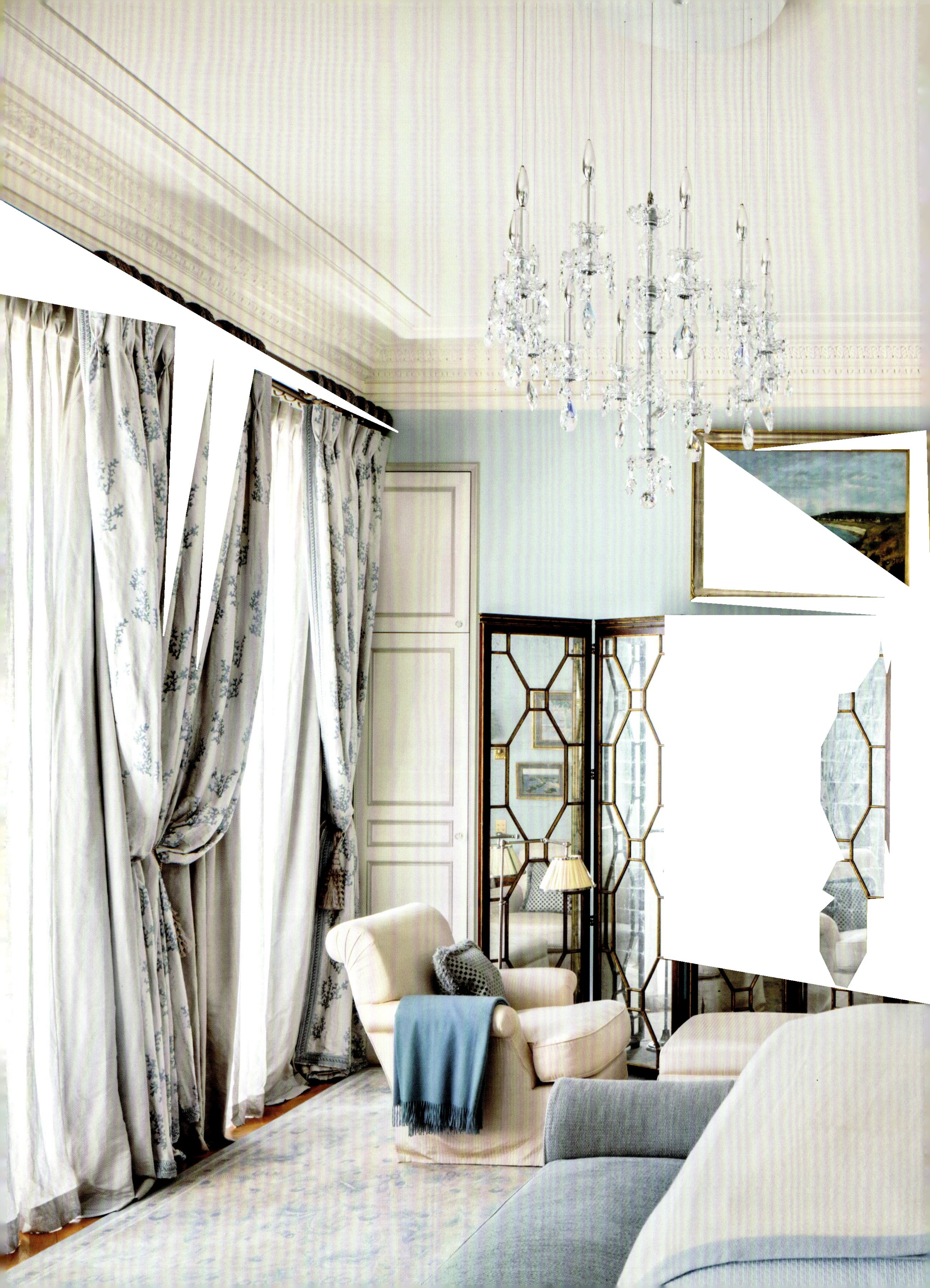

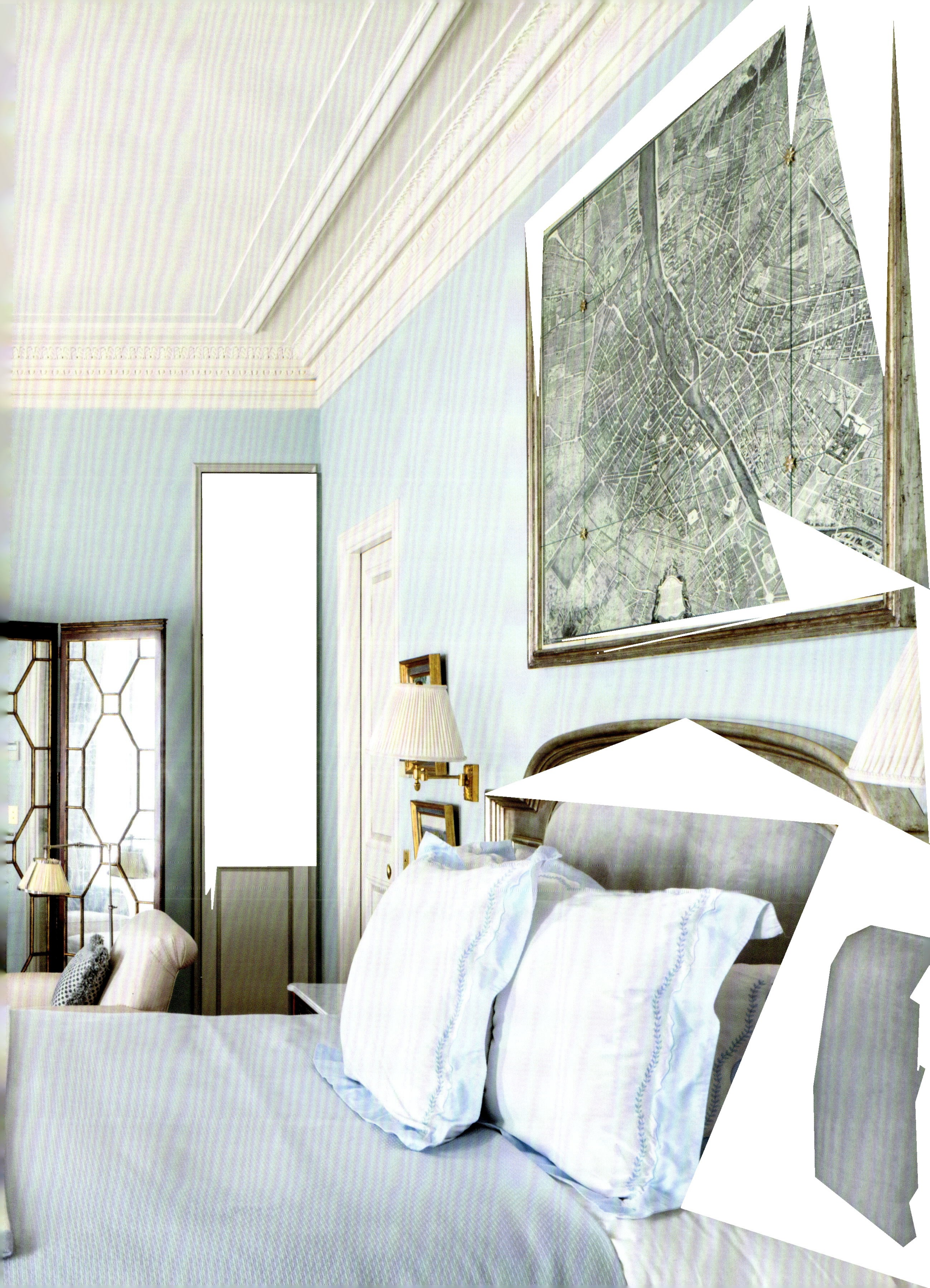

INTERLUDE
DETAILS ARE THE DESIGN

Everyone loves dramatic rooms, bold gestures that grab your attention, overscale furniture, and crystal-encrusted chandeliers and light fixtures. This is why it is often so much fun to go to a theatrically designed restaurant, bar, or hotel lobby. Over-the-top gestures, go-for-broke elements, and bravura design make for a spirited evening.

But when it comes to our homes, the spaces we live in and use every day, too much is usually too much. I have found that it is actually the subtle details that make any room more interesting and a more compelling place to spend time. Elements you might not even notice right away are what help a home feel special. It is the little extra unexpected or unnecessary touch that adds a bit of oomph, that pleases the eye and the hand. You may sense this kind of subtle detail before you see it, but inevitably you will come to appreciate it. To quote the great American designer Charles Eames, "The details are not the details. They make the design."

There are any number of opportunities to bring that level of richness and finish to a room. You can do so via fabrics, trims, carvings, embroideries, paint, wallpaper, pillows, or finishes. Details can be added in ways as grand and sumptuous as curtains or as simple and unobtrusive as backing a bookcase with fabric or a mirror. However you choose to enhance your rooms, remember these details are what will take a space from everyday to extraordinary.

1

I have such a weakness for passementerie and other elaborate trims, braids, cords, beads, embroideries, and fringes that my staff sometimes jokes they should call me Trim-othy. These embellishments add richness and visual delight on an intimate scale. They beckon to be touched. In this Los Angeles dining room, we added a tassel fringe to the brocade curtains, after first checking to see how the fringe would fall when hung vertically (an important consideration). We also added a ribbon-brush fringe to the chair cushions to play off the elaborate caning of the seat back. These kinds of dressmaker details take a room from off-the-rack to couture.

2

In a fanciful Beverly Hills home, a seventeenth-century Italian frame, rich with carved and gilded shells, foliage, and putti, is enhanced by a backdrop of striped fabric both real and faux. The tented effect of the walls is amplified by painted plaster behind and above the gilded carvings that replicates the actual fabric on each side. And the background mural further reiterates the colors of the fabric.

3

The items on the table in this Los Angeles study compose a fascinating still life, full of international influences. The array is clearly owned by someone who takes a global approach that traverses time. The architectural model looks contemporary, but is from a flea market in Brussels. The marble sphinx is French, as is the Empire model of a monument. The eighteenth-century ivory bracelet is from India, the nineteenth-century watercolor was found at a Paris flea market, and the small silver coins and pillbox are from Jakarta. Shedding light on it all is an ostrich-egg lamp that I designed.

4

Sometimes the most powerful details are those that make their presence felt over time. I designed this chest for a very traditional room and embellished it with carved and gilded wood, like a curtain flowing across the front. It is not the first thing you notice, but the detailing adds an unexpected bit of luxe and somehow makes the room feel more contemporary—a golden moment, reinforced by the gilded frame of the painting above it. However, the more rustic inlaid box and vase of simple country flowers on top banish any sense of stiff formality.

1

2

3
The Language of the Body
Drawings by Pierre-Paul Prud'hon
Elderfield

4

Acknowledgments

I want to thank two people whose talents, vision, and passion made this book possible: my dear friend Michael Boodro, who was able to beautifully express my thoughts and ideas in a manner that completely reflects my voice. Working with Michael was a total joy. Secondly, I would like to express my gratitude to Elaine Maltzman, who was tirelessly involved with every aspect of this book from inception through to completion. I cannot even imagine a day without Elaine's valuable insights.

A huge thanks to all my wonderful clients who have shown their confidence in me by allowing me to help them create their very personal embodiments of their concept of comfortable elegance. Only through our true partnership could these special places have come to life.

From my own staff, past and present, I would like to thank those who worked on the projects in this book: Alissa Arnold, Jamie Atterholt, Dan Baer, Nicole Choy, Carolyn Chris, Ruth Corrigan, Erin Cunningham, Karen Dardick, Alison Duboff, Eve Durando, Julie Feehan, Stephen Ginnegar, Lauren Goldberg, Rachel Goldberg, Cecile Haddouche, Andrew Horn, Ajanta Kalyanpur, Shelby Kass, Laura Kay, Camille Kurowski, Elaine Maltzman, Nicole Perry, Kristina Roach, Beth Rossi, Kathleen Scheinfeld, Sylvia Skylar, Bobby Thoren, Genevieve Trousdale, Amanda Valli, Laura Van Der Spek, Paul Van Kampen, and Merissa Whitney.

None of these projects would have been realized without the contributions of an incredibly talented group of artisans and craftsmen from around the world; I am full of appreciation for all of the immense dedication and skills that they exhibit every day.

I would especially like to thank my great friends in the design community who have given me their support, including Stacey Bewkes, Michael Boodro, Dara Caponigro, Jill Cohen, Sophie Donelson, Carolyn Englefield, Cynthia Frank, Pamela Jaccarino, Rocky LaFleur, Ann Maine, Susan McFadden, Deborah Needleman, Paige Rense, Whitney Robinson, Krissa Rossbund, Robert Rufino, Margaret Russell, Susanna Salk, Clinton Smith, Jennifer Smith Hale, Newell Turner, and Vicente Wolf.

I have been lucky enough to work with some of the finest photographers of our day, and I am so very thankful for their enormous skill and artistic vision. Their work in these pages attests to their great talent.

I am deeply indebted to Doug Turshen and David Huang for the beautiful design of the book and my dream team at Rizzoli; Charles Miers, my editor Kathleen Jayes, and Pam Sommers . . . you are all best in class!

Finally, I would like to thank all of my readers, who understand that every day is special. Don't wait for company to live elegantly today!

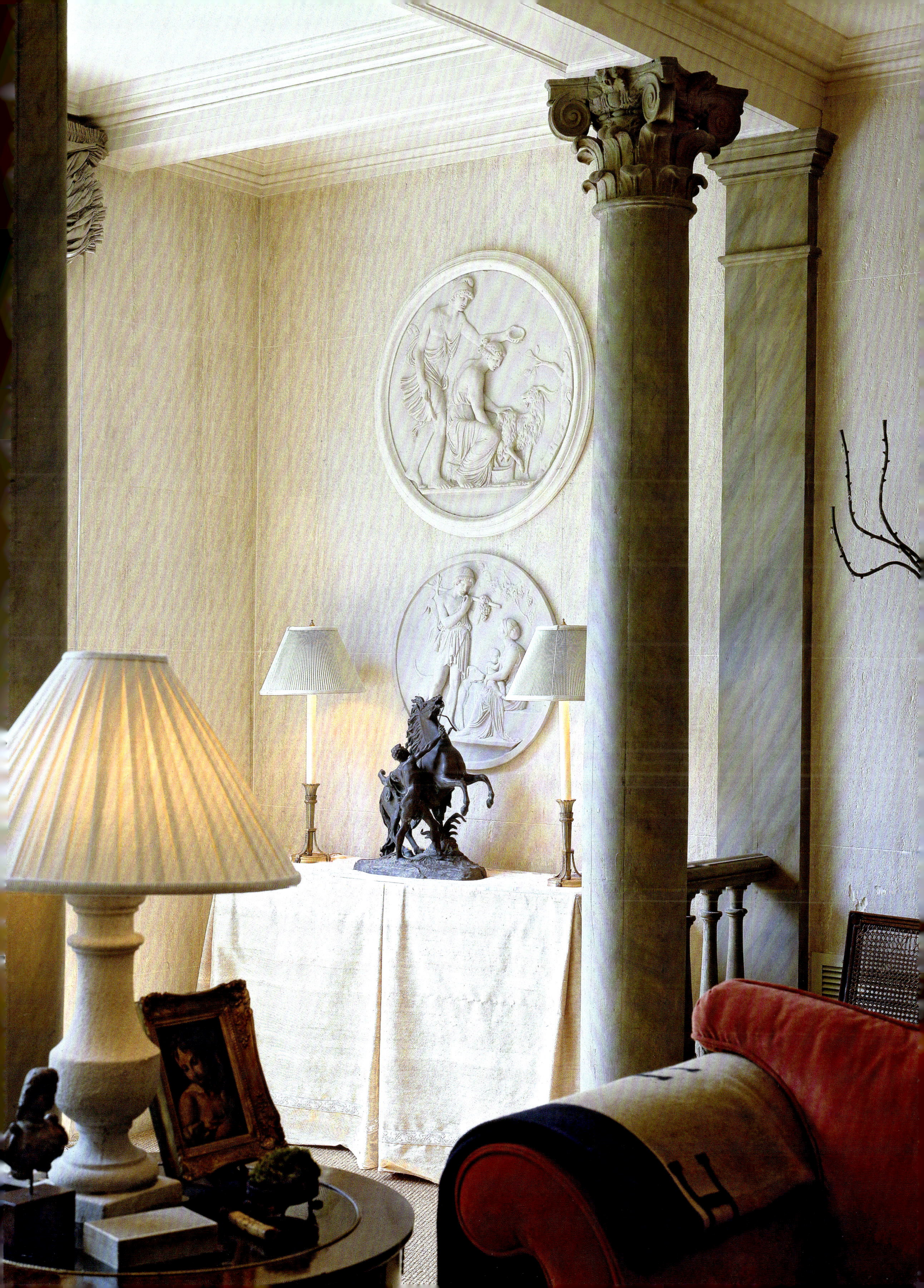

CREDITS

Endpapers: Jardin Francais by Timothy Corrigan for Fromental

Melanie Acevedo: 171 (5)

Amy Barnard: 67, 69, 70, 72-73, 76 (2), 79 (5 & 6), 105 (1), 151 (4), 152, 155, 156-157, 158-159, 160-161, 162-163, 164, 165, 166-167, 169 (2 & 4), 173, 174, 175, 176-177, 178, 179, 180, 181, 182, 183, 184-185, 253 (2)

Alexandre Bailhache: 33 (2), 35 (6)

Jim Bartsch: 35 (5), 55 (1 & 4), 57 (7), 129 (2 & 4), 171 (6), 207 (3), 231 (4)

Cordero Studios: 33 (3)

Timothy Corrigan for Fromental: 105 (2)

Roger Davies: 79 (7), 105 (3), 116, 122-123, 125

Marina Faust: Author Portrait, 151 (3), 171 (8)

Gianni Franchellucci: 37, 42-43, 44, 48-49, 50-51, 53

Nadine Froger: 217, 218-219, 220-221

Emily Jenkins Followill: 6

Mark Edward Harris: 58, 62-63, 75 (1), 253 (1)

Nicole LaMotte: 5, 55 (3), 77 (3), 105 (4), 112-113, 114, 115, 117, 118-119, 120, 121, 124, 126-127, 129 (3), 169 (1 & 3), 231 (1 & 3), 253 (3)

Massimo Listri: 212-213, 255

Mark Luscombe-Whyte: 55 (2), 57 (5), 81, 82-83, 85, 86, 87, 88-89, 90, 91, 92-93, 94-95, 96, 97, 98, 99, 100, 101, 102, 103, 107 (5 & 6), 151 (1), 233, 234, 235, 236-237, 238, 239, 240-241, 242, 243, 244, 245, 246, 247, 248, 249, 250-251, 253 (4), Back Cover

Lee Manning: 2, 35 (7), 109, 111, 187 (2 & 4)

Michael McCreary: 35 (4), 57 (8), 61, 64-65, 66, 68, 71, 75, 107 (7 & 8), 151 (2), 187 (1), 187 (3), 187 (5), 207 (1, 2 & 4), 209, 224, 226

Mary Nichols: 222-223, 228-229

Eric Piasecki: 171 (7), 188, 190, 191, 192-193, 194-195, 196, 197, 198, 199, 200, 201, 202-203, 204-205

Julio Piatti: 8, 40

Richard Powers: 38-39, 41, 45, 52

Marjorie Preval: 46-47

Lisa Romerein: 210-211, 215, 216, 225, 227

Nick Springett: 33 (1)

Simon Upton: Front cover, 13, 14, 15, 16, 17, 18, 19, 20, 21, 22, 23, 24, 25, 26, 27, 28, 29, 30 31, 57 (6), 79 (4), 129 (1), 131, 132, 133, 134-135, 136-137, 138, 139, 140, 141, 142-143, 144, 145, 146, 147, 148, 149

Firooz Zahedi: 230 (2)

First published in the United States of America in 2019 by Rizzoli International Publications, Inc.
300 Park Avenue South
New York, NY 10010
www.rizzoliusa.com

Copyright © 2019 Timothy Corrigan
Text: Michael Boodro

Publisher: Charles Miers
Senior Editor: Kathleen Jayes
Design: Doug Turshen with David Huang
Production Manager: Barbara Sadick
Managing Editor: Lynn Scrabis

All rights reserved. No part of this publication may be reproduced, stored in a retrieval system, or transmitted in any form or by any means, electronic, mechanical, photocopying, recording, or otherwise, without prior consent of the publishers.

Printed in China

2019 2020 2021 2022 / 10 9 8 7 6 5 4 3 2 1

ISBN: 978-0-8478-6361-7
Library of Congress Control Number: 2019936654

Visit us online:
Facebook.com/RizzoliNewYork
Twitter: @Rizzoli_Books
Instagram.com/RizzoliBooks
Pinterest.com/RizzoliBooks
Youtube.com/user/RizzoliNY
Issuu.com/Rizzoli